This is the true story of a woman's will to succeed and overcome all obstacles to find a better life.

Born and educated in USSR, she qualified as a Geodesic Engineer and then, after obtaining a degree in law, worked for the communist party in Siberia for 20 years.

During this time she worked her way up the party hierarchy to the level of "nomenklatura" (senior position), all the while enduring the hostile environment of the Siberian Frontier.

Eventually with the breakup of the U.S.S.R., and after establishing several businesses, she realised that the only hope for a better life was to emigrate. She met and married an Englishman and moved to the UK experiencing all the problems of learning a new language at the age of 53 and adapting to a very different culture.

To my loving husband Dyfrig for his help and support.

Mila Jones

From Communist to Capitalist

AUSTIN MACAULEY
PUBLISHERS LTD.

A CIP catalogue record for this title is available from the British Library.

ISBN 9781786123107 (Paperback)
ISBN 9781786123114 (Hardback)
ISBN 9781786123121 (E-Book)

www.austinmacauley.com

First Published (2017)
Austin Macauley Publishers Ltd.
25 Canada Square
Canary Wharf
London
E14 5LQ

Acknowledgement

For the help and courtesy of the photos about life in Siberia in my book, I would like to sincerely thank my good friend Alexander Mekheda and his wife Ludmila, who lived in the village of Zyryanka for 20 years, the same period when I lived there.

Alexander Mekheda worked as a helicopter pilot at Polar Aviation and during all those years had admired and been fascinated by the beautiful scenery and landscape of northern Siberia and later began taking aerial photographs showing all the beauty of the Kolyma region.

Contents

Chapter 1

Siberian Welcome

When I first stepped off the plane into that Siberian summer of July 1971, little did I realize what a dramatic change would take place in my life over the course of the next few years, eventually leading to a whole new career as a lawyer and a senior position within the communist party. At this time I was a newly qualified Geodesic Engineer, freshly married with a new son, but already had decided that I no longer wished to pursue a career in this discipline.

However, the prospects, in Ukraine, outside this profession did not seem particularly good for me and so the decision was taken, that together with my husband we would try to find a better life in Siberia. It was an extremely risky undertaking, leaving my home and friends in Ukraine to search for a better life in far off North East Siberia, as was said at the time "to go to nowhere".

We had no friends, job or money and no place to stay in Siberia, but we were young, energetic and well educated, and somehow I knew that we would be able to find a new life in this developing region of the USSR, this new frontier on the edge of the arctic circle. This optimism did eventually prove to be well founded.

It was only when the plane was already flying to Magadan, that for some reason I had sudden attack of doubts and fear. After the farewells to my parents and my son I felt heavy-hearted and the tears blurred my eyes. My husband and I were going to a completely unknown place in the north- east of Siberia and we didn't know what was waiting for us there, how this severe land would meet us and whether we would be able to settle and adjust to life so far from our homeland.

During the 11 hours of the flight from Moscow to Magadan, the plane traveled a distance of 6400 km., crossed 9 time-zones and almost the whole country before landing in Magadan Airport. We left Ukraine in the middle of July 1971 when it was 30 degrees Celsius hot outside and had no idea of the temperature in the North of Siberia, but assumed, that it must be very cold there, and we had dressed accordingly with our warmest clothes.

To my surprise, the weather in Magadan was wonderful, it was very warm, sunny and all the people were dressed in light summer clothing. The first thing that struck me was the huge number of mosquitoes that were everywhere, they seemed to particularly take a liking to me and after a while my whole body was completely bitten by them.

Magadan is located on the shore of Nagaeva bay by the Sea of Okhotsk in the north-east of Siberia, and the fact that it is so close to the sea has an impact to the unique microclimate of the city, it is humid and one can smell a tang of sea. Magadan turned out to be an ordinary city with tall buildings, wide streets, and a beautiful area in the center, where, like almost all the other cities of the country, a monument to Vladimir Lenin was situated towering above all else.

I was so glad that we appeared to be in such a decent place, but we had to find a job and a place to live quickly, in order to stay there. In the center of the city we saw an employment office, but when we came closer, my spirits sagged, because there was a huge amount of people who wanted to find a job just like we did.

We reserved a place in the queue and began what we expected to be a long wait. However, the man, standing in front of us said, "Don't worry, it goes quickly, but they will take only a few of us. They need professionals with working experience in the logging industry or in the goldfields quarries." 'What about us then?' I thought.

When it was our turn, my husband and I went into the office where two officers were sitting at a table. We put our diplomas on the table in front of them, but they didn't even open them, and said:

"Take your diplomas away we don't care what specialties you have, just tell us, what skills you have and why you came here." My husband told them that he was a building technician and served in the army in the Construction Corps. The officer interrupted him and said, "We have nothing to offer to you, and actually, I advise you to go back home. You are so young and inexperienced and life here is not for you."

After this setback we decided to look for work on our own in the Construction Department of the Magadan city, but when we found this company we did not even enter. On the door was stuck a note which said 'Apply at the employment office if you are looking for a job.' But we had just been there! That was a never-ending circle ... It turned out that hundreds of people were going every day around the city in search of job, but the city simply couldn't accept all newcomers.

Everything became confusing in my mind, and I didn't know what to do and what would happen to us, because we could not even go home. We had spent 430 roubles, out of the 500 roubles that my parents had lent us for the tickets to Magadan, and remaining sum of money was only enough to allow us to spend a couple of days in this strange city.

I was walking next to my husband with my head down, being afraid of even looking into his eyes, because it was my initial idea to come here. And now I'm here and what could we do next? We both felt so miserable and tired that we weren't even able to discuss our situation and the moment we sat down on a nearby bench I immediately fell asleep.

A bit later, a man sat on our bench next to us; my husband lit a cigarette and started to chat with him. Having learnt of our problems he said, "You came in vain. It's impossible to find a job here. I advise you to go to Zyryanka village. I've been living there for many years already. It is situated on the bank of the Kolyma River in Yakutia."

He started to speak and praise that place, describing how life was very good there: taiga (north-east Siberian forest consisting mainly of coniferous trees, which can endure the subarctic frosts with rivers, swamps and lakes), a river, very nice people and a possibility to find a job. One could go there by aero plane only.

"And how much is the ticket?" I asked. "27 roubles," he answered. My husband and I looked at each other and had exactly the same thoughts. Our money was enough for two tickets and a little more. Let's go! We came back to the airport, bought the tickets and began to wait for our flight.

We spent the whole night at the airport of Magadan, because the only flight to Zyryanka was the next morning. I felt very exhausted, but because of many thoughts that one after the other uinhabited my mind, I couldn't sleep a wink the whole night long. I was in a state of shock because of what had happened to us on our first day in Siberia.

I had assumed, of course, that it would not be so easy for us to get used to a new life at first, but I didn't expect that everything would turn out so badly that we would be forced to leave Magadan. I thought that the next day we would be in another new place in Siberia but I still had no idea how everything would turn out. It turned out that Zyryanka village was to be our final destination in our journey, because we had only 20 roubles left and that would only be enough to buy food for a couple of days.

Our plane took off at 10 a.m. and, and although the distance to the village was about 700 kilometres, compared to the previous flight across the whole country it was almost ten times shorter, but more difficult for us because of the types of aircraft we were flying in. It was in two stages and we would be flying in small planes built to carry only a few passengers, and flying at relatively low altitude. However, the weather turned out to be cloudless so that it was possible to see the landscape below quite clearly.

Under the wing of the plane, there was for me, a strange landscape. At first there were small snow-capped mountains, and then there appeared the taiga, with rivers, swamps and lakes. These lakes and swamps were very close to each other, and it seemed that the land underneath was covered with blue-green lace, created by nature itself.

After a while we landed at the airport of Seymchan, which was just a landing strip with a small two-storeyed wooden building. As soon as we left the plane mosquitoes surrounded us, and we were bitten mercilessly. We didn't have any insect repellent, as we did not expect this kind of thing; however we quickly boarded the other plane for our onward journey to Zyryanka.

Our new plane was an Antonov AN-2, which was even smaller than the previous one, and there were no proper seats but just metal benches down both sides complete with seat belts. There were only 10 passengers for this leg of our journey. The plane flew at a very low altitude and it was buffeted and shaken so much that I was almost sick. I felt so awful that I could not summon up any inclination to watch the landscape below. Although, in reality it was not a particularly long flight, to me it seemed never ending.

Chapter 2

The Village of Zyryanka

The village of Zyryanka appeared on the horizon abruptly and the plane started its descent and prepared for landing. I had recovered enough to take an interest once again and started to watch through the window at the scene evolving. The whole scene below right up to the horizon was just taiga with a large river immediately below us. I thought we must be making a landing approach, but where could we land? The plane continued to descend quickly, it was very low, but there was still water from my side. 'Maybe we're landing on the river? Maybe we are falling?' I thought. And suddenly I felt that we landed on solid ground.

After the plane came to a halt and the door opened I descended the steps into the dust and unexpected heat of the North- East Siberian summer. It was terribly hot and so dusty that I couldn't see anything. "Where is the village? Where's the river and taiga?" there was nothing but dust and heat. After a while the dust settled down and it was possible to look around. The runway was actually along the river Kolyma. It wasn't a runway at all; the plane had landed right on the sand beach of the river. The beach was covered with fine sand and that is why it caused such a dust.

There were other small planes on the beach, and here, between them, people were sunbathing and swimming in the river. The airport terminal was situated in a small one-storeyed wooden building, coloured in blue. We went through this building with minimal formalities and out straight into the village. The road starting outside this terminal ran straight through the whole village. There wasn't a left luggage office at the airport and so we went into the street with our bags in our hands.

My first impressions of the village were favourable. On both sides of the street there were two-storeyed wooden houses painted in different colours: brown, blue, dark blue, green. I saw shops, a school, a kindergarten, gym and a stadium. My mood improved and there appeared hope that we would be able to live here. "Look, Victor, here's everything for a living: a school, shops, a kindergarten, a stadium," I said. We walked through the whole village and we eventually came to the bank of the river. This was not the same river on whose shore we had arrived, but another river.

The village was situated at a confluence of two rivers: the Kolyma and Yasachnaya. We stood on the bank and looked around. Over on the other bank there was a similar village but seemingly a much smaller than the one on this side. A ferry which carried both people and cars linked the two villages.

It became obvious to us that these were navigable waters because not only was there a ferry we could also see a river port, complete with larger vessels and cranes for unloading. There were also many other smaller craft darting about on both rivers.

I turned to my husband and said, "Victor, I like it already. Look, the village is fine, everything we need is here, people have time to sunbathe and go on boats to the wild. Let's go back and find a job centre office." We went back down the same street up which we had walked. We passed many local Yakut people during our walk. No wonder – it was Yakutia.

In a couple of minutes, a Russian woman appeared in view. We stopped her and asked about the whereabouts of the local job centre office. She replied to us in Ukrainian language. We were so pleased to see her, someone from our homeland, and greeted her as if she was a relative, my husband talking to her in Ukrainian. She was glad as well and asked us where we had come from. It turned out that she had lived in Ukraine, only 100 km from city of Chernovtsy. When she found out that we had just arrived and didn't know anybody she said – "I won't leave you, I'll help you. Come with me." It turned out that there was no job centre office in the area.

The village of Zyryanka Yakytia Regeon

She brought us to the Offices of a building company. My husband went to see the director of the company to seek if any positions were available and we were left waiting at the reception area. Whilst we were waiting I got to know the woman a little better. Her name was Galina. She was 50 years old, and had come to Yakutia with her husband 15 years earlier to join her husband's brother who had been a prisoner at the Zyryanka prison camp. He had been taken prisoner by the Germans during WW2 and on his return to Russia had been sent to the Gulags. After the camp had been closed he had stayed to live and work there.

Galina and her husband came just to visit him originally, but decided that they would like to live there as well. She said that they had no plans to return back to Ukraine. Suddenly I realised and thought,

"My father was worried that we originally said we were going to Magadan, but we were now thinking of living in Yakutia, the place where Gulags were formerly situated.' Galina probably noticed that I felt awkwardly and started laughed and said, "Don't worry! There aren't any prison camps anymore. The village is cosy, people are nice, and it's very interesting to live here."

Eventually my husband reappeared looking very happy. He was to be hired as an office based engineer with the promise of being promoted to the main construction division and sign a contract for three years. This position would also entitle him to a room in a hostel. The director refused though to hire me for the position of a land surveyor. He said that in such conditions a woman wouldn't be able to work and advised me to look for something else. I wasn't upset. Frankly saying, I didn't want to work as a land surveyor any more.

The Lenina Street is the main street of Zyryanka village

After this success Galina took us to her home. Her house was outside the village on the Yasachnaya river bank with a small yard in front of the house. There was a wire between posts on which fish were hung to dry. There were a lot of fish, big ones and smaller ones. The big ones were split open and were

21

held apart with thin sticks so that it couldn't fold back. It was covered with cheesecloth. "So that flies don't sit on it," explained Galina. Small fish just hung on the hooks. Fat dripped onto the ground and the smell was very appetizing.

Behind the house were steep steps down to the river on which was moored a motorboat. "We've got two boats and my husband's gone fishing in the other, but he will be back tomorrow. Now make yourself comfortable in this room, and I'll prepare dinner," said Galina. She gave us a small room, which could only fit a small bed. She had a small house and all the rooms were small. In the middle of kitchen there was a big Russian stove made from bricks. It was heated with coal and kept the whole house warm. There weren't any modern conveniences in the house. Running water and a toilet were outside.

Galina prepared dinner quickly. She sliced a big stock fish, and put lots of small fish on the table, "This fish is called 'Chebak' and is tasty with beer. All who go on holidays to the mainland take it with them," she explained. She also put on the table a jar with Hungarian pickles and marinated tomatoes, and cans with condensed milk. She sliced bread, good salami and 'salo' (pork fat with a skin). She also put onto the table a pile of expensive Moscow chocolate candies and brought out a bottle of vodka and Bulgarian wine.

"Welcome to the table. Let's celebrate your arrival to the Kolyma land," she said.

This dinner differed greatly from the food which we had in Ukraine. Everything here was from jars and cans and at the same time these were quite expensive delicacies for us. I always loved fish and that's why I immediately grabbed it. I drank wine and Galina with my husband drank vodka.

Galina talked nonstop. She tried to tell us as much as possible about this land and prove that this was the best place in the world. She told us that everybody there lived well. There was everything we could want: A taiga rich with mushrooms and berries, rivers and lakes full of fish. The best products and goods were delivered there from every corner of the Soviet Union. My head was spinning from the wine and her words. I listened to her and thought – "God, how good that we came here. Everything here is so interesting and unusual."

The next day, when Galina found out that I was fully competent as a seamstress she told me that I should seek employment at the consumer services centre, where there was a department that produced clothing. This was good news for me, as I had always been a keen dressmaker and seamstress and this was an opportunity to get employment doing a job which I loved. Although I had never been a professional seamstress, but for as long as I can remember I had always had a passion for sewing and needlework.

Perhaps I inherited the love to do this work from my granny, who was a good seamstress. By my early teens I had finished several sewing courses and was preparing to become a fashion designer, but my plan was destined to fail. Now, perhaps, was the opportunity to do the thing I was fond of.

The Consumer services center was located just in front of a building site, coincidently, where my husband going start to work, so I joined my husband and together we went to meet the director and ask for a job for myself. The director was an older lady, and she immediately asked me what experience I had. I showed her the certificate I had been awarded from my sewing courses, which I had received ten years ago and telling her that I had sewed regularly since that time. So you haven't got any experience. Those courses are not professional," she said, openly disappointed.

That moment my husband stood up for me. He started to explain to her that I sewed well and had made things for many people: himself, relatives, neighbours and for all of them were satisfied. She laughed and said, "Alright. If everyone was satisfied I'll take you as a master of the second category to the women clothes sewing department. Let's go with me, I'll lead you to the department."

The department was big. There were 15 professional stitching machines and several special machines which I had never seen before. At each machine there worked a woman. When they found out that I had no experience they started to teach me how to use the machines and the other equipment. A tailor's cutter brought me an order and I started to work on it.

I saw that women were watching me. After a while they stopped me and showed me how they sewed. Their goods were of much better quality than mine. After seeing that, I felt upset.

I understood that compared to them I couldn't do anything. I ripped it up and started to sew from the start. They calmed me down and told me not to worry as this was just my first day and that I would soon become proficient.

The next day my husband and I got an advance of salary and so had money to spend. We listened to Galina's advice and went to the shop to buy warm clothes. We bought a warm sheepskin coat for my husband, a warm blanket of camel's hair and other items we deemed necessary.

It was the middle of summer – July. It was hot – plus 36 degrees above zero (plus 96 degrees F). People swam in Kolyma River and got a suntan. But everybody said that it was not for long. In the middle of September the snow would fall, the river would freeze and a long winter with bitter frost would start. It was hard to believe but we needed to be prepared.

We lived at Galina's place for two weeks and then rented a room in the centre of the village closer to work. When we were leaving Galina's house I wanted to pay her for home and food but she refused. We were very thankful for all she had done for us and became friends with this family. That is how easy we settled down in Yakutia, I think it was God who helped us.

Chapter 3

My First Siberian Winter

So, my new life in Siberia began during the summer time, when the temperature was about 36 degrees C and the local residents took full advantage of this by swimming in the Kolyma River and lying on the bank getting a suntan. The fact that it was so warm was big surprise for me, because I had always thought of Siberia as a very cold place, even in summer. I was, however, quickly advised by my work colleagues that summer was finished by September, and that the first snowfall would arrive by the middle of that month. By the middle of October the rivers would be frozen over and the long severe Siberian winter would have started.

It was difficult to believe that temperatures could change so dramatically, but I realised that we must make preparations for the winter ahead. A few days later we both received an advance of wages, it was not a big sum, but it was first our money in Siberia! Nearly all that money we spent on warm clothes ready for the long cold winter.

Our first winter in Siberia was spent in a small room at a family hostel, which belong to the building company, where my husband worked. This family hostel was a wooden, one- storeyed building in the centre of the village, and the room which we occupied was only 10 square metres. The previous occupants of the room had left behind their furniture: a single bed, a coat rack, a table and one chair. There was also a small table, on which we put an electric cooker. That table, where we cooked, was our 'kitchen'. The 'kitchen' was separated from the room with a printed cotton curtain.

A tap for cold water was situated in the hostels hallway and warm water had to be taken from the radiator which also had a tap for this purpose. At that time there wasn't a single house in the village with all the modern amenities one would have expected.

The only inside toilets, and therefore warm, were in the building occupied by the district committee of the party, district executive committee and the other enterprises. In all other occupied buildings in the village, people had to use public conveniences outside and in any weather.

The frost about minus 58 degrees C (minus 72 F) on lunch time

Even bathing had to be done in the public baths which were situated in a very old wooden building, constructed by prisoners during the Gulag years. There was only one bathing room, that's why there were men's and women's days. A couple of years later a fire destroyed this building and as a result a new larger one was constructed of concrete. Inside not only was there a separate room for men and one for women but also there were steam rooms, a hairdresser's, a laundry room and dry cleaning room.

People usually went to the public baths on Saturday and Sunday, although the baths were open throughout the week. The weather didn't matter, even when there were frosts of minus 50 degrees C (minus 58 degrees F) everybody still went, even little children were taken. For hygienic reasons we all took our own wash basins and also a bunch of green birch twigs for use in the steam room. We usually returned home red faces and our towels twisted round our heads. It was a popular meeting place and perhaps used more like a social club than just for bathing. After meeting up with people one was acquainted with it was commonplace to go to someone's house to eat and drink for the rest of the day.

In the hostel where we lived there was central heating and the radiators were always very hot and it was nice and warm in the centre of the room, but a little bit further away in the corners of the room the walls froze solid. They were covered with ice up to a thickness of 5-10cm (2-4 in). If we went to bed with our head to the window – hair froze to the wall. If with legs next to the window our legs never got warm. We didn't have a fridge and it may seem peculiar to some people that with temperatures as low as minus 50 degrees C, we would actually need one. It should be remembered that this was the outside temperature and the inside temperature could be quite high and food still had to be preserved.

Most people, like us, could not afford this type of appliance even if they had been available to purchase. To overcome this problem, people would place whatever they wanted to freeze into a string bags and hang them out of the ventilator windows. All the houses were covered with those string bags full of products, but due to the temperature difference outside and inside the houses ice eventually formed round the ventilator windows. The opening in the ventilator windows became smaller and smaller and by spring they were totally covered with ice.

It was in this room that I and my husband Victor celebrated our first New Year in Siberia. We had our small flat decorated with a Christmas tree provided by our employing organisations who sent workers into the taiga and who brought back pine trees. People could choose what size they wanted and as many as they wanted for free. The taiga is so big our few trees taken from the wild was of no ecological importance. I brought just a small pine tree home, put it on the table and decorated it as a Christmas tree with cotton wool. The aroma of fir spread all over the room and put us both in festive mood.

Winter time in Zyryanka, Kolyma region

By this time we had plenty of friends, and we agreed to celebrate New Year together with my friend who was also a work colleague. We would walk to my friend's place which was a two-room apartment opposite the social centre which everybody simply called the club.

My colleagues from work had told me how they celebrated New Year and I wanted to see it with my own eyes. Victor took a bottle of champagne and I took some food which I precooked and we went on our visit. It was such a tradition here that if a group gathered for the New Year, everybody had to take alcohol and food with them and then a big table was laid.

It was 10 p.m. when we left home and the frost was so bitter, that visibility was only about 3 metres. There was a thick fog, white as milk. It was fortunate that we knew which way to go as we could only see the road immediately in front of us. The light from the street lamps and house windows could only be seen only if we approached it closely. I had a big shawl round me made of goat's fur and called a 'Russian shawl'. I twisted it round the whole of my head and left open only one eye, but it didn't help and my whole face was frozen and it was almost impossible to breath.

In those conditions if you breathed out the air fast – your breath turned into tiny pieces of ice. We came to our friend's house as fast as we could relieved to get out of the cold. It was very hot in the flat, even though the ventilator windows were open. There must have been about fifteen other people in the flat and everybody had brought with them alcohol and some food. The women laid up the table and we started to see off the Old Year. According to the Russian tradition, the Old Year had to been seen off starting from 11 p.m., and then at midnight the New Year was celebrated. Everybody was in a festive mood and all had fun.

We switched on the radio full blast (at that time there was no TV in the village) and listened to the local radio station. Right on midnight, according to local time, the chairman of District Executive Committee congratulated all people with the start of the New Year. In Moscow it was only 4 p.m. and it would be another 8 more hours before receiving the congratulations from the Chairman in Moscow. We celebrated the new 1972nd year the way it should be with champagne and the cries of "Hooray!"

After that all men went out and let off rockets into the sky whilst the women stayed indoors and looked out of the windows. The rockets were not ornamental fireworks, but were those that were given to the flying personnel at the airport, to the workers of the river port, lifeguards and hunters. They were used when needed as signal flare, because when there was a bitter frost or fog only those signal rockets could be seen from distance. However, everybody saved some of them up for the New Year as at that time fireworks couldn't be bought at shops as today, in fact we did not know that such things even existed.

When this happened the sky illuminated at once with different colours and it almost became daylight. This was a real firework display the rockets of different kinds and colours were fired none stop from almost every house. It seemed as if the fog had disappeared altogether. The whole display lasted for about ten minutes and then the village was captured with fog and haze again. I'd never seen such before. This was a real firework display.

After that everybody started to prepare for the New Year's party at the club. The club was situated in a big two-storeyed wooden building that was constructed in 1947 as the recreational centre of the village. On the second floor there was a library, a café, several rooms for hobby groups: dancing, vocal, folk arts of the native people of Yakutia among other activities.

On the ground floor there was a cinema for 400 people, a dance hall, where each Saturday after the cinema closed a dance was held.

For the New Year all the chairs were taken away from the cinema, a Christmas tree was set up and a New Year's party was held in both rooms. It started at 11 p.m. 31st December and finished at 8 a.m. 1st January after the celebration of New Year according to Moscow time. Our friends told us that it would be better if we go to the club without wearing our heavy outdoor coats, as there would be quite a lot of people and there weren't enough places in the cloakroom to contain everybody's coats, and we would not be able to find our coats later.

All the men from my organisation were dressed in suits and the women wore dresses and nylon stockings. I wore a white dress of taffeta without sleeves and white shoes. The house where my friend lived was opposite the club and you only had to cross the square to get there. My husband took my hand and we ran as quickly as we could across the square. It was so cold that I instantly froze, gasping for breath. The cold paralysed my body and within a couple of steps my shoes beat the road as if they were wooden and my whole body became stiff with the cold.

The Palace of culture (Club), 1971

When we entered the club, it was very warm, and my husband turned and asked me how I felt and whether everything was alright. I couldn't answer. My face was literally frozen; the muscles on my face didn't work. I touched my forehead and knees and didn't feel anything. All my girlfriends froze as well and it was only after we had warmed ourselves and drank some champagne that we were warm enough to be able to dance.

As my friend had predicted there were so many people in the club that it seemed as if the whole village had gathered there. People danced everywhere – in the hall, in rooms, and in corridors. The party was hosted by Dedyshka Moroz and a Snegyrochka (Grandfather Frost and his granddaughter). It was fun. Some people had come in fancy dress and a competition was held for the best costume. Volunteers went on stage and performed songs or recited poetry and the best ones received presents.

At various times during the evening, as was usual, many of the men, among them my husband went out of the room for a smoke. At the very moment that my husband went for a smoke the host announce a competition for the best dance. Nobody went up onto the stage. I without thinking jumped up onto the stage and told the musician what music to play and performed an Ukranian dance, a dance which I had previously performed at college in Chernovtsy.

Dancing had actually been a hobby of mine from primary school, when I had been included in the dancing group which danced on stage at special occasions, and continued until I finished school. My dancing continued while I was studying at Chernovtsy College and in fact became the soloist of the college dancing ensemble. After this I always took advantage of every opportunity to show of my dancing skills. At the end of my dance, Grandfather Frost presented me with a big doll as a prize.

When Victor came back I stood with the doll in my hands and thinking, 'How great that my husband wasn't here, he would never have let me go onto the stage.' When he found out that they had given me a doll for my performance he was surprised and said, "Don't drink any more, you must be drunk." But I wasn't drunk; I was just in a good mood and happy.

The night passed very quickly. When it was 8 o'clock in the morning we celebrated New Year according to Moscow time. This was the signal for the end of the party. I then refused to go outside without my coat and my husband went over to my friend's house and brought me my outdoor clothes.

My friends, who told me about their celebration of New Year, were right. There were really lots of people at the club and as predicted there weren't enough places in the cloakroom: fur coats, hats, boots were put right on the floor. The whole corner of the hall was piled up with clothes. How, on earth, did people find theirs afterwards, I don't know; everything was almost the same. They say, that after such parties people often came home wearing someone else's clothes. The last ones wore what was left.

After the New Year holiday I told my colleagues at work how bitter cold it was and how I froze when we ran to the club. They told me that it was minus 60 degrees C (minus 76 degrees F) that night. Many of them had thermometers behind the windows and they knew exactly what the temperature was each day. That was how, as fate had willed, I experienced minus 60 degrees that first New Year's night in Siberia. I will never forget it!

Chapter 4

The First Flat and My Husband's New

Job

We were lucky, my husband worked for the construction company and he had an advantage in getting a flat. It was even less than a year when we got a separate flat in a new house. This flat was on the ground floor of a two-storeyed house in the centre of the village. There was only one room of 15 square metres, a kitchen of 7 square metres. There was a stove in the kitchen which was heated with coal. I heated it in order to cook.

This house was new, it was always warm and dry and the walls never froze solid. There was central heating in the flat and a tap with cold water. It was very convenient, because almost nobody had cold water. The majority of houses only had hot water on tap which they took from radiators; and when they needed cold water they waited till the hot one grew cold. For those times it was a very good flat and all told us we were very lucky. At that time we didn't have much money and we only bought the most necessary things: a bed, two tables with chairs, one for the main room and one for the kitchen. Two wooden shelves nailed to the wall and curtained with a blind replaced a wardrobe for us.

I had my first flat in this house

30

Such wardrobes could be seen in every flat. They were called jokingly 'Kolyma wardrobes'. I sewed the curtains for the window myself, and added pot plants to the room, making it very cosy and comfortable. We lived there happily for 5 years.

We got the flat because my husband was promoted to a new position within the main construction company. He earned much more money at this job, but it was not without its problems. The climate in the north-east of Siberia was very inhospitable, people worked under extreme conditions, and the work of construction was carried out at all times of the year.

In summer workers worked in the broiling sun and were constantly plagued by mosquitoes which bit them relentlessly. Everybody received an insect repellent, but it was not effective enough. During the summer months when there was almost perpetual daylight or 'white nights' when it was light all the time, they worked day and night in shifts, trying to complete as much work as possible and consequently earn a little extra money.

In winter, they worked even when the frosts were the most bitter and when the daylight was almost non-existent. According to the labour legislation of the country work stopped in the north-east parts of Siberia only in those days when a temperature was equal to minus 50 degrees C (minus 58 degrees F). Workers used to joke: "We can work in such frost, but the equipment can't." The construction company constructed buildings for the social needs such as: schools, kindergartens, hospitals, industrial and agricultural units and housing.

Not only was construction carried out in administrative centre of Zyryanka itself, but also in outlying villages, sometimes as far away as 130 kilometres. This may not sound too far away, but ground access to those places could only take place during the wintertime from November till April. In this period all the construction materials and equipment required had to be delivered.

At the end of October, when the rivers and lakes froze, heavy machinery carved out a road through the taiga and on frozen rivers and swamps. Such roads were called 'a winter road' because it was used only during the wintertime. During the snowfalls and snowstorms the roads were totally covered with snow and it caused big troubles. For example, it was 130 kilometres to the village of Arylakh, and if everything was fine the journey would only take about twenty-four hours, but if there were troubles it could take a couple of days or more..

Closer to spring, partial thawing would occur on the lakes and rivers over which the winter road ran, and this created a layer of water under thin ice, but thicker ice at a depth of about one metre. This could cause vehicles with heavy loads to fall through the top layer of ice into the metre of water above the thicker ice. To pull such a vehicle fully laden out of there was almost impossible. The load had to be transferred to another truck and even then it took a long time to get a truck out of the frozen river. Despite those troubles everything was done to ensure that everything needed for construction was delivered during the winter season.

When spring came the winter roads were destroyed and land communications ceased. During summer time you could only get to outer villages by plane or a helicopter, although those villages situated on the riverbank could be reached by boat. It was my husband responsibility to supply working teams with documentation, uniform and dwelling for the period of work and for ensuring that construction materials were delivered to the construction site.

He also took care of quality control and recorded the hours worked according to which the workers were paid.

He was practically responsible for any problems that occurred on site and, therefore, spent most of his time at the construction site, only returning to his office at the end of the month to complete paperwork. In the one cold December he was working at a site in the village of Nelemnoe, which was 65 km from Zyryanka. This was a small village with population of 350 people, where there were only two streets only and around forty houses. But it was a special historical place for our region, because Yukagirs – a small population of people of the north-east of Siberia with mysterious and interesting history, lived there.

In 1970s there were only around a thousand people of this nationality was in the USSR, and around 200 of them lived in Nelemnoe village. Despite the remoteness of this village all conditions for normal life were provided for. There was a post office, a shop, a club, a museum, a kindergarten, a first-aid post and the construction of a school, a boiler house and the other social projects were in progress, that is why my husband often travelled there on business for several of days.

My husband travelled to this site quite regularly by car which was usually driven by his chauffer. On one occasion he promised to return in 3 days, because it was my birthday and he wanted to be there for me. When he left I asked him to buy a fur coat for our son as I had heard that a shop there sold great kids' fur coats. After three days he called me at work and told me that he had done everything he needed to do at the site, bought a fur coat and if everything will be alright, he back home tomorrow evening.

The next day it was my birthday and I cooked several tasty dishes and waited for my husband. Time passed and he did not arrive and I started to worry. I was alarmed as I knew that conditions were bad outside and something must have happened on his way back. However there was nothing that I could do, it was a dark winter night with sub-zero temperatures and nobody can help during that time. After midnight, still waiting for him I fell asleep.

He eventually arrived back home at 4 a.m. When I opened the door I almost fainted. There he stood like a block of ice with a bag in his hands. He looked ghost like because his face, eyebrows, hair, a hat, collar of the sheepskin coat was covered with ice and white frost. His trousers, felt boots and bag were covered with snow and he couldn't talk because he was shivering with cold. I quickly took off his outer garments and wrapped him up with a warm blanket and started to massage his face with a wool scarf. He refused to eat. I forced him to drink some hot tea with some cognac and he immediately fell asleep.

I untied the bag and inside there was a fur coat for our son, a very nice sheepskin one of brown colour and a hat to match the coat. There was also a present for my birthday – a small beige collar of mink fur. It was the first fur collar bought for me in Siberia. I cried involuntary at seeing all this. In the morning my husband related to me how he and two others, including his driver had departed from the construction site in good conditions and headed home to Zyryanka. However, just over half way home the car broke down and the driver was unable to carry out repairs.

The driver, assessing the situation decided that it would be better to stay with the vehicle overnight, realising that in the morning because people in the village knew they were on the way back, they would launch a rescue party to find them. He therefore, proceeded to light a fire and prepared for them to stay the night. Despite the temperature being minus 30-35 degrees C, the weather was fine with a good moon that lit up the countryside, my husband foolishly decided to walk home. Telling the others to stay with the car and he would send another car for them in the morning.

They tried to talk him out of the idea but he grabbed a bag and left them. He told me that he walked fine at first, but then he began to tire and feel the effect of the cold.

His face became covered with white frost because of the cold, his eyelashes stuck together and it was hard for him to breathe. He said that there was a moment when he was afraid that he wouldn't reach the house and he didn't know exactly how far away from Zyryanka the car was broken down, how many kilometres he had already walked and how many still had left to reach the village.

However, he did know that if he did stop to rest he would freeze to death in a very short time so he just continued to walk, walking for what seemed like hours. He did not even remember arriving home or how long it had taken him because when he woke up in the morning he asked, "Did I bring a bag with me?"

"You did. The fur coat for our son is gorgeous and the collar, too. Thank you so much for the present," I replied. He then made immediate preparations to leave to rescue his comrades still marooned in their car.

After this near tragedy for my husband, I realised that our future life in Siberia would be not easy. Because of its poor infrastructure, lack of roads, boundless taiga, rivers and impassable swamps, what in normal circumstances would be an insignificant incident, in this severe land it could be quite a serious catastrophe. We both, however, understood that we had come to this dangerous place as a result of my previous life in Ukraine, which I will briefly introduce to you in the next several chapters.

Chapter 5

My Background

So, I was born in Eastern Ukraine, in a small mining town about 60 kilometres from Donetsk. The history of Donetsk is very interesting and unusual. It may seem strange, but the city was founded by an English industrialist and engineer named John James Hughes, who was originally from Merthyr Tydfil in the Welsh coal mining area. His father was the head of an iron and steel works in the city, and John Hughes was also engaged in metallurgical and foundry engineering for the whole of his life.

Since 1860 he was the director of a big steel rolling works, some the products of which were used in the construction of warships. The works executed orders from Europe, including Russia, and thanks to that John Hughes met Russian military engineers, who considered him to be a purposeful, energetic, knowledgeable engineer and experienced business partner. Then, as a result of geological investigations, in the south of Russia, huge reserves of iron ore, coal, rock-salt, limestone and many other minerals were discovered and, presented the opportunity to develop heavy industry in the region.

The Russian government offered John Hughes the chance to become a chief executive of a New Russian joint-stock company charged with the development of metallurgic works and coal mines. He gladly accepted the proposal and moved to Russia. He explored the whole area and decided to develop a production in a small riverside village called Aleksandrovka. He took all his family with him to this place, together with about 500 experienced welsh miners and metalworkers and their families.

After three years of toil, he established an iron and steel works, together with mines to supply the power for this activity. The construction of a new town was started, to be called in his honour – Hughsofka, instead of Aleksandrovka. John Hughes was very famous in Russia at that time, and as a consequence, his metallurgical works and the town became the main industrial centre of Russia and later Ukraine.

The legacy of John Hughes still lives on in the area in the form of two buildings, constructed in the British styles which still stand to the present day. One a nearly ruined house where John Hughes and his family lived is now a historical monument. The second a hotel called "Great Britain" which although constructed in 1883 is still operating as a hotel.

He and his fellow countrymen not only developed the works and the town, but also trained local people in the skills needed to work in these new industries, and promoted the development of cultural institutions. Amongst these were a commercial college (which is now the 2nd department of the Technical University of Donets) and a British school (now it is an evening school for young people who work).

A monument to John Hughes was erected in 2001 at the territory of National Technical University. The city had borne this name up to 1924, when it was renamed to Stalino, but since 1961 the city was renamed Donetsk, and has preserved this name up to the present time. During the Soviet period the town developed rapidly, and became a heavy industrial centre, with the enterprises of iron and steel making, coal-mining and chemical industry.

Monument of John Hughes, 2009

Coal mines with their waste tips and other industrial plants are situated all over Donetsk, but despite this the town is very green and has many parks, boulevards and squares richly planted with flowers. The especially of these parks was roses of every variety, which has become a kind of a symbol of the city This way, at the end of 1970s, when the population of Donetsk reached 1 million people, a million roses were planted all over the city, that was a rose for each city dweller.

I particularly remember the city from my childhood, when it was called Stalino, because sometimes, during weekends, all my family would travel into the city and spend time in a park named Shcherbakov. This park was situated in the Centre of the city on the town lakes and was big, beautiful and well-tended. Amongst the many other attraction in this park, was a boat-station, where father used to rent a boat and take us boating on the town lake.

The park was a wonderland for me at that time, with so many attractions: a hall of distorting mirrors, swings and roundabouts for kids. This was the happiest time of the week for me. I lived in a small mining town, where there was nothing interesting except the two mines with waste banks, a small park and an entertainment complex, consisting of cinema, dance hall and library and that is why the trips to Stalino (Donetsk later) was always a great joy for me.

My parents were both born and lived in Donetsk region. My mother descended from a mining family. Her father (my grandpa) worked at a mine for his whole life. During World War II he volunteered for the army. Although he was wounded twice, he fortunately came back home alive. He was awarded several medals which he cherished and wore only once a year on 9th May – the Victory Day of the Great Patriotic War (WWII).

Every year on this day we visited our grandparents. Grandpa loved telling us front-line stories: How he fought and survived, how and when he was wounded and, sadly, he always cried when he told us those stories.

My grandmother (my mother's mom) gave birth to eight children, but six of them died, due to the famine in Ukraine during 1933 and the subsequent illnesses. Only my mother and her sister, who was three years younger, survived. Grandma was a very good seamstress. She sewed at home and always had plenty of orders.

Mother studied very well at school and dreamed of becoming a teacher, but her dream didn't come true. In 1941 the War began and all schools were closed. I do not know much about the Second World War and my main information came from my mother and the depravations which she suffered, and I can only imagine what she went through.

She was 13 when Germans invaded Eastern Ukraine. Her father volunteered for the army, leaving my grandmother, my mother and her sister at home alone to fend for them. These were very difficult times for everybody. Thankfully, due to the skill of my grandmother at sewing, at the start of the war she had some work which enabled the family to survive. However, when the Germans invaded the town she had to give this up as it became too dangerous to live in the city, and eventually managed to travel to a nearby village in which her relatives lived.

The Germans carried out raids in the town, on people's houses and homes, turning out the people onto the streets, from where, the women were rounded up and taken to the freight cars on the railway, and sent to work in Germany. Those who refused were simply shot. In order to avoid this fate, my grandma with her daughters hid in the cellars of the houses or in the house of her relatives who lived in the village.

Teenagers had their own role to play during the war. My mother told me that in the city, near to the school, was a concentration camp for Russian soldiers. She, together with the other children, brought and passed through the wire fencing some bread for the prisoners, although she was always hungry herself. The guards naturally disapproved of this and did their best to stop them, even threatening to shoot the children.

Very often after a big battle in the area there were many casualties just left on the battlefield. Many teenagers assumed the responsibility of gathering the IDs of the Russian soldiers and saving them ready to hand over to the appropriate military authorities. After one particularly devastating raid during which almost all the women were taken from their homes and sent to Germany, my grandmother gathered up her daughters and they escaped to the village where her relatives lived.

But this didn't save them. Not far from this village, however, was a quarry, where imprisoned Russian soldiers extracted stone and chip for the construction of a road to Krasnoarmeisk. Every day the Germans drove all the woman and teenagers from the neighbouring villages to the quarry to work. They were treated like slaves.

Some of them lugged stones from the quarry face to the waiting trucks and the others loaded these vehicles. If someone stopped to have a rest they were lashed. My mother was small and fragile and could not continuously work for long periods and was therefore constantly whipped. Because of this constant beating there appeared wounds on her thigh, which didn't heal for a long time leaving her with permanent scarring. Despite this brutal treatment she did say some of the Germans were a little compassionate, giving a little bread or chocolate to the teenagers when their officers were not looking.

In September 1943, east of Ukraine was set free as a result of the Soviet Army's attack. Mother said there was such a battle that she thought that the end of the world had come. Tanks went in solid rows across the fields, without choosing a road or avoiding the villages. Everything exploded and was on fire, it seemed as if the Earth itself was on fire. During the battle day turned into a dark night. When finally the Germans retreated nothing but ruins were left behind, most of coal main were flooded or ravaged.

After the war, when the region started to get back to some sort of normality, mother completed a course in bookkeeping and started to work as an accountant at a mine. There she met a local young miner-man and married him after two years. That was my father. I was born a weak child, because my mother was in poor health due to the depravations she suffered during the war. When she was pregnant she often fainted due to the starvation.

Even in the post-war period there was a period of starvation, there was very little to eat. As a working person she received a small ration - 200 grammes of bread per day. The diet of many at this time was mainly vegetables from their vegetable garden. Most of all they ate beetroot. It was cooked in different ways: boiled, fried and dried. There after my mother couldn't eat beetroot for a long time. When I grew up and I told her that beetroot is very healthy, she replied: "I have eaten enough of it in the wartime and I can't even look at it right now."

I don't remember my father at all. He died due to the accident at the mine, when I was only two months old. My mother got married once again in three years and gave birth to my sister. My mother concealed the truth from me for many years. For a long time I thought that my stepfather was in fact my own father and he treated me as if I were his own daughter.

He was a really good man: kind, tactful, patient and always treated me as if I were his natural daughter. I considered him to be my own father for my whole life. He graduated college of mines and worked down a mine operating a mining machine at the coalface.

I was lucky, my mother and my father lived in harmony and I grew up in a tight-knit family. I had a happy childhood. After my sister was born my mother didn't work. She kept house and brought us up. Father worked at a good mine and earned a good wage, for those days. My parents indulged us both and kept saying: "We didn't have a happy childhood but our children must be happy." And we were really happy. We lived well. My sister and I had the best clothes and the best toys and the house was always full of food.

Father worked very long hours. His job at the mine was really hard. He used to come back home so tired that he ate and went straight to bed. Then he woke up, ate and went to work.

He worked different shifts and sometimes we didn't even see him for days at a time. Even so on some weekends in summer we had some pleasant times.

My mother and stepfather, 1950

Easter in Ukraine is situated in the steppe zone with a distinctly continental climate. There are frosts with more than -20 degrees C in winter and heat of 37 degrees C in summer. Summer is hot and long here. Donbas's nature has stuck in my mind – steppes, mines with slag heaps, dry winds, heat, and dust.

We had our own family traditions, which never changed, for example, once a year my mother went shopping to Moscow. Father's sister lived there and we stayed at her apartment. Mother saved money for that trip for a whole year. During this visit, mother used to buy us plenty of smart clothes: pullovers, woollen knitted hats, shoes and fur coats. These were enough to last us for the whole year and we were always smartly dressed. Once she brought back for us dolls, which could open their eyes and say "Ma-ma" My sister and I were so happy. At that time children didn't have as many toys as they have now and those dolls were like a fairytale for us.

I remember, very well, the days when my father got his wages. It was once a month and for every family this day was a celebration. And everybody looked forward to it. Once my father got his wages he went to the shop and bought a bottle of vodka, a bottle of good wine, and a kilo of the most expensive chocolate candies: "Kara-kum (Dessert)", "Belochka (Squirell)", "Mishka na Severe (a bear in the North)", canned food: sardines, sprouts, cod's liver, Dutch cheese and many other delicacies. He did this all the time whilst he worked at the mine and nothing changed.

On payday my sister and I were glued to the window looking out and waiting for our father.

When he arrived in the yard with handfuls of tasty food, we screamed: "Mommy. Mommy, Daddy is coming," and we jumped for joy. He came into the house, put all his money on the table and laid out the treats he had bought. Afterwards we had a holiday dinner. Mother always cooked a lot of very tasty food but that day she did her very special best.

We always had borsch for dinner. Borsch is a traditional Ukrainian dish. In order to cook it you have to take a good piece of meat, mainly beef. It is boiled, then some potato, cabbage, onion, fried in "salo" (lard), then pepper, carrot, beet and tomato sauce are added.

Borsch is eaten with sour cream. Everybody loves borsch and it is the main course for dinner in Ukraine. My mother also cooked a casserole with chicken or duck. She made a salad of fresh vegetables with sour cream and served up sweets and pastry. Stewed fruit compote drink was also served, made with fresh fruits in summer and dried fruit in winter. It is made by boiling the fruit and then adding sugar. It is drunk cooled. This is a traditional Ukrainian drink.

Father used to drink vodka and proposed his favourite toast "Let's drink to a life and health." The meaning of the toast I understood later when I grew up. Work at the mine was hard and dangerous. Accidents happened often and people died.

My sister & I, 1956

41

Every time, when father left for work we didn't know whether he'd come back. Many of his friends died at the mine or were disabled by these accidents. But there were also accidents with the people who didn't work at the mine. We had several mines in our little town and even more slag heaps. When the coal arrives at the surface it contains impurities of stone, coal is taken out of it and the rest is taken away and tipped on a waste heap.

With time this heap takes the form of a big cone-shaped mountain – a slag heap. The old slag heaps are often left and the new ones are made. This way wherever you look you can see them. This is peculiar scenery of Donetsk region and many other coal-mining areas of Ukraine.

Slag heaps are very dangerous, because the remains of the rock mixed up with the coal can start to burn inside and creating gas which pollutes the air. Rain water falling on these heaps can little by little wash away the rock allowing the water to get inside which can cause explosions. This happened in our town, at a very old waste heap which was only about 100 metres away from where people lived.

The Shock wave from this explosion devastated the first houses in the nearest street and around 60 people died, including the family of my father's friend. Father's friend was at work in the mine at the very moment and survived. We thanked God for saving our father, but he was once injured in a rock fall. He was treated in the hospital for a while after which he was prohibited from going down into the mine, and was restricted to other jobs on the surface of the mine.

Chapter 6

Life Under N. Khrushchev's Years

I was born and lived my early childhood during the Stalinist regime, but as I was a very small child at that time I didn't really understand anything. Remembering only in 1953 when Stalin died, all the neighbours gathered in the yard discussing something and with many of the women crying. When my mother came home she said: "Don't jump or laugh, just sit still, Stalin died." I was hazy about who Stalin was, but I understood that something bad had happened.

I knew Stalin and Lenin from children's books. All the books that our mothers' read to us contained stories and poems about Stalin and Lenin, together with their portraits. My sister and I learned one by heart:

I'm a little kid

From boredom I get rid

Who Stalin is I don't know

But, I love him deeply though

Sometimes in a poem I would change the word Stalin to Lenin but the meaning was left the same. When father came home from work, he discussed something for a while with my mother and after that dad always repeated: "No matter how good or bad Stalin was, it was thanks to him we won the war."

When Stalin died, for the next 11 years the General Secretary of Communist party was N. Khrushchev and I remember these years very well. In these years I was more grown-up, studying in school and listened intently to what my parents were talking about I understood about the changes in my family's life. I also began to appreciate what changes were happening in the country as a whole.

I want to say, that when N. Khrushchev came to power, life did change for the better. For the first time in many years of the Stalinist repressions people stopped being scared and felt that they were safe and more free, particularly when the rehabilitation of political prisoners began. Although in my family we had no one suffering as a political prisoner and this grief had not touched us directly, my father was very interested in this question, and could hardly wait to read the fresh newspapers such as "Izvestiya (News)" and "Pravda (The truth)".

It was impossible to comprehend how this had been allowed to happen under the Stalinist System – a system that had repressed thousands of innocent people, many of whom had died in prisons or the Gulags. The truth about that tragic period had been completely hidden from the population in general. Of course in those days there was no television and radio was heavily censored.

During the Kruschchev era, although we did not have television yet my father would listen every day to the radio, which was on all day long, and was the main source of instant news.

My parents were afraid that if something serious happened it would be broadcast on the radio and we wouldn't know about it if the radio was turned off. Even in those more "enlightened" days, little of the horrors was actually revealed to the general public.

A USSR radio announcer Yuri Levitan had been the voice of the country for many years, informing us of all the important issues in the country. He had a very nice, eloquent and unique voice. It was he who had made announcements about the beginning of the Great Patriotic War (WWII), and also gave operational summaries from the battlefront and Stalin's orders in the time of the war. It was he who also announced of the ending of the war.

When something important was happening in the country all the regular broadcasts from each radio station were broken off at the same time and we could only hear the voice of Yuri Levitan. He always started all his announcements in the same way, that's why nobody could guess what he was going to say, whether it would be good or bad news. He began "Attention! All the broadcasting stations of the USSR are working. Today in ..." After these words my mother would start to cry, thinking that every announcement was bad news, like that a new war had started.

In fact in the middle of 1950s there really was a period of "Cold war" between capitalist and socialist countries. Civil Defence classes were taught in schools so that we knew what to do in case of war. I was taught to wear gas mask and had practical training in giving first aid to wounded people and victims. All schoolchildren were led to bomb shelter and told what to do in case of an air raid.

A confrontation between our country and USA was especially strong in 1962, when USSR tried to put rockets in Cuba. In the course of two weeks, while negotiations between the two countries were being carried out, the USA instigated the blockade of Cuba. At this time the world appeared to be on the brink of a nuclear war.

We must be grateful to the leaders of both countries – N. Khrushchev and J. Kennedy, who had enough self-control and strong mind to negotiate, make concessions and avoid self-destruction. This period is called The Cuban Missile Crisis in history. At this time we had panic among the population. All our neighbours stored bread by drying it, no freezers, of course. They also bought lots of salt, matches, soap and other goods which might be needed in case of war. My father stopped mother from doing this, saying: "If there was a war, we'd all die and wouldn't need anything."

I personally, have only good memories connected with the voice of Yuri Levitan. He announced of the launching of the first Soviet satellite 'Sputnik', of the space flight with the dog Layka on board. I remember, best of all, 12th of April 1961. All the classes at school were stopped and all the pupils were lined up in the yard and the radio was switched on.

Within a few minutes Yuri Levitan announced the space flight of Yuri Gagarin, the first man in space. The next minute all of us together, teachers and pupils, cried, jumped and embraced each other. All the classes were cancelled that day and we all went home to continue our celebrations. All around the city pictures of Yuri Gagarin and the sputnik were hanging in schools and shops.

It seemed that there weren't any other issues in the country. Everybody discussed only the space flight of Yuri Gagarin. All the boys wanted to become astronauts and newborn babies were named Yuri. I didn't dream of becoming an astronaut, but I was very proud that the man who made the first space flight was from USSR. It made me wanted to better myself and to do something special, in order to be worthy of my country.

The life under the reign of Nikita Khrushchev was interesting and every single day brought something new. The reforms aimed at social development of the country were unveiled, with plans that would provide people with clothes, shoes and food and create decent living conditions. Animatedly people accepted the program of agricultural reform and development and in my opinion everybody, not only in our country, but also in the whole world knew Nikita Khrushchev's slogans "Let's catch up and leave behind America in production of meat, butter and milk."

In order to achieve his aims more land was needed to be developed for agricultural use, and to this end, new virgin land development had begun in Kazakhstan for the growing of grain. People were cajoled and persuaded to move there. My mother also wanted to move to one of these virgin regions in Kazakhstan, but father wouldn't go. He said: "I won't go anywhere. I was born here, I will live here and I will die here." However, mother's relatives did move and were happy living there.

The virgin farmlands were developed very quickly, because the whole country was encouraged to provide everything necessary to develop these regions. The best agriculture equipment, machinery, construction materials, and food were sent there. Thousands of students and skilled volunteers from all over the country worked in the virgin areas during the summer time. Villages and towns were constructed, infrastructure and roads appeared and in a matter of a couple of years millions of hectares of virgin land were ploughed up and planted.

Literally hundreds of sovkhozes (*a state-owned farm in the former USSR*) were established and thanks to them it was possible to get big cereal crops, but on the horizon there appeared unexpected trouble. The reason was that Kazakhstan is situated in the steppe zone which is predominantly grassland and is not supposed to be subject to regular ploughing for farming crops.

As a result there was soil erosion and dust storms, and sometimes everything was swept out of the fields. Crops became smaller and as a result expectations were not met.

Bread is good but corn is better! Khrushchev's idea was to use maize more. It was possible to farm it almost all over the USSR. It gave big crops in almost any weather conditions. Consequently, all free fields from Ukraine to Siberia were planted with sweet corn. Before that corn was mainly used as an animal produce, but from that time on it was introduced into the food industry. Corn meal and flour appeared in the shops. Corn flour was also added to bread.

Wheat flour became very hard to get, almost extinct. Everybody had to use corn flour. My mother used it to cook pancakes and omelettes, and these were not bad I even liked the pancakes. But the situation was much worse with bread. Bread baked with this flour was rough, hard and not at all tasty. It was only when Nikita Khrushchev was removal from power, did white bread made from wheat flour become widely available.

My mother brought a whole tray full of buns which were small with raisins, but very fresh and the smell of it spread all over the house. She put them on the table and told me, "Eat them, as many as you want." We missed ordinary wheat bread and buns so much, that I will never forget how tasty these new buns were. I distinctly remember the changes which happened after the 21st Congress of Communist Party of the Soviet Union, which took place in October 1961.

People couldn't believe that Stalin's body was taken out from the Mausoleum and his portraits and monuments were taken away throughout the whole country. We had a monument in our park and it was taken away during one night. It was there in the evening and there was nothing in the morning. Everything that was connected somehow to the name Stalin was renamed: towns, streets, etc., even the city of Stalino – the regional centre of Donbas – was renamed to Donetsk.

I will never forget the consternation and emotion, when N. Khrushchev announced at this congress that by the year 1980 communism would have further developed, and that everybody able to work would be employed and contributing as much as they were able, and receive, in return, everything that they needed for life. Even, if somebody can't work full time or is unable to work at all, they would still receive everything necessary! In connection with this matter, the program would last for 20 years and involve the studying of communism development and moral code at schools. To this end posters were introduced with the title: "Present generation will live in communism!" and these were hung all over the country.

Posters with the moral code were hanging everywhere in schools, clubs, and in the factories. They were before our eyes all the time, but I for one found many things hard to understand: what exactly was communism, how could we develop it and how could we live in it? Dad was very interested in politics and he knew everything. He tried to explain to us that the development of communism depended on each of us. The better we study and work the faster we could live in communism.

Mother couldn't understand either: How can a person work as much as they can and get as much they want? And who will be able to estimate how much and how good you can work.

I also couldn't understand: Why should I study at the university and work if I can get everything I need anyway? Everything was depending on the people's consciousness. But people are different and not all of them are good. I sat and counted how old I would be when communism came.

I thought 20 years isn't so much time I'd only be 32, so I could see what communism is and live it for a while.

What else can I remember that happened in the time of N. Khrushchev? – The mass accommodation construction, because Nikita Khrushchev wanted to give as many people as possible a separate flat and as fast as possible. The construction of blocks of flats started all over the country. To start with they were mainly five-storeyed brick houses, but later they were made of prefabricated concrete panels. Flats in such developments were small in area, the kitchens being particularly small only 5 - 6 square metres, with low ceilings. However, people were happy to get a flat in such developments.

The house that I lived in with my parents had been constructed by them over a period of time. It wasn't normal to hire builders at that time.

Father and mother worked very hard and did everything by themselves and when the work to be done was very hard relatives and neighbours helped. In four years a house was constructed. This house wasn't big: a living-room, kitchen, two bedrooms and a small veranda. The house was heated with the help of a stove which burned coal. There were no bathroom or toilet facilities. In the 1950s - 1960s almost every house in our town lacked these facilities. All our water was taken from the draw well in the garden. People had to bath in a tin bath in front of the stove. The toilet was outside in the garden.

The house where I grew up, 2008

Despite this I loved my house very much and my childhood passed very happily here. Eventually we wouldn't live a long time in this house. The reason was as follows: right under our house there were mine tunnels from where the coal was taken, they were everywhere in this region, but we hadn't known about it until we started to live in the house. The problem was that those tunnels were interconnected and we thought that we could hear noises and sound of footsteps and the voices of people below the house.

My mother remembered that during the war the mines were flooded together with people who worked there. It was especially unpleasant and scary to hear those noises at night.

Later when the "Khrushchev-era" apartments were constructed in our town as well we sold the house and got a two-room flat on the 3rd floor in a new panel block of flats. Such blocks of flats were constructed in the suburbs and they had no street names but numbers only. The address for example could be as follows: Gorlovka city, block 41, and house 15, apartment 7. Years after, blocks were renamed as neighbourhoods and received names, like: Sunny block, West block, South block and other. Our flat was small; it had all the facilities though: a bathroom, a toilet and a balcony. It was considered to be a very good flat at that time. Since that time many years have passed. My sister and I after finishing school left home, father died and my mother continued to live there until her death.

Khrushchev era block of flats where my parents lived for more than 40 years

Chapter 7

The First Courses

I already told you that my grandmother was a very good seamstress and tailor and this may be where I inherited my passion for sewing. For as long as I can remember I always wanted to sew. She told me that when I was a little girl I often visited her house and there I would always spend most of my time playing with her sewing machine. This machine was a hand crank Singer sewing machine which was very old, and she used to joke that it was almost as old as her, but despite this it worked extremely well.

So that I would not have to continually bother her she placed a stool in front me together with some pieces of cloth, threads and a big needle and would tell me, "Learn to sew if you want." I knelt before it and "sewed." As a result, all the cloth pieces were tangled with the threads and I would fall asleep with my head bent over the stool.

When I grew a bit older I dreamt that one day I would be able to sew like my grandma, because I didn't like the clothes they bought or sewed for me. I always thought that there was something wrong with each outfit, wrong size, wrong colour or even bad design. My mother used to tell me, "If you learn to sew, when you grow up you can make all the clothes you want for yourself as well as for other people. If you succeed at it you'll make your living, this talent will always earn your daily piece of bread."

One day my father told that he had seen an advertisement about the opening of some new sewing courses at our local culture centre. Girls and young women from the age of 18 upwards were invited to apply. These studies lasted for ten months. My father said, "You may start when you are eighteen." My heart was panting. God Gracious! Why am I only thirteen? I can't wait until that time! It's too long! And I started to beg my mum to let me take the courses.

She did not agree. Neither did my dad. They said, "The most important thing for you now is your studies. You can do it when you finish school." I did not calm down. "I want to sew, let me take the courses!" I insisted. At last my mother gave up. Next day we went to the culture centre to talk to the teacher of sewing. The teacher was an elderly woman with beautiful eyes and a lovely smile, but she told my mum that I was too young to take the course.

The course was quite intensive and she would give out a lot of homework and I would also need some time to sew at home. Besides this, it was necessary to have a sewing machine at home, because in the centre there was only one machine for a group of 30 people. I was very upset and unwittingly started to cry. The teacher looked at me and said: "All right, I'll go and talk to our principal, if he allows, I'll take you." The principal did allow, and I was accepted onto the course.

A few days later my father bought me a treadle sewing machine! It was made in Germany by a firm called "Keller". It was very expensive and cost 180 roubles (while the average monthly salary was about 70 roubles in those times). It was one of the most modern and up to date models available. It could perform 24 different operations; zigzag stitches, embroidery, button holes and many others.

The entire machine was enclosed in a wooden cabinet which had to be opened when I needed to use it. My father also gave me big pair of heavy scissors for cutting, and which I have used for nearly all my life. This machine brought me great happiness. In the evening when it was time for bed my mother could hardly pull me off my sewing machine. I was ready to sew the whole night through. To tell the truth I was interested in sewing much more than in my academic studies.

It was very easy for me to study at the sewing courses and I was very diligent. I did my home assignment better than all of the other students and I received much praise from the teacher. She told me that I had a God given talent. At the end of the course I took exams and got an excellent mark. So, at the age of thirteen I got my first certificate. Since that time I've been sewing for all my life.

Whilst at home, I sewed trousers and shirts for my father and a lot of clothes for mother, my sister and myself, choosing both the fabrics and designs. When my mother revealed to her neighbours that I had made a suit for her, nobody believed it, but later, as the news spread among our friends and neighbours I began to receive commissions to sew and make clothes for an ever-widening circle of people. My mother had been right, and from this time I always had money. Although at this time I was already a very good seamstress I was still a little unworldly and very shy in collecting the payment for my work, instead they paid my mum!

Since the mid-1960s, when career education was introduced at schools, I chose "Tailoring" without a moment's hesitation. I already sewed well by this time and so the teacher assigned me to more complicated tasks. While my classmates were just learning to sew, I sewed gloves and aprons for the workers, white coats and hats for the hospital and health care workers, etc. Once, the school received a large order to make uniforms for employees of the city's cafes and restaurants.

Our reward for this was to be a guided tour to the Crimea for a group of 20 people, paid for by the restaurants for whom we were making the uniforms. I was fortunate to be one of those twenty selected. It was a particularly great joy for me, because I had never before been to the Crimea.

The Crimea is a peninsula in the south-east of Ukraine, surrounded by the Black Sea and is the most popular area for holidays in the country, the main resort city being Yalta. Yalta is situated on the south coast of the Crimea peninsula and is both a port and holiday destination. The city is situated at the foot of a small mountain with all roads leading down from the hillside to the long seafront promenade.

There are also many beautiful buildings, hotels, wonderful parks and beaches. Our visit to Yalta lasted for 10 memorable days, during which time we stayed at the local school, which was turned into a simple hotel for the summertime. It was great that we had our own bus and every day it took us out to visit almost all the towns and resort-places situated on the shore of the Crimea. We were shown remarkable architectural landmarks and historical sites.

One of these was a castle called a "Bird's nest" which is the symbol of the southern seashore of the Crimea. It is constructed on the top of a 40 metres high promontory surrounded on three sides by the sea, approachable only from the landward side up steps.

However, what impressed us the most was an excursion to the international pioneer camp "Artek". It is situated not far from the village of Gurzuf. I never thought that a camp could be so huge, almost a town by itself. It had whole streets of cottages and other buildings, a stadium, swimming pools, different playgrounds, a school and even a film studio.

The camp was operating the whole year round, and only the best pioneers from our country and the other countries had holidays there. It was almost impossible to get a camp voucher. We were all incredibly pleased to have at least an excursion to this camp.

We also visited the Livadia Palace situated in the village of Livadia not far from Yalta. This is a big and very beautiful building with a splendid park and avenues which lead to the sea.

The palace is both a landmark and historical site. It was constructed in 1861 for the family of the Russian tsar Nikolai II who used it as a dacha during the summer time. After the 2nd World War the Livadia Palace became even more famous all over the world being the venue for the Yalta Conference held here in February 1945.

During this conference the General Secretary of USSR Joseph Stalin, British Prime Minister Winston Churchill and President of USA Franklin Roosevelt signed an historic agreement as the leaders of three winning countries: It established the world order for the next 60 years, the partitioning of Germany and division of European countries between the winning nations.

Nowadays part of the Livadia Palace is a historical place-museum, where all the documents and photos of that time are kept. The other part of the palace is a sanatorium, where people spend their holidays for their health.

The Livadia Palace in Yalta, 2005

That trip left me with the most vivid impressions of the southern coast of Crimea, with its stunning scenery, warm sea, sun, palm and cypress trees, and the abundance of fruits and vegetables, many of which I tried for the first time in my life.

Chapter 8

Choosing a Profession

Before finishing school all the pupils started to think about their further education, and choosing between the different professions. I for my part applied for admission, and started to prepare for the entrance examinations to the College of light industry in Donetsk city. From an early age I dreamed of being a fashion designer and so was preparing for that. I had finished a course of sewing, and had several portfolios of my fashion design drawings. I knew that to be a professional designer was my dream and destiny and therefore I did not even think about any other profession.

But there is a saying: 'Men make plans God makes ways'. And in the week before the exams a neighbour visited me. We had been friends since our childhood. She had finished the school a year earlier than me and was already studying at Chernovtsy College. She told me about the beautiful and unusual city of Chernovtsy, about her college and about her future profession of land surveying (geodesy). She told me that this profession was very interesting. The land surveyors take pictures of the land, make up the maps, and do field work all over the Soviet Union.

I felt confused. I had no idea what geodesy meant, but that already was not important. It seemed as if somebody pushed me, and I woke up. "God what am I doing?" I thought. It's good to be a fashion designer and that was my dream, but where will I work? There seemed little prospect of employment, possibly at a garment factory in our town, or as a dressmaker, or in a fashion house at the best. There was no romance in this. But I had been dreaming since my school time that I would leave home for some other places possibly in the Northern part of the country.

I now realised that fate had given me the possibility of acquiring another profession that would hopefully give me the opportunity to travel to the places that I had longed dreamed about, and took the decision to move to Chernovtsy college to study geodesy engineering. However, at that time I didn't know that this profession was not for me and I would never work as an engineer in geodesy, but sure that my decision was correct. I was scared even tell my parents about my change of opinion, because I knew it would cause them distress. When I did tell them, my mother started to cry, realising that I was now going to leave home.

Father could not understand anything; he repeated only one thing that it was impossible to change one's plans so quickly and radically. "You have the talent! And to be a fashion designer is your dream since your childhood. I do not understand how you can change your mind so quickly "Do whatever you want!" He said and left the room. That meant he agreed.

I went to Donetsk immediately, took my papers away from the College and sent them to Chernovtsy. In a week I got the invitation for the exams and started to get ready for the road. I was 17 and I had never gone so far by myself. My mother was very anxious about my trip, but I wasn't afraid at all. I bought a ticket, took my things and left my home for good …

And that was a right decision! Otherwise I would not have lived such an interesting life as I did.

The territory of Ukraine makes up 603.5 thousand square kilometres (380 thousand sq. miles) and after France it is the biggest country in Europe. I only understood just how big it was when I bought a train ticket, and had to spend one night on the train to Kiev from Donetsk and after one day in Kiev, and another night on the train from Kiev to Chernovtsy.

Donetsk region is situated in the eastern part of Ukraine and Chernovtsy is in the west, only about 43 kilometres from the Romanian border. The distance between them along the straight line is 1200 kilometres (750 miles). But, without a direct railway line between I had to travel with a change for another train in Kiev, and this way was a much longer journey.

The journey from Donetsk to Kiev took 13 hours travelling in a sleeping wagon, which was served by two women conductors. They were responsible for passengers' boarding; they checked tickets, provided bedclothes and kept everything in order. In wintertime they had to heat the sleeping car. Even though, at that time the train was propelled by an electric locomotive, the carriages were heated by a coal-fired boiler in each wagon.

Although the journey was long I wasn't bored. Passengers soon got acquainted, and told each other their life stories and things that had happened to them. Some of them read, and many of them played cards. All passengers took some food with them for the journey, and conductors always served hot tea. Tea was served in metal glass holders in all trains all over the country and it always seemed to be tastier than at home. After this supper, and like other passengers who stayed on the train all night, I made my bed and went to sleep.

There were four sleeping berths in each compartment: two upper and two lower ones. I was allocated an upper berth, but could see out through the window and lay there thinking about how it was going to be in Chernovtsy. If I pass the entrance exams well, I would enter the college and study there for three years. Three years of life by myself far away from home. It was very interesting, but a little scary at the same time.

At the 8 a.m. in the morning the train arrived at Kiev. As we approached the city the conductors turned on the radio and played the 'Kiev Waltz', which was the hymn of the city. By the tradition this waltz was played in all the trains, which approached the city. So, with this song and in good mood I entered to Kiev – the capital of Ukrainian Soviet Socialist Republic. First thing that impressed me was the railway station. It was an impressive building very big and beautiful. On the first floor there were a booking hall and atrium. On the second floor there were a mother-and-child room, a restaurant, a café, and a platform entrance.

By tradition, all the railway stations over the former USSR are quite impressive and prestigious buildings. Many of them are solid buildings, with walls and ceilings decorated by modelling and paintings. There is a saying in Soviet Union that a theatre begins from the cloakroom and I believe that a city begins from a railway station. This is like a business card or a gate through which we enter the city. The more beautiful is the city – the more beautiful is the railway station.

Kiev railway station is more like a palace, a theatre or a church. The height of the main hall reached about 37 metres, and when you looked up at the ceiling, all painted with pictures you could feel dizzy. When I had finished admiring the railway-station building I ventured out into the city. I had a whole day free as the train to Chernovtsy did not depart until 5.30 p.m. Just outside the railway station across the square was the office of a company offering tours around the city. I had never been to Kiev before and was very happy to see it. The tour lasted three hours.

During that time I saw and found out many interesting things about Kiev, its historical and architectural places of interest. I turned my head right and left and was amazed by the beauty of that city. I had a desire to see and know many more things about it. Kiev is a most ancient city and was originally the main city of a state known as Kiev Rus. According to the legend the city was founded by three brothers – Kyi, Shchek and Khoryv. The city was named Kiev in honor of the eldest brother and since the formation of the state of Kiev Rus in 882, Kiev has been the capital of Kiev Rus. It was written so by the historians in Old Russian chronicles.

The foundation of Kiev started on Starokievsky hill on the right bank on the River of Dnepr – the biggest river in Ukraine. This area is still the most beautiful part of the city and the history of the entire city starts exactly from this place. It is here there stands the greatest building of Kiev – St. Sofia Cathedral, founded in 1037. During the restoration of the cathedral at the end of 19th century, there was a three-level bell tower built, which had a bell which weighed 13 tons.

Also in this area is the beautiful church of St. Andrew, built in the baroque style in the second half of 18th century. The biggest pride of Kiev is the most ancient monastery of Kiev – Pechersk Lavra which was built in the middle of 11th century. This monastery complex is so large that it would take a whole days sightseeing on its own. Of course, a visit to Lavra was not included in my tour that day, but its buildings and golden domes could be seen from the bus during my tour of the city.

The waiting room in Kiev's railway station, 2007

In 1934 Kiev became the capital of the Ukrainian Soviet Socialistic Republic. It became an important administrative, scientific and cultural centre with the population about 2.4 ml. people.

There are many memorial buildings and monuments, beautiful streets, squares and historical sites.

Kiev is a very green city, when we were at the Dnepr hills, I could see a view of the city with the churches and their golden domes, sinking in greenery. All the domes of the churches were covered by the thinnest layers of gold.

The tour ended in Khreshchatyk – the main street of Kiev. From one side of the street there was a chestnut tree alley with the benches for resting in the shade. Chestnut trees had been planted since the beginning of the 19th century. Now they are growing everywhere: in the parks, public gardens and streets. They have become like a symbol of Kiev.

But Kiev is not only about chestnut trees. There are some other things typical for Kiev. For example, the Kiev cake, first made in 1956 in the city's Karl Marks candy factory. The cake is very light; it's a kind of meringue sandwich between sponge cake with nuts and chocolate. These cakes are sold everywhere – in cafes, stores and especially in the railway-stations and airports. Almost every person buys that cake as a memory of Kiev.

Another example of a traditional dish is the Chicken Kiev. Many people think it's just the name of the dish, but it is an interesting fact, that this recipe was invented in one of the Kiev restaurants and that's why it takes its name from the city. There is also a song or hymn written in praise of the city, known as the Kiev Waltz. It is sung and played at festivals and parades and in radio programmers about Kiev, in all trains arriving in Kiev, and it became a favourite waltz for millions of Ukrainians and citizens of other socialist republics.

I was amazed by Kiev and did not want to leave. I thought about the people who lived there, how they must be very happy to live in such a city and see its beauty, not at all like the mines with slag heaps, that I saw every day at home. I travelled by subway (Metro) back from downtown to the railway station. The Kiev subway was relatively new and every subway station was very beautiful and unique just others all over the USSR. Almost all stations were decorated with marble of different colours and other natural materials. Happy and satisfied I came back to the station, got into a train and carried on my 14-hour way to Chernovtsy.

The train arrived in Chernovtsy at 5 a.m. My neighbour, who had advised me to study in Chernovtsy, had told me how to get to the college from the station. I could either take a tram or walk down the street and then go through the park. I could see from the timetable that trams only started at 6 a.m., but people who did not want to wait walked in the direction of the city. Neither did I, so, I just followed them. When I left the station I seemed to have arrived in some other world. This was western Ukraine, completely different from any city in Eastern Ukraine or Kiev.

Even the roads were not like in other cities. The road was a cobbled street, faced with masonry, not very big black stones 10/10 cm. They were very well polished and laid thick. The cars rattled going down that road. It was also not very comfortable for walking. The heels stuck between the stones. All the central roads in Chernovtsy had this kind of cobbled construction.

The main street of the city, called Lenin Street, began at the railway-station and went through the whole length of the city. Lenin Street went uphill from the railway station towards the centre of the city. The street was lined with houses that were also unusually built, with very beautiful facades, decorated by ornaments and statues of stone. At first I did not understand they were also shops, which were situated in the apartment buildings' basements. Their windows rose from the pavement. They were both windows and shop-windows. To enter the shop you had to go down the stairs like into a basement.

The Railway Station of Chernovtsy City, 2008

Lenin Street – the main street in Chernovtsy

The first shop I noticed was a butcher shop. I stopped and looked for a long time, looking at everything there through the window. I saw smoked gammons hanging on the hooks, sausages, smoked lard seasoned with red pepper and other delicacies, which I'd never seen or eaten before. On both sides along the street there were other shops in the basements.

At the top of the street I assumed there was a market nearby because I saw people who were carrying heavy bags and sacks with produce, probably taking them for sale. Some of these people were wearing interesting clothes. The women had white nicely embroidered blouses, vests and thick, striped woven skirts of different colours. There bags apparently made from the same or similar materials.

The bags were carried not on the shoulder as is usual, but hanging from their neck in front of their bodies. Later I found out these were the national costumes of people from this part of Ukraine and was traditionally still worn by people living in nearby villages. Further on I arrived at the central square, in the middle of which stood a monument to Vladimir Lenin and the square itself was called in his honour – Lenin Square.

I finally reached the park which my friend had told me about, and followed an alleyway straight to my college, which was situated behind the park in a solid two-storeyed old patrician building, in a quiet and beautiful street.

The entrance examinations took ten days and during that time I lived in college together with other students, I had great time and made new friends. At first I could hardly understand some of the students, who came from villages of the West Ukraine region and spoke Ukrainian, but with a local dialect, which had many words from German, English, Romanian, Moldavian and Polish languages.

Fortunately for the students entry exams at the college used both Russian and Ukrainian languages and, although I had studied Ukrainian at school, it was easier for me to take exams in Russian like the other students who actually lived in Chernovtsy city.

Chapter 9

Student's Life

I passed the exams quite well and afterwards became a student at the college. I lived in the students hostel accommodation provided by the college, and which cost me the princely sum of 5 roubles a month for the pleasure of living there. The hostel was a new a five story building, situated in a nice area, not far from the college.

Our college specialised in the teaching of only two subjects – Geodesy (engineering and Land Surveying) and Civil Engineering. Both these professions were traditionally done by men and that's why there were more boys than girls attending this college. Girls occupied only the fifth floor of the hostel, and the four other floors were occupied by boys.

In my group there were 25 students consisting of 20 boys and 5 girls. I liked that ratio, because not only were we paid more attention by the teachers, but also by the boys. I shared my room with three other girls and between us we had four beds, one wardrobes and a small desk situated by the window.

Each floor of the building had a kitchen with two stoves, a table and one cupboard. There were no refrigerators as they were not considered essential and very few homes had one at that time.

There were also two toilets, but no bathtubs or shower and we had to use the public bathhouse for a wash.

Those, who have ever been students, will know what it means to say this was the best time in every student's life, as we were young, free and happy.

Whilst living there we had both good times and hard times but we were always happy and full of fun. There were some rules at the hostel, which every student had to keep.

For example, everyone had to be in his room by 10 p.m. because after that time the entrance door would been closed and locked.

Together with friends by the student's hostel, 1968

At 11 p.m. the lights were switched off and we were expected to go to sleep immediately. After this time, every night, a teacher on duty went up onto every floor to check if everyone was sleeping. We knew about this rule and would sit or lay as quiet as mice. As soon as the teacher left the building, this was our favourite time, everybody get up and the 'show' began.

We lit up candles, laid a blanket on the floor in middle of room, sat in a circle and put some food on the blanket (actually there was hardly ever anything to eat). We often had a bowl of cut onions seasoned with oil and vinegar, and ate it with bread by the spoonful. It was my favourite dish at this time of night. Then we sang songs popular in the West Ukraine region, which I learned and liked very much. Often when the other girls sang I danced to the rhythm of the songs.

There was a long corridor on our floor to connect all the rooms and we ran in and out of our fellow students rooms with candles in our hands, and also into the kitchen, where many girls were cooking meals at this time. When we became too boisterous the boys from the floors below would come up onto our floor and scare us, and in response we would scream the roof off the hostel.

Despite all the noise, the man in charge of the hostel who had a room by the entrance door hardly ever checked the upper floors. We did whatever we wanted and it was a great fun, but after this was very difficult to get up in the morning, we could never sleep enough.

Our group was very friendly and I had many friends amongst them, but my best friend was Oksana. She was born and brought up in a small village near Lvov (it's a city in the West of Ukraine, 70 km from the borderline with Poland). Oksana was shy, modest and honest; she studied very well and was especially good at math. We both lived in the same students' hostel for 3 years and became the best friends for the rest of our lives.

Student life was not easy; the main problem was money or rather the lack of it! We received a student grant of about 20 roubles a month, and paid a 5 rouble fee for living in the dormitory, that left 15 roubles to spend for everyday life. It was almost impossible to survive a month on this sum, so parents helped every student.

Those students who were from villages brought some food from home: potatoes, tinned meat, onions, honey, lard, jam, etc. Their parents could not give them money because they were paid mostly by food products throughout the year, and only a little part of their salary, at this time, was actually paid in money. The income of people from the villages was generated by the products of their gardens and domestic farming.

The best time for students was during holiday time and this was twice a year. Winter holidays for 2 weeks and summer holidays for 1.5 months in July and August. After the holidays everybody came back with heavy bags stuffed full of food and all kinds of home delicacies, they very quickly ran out of everything and again lived on pennies each day, trying to economize.

I lived very far away from the college, and my parents had never done any farming, but my father worked at the mine and had a good salary. They managed to send me 50 roubles a month, and that was a great sum of money, especially for a student. That time the average salary in the country was about 90-120 roubles a month, and the minimum one was 65 roubles.

The money I was given was enough for a good life. My mother told me, "Eat well, look after yourself, and buy whatever you need." So I did, I bought everything I wanted except for the food I should have bought, I was a woman! I always liked to wear smart clothes.

As soon as I received the money I went to the clothes market, there were so many things that I wanted to buy and I didn't know where to look first and no amount of money was ever enough.

Chernovtsy is situated just 43 km from the Romanian border; Romanians brought and sold on the market, beautiful and smart clothes, the like of which were not available in the State shops. Many other items were brought in from Poland; at that time many Poles travelled around the Western Ukraine by car, visiting local markets selling clothing.

I preferred to buy imported clothes, they were more fashionable but very expensive. It would be better for me as a poor student not to go to the market at all, but Oksana and I always went there and bought everything that our allowances would stretch to. I wanted to buy everything fashionable: nylon stockings, crimplene dresses, nylon blouses, and pearl lipstick, etc.

One day, having received 50 roubles, I went to the market and spent 53. I borrowed 3 roubles from Oksana, bought a very beautiful pair of white high-heeled shoes and a white turtleneck jumper, which was very fashionable at that time. Oksana bought the same kind of turtleneck jumper for herself. This resulted in us having very little money left with which to buy food, and for the rest of the month we were on a starvation diet.

Oksana and I in 2013 - still the best friends after 49 years

My 15 roubles grant was enough only for bread, but in the kitchen cupboards there was always some lard (melted pork fat) in jars; it was brought in from the villages by other students. Nobody liked it, that's why it was left for common use; for breakfast we had a lard sandwich and a cup of tea. We had lunch in the student canteen of our college, we both took half a portion of soup and 5 pieces of bread and for dinner we had lard and bread again. There were days when we had only a loaf of bread and pickled cucumbers, life was really hard. But we were always the best-dressed students and had nice thin figures!

We swore that we would never spend all of our money again, we were going to go shopping next month and buy all kinds of foods – sausage, butter, cheese, candies, cakes … But having received the money, we left a little for food and went to the market again …

This was the way we lived for 3 years becoming real friends, helping and sharing to the last piece of bread, dreaming of the time when we finished studies and went to work and lived a nice life.

Chapter 10

A Little of History

Every group in college had its own teacher/mentor – a group master or mistress. Our group mistress's name was Zinaida Likhacheva, a woman about 40 years of age, the teacher of Russian language and literature, who was originally from Kazakhstan. Her father was Russian and her mother was Kazakh woman. In 1949 after her graduation from Moscow State University, she got a job assignment to our college for three years, but she liked the job and the city and stayed to work in Chernovtsy forever.

Zinaida Likhacheva was a very good teacher, a talented instructor and a very generous person. All of us were still teenagers and did not have any experience of independent life. She became like a mother to all of us. She taught us those things, which were not even part of her duties: how to keep our rooms clean, how to wash clothes, how to buy and cook the less expensive foods, how to survive a month on our scanty grant. She gave us the lessons in personal hygiene, of course, talking to the boys and girls separately. She taught us "life".

Zinaida Likhacheva did not let us get bored and our free time was usually busy too. Our group consisted mainly of students from other parts of Ukraine and nobody knew much about Chernovtsy. To remedy this she arranged to take us on tours around the city, telling us about the many interesting places and beautiful buildings. I still remember that when I first arrived there I was curious why everything was not like other cities of Ukraine. I finally understood why it was so different when I had lived there for some time and got more acquainted with the city and people.

The history of Chernovtsy is so unusual and interesting that I could write another book about it. I can't tell about it in details, but I'll try to highlight the main historical events of this region just to let you understand and feel its atmosphere. Chernovtsy stands on the Prut River, in an area that was first settled in the 12th century. This original settlement was situated at a crossroad of the silk trade routes and was therefore, of great interest to many other nations. Over time it was ruled by Tatars, Turks, Poles and Hungarians. Later, the area became known as Bukovina and came under the rule of the Moldavian principality for a long time.

In 1775 Bukovina became the part of Austria and the Austria-Hungary Empire and Chernovtsy its capital. Austrian rule lasted until 1914 and during that time Chernovtsy developed into an economic and cultural centre, expanding more rapidly with the arrival of Jewish immigrants. Jews made a great contribution in the development of the city, setting up banks, companies, and they were sponsors of many important constructions in the city. Chernovtsy later became more cosmopolitan with arrival of Germans, Romanians, Poles, Ukrainians, Russian Old Believers, and people of other nationalities.

Such a substantial inflow of different people into the city worked well for the development of the whole region, opening new schools, gymnasiums, the teacher seminary, and the university. Originally the teaching in almost all educational institutions was carried out in German and Romanian languages and it was only after 1850 that the Ukrainian language was used in these establishments.

Panorama of the University, 2008

In the Austrian period, many buildings were constructed in the neo-renaissance and neo-baroque style. Many of these buildings still survive such as The Bukovina Metropolitan (now the Chernovtsy National University), the Palace of Justice (now it is the State District Administration), the Music and Drama Theatre, the synagogue and Jewish National House (now the Palace of Culture), the railway station building and the central post- office building.

After the First World War Chernovtsy became part of Romania, but when in 1939 a non-aggression pact was signed between Germany and the Soviet Union, this pact, which is known in history as the Molotov – Ribbentrop Pact, among other things, ceded the northern part of Bukovina to the Soviet Union, but not for long, because during the first days of WWII it was recaptured by Romania. In March 1944 Soviet troops set Bukovina and Chernovtsy free.

After the war was ended, Northern Bukovina became part of Ukrainian Soviet Republic as a separate district and Chernovtsy became the administrative centre for it.

During the Soviet period in Chernovtsy many industrial factories were established and many blocks of flats were built. I came to Chernovtsy in 1966 at which time the city was a cultural and administrative centre with a population of 260 000 people.

Because of historical events, Chernovtsy has always been a multinational city, where lifestyle, customs and traditions of the local people mixed together with those of other different cultures, religions and languages and thereby created a special atmosphere. With so many different nationalities and languages spoken, it was not long before everything became mixed up, creating a local Bukovinian dialect.

With so many different building styles, Chernovtsy is more like an open-air museum, where every block or street in the city differs in architectural style, reminders of the cities rich history. Many buildings have plaques, with date and name inscriptions, referring to the period and authors of their construction. All buildings constructed during the Austro- Hungarian and Romanian periods are preserved as cultural and historical monuments. They are the best and the most beautiful buildings in the city, and to which the city owes its unique ethnic flavour. Many of the tourists who have visited the city have called it "a little Vienna" or "a little Paris".

Outside of the city, the countryside is very beautiful, situated as it is close to the Carpathian Mountains, where in winter we went skiing or played sports. Zinaida Likhacheva tried to show us the beauty of Bukovina by organizing tours throughout the area, including to the Carpathian Mountains. She did this not only to show us the beauty of the area but also to encourage us to socialize and for us to know each other better.

It was not necessary for us to travel very far from the city, because Chernovtsy is situated at the foot of the Carpathians. The mountains begin just in few kilometres from the city and stretch throughout the territory of the western Ukraine regions and into such countries as Romania, Czech Republic, Slovakia, Hungary and Poland. They are not very high mountains, as mountains go; in fact the highest point in Ukraine is mount Hoverla (2060 metres above the sea level).

The Carpathian Mountains which are situated closest to Chernovtsy have a specific feature, which differentiates them from other area of the Carpathians, in that this area has many forests of Beech Trees, which grow very slowly, up to a height of 20-30 metres and may survive for up to 400 years. The Beech forests of the Carpathian Mountains are on the List of Worldwide heritage sights of UNESCO, and their felling is strictly forbidden. The name of Bukovina, the area where Chernovtsy region is situated, comes from the name of these trees which in the Ukrainian Language is Buk.

Besides the Beech Forests there are also areas of mixed forests, interspersed with area of alpine meadows, where many different herbs grow. All over the mountain hills there are small villages or just houses with sheep grazing around. The Mountain people of Bukovina live mostly by sheep farming, growing sheep not only for food, but also using the wool and skin for the manufacture of national costume which was worn every day. Local people are very talented and know the art of making wooden souvenirs and national clothes embroidered with glass beads or colour threads.

During my tours I found out many interesting things and got many impressions from charming landscapes of the Carpathians.

One time Zinaida Likhacheva told us "When you get your diplomas and go all over the country I want you to always remember Bukovina and Chernovtsy and the years of studies in the college." And we didn't forget anything. You can't help loving Bukovina and it's impossible to forget it. We loved this land once and forever.

Chapter 11

Practical Experience

Twice a year, at the beginning of summer and in the autumn, we had practical training in engineering and higher geodesy. It was an interesting time for the students. We were gaining the work experience of a land surveyor and could see what we would have to deal with in future. Our college cooperated with the Institute of Planning in the organizing of this work. The institute provided the students with simple design projects which were usually carried out in the rural areas.

The period of work depended on the difficulty of the project. Sometimes it took only a few days, sometimes a few weeks. My group of 25 students was divided into 5 brigades (teams). Every brigade had 4 boys and 1 girl. During the practical training we lived in various types of accommodation – in hotels, in schools, or in the houses of local people.

Once, we did the survey of a garden territory in a small village, and for two weeks we lived in a kindergarten. We were very lucky here. There was a big stove in the kitchen, and the workers in the kindergarten told us. "You can eat everything you see on this stove." They cooked so much food for the children that much of it was always left. When we arrived back from work in the evening, we always found a lot of food waiting for us on the top of the stove. We enjoyed working here so much that we didn't want to leave at the end of our assignment.

On another occasion we worked in a vineyard and lived in the house of a watchman. There was also a winery with special equipment where they made wine. It was interesting to watch how they made the wine and to listen to the secrets of their skill. These vineyards exist throughout Bukovyna as the climate is favourable for growing grapes of many different kinds that are why wine production developed in this area. During this practical training we were often left to our own devices and without our teachers which enable us sometimes to do whatever we wanted.

Usually we had different adventures, both funny and the sad ones. When we arrived back at the college we would often tell each other about our adventures. I'll tell you a few interesting stories which happened to me and my brigade. Our geodesy teacher was very exacting and strict. During his classes we worked hard and intensively. "Geodesy is a difficult profession. A land surveyor should start his work from 5 a.m. with the sunrise and finish it after the sunset," he used to tell us. Our brigade got the task of planning the land for a dairy factory building.

We had to work during the week in a small town, about 100 km from Chernovtsy. Teacher took us there by a college car and checked us in at a hotel. "I hope you will cope with the work well. I'll come in a week and take you back," he said and left. Next morning we got up at 7.30 a.m., because breakfast in the hotel restaurant started its work from 8 a.m. After breakfast we took our equipment and left the hotel. When we went out of the hotel, we saw a cinema across the road with a huge poster on it. It was the advertisement of a new French film *Angelica – the Princess of Angels*.

The first show started at 10 a.m. It was always better to watch a film in the morning, because the tickets for evening or night shows were twice as expensive. We didn't know what to do – to go to work or to the cinema. We couldn't resist the temptation and altogether decided to go to the cinema first and then to work. Thinking that the work is not going anywhere and we would have the rest of the week to complete our assignment. We went back to the hotel, left the equipment in the reception and went to the cinema.

The film ended at noon. By that time we were hungry and decided to have lunch before the work. When we were eating I sat with my back turned to the entrance door. Suddenly I noticed that the students who were sitting facing the entrance door became terrified. Their faces were changed as if they met a ghost. Looking back I saw the teacher of geodesy approaching us. He was furious. "We shall talk about your behaviour later in college and now in 5 minutes get to your working place!" he told us. We left everything and ran to get our equipment.

He had returned, unexpectedly for us, to bring another group of students on another project, to the hotel. It was then that he saw our equipment and went to look for us. We were very worried about what awaited us on our return to college after the practical training. We though this incident would mean big trouble for us all, but everything turned out all right. He did not complain about us and we were very thankful to him for that.

I remember one more funny story: We had to make a survey of a garden at a Lenin collective farm, which was situated a few kilometres away from Chernovtsy. The boys from my brigade went there a day earlier than me. They gave me one day to have a rest. "We go today and you come tomorrow. You will find us in the garden," they told me. Next day I went there by bus. I came to the office of the collective farm to ask where the garden was situated.

The chairman of the collective farm was an elderly man. He was talking on the phone. Better to say he was shouting on the phone, paying no attention to me. Then a bookkeeper came in and they went on discussing some questions for a few minutes. When I eventually got his attention and told him what I wanted he looked at me like at a ghost. Then he looked away, as if thinking of something different. "Students are in the garden. It's 6 kilometres away from here," he answered at last.

"When you get to the end of the village, turn right and go down the road until you see the apiary. Behind it there is a garden. You will find the students there. "Six kilometres? How can I get there on foot?" I asked in a disappointed voice. "I don't have a car to take you there. I don't have anything!" he shouted and the he looked through the window.

Outside, next to the building, stood a horse and cart, the like of which I had seen only in films about the Revolution. The Red Army used those carts for fixing machine-guns during a battle.

He told me "Take the cart and go. Leave it at the apiary. The foreman will bring it back." I was scared and said, "How shall I go that way? I've never used the cart and never dealt with horses."

"It's easy. If you pull the reins, the horse will go straight ahead. If you pull the right rein, it will turn right – the left rein, it will turn left. Ok. Go! I'm busy," he told me and picked up the telephone receiver again. I went outside. It was the end of June, very hot and sunny and I was just wearing trousers, a red T-shirt and sunglasses. Besides I had long blonde hair and quite frankly speaking my appearance did not fit in with the countryside, or the ride on a cart. I felt conspicuous and funny.

I imagined how I would appear to my fellow students by riding on that cart. However, I got on the seat and pulled the reins a little. The horse moved ahead. Hurray! It worked! I pulled more intensively and the horse rushed along through the village, leaving the dust behind. It was a sight that not many people in the village had witnessed before. Having gone through the length of the village I entered the main road and turned the horse so sharply that I nearly turned over. Approaching the apiary I speeded up even more and entered the garden happy and pleased with myself. The boys stopped working and ran to meet me.

On other occasions we had practical training just a few kilometres away from Chernovtsy. We lived in our hostel and every day went to work by bus. On one particular local project, the teacher just showed us the location of our project on the map and explaining how to get there said, "You go to the village Chagor. Across from the bus stop you will see the hill. On the top of the hill there is a geodesic tower where you have to start the land survey. It's a task for one day. Is everything clear?"

"Yes," we answered and went our way. When we got off the bus we saw a hill right in front of us, but we had to walk to it. First we walked along the path, and then we went across a brook with stepping stones. It was not so easy because the stones were very slippery and we carried heavy equipment. One of the very unpleasant things in our profession was the necessity to carry very heavy equipment.

We had to carry a micrometer theodolite TT-30, which we used for topographical survey. It weighed about 12 kg together with its box. The tripod on which to mount it weighed another 7 kg. We also had a level staff (levelling rod), which was 3 metres long and also quite heavy. The boys carried all those heavy things and I carried an umbrella, a stool, a bag with the workbooks and sandwiches.

Behind the brook there was a field which extended up a steep hill in which had been growing white beet that had been recently harvested, the remnants of which still remained on the ground. It was autumn, October in fact and with recent rain the ground was very wet. It was very difficult to walk on. The mud stuck to our shoes and we could not move. We stopped, took the mud off the shoes and went on. But in few steps it stuck again. We progressed very slowly up this hill.

The boy who carried the theodolite was sliding and slipping all the time, the heavy box dragging him back. We went up and up but still could not see the tower. It started drizzling with rain, and as the weather got worse, we got thoroughly wet and cold.

Almost giving up hope of ever reaching the top I enquired of one of the boys "Maybe it isn't here at all?" "Calm down" he said, "we can't see the tower because the hill hides it. As long as we reach the top of the hill we will see it."

We did eventually arrive cold and exhausted to the top. And looking around we could see the geodesic tower … But it was on the top of the hill opposite! The brook we had crossed was between the two hills. From the bus stop we had set off without consulting the map, and headed off in the wrong direction and climbed the wrong hill. I don't know why, but it was our mistake. We were shocked at our discovery and didn't know what to do, whether to laugh or to cry.

Everybody was guilty. It was awful to think that we would now have to go all the way down, across the brook and climb the other hill. I sat on the stool and said, "I will not move from this place!" But what was I supposed to do? It was necessary to fulfil the task. So, I dragged along behind the boys. Going down was even more difficult than to going up. We joined our hands to try and prevent us falling and sliding down to the bottom. We crossed the brook and went up the right hill. When we eventually got to the tower it was already afternoon time.

Everyone was tired, wet and hungry. We had a quick lunch and got to work. We had to hurry up. The days are short in autumn. It would be getting dark about 5 p.m. The boys carried out the necessary readings and I sat on the stool and recorded this data in the logbook. It was still raining and we had to use the umbrella to cover the theodolite to prevent it from getting wet. I sat in the rain and got soaked. My hands were so cold that I could not write. I was all chilled through.

At that moment I first had serious doubts about the career I had chosen and began to think that I would never work as a land surveyor. This type of work was not for me. It was for strong, capable people who had great endurance, and who could work and live in extreme conditions. Besides this, I didn't like maths. And there were lots of calculations and formulae to remember. I was sick and tired of it. "Why did I ever come here? I wanted romance. So, here it was!" I rebuked myself. But I decided for my own pride to graduate from college and get a diploma and because I didn't want to upset my parents.

Chapter 12

The First Love

During my time at college many things happened that changed my life completely. I not only successfully graduated as a Geodesic Engineer, but also got married and gave birth to my son. My future husband was also studying at the same college, but for the profession of construction engineer. I was married by love, but honestly speaking he was not my first love. In my teenage years I had my first real love, which had broken my heart and left me with sad and hurtful memories.

It happened when I was studying in 9th grade in school, when I, together with my friend, was walking down a hallway. I saw boy from 11th grade and fell in love with him from first my look. What happened to me is difficult to explain – my face was flushed, head was spinning and I shivered like I was frozen. "Did you see that nice tall blond boy?" I asked my friend later.

She replied "I saw him. I've seen him several times before, he often talks to Marina from our form. What about him?" I then told her that I thought that I had fallen in love with him and that I had a nervous trembling and shivering as if I was cold. When I arrived home my face was red as fire and my head ached. My mother thought that I had caught a cold and put me straight to bed, but I couldn't sleep that night.

I had never thought that nights could be so long and could not wait for the morning to ask Marina about this boy.

The next morning when I arrived at school I told Marina about my feelings and asked her if she knew this boy. She answered "Of course I know him. His name is Peter. He is a friend of Sergey, the boy with whom I go out. But you have fallen in love with the wrong guy because he's very popular at school. He has had many girlfriends, but he hasn't gone out with anybody for a long time now, and he is not serious about any girl." Oh my God! What had I done? I shouldn't have told her about my feeling for this boy. "OK, Marina, if he's really such a bad guy as you told me I'll forget about him. And please don't tell anybody about that," I asked her.

But she, of course, like any woman with gossip to tell, told him everything. A couple of days later there was a party at school with dancing. When the dancing started, me and a friend were stood by the wall when suddenly we saw that Marina, Sergey and Peter were coming towards us across the whole hall. I didn't know what to do; it was even too late to run away.

Marina introduced me to Peter and then left us together whilst she and her boyfriend went off to dance. Peter then also invited me to dance, but I don't remember anything we talked about during this dance.

My photo at the time, 1965

My heart was beating so hard that I could hear the beats. My head was spinning and my feet almost gave way under me. I was ecstatic with joy and after the party he took me home, but later, considering what Marina had told me, I didn't know whether I should be happy or not. Thinking about what Marina had told me about him I tried to keep some distance between us, thinking that it could not be a serious romance and would soon end. But this was the first bright and true love in my life and like all first loves it seemed like it could go on forever.

We met every day, visiting cafes and the cinemas. Sometimes we just sat in the park and dreamed of our future. It was so delightful and interesting to be with him. He sang well and played the guitar, he was funny and joyfully romantic. He was very popular with everybody and romantic, particularly towards me. One morning my mother opened the door, and to her astonishment found on the porch of the house a huge bouquet of flowers, on top of which there was his photo. I then had to tell my mother and father everything after which my Dad asked me to invite Peter to have dinner with us and be introduced to him. When they met him they liked him very much. His parents liked me as well, and I often visited his home where his mother always treated me with something tasty to eat.

Peter was two years older than me. When he graduated school he tried to enter Donets Institute of mines, but he failed to gain entry, but as he was eighteen he knew that he would soon be called up to do service in the armed forces. It was the law at this time that all men of that age be required to serve at least two years. In the army it was the minimum of two years, but in the navy this was increased to a minimum of three years.

I had already seen off my various male relatives into the army, and it seemed to be a routine course of events, but when Peter told me that he had received call-up papers I had a panic. He would be away for two whole years! "What about me? What do I do for two years without you? I love you! I will die without you," I cried. He stood all helpless and confused ready to cry himself. "You will study and wait for me and I will write to you every single day. Two years will pass very quickly and we'll be together again and forever. Promise me that you'll wait for me? Will you?"

There remained ten days for us to be together and they passed as if it was single day. He repeated again and again: "Wait for me and everything is going to be all right." I remember every single detail of his departure. September 18th, 6 a.m. all the draftees had to arrive at the District Military Registration Center. It was situated 7 km away from our town. The day before on 17th September Peter had a farewell party at which, according to the traditions there gathered many people: neighbours, friends, relatives about 100 or more in total.

Peter's family lived in the suburbs of the town, and they had a big garden in which they assembled long tables with benches on both sides. The women of the family cooked and laid the tables preparing many different dishes which would be washed down with vodka and other alcohol. People who came to the farewell party all brought presents with them: cigarettes, socks, handkerchiefs, or money. All the guests drank, ate, and danced to accordion from 10 p.m. till 5 a.m., but I and Peter didn't eat anything, we just sat hugging and holding each other's hands the whole night long. I gazed at him and thought, 'They will take him away in the morning. They will break my love apart, my heart, and my life.'

Later in the night the rain started. Despite this the celebrations continued, the men stretching a rubber sheet over the table to protect it from the wet. At 5 a.m. a lumber truck arrived to collect those leaving for military service and take them to the District Military Registration Centre. It was announced that only 20 people could travel on this truck as there was no room for more. Friends and relatives started to get into the truck which was completely open, with just benches down each side to sit on and small sides, on to which we could hold.

The accordion player was also dragged onto the truck and as the rain became heavier a rubber sheet was held over him to protect his accordion from wet. The accordion player continued playing and guests, who were a little worse for wear, sang songs the whole way to the District Military Registration Centre. Despite the rain it was a warm night and as nobody had umbrellas, and everybody was drenched to the skin due to the rain.

When we arrived at the District Military Registration Centre we found two buses waiting to take the draftees to army. All the draftees were lined up in ranks and the commander read an Order about conscription into the soviet army and gave ten minutes to say goodbye. Everybody rushed to say goodbye. He came to me last of all and with very little time left he just hugged me and ran to the bus.

I arrived back home very tired, drenched and very unhappy. I thought it was the end of my life. I didn't want to go to school, and I didn't even want to live. My family worried about me and tried to calm me down, but nothing consoled me and I was in tears for many days after Peter left. I received a letter from Peter about three days later, which instead of comforting me upset me even more. In his letter he told me that he was being sent at a navel establishment just south of Murmansk, and that he would have to serve for three years at this atomic submarine base.

This news was devastating for me, I was beginning to be reconciled to the fact that he would be away for two years, but now the probability of three years away made me feel faint. I had worried how I was going to live without him for two years and now this news that it was to be three years nearly polished me off. He had promised to write every day and he kept his word and I received a letter every day. In these letters he described his daily routine, so much so that I knew about every aspect of his life from morning until night as if I was serving with him.

On my birthday he sent me a big green velvet photo-album on the front of which was a plastic submarine, which he had carved out of a plastic comb, and in the bottom corners were two gold anchors like the ones worn on the uniform of submariners. Finally I got used to the fact that he was far away from me and I lived with a help of his letters and the hope that we would eventually be together once again.

During his absence, he knew that I was going to enter to the college in Donetsk to study design, but I change my mind without the chance to discuss this with him, and entered Chernovtsy technical college to study geodesy/surveying. Everything had happened so fast that I didn't have time to talk things over with him and when he found out he was disappointed.

He wrote to me that he could find a college in Murmansk to which I could be transferred and study the same subjects. This way I would not be far from him and he wouldn't have to worry about me. This was the last letter I received from him. I wrote to him but he didn't answer my letters.

After about two months I received a letter from his sister informing me that Peter had got married. To be more accurate he was forced to get married. He had been dating the daughter of his commanding officer and had gotten her pregnant!

The laws that govern the armed forces were strict and there was nothing he could do about it, and he was expected to get married. He had asked his sister to write this letter and tell me this and other things, but I could read no further. The tears covered my eyes. I rushed out of the room and ran to the gym where I fell crying onto the mattresses that were lying there. My best friend Oksana who was with me when I read this letter ran after me and grabbed the letter from my hands; she read it and then also started crying. After having a good cry we dragged ourselves along to our room.

Nobody knew just how miserable I was! He had only to serve another year and I was still waiting for him, but at that moment all my dreams had been cruelly shattered. The time passed quickly, and I completed the first course of my college education and went home to my parents for the summer holidays. God, it was so good to come back home, not having been home for almost a year. I missed my family, my friends, my house and home. I enjoyed myself during this time and was happy, but the pain Peter caused me, didn't leave me completely.

During the holiday I received a note from Peter's mother asking me to come round for a talk, but I didn't go. At the end of the summer holidays, just before my departure to Chernovtsy, I went to the cinema with my friend Anna. When we came out of the cinema I saw Peter coming toward me and I couldn't believe my eyes. We had not seen each other for nearly three years and during this time he had change quite a lot. He was no longer the boy that I had known, but he was now obviously a man and a married man at that.

I was determined to ignore him and go past him proudly with my head held high. But as he came near to me he rushed up to me and started to hug and embrace me. I cried! I repeated the same question over and over again: "How could you do this to me?" We found a convenient bench to sit on and he started to tell me, how everything happened. He told me that his life was now broken.

He didn't love his wife and he had never loved her. It was due to the circumstances of her pregnancy that he had to marry her, though he wasn't even sure if the baby was his. He said that a week ago his son was born and that is why he couldn't get a divorce yet. The very moment his son was one year old, he'd get a divorce.

He also told me that he would not be coming back to home to live. When his required national service in the Navy was finished he planned to stay and continue working on the submarines as a regular sailor. He adored Murmansk – a town within the Polar Circle. He told me that he had fallen in love with the Artic Sea and the local people. He did, however, repeat that he still loved only me and wanted to spend a lifetime with me.

"Wait for me for one more year. I'll get divorced in a year. I'll come in autumn and will take you to Murmansk. You'll continue your education there. Remember how you dreamed of living in the North," he reminded me. I wanted not to trust him, but I couldn't. Despite all those things he'd done to me I continued to love him. "I'll wait for you till the next autumn. No longer," I promised.

When I told my parents about our meeting there was a scene. My father disapproved of my behaviour, he told me that I would be breaking up a family, and taking Peter away from his wife and son. "I take him away?" I gasped. "It was she who took him away from me. I am just reclaiming for myself the thing which belongs to me, because I love him!" I replied and cried.

My mother didn't say anything, but I felt that she wanted to talk to me, and I gave her the opportunity the next day. I asked her: "Mother, what would you do if you were me?" She said, "I don't know. But before you left I want you to remember that you will be his second wife. After his first marriage he'll have a son, whom he'll pay alimony and whom he must take care of. You can't strike out his wife and son from his life just like that, moreover he wants to stay in the same town they are. Think whether you need all that."

I came back to Chernovtsy with a heavy heart. Two feelings fought inside of me; the first one – I loved him and wanted to get him back; the second – I had resentment against him. I couldn't forgive his infidelity. He betrayed our love, our dreams of our life together. The words of my mother and father also stayed with me. And, frankly saying, I didn't believe that he would do all that he promised.

And now, leaping ahead, I'll tell you how the story ended. As soon as I came back to the technical college I got it off my chest. The students' life and youth did their part. I remembered Peter, but without feeling pain in my heart, and I soon fell in love again. A year or so later I found out from the neighbours and my friends what happened to him. It turned out that he kept his promise. He divorced in autumn and at the beginning of November he came home on leave. He was about to travel to Chernovtsy where he hoped to find me and take me back to Murmansk with him.

However, before travelling he decided to go and see my parents in order to get their consent. When he arrived at my parents' house there was nobody at home. He returned the next day and again there was nobody in. He then spoke to their neighbours and asked whether they knew where my parents were. Neighbours said: "Of course we know. They went to Chernovtsy to Luda's wedding."

My wedding was 28th October.

He didn't expect that and decided to take a vengeance on me. The next day he visited one of my old school friends and offered to marry her. Of course, she agreed, because she had always liked him. They went to Murmansk together and I never saw either of them again.

Life takes us on different ways.

Chapter 13

My Wedding

As soon as I came back to the college I got it off my chest. The students' life and youth did their part. I remembered Peter, but without feeling pain in my heart, and I soon fell in love with Victor, the boy from my college. He studied in the construction department and destined to become a construction engineer. He was born and brought up in a village situated just 27 kilometres (17 miles) from Chernovtsy.

One could not help falling in love with him as he was very handsome. I gazed at him enchanted and could not take my eyes off from him. He was a good sportsman, playing basketball and volleyball which gave him great authority with other students. Many girls were in love with him. We had been dating for a year and were happy together when I first met his parents, brother and sister. They were simple, nice people. I was pleased that we were able to visit them together on weekends. His parents gave us the food to take with us back to college, which was enough till our next visit.

This was a great support for us as we were only students. His parents liked me and hoped that we'd be together forever. He was a year older than me and was preparing for his graduation. After which he would have to leave for some other city to undertake his final work qualification. Nobody knew which one; it could be the city in Chernovtsy region or in any part of the Soviet Union. It all depended upon which cities needed construction engineers.

I, however, still had another year to go to complete my studies. In order not to lose each other, we decided to get married in my 20 year-old. In Ukraine at this time people married early and it was not unusual for an 18 year-old girl to get married. If a girl was not married by the age of 25 she was considered an old maid and would find it was more difficult to find a husband. Nobody lived together before the wedding, society condemned such a thing it. Many young couples had sexual relationships only on the first night of their wedding.

In the villages of Bukovina according to the tradition people organized big wedding parties and prepared for them about a year in advance. They prepared a special alcoholic drink – homemade vodka, called 'samogon' and set aside pigs, geese, ducks and chickens for the wedding feast. Every village had teams of cooks, women who had a great skill in preparing special food for weddings.

Usually the team consisted of three or five women. They were very efficient in their work and were much in demand although they were not paid a great deal of money for their services.

The menu and the serving of the dishes was almost the same for all weddings. They made many meat dishes – a home-made and smoked sausage, roast meat, chops, cutlets, meat pies. There were many fish dishes: herring, sprats, stuffed and fried fish. There were many vegetables too. There were different salads, stuffed pepper, cabbage rolls, beetroot soup (borshch), stewed vegetables, etc. They made a lot of bakery: sweet pies with jam, poppy, walnuts, biscuits, waffles with cream.

One of the main traditions at a wedding feast was the serving of fancy ring loaf of white bread, called "Kalach". They were different sizes of the loaves. The biggest one was for the bride and the groom. The smaller loaves were given to the guests. Everybody had to receive a loaf. There was much food on the wedding tables. The dishes were arranged in such a way there was no space left on the table. Sometimes there was so much food that the plates had to be overlapped. As soon as a plate was empty, it was taken away and the full one was served instead.

The Wedding's Kalach (ring loaf), 2005

In the garden of a house in which a wedding was being celebrated a stage would be assembled on which a band of musicians would stand. These musicians were experienced, they knew wedding customs and traditions, and could play folk as well as popular music. In Bukovina they play traditional

Ukrainian, Romanian and Moldavian wedding music. If the garden was not big enough to accommodate all the people invited, they could choose another special places in the open air for the wedding dance to take place. It could be a meadow, beside a lake or a river, or some territory between the streets.

These special meadows are in every village and they are called 'toloka', and at the weddings people dance for a long time and at a very fast pace. Anyone who happens to be at such wedding for the first time may find it difficult to keep up with the dancing. To dance those dances you must have special skills. Local people all dance and sing very well and are very skilful in their performances. The weddings will usually last for two or three days according to tradition. Before the wedding a couple must choose a wedding mother and father. They must be a wife and a husband – a family, usually relatives or good friends.

These wedding parents are very important and honoured people at the wedding. They usually are the hosts of the wedding and later help the married couple to arrange their family life.

Tradition also dictates there is also a best man and a bride maid – a lady and a young man who are both single. The bride and the groom sit at the top table and next to them on each side the wedding parents and best man and bridesmaid.

The couple of parents, relatives and other guests are seated at other tables. On the first wedding day there is a marriage registration, a civil ceremony, because in the Soviet period a church wedding ceremony was strictly forbidden. After the official registration of the wedding, everybody sat at the tables and that was the beginning of the celebration. At this time there were some other traditions common to every wedding. Late in the evening after much dancing, the guest would return to the tables again.

The wedding father and a few assistants would then come to every guest with big trays containing small glasses of vodka, which the guest had to drink straight off, and after this had to give their present. It could be a thing or money. Every present was opened and shown to all guests and the sum of given money was announced, too. When all the ceremonies of the first day were over the newly married couple were allowed to retire for the night, but the guests usually went on celebrating by eating and drinking and dancing until the morning.

Next day the guests usually returned in the evening and the wedding celebrations continued. The bride discarded her wedding dress and wore more normal clothes; she also donned a scarf over her head and helped to lay the table, to clean, and to wash up. That meant she wasn't the bride anymore, but the young hostess of the house. The second wedding day was more interesting, with groups of young people dressing up into national or carnival clothes and masks. There were games and entertainments till morning. I've been to such weddings many times and loved it each time. All people loved weddings and went to them with pleasure.

When I and Victor decided to register our marriage we had no time for preparation. His parents were in panic when they learned we want to make everything quick. They asked us to postpone it to the next year, to give them time for preparation. But we didn't want to wait and decided to be modern people – to have a student wedding in our student café. My parents sent me some money and we made everything by ourselves: ordered the menu, made up the party program, and invited a best man and a bridesmaid (we did not have wedding parents).

I bought a length of very nice white guipure material and sewed a wedding dress with the veil by myself. In those days a short wedding dress and a short veil were in fashion. I already had a pair of white shoes. Victor's parents bought a suit and shoes for him. And that's it – without any problems we were ready for the wedding! My parents and my sister travelled from Donetsk for the occasion, and an old school friend also came and acted as my bridesmaid. There were also Victor's parents, relatives, friends, teachers and our student group friends. There were only 70 guests in total, a small number by Ukraine standards.

Our wedding was registered in the Hall of Ceremonies also called the "Palace of Happiness" in Kobylianska Street which has always been a pedestrian's street and the very upmarket centre of the Chernovtsy City.

The registration was very solemn and was attended by only fifteen guests. We went up the beautiful stairs to the music of Mendelssohn's 'Wedding March'.

By the local tradition, during the ceremony, we had to step on a beautiful embroidered towel. It was called "rushnyk". We stood facing each other and made vows to be committed to each other for our whole lives. When the registration was over we went to another hall in the Palace of Happiness, where a table, laden with champagne and sweets, waited for us.

Then we went to the student's café, where all the other guests had been. As I've already said, our guests were mostly students. It was a very happy and merry occasion and we felt completely at ease surrounded by all our friends. The wedding lasted only one day, until 4 o'clock in the morning! Victor's parents did not agree or understand that kind of wedding and they always said: "Victor married without a wedding."

My wedding, 1968

Chapter 14

The Beginning of Married Life

Though we were a husband and a wife, we continued to live in different rooms as it was a student's hostel, not a family hostel. All our spare time was, of course, spent together. Soon I became pregnant, but I continued to study in college. Sometimes, life was difficult with morning sickness, but I didn't want to quit studying and have the sabbatical leave, which was entitled to do as an expectant mother.

I somehow, felt from the very beginning of my pregnancy that I would give birth to a boy and I always said to my husband, "I want to have a boy who'll be like you." And so it came about.

By the end of the year I had given birth to a boy, who was as like as his father as two peas in a pod. We named him Alex. It was forbidden to live in student accommodation with a child and that's why I had to move out and live with Victor's parents.

Victor continued to live in the student hostel and continue his studies without interruption. Our separation was to be further extended because as soon as Victor had graduated, on finishing his studies he was called up for national service in the army.

It was the second time in my life that the army took the man I loved. Again I would have to wait for two years, but this time I was married and with a baby in my arms.

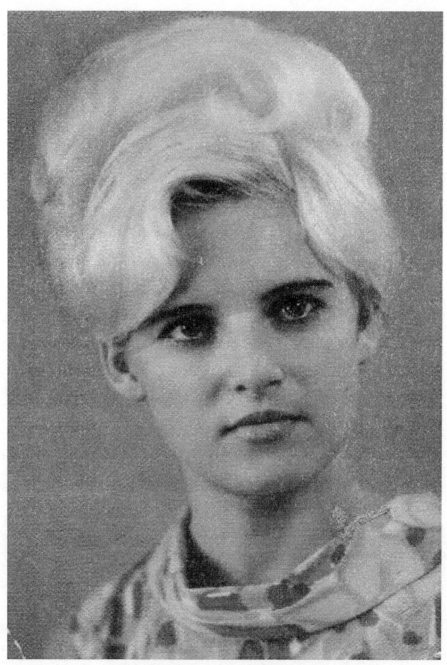

My photo at pregnancy time, 1969

After seeing off my husband to the army there was no point in staying in Chernovtsy. I took my exams at college ahead of schedule and together with my son went home to my parents flat in Donetsk Region. On arrival back home I found that my parents were anxiously waiting for us to arrive. Father had already bought a pram and a cot and the whole family were delighted with my new son. I was lucky to have such very good parents; they took great care of us and did everything they could for us.

This was, perhaps, the hardest period in my life, because I was almost without means of subsistence. I didn't receive any cash maternity benefit, as it was given only to women who worked, but I was, so far, only a student. My husband in the army received only a couple of roubles a month for cigarettes and wasn't able to help me financially. One my friends told me, that I might be eligible to receive maternity benefit from the military registration and enlistment office, as my husband bore arms. I went to the local Military Registration Office and asked about the maternity benefit for the child of a soldier.

A military commissar didn't even listen to me properly; he interrupted me right away and told me that the maternity benefit is given to women who can't work. "And you are a young and healthy woman and can work and support your child," he said. "But I can't work. I'm still studying and will graduate the technical school only next year," I explained.

"Under such circumstances as yours you have to work. You'll continue studying when your husband comes back from the army," answered the commissar in a rude manner. I was so ashamed and ran out of there like a bat out of hell. I'd never ever go to a Military Registration office again. I understood immediately, if you are having hard times – those are your own problems.

This meant that I was expected to quit studying and go to work, but there was only seven months till graduation. Fortunately, for these seven months I had to undergo practical training which I was allowed to complete in my home town, thus avoiding having to return to Chernovtsy. This way I could stay beside my child. After the practical training I had to go to Chernovtsy for a couple of months and pass the degree examination and receive my diploma. I didn't want to lose this opportunity. It was great that my parents supported me and promised to take care of my son until I could "find my feet", as my mother used to say.

My husband did his military service in the building battalion based in Moscow. Soldiers who served in the building battalions worked both at military and civil construction projects. Construction engineers were needed all over the country as there was a chronic need for more housing.

Since 1964 Leonid Brezhnev had been a General Secretary of the Communist Party of the USSR, but small 'Khruschev-era' apartments from pre-cast concrete construction were still being constructed over the whole country.

My husband Victor was well qualified in construction techniques and was soon promoted to an officer, being awarded the rank of a battalion commander. It was hard for me to cope with the separation and I missed him very much and worried.

Every month I sent him the photos of our son and Victor saw how his son was growing up. He missed us as well and counted the days until his homecoming. The six months of practical training passed really quickly and I only had to go back to the collage to pass the degree examination. I left my son with my mother and went to Chernovtsy. I passed the exams successfully and after that, the college organized a gala night at a restaurant to congratulate us on our graduation.

We were presented with our degree diplomas and photo-albums containing photos of all our teachers and students from my group and pictures of Chernovtsy. To be more exact we weren't students anymore. We were young specialists with the degree of an engineer land-surveyor.

My son Alex and I, 1969

After we had received our diplomas at the beginning of May, all the students received their assignments as to where they must work. There was a single rule in the country for all the colleges and universities: when a student got a degree he or she became a "young specialist" and they received an assignment to a job in those regions of the country where such specialists were currently needed. Every young specialist had to work there for three years. If they refused to go or quit before the appointed time – the degree would be cancelled.

Most students or "Young Specialists" would wish to stay in their home towns or districts, close to parents, but it was impossible. Very often they were sent to distant places, where people were not naturally willing to live, to the North, to the scarcely populated regions of Siberia. After working in these allocated locations for three years, it was then possible to leave, and look for a new job in other parts of the country. But people often got used to the places to which they had been sent started families and stayed there forever.

Four people in my group received assignments to the North of the country, to the Tyumen region of West Siberia. The rest were assigned all over the territory of USSR and the cities of Ukraine. When I was due to receive an assignment for a job I was at an advantage, as I had a baby. In such cases it was usual for the authorities to try and assign a job closer to home. I was particularly lucky as there was only one assignment in the Donetsk region and I was assigned there.

Throughout our course, everybody had dreamed of graduation and the beginning of work. But when that moment arrived everybody was sad. We had studied and lived together for three years, and had got to know to each other very well over that time, and it was so hard to lose each other. Everybody understood that the next day we would depart and go our different ways forever. However, we wanted to think of some way in which we could always be reminded of this special time in our lives. After a little deliberation we thought of two small, but significant things that we could all do.

Firstly – we decided to wear our wristwatches on the right arm, as most of the people wear watches on the left arm. So we all took off our watches and put them on our right arms. Since that moment I've always worn a watch on my right arm. Many people ask me why I wear a watch this way and I always tell them the story with pleasure. Secondly – we decided to meet at our college in Chernovtsy once every five years at the beginning of May. It was not to matter where we eventually settled, but we agreed to return to meet at the college on 9th May, which was the same day that the Soviet Union celebrates Victory Day after the finished WWII.

Many years have passed since that moment, but we never forgot each other and according to that decision we have met at our polytechnic school once every five years, but unfortunately the first few meetings were without my presence because due to weather conditions in the regions of North-East

Siberia I couldn't come. But I regularly sent letters in which I gave details about my life in Yakutia and the events that had happened in my family during the previous year, I also attached photos, and in this way it seemed that I was present among my fellow ex-students, because they knew everything about me.

When I finally returned back to Ukraine I didn't miss a single meeting. I particularly remember our last reunion meeting which was in 2010 and commemorated the anniversary of 40 years since our graduation. This was a very emotional meeting because it allowed all of us, as 60-year-olds, to travel back in time to our youth and happy student days. Each of us had a different fate and each of us had lived his/her life differently, and though all of us had changed outwardly, we had somehow stayed the same inwardly.

According to our meeting ritual which had remained the same for the last forty years, after the bell had rung we entered a lecture-room, just the way we did during our student years, sat at the desks and began the lesson. We checked the register of those present, as was usual at the start of lesson in our student days, and then each of us stood up and told about what had happened in his/her life during the previous years. It was a very emotional moment for everyone in the room.

Everybody without exception spoke with tears in their eyes. Each person spoke about their individual experiences as a student, but we all shared the same memories and were an integral part of each other's memories from those days. One of the surviving lecturers from our student days was also present and she also shared her memories from those days and explained what she particularly remembered about each of us.

I was impressed when the lecturer remembered a particularly funny episode about me, but I couldn't laugh because of the feelings that it evoked within me, bringing tears to my eyes. I was immensely grateful to our lecturer who still remembered us all after so many years. After the emotional lesson we traditionally visited a local cemetery where we put flowers to the graves of our lecturers and some of the students, who were no longer with us.

The same evening we had a solemn dinner at a local restaurant and the next day we all went out into to the beautiful Bukovinian countryside where we had organized a picnic and barbecue with traditional shashlick (shish kebab). It was a more social affair and many ex-students brought their partners, children and grandchildren.

Many of us had achieved quite high office within our profession and organizations, but we called each other by Christian names as usual and others even by their nicknames. This was an unforgettable meeting for me, which brought plenty of positive emotions to my life and an inexhaustible supply of energy for many years ahead.

Chapter 15

My First Job

So, after finished my college, I came back home with an assignment for work placement, as a land surveyor / engineer at a construction company, in the city of Makeevka. The town is situated 13km from the city of Donetsk, and is an important industrial city in the Donetsk region. This was my first employment and the rate of salary was very good – 135 roubles per month which in the 1970s this more than enough to live on. I was also given a room in a five - storey hostel. The room was small, with just enough space to fit a bed and a wardrobe and had shared facilities; but at that time I didn't need any more because I lived there alone.

On the first day of my work I was given a uniform – canvas pants, a jacket, gauntlet, big rubber wellington boots and a hard hat. Although I worked as a land surveyor / engineer I got the same uniform as all the workmen at the construction site. The main occupation of the company was to build accommodation for the local people.

This was to be in the format of an out of city development, building self-contained neighbourhoods within a residential area, together with the infrastructure for kinder gardens, schools, shops. These were mainly "Khrushchev-era" blocks of flats and apartment houses of between five and nine stories high built mostly from pre-cast concrete. It was a big building project, with heavy machinery such as excavators, bulldozers and cranes all over the construction site.

The whole territory of the construction site was laced with trenches and foundation works. Lorries with building materials were constantly crisscrossing the site and churning up the mud ever more than it already was. The whole site was a cacophony of noise and dirt, and I found the whole experience quite horrible

Despite all the men swearing and cursing at every little thing, they all treated me as an equal because I was their colleague. Equality of the sexes was almost taken for granted; I was doing a man's job in a man's world and was treated as such. However, when I stopped them from using bad language they used to tell me: "Never mind, you'll get used to it and will swear as well ..." I felt myself so miserable because of everything, and wanted to cry. This perhaps was really not the kind of industry that I would be happy in.

There were two land surveyor engineers: myself and another man who had worked there for a long time. He looked at me disappointedly and said: "Why, on earth, did they send you here? I asked for a man! Take this the levelling rod and let's go." He himself took an engineer's level together with a support. He went on muttering: "Why did they send her here?" I understood why he was dissatisfied when we started to work.

Our task was to project (place marks) for the run of sewage pipes and water supplies. In order to do this one had to go down into the trenches, which were a couple of metres deep, necessary because the pipes were around 1.5 metres in diameter. I was quite short and weighed 52 kilos. It was hard for me even to walk wearing the uniform and the wellington boots. When I got down into the trench mud stuck to the boots and I couldn't lift my leg anymore.

Workmen lowered me into the trench by holding my hands and got me out of it the same way. My colleague went down there by himself, with a surveyor's level in his hands, and he ended up all covered in mud. After work, when I came back to the hostel, I fell down on the bed half-dead; the following morning everything started all over again.

Getting up very early and walking to the building administration centre where the bus was waiting to take us back to the site. On weekends I went home to my parents, who lived 60kms from Donetsk, and who were looking after my son, I practically didn't have any rest at all with the constant travelling. What impressed me the most about this city, were the smokestacks at Makeevka metallurgical plant which I could see from my room in hostel. This was the biggest enterprise in the city which occupied a huge factory site where huge, stacks rising from the iron and steel works stood in a row and were different in size. Some of them were tall, the other short, some of them were wide, the others narrow. Clouds of different coloured smoke belched from each stack, according to the process carried beneath it, some of it was pure black whilst others emitted, grey, red, or even white smoke and I could see all this from my window.

My hostel was situated in the lower part of city, and when I came back home I walked down the street past the plant. When there was no wind, smoke didn't go straight up, but enveloped the whole city. On one occasion as I walked home smoke from one of these chimneys swirled all around me like a red fog.

I was young then and didn't understand a lot about the matters of environmental pollution. I was born and grew up in the Donbass region, and understood that it wasn't the most environmentally friendly region of the country. In fact it was one of the most polluted areas of the USSR, but what I experienced here really frightened me. "How can people live here?" I thought. My heart ached when I remembered Chernovtsy, which was such a beautiful city and the nature of Bukovina, and I longed to return away from this place. I disliked everything about my awful job and the place I was currently living, and just couldn't accept it.

After a month of working in these conditions, and in such a polluted place, I didn't want anything; the job, the money; not even the completion of my assignment which would confirm my certificate of degree. I went to my boss and asked him to transfer me to another job. I agreed to take any job in the office, but he told me he couldn't do anything about it, if they'd sent me here I had to work here for three years, otherwise the certificate of degree would not be valid. He was, however sympathetic to my situation and advised me to apply to the Ministry of Education in Kiev and ask them to relieve me of this work.

If they would do that my certificate of degree would remain valid, but added that I must not say that I did not like my current position, but explain that I had a little baby in another town. So I did. I went to Kiev, and at the information desk at the railway station I found out the address of the Ministry of Education and went there. I told my story to the officials and was asked to write an application; I waited for a couple of hours and then was handed a document, – an authorization for a free certificate of degree. Yippee! No need to return to Makeevka.

I was so happy that I jumped for joy, all this horror was in the past, now I would be able to find a job myself and in a town that I wanted to live in. My parents were also very happy, I could now live at home with my son and I will see him every day and not just on the weekends.

When I arrived back home I began to look for a job, I'd never thought that I would be confronted with such difficulties. I visited all the establishments, which advertised they were hiring Surveying Engineers, and then I just simply visited every enterprise, where I could possibly find a professional job. Nobody wanted to hire me; they found any excuse, in order not to hire me.

I understood well what the cause was, firstly the job of a surveyor involved travel trips all over the area, working in similar situations to those in Makeevka and that is why everybody preferred to hire a man.

Secondly: I was a young specialist and I didn't have the experience. Thirdly: I had a baby, and that was the main problem. They tried not to hire those women who had babies.

Babies often got sick and mothers had to stay home with them instead of going to work. That's when I understood why the young specialists were assigned to a job after their graduation: If everyone went to look for the job themselves, many of them would never find one.

I couldn't find a job in my town, after two weeks of distressful searching and visiting any place where I could find a job. I was eventually forced to go to Donetsk where I was finally employed in a design office. The salary was minimal, only 70 roubles per month, which was half as much as my previous salary.

The coat & hat I made myself, 1971

However, this work was a white-collar job and not so hard. It involved working in a large drawing office fitted out with big sloping desks. The whole working day lasted for 8 hours and during this time I stood bent at the table and made drafts and designs of land surveying.

I liked the job, I liked to draw, but it was hard to stand bent for the whole day. After the work I couldn't feel my legs or my back and I couldn't straighten myself up straight away. So I had to walk this way until I got to the bus stop for my journey home.

Chapter 16

What to do Next?

Whilst I was working in Donetsk temporarily, and waiting for my husband's return from the army, I thought, with a little trepidation about our life after his return. My minimum wage was just enough for a very modest lifestyle and only just because my son lived with my parents, who fully supported him. How would we manage to live on our own when my husband returned from the army? We had no house, no furniture and no money. We did not have much of anything.

My parents would allow us to live temporarily with them until we managed to get a home of our own, but no one knew how long this would take. Some people, especially those who worked in government offices or in the public service sector, had waited for 10 or even more years on a waiting list before being allocated an apartment. Of course, it was possible that my husband being a building engineer that we might be given some priority, and perhaps be allocated an apartment quicker.

However, in order that this might happen he needed first, to find a job at a construction company in Donetsk, but I was painfully aware from my own experience of looking for a job that it was impossible to get a job without first obtaining a permanent residence there. The thought of living in the Donetsk region was not particularly appealing to me anyway, having dreamed of living in Chernovtsy since my college days, but we knew no one living there either.

At that time, according to the law, we could get a permanent residence in Chernovtsy, or in any city, if we bought a private home there, but house in Chernovtsy were very expensive. Even a combined income would make it almost impossible for us to buy a private house in Chernovtsy, then or in the future. Realizing that our options were strictly limited, I began to think and look for the other options for my future life, but always came to the same conclusion – to go to Siberia.

I am Sagittarius by star sign – a sign of fire and traveling, and probably, therefore, the passion to change places in search of a better life, had been with me since my school days. I remember when I was in school; geography was my favourite subject because I liked our teacher, who was an extraordinary and interesting person. He was from Siberia and had served in the Navy on the Kamchatka Peninsula.

I was so fascinated with geography that besides the main lessons, I became involved in a geographical group, where the teacher told us many interesting things about the North of Siberia, the North Pole, the Arctic Ocean and other interesting places on the planet. I watched the movies about brave explorers, about the lands and islands that they discovered, learned how to work with a map, a compass, and studied all the continents.

When I arrived back home from school I used tell my parents about all those new things he had taught us. Once my father said to me, "One day, when you grow up, you will also be able to travel and live where you want. Our country is huge and it is not necessary to live all your life at the place where you were born."

It was a great piece of news for me, and I said, delighted with his words, "I would like to live on the Kamchatka Peninsula, where our teacher served in the army, because I want to see the sea!" Everyone laughed at me. But from then on, I had a dream that when I grew up I would definitely move and live in a more interesting place, wherever that might be.

It now seems to me that this very fact played some part in my decision took when I was choosing the profession of Geodesic Engineer and went to study in Chernovtsy. Now my life had reached another turning point and the moment when I had to think what to do next. There were only six months before my husband's return from the army, and I realized that it was necessary to take a bold decision quickly – as long as we had nothing, nothing kept us in Ukraine.

I'd heard that people moved to Siberia, where they worked under the contracts in the oil, gas, gold extraction teams and earned a lot of money. In addition to this, my fellow students, who worked by the assignment of the college, in Tyumen West Siberia, wrote me letters and told me how great it was there: much easier to live, find a job and get an apartment.

I began to write to my husband and persuade him to leave for the North of Siberia and work there under the contract at least for three years. "For this time, we will earn enough money for the house and the car and go back to Chernovtsy," I wrote. At first, he did not like my idea and started looking for other options, for example: to live with his parents for a while and work in Chernovtsy I didn't even want to listen to this or any other option that he thought of and continued to press my point. Finally he agreed!

I decided to prepare for his return and spent hours looking at the map of the USSR and thinking about the places we could go to. Siberia occupied a vast portion of the country and our choices seemed endless. We could go to Tyumen, to my fellow students or to any northern city in the European part of the country, but my eyes were looking to the Far East, where the Kamchatka Peninsula is situated.

'No, it's very far, close to America. We have to go somewhere closer,' I thought, and chose Magadan city, which is located in the north-east of the country on the shore of the Sea of Okhotsk.

I remembered from an article that I had recently read in a magazine about Magadan that Magadan was a regional centre of the Magadan region and prisoners worked there during Stalin's repressions, but had left this place in the middle of the 1950s. It also said that skilled workers were invited to work in the gold mines and other important sites in the region.

I was going to tell my former teacher about my plans, and I telephoned her in Chernovtsy, but she did not support me – "No! You're crazy! Do not even think about it! North is not for you, because there are no normal conditions for life. Severe frosts and heavy life without fruits, vegetables and vitamins – that's what you'll get." She continued, "You do not know what place you will get to and what is waiting for you there. Maybe you will wear skins like Eskimos do, or maybe you'll melt snow in a basin to wash in it. Is this what you want?"

Despite the fact that her opinion was very important to me, I did not agree with her and said, "Yes. I want! I want to see Siberia and try to live there. I do not know what is waiting for me there, but I know exactly what is waiting for me here."

My husband Victor eventually arrived home from the army and united again we were very happy. It was hard to believe that two difficult years of our lives had passed but we were now together again. Our son Alex was more than two years old, he grew up without a father and had seen him only in the photographs that I used to show him and told him that this was his dad and that he would come home soon.

Despite this, when Victor came back, Alex did not recognize him, ran away and hid from him. He was also jealous of my affection for my husband, and when I was sitting next to Victor on the couch, Alex tried to push him apart from me.

However, after a couple of days, our son started to get used to his father and was running around the room wearing his military cap. I was glad that my husband agreed to go to Magadan, but I did not dare to start a conversation about this with my parents. I knew in advance that they would be shocked, but I eventually had to tell them about our decision.

At first, my father listened to me quietly, but when I said the word "Magadan", he was horrified. "What do you mean? Magadan is Kolyma. This is the place where Gulags were and where prisoners were forced to work during the Stalin era. Do you know about that?" He asked.

I told him that I had read a little bit about it in a magazine, and that now all the Gulags and the prisoners were no longer there and that it was now just an ordinary city. My husband began to explain that we were only going there for three years, and if it was very bad we would come back.

Mother began to cry and say that she would not let Alex go with us. After hours of discussion of the issue, my parents finally agreed, but insisted that we initially leave Alex with them.

Just one day before me & my husband went to Siberia, 1971

If we managed to settle there, then we should bring Alex to live with us, but for now he was to live with my parents. At this discussion I started crying, because I realized that I would not see my son for such a long time.

My husband and I decided that the minimum amount of money we needed to get to Magadan was 500 roubles. It was a lot of money for those times because my salary was only 75 roubles a month. In addition to this, the week before the arrival of Victor, I actually quit my job, as I was already preparing to move to Siberia. We borrowed 500 roubles from my father and bought tickets to Magadan, spending 430 roubles.

All our belongings fitted into 2 small suitcases, because I did not possess a lot of things at that time, and my husband had only the one suit that he was married in, and the soldier's uniform he returned home in from the army. I continued to be worried about the fact that I had to live far away from my son for three years, but I tried to calm myself by referring to the fact that if I wanted to change my life, there was no other way out. I wasn't particularly worried, though, about our future life in such a distant place, probably because I was young and carefree.

I often think back to that hard period of my life, with the lack of money, insecurity and fear for the future. I think, however, that everything that had happened in my life before I left Ukraine, contributed to the decision to go to Siberia, and as they say "Every cloud has a silver lining". I am thankful that fate pointed me in the right direction, and to my husband, who supported me, because life in Siberia was unusual and extraordinary. You don't believe me? Then read on and make sure by yourself.

Chapter 17

GYLAG legacy of Kolyma

Before telling you how my life was going, I'd like to familiarise you with the history of the north-east of Siberia, where fate had brought me. It is hard for me to write this chapter of the book but I must tell you, about that tragic period of the history of my country and about those places where everything happened, because I had lived there for 20 years of my life.

So, the north-east of Siberia is a huge territory, situated in the zone of a severe subarctic climate and is thousands of kilometres away from the centre of the country. Since long ago these mysterious and unexplored lands had been of great interest for explorers and prospecting expeditions; they discovered abundant reserves of gold, tin, uranium, coal and other mineral resources, in basin the of the river Kolyma, at the beginning of 20th century necessary, for the developing industries of the Soviet Union.

At the beginning of 1930s, a task was given by the Government of the USSR – to begin the development of the Kolyma region, and started the construction of mining and smelting enterprises, production plants, settlements, roads, and commenced the mining operations as soon as possible. This required big material resources and a large work force because this territory wasn't habitable and didn't have any infrastructure – only a small number of indigenous people of the North lived there, who pursued a traditional trade to survive.

Of course at those times and under such extremes, few would agree to live and work there. However the exploration and development of the North and distant territories of the country coincided with the period of Stalin's repressions in 1931-1953. From the very beginning Joseph Stalin planned to use the labour force of prisoners for this task and sent them there by force. In order to do this job they needed new authorities, and that is why the government of the USSR made the GYLAG (Chief Administration of Corrective Labour Camp and Colonies) that dealt with camp network creation and prisoners' work organisation.

By the way, the camps of GYLAG were created all over the territory of the USSR at the time of Stalin's repressions: in the central part, in the north of the Arctic Circle, in Siberia, in the Far East and Central Asia. Prisoners of forced labour camps, as well as political ones were used to work at the most important construction projects of the country: canals, hydroelectric power plants, military installations, roads, and timber and logging operations.

The prisoners constructed new cities in the north of the Arctic Circle and Far Eastern regions of the USSR; metallurgical works were constructed in the central part of the country, near to Leningrad and Moscow; but for some reason the word GYLAG was associated with Siberia, Kolyma and Magadan only. Maybe, because the worst conditions for peoples' lives were at these camps, and more prisoners died there, than anywhere else.

As I have said before, the north-east of Siberia was an undeveloped region, most difficult and inhospitable to reach. There wasn't anything except for taiga, swamps and mosquitoes. The only place where you could get from the mainland was the Nagaev Bay in the Sea of Okhotsk. That is where the small village of Magadan was founded in 1929 and from that place, the development of the Kolyma lands began.

A Trust for industrial and road construction in the region of Upper Kolyma was established for the future work arrangement; it was called the Far North Construction Trust. This Trust was supposed to create and organize immediately the work of a forced labour camp network on the huge territory, which started from Magadan, stretched into the depths of the mainland and included the whole basin of the River Kolyma, the seashores of the Sea of Okhotsk and the East-Siberian Sea: also the arctic regions of Chukchi Peninsula – the farthest north-eastern part of the USSR.

Gold mining regions of the river Kolyma were the most important resources that are why the whole territory of the camps that surrounded this region was named as the Kolyma. This way, the words Kolyma, Magadan, and GYLAG came at the beginning of the 1930s and remained about of Joseph Stalin, political repressions, gold and death of many innocent people.

At the beginning of 1932, the first prisoners arrived to Nagaev Bay on a steamship, and were sent immediately to the construction site that would become the town of Magadan. At first, they constructed temporary one-storeyed wooden houses, which were called barracks. In 1933 mass arrivals of prisoners began, and since that time the town had turned into a huge construction site, where everything was constructed at once: a sea moorage and the road to it, a timber mill, a bathhouse, a first-aid post, a bakery, a engineering works, and office buildings.

In 1937, during the period of mass political repressions, thousands of Soviet citizens were convicted on false charges as public enemies and sent to the labour camps of GYLAG. In those years, eminent people of the country worked at the construction sites of Magadan, among them political prisoners – managers of the big enterprises, scientists, professors, writers, generals.

Thanks to their hard labour, a town was constructed; unfortunately many of them, due to the harsh conditions, never lived to see the completed town. In June 1939 the area achieved the status of a town. This way Magadan appeared

– the first town in the north-east of the country, an administrative centre, the base of the Far North Construction Trust, and the main transit camp of the GYLAG of the Kolyma region.

The important task of the Far North Construction Trust was a construction of Kolyma road, which would be used to deliver prisoners, equipment, and food to the labour camps and gold and other minerals from the camps.

According to the initial project, the road was supposed to go from Magadan to the border with Yakutia with the brunch roads along its way to all the gold-mining fields and villages of Kolyma.

In consideration of the fact that the work was supposed to be carried out in scarcely populated regions with subarctic climate and severe frosts, snow slides, and snowstorms in winter and spring floods, it seemed to be an impossible task to do. But the task was set and they had to perform it at any cost. And the cost of this road was really high – it cost lives of thousands of people.

The first years were the hardest ones in the history of the Kolyma road construction and during that time the biggest amount of prisoners died. They constructed the road by hand using spades and wheelbarrows, because there wasn't any equipment. Even under hard frosts, prisoners lived in tents without warm clothes, they got frost bitten, caught cold, had the scurvy and tuberculosis.

As soon as the first kilometres of the road were paved, truck with prisoners drove them along this road to the camps, which were opened right there along the future road. Prisoners were assigned to different camps of Kolyma and depending on the destination they were transported further by ground along the Kolyma Road which was being constructed, or along the northern sea route, which prisoners passed leading on to the Kolyma labour camps, and for many of them they had entrance only and no exit.

Shipping convoys that were on their way from Magadan to East Siberian Sea across the Bering channel which separated the extreme points of two countries: Chukchi Peninsula (USSR) and Alaska (USA) and after they transported by river steam-boats with river barges to the camps, situated in the upper reaches of Kolyma river basin.

Since that time, the history of development of Zyryanka village had started, which came into existence the same way as the rest of the settlements of Kolyma as a labour camp of the GYLAG. In 1933, there the development of coal fields, situated 65 kilometres away from Kolyma River on the bank of the small river Zyryanka. After the development started, they planned to develop a settlement there as well.

But in 1936, the first director of the Far North Construction Trust came there; he thought it to be more advantageous for a settlement to be built on the banks of the Kolyma River at the estuary of the River Yasachnaya. In order to transport coal, they planned to construct a river port on the bank of the river

Yasacjnaya. This way, a settlement of Zyryanka started to develop in the new place, which was charted on the map of the USSR as a village in 1937.

Since that time, fast development of the Zyryanka coal fields had started by the efforts of prisoners, who mined the first tons of coal that very same year, which were transported down the Kolyma River. Prisoners not only mined for coal, but also constructed barracks where they lived afterwards, industrial premises, a pendant bridge over the small river Zyryanka, residential houses for the wardens and free-lance workers – they constructed the future village for the miners.

There was open-cut mining, where the coal stratums was not very deep in the ground and in order to mine they just had to take away the upper ground layer forming an opencast mine.

In those years, this work required big human efforts because of the climate peculiarities, imperfect equipment and the exhausted condition of the prisoners. It was even harder to transport coal from the mine to the shipping point, where it was transported along the river of Kolyma to the north-east of Siberia.

The distance between those two places the mine and the shipping point, was around 65 kilometres of taiga, swamps, the lack of roads, contributed to the difficulties encountered.

The construction of winter roads stretching across the icy landscape could only be used during the winter months, having melted away by the beginning of May. Starting from early spring until the hardest frosts, prisoners mined for coal and when everything around froze they transported it to the village of Zyryanka and stored it on the high banks of the river Yasachnaya.

During the first years, coal was transported by horse and cart, and then later on small trucks were used. When the river ice had melted (from the middle of May until the middle of September), coal was loaded on to barges and sent down the river for supplying all the labour camps and gold fields situated in the basin of the Kolyma River and also the Northern part of Chukchi peninsula. This way, steam-boats and barges loaded with equipment, construction materials, food and prisoners arrived to the settlement and departed loaded with coal.

Several labour camps were established in the village Zyryanka and around it, each of which had their own specialisation: mined for coal, constructed road, logged wood, and even grew vegetables on the open soil. The camps were surrounded with barbed wire; they had gates, gulag watchtowers, soldiers with dogs, wooden barracks, each of which contained several tens of prisoners, who slept on double-level wooden plank beds.

The construction of the village was started after the construction of the GULAG camp on the banks of the river Yasachnaya, where wooden barracks, industrial buildings, a two-storeyed house for militarised guards, a first-aid post, and a bathhouse were constructed first. The Administration headquarters of the North-East Department of Forced Labour Camps was situated in

Zyryanka, with responsibility for all the camps is the region including Chukchi Peninsula and Ambaerchik.

Native people of the north had lived all over the territory of the north-east of Siberia before its industrial development: Chukchi, Yakut, Yukagir, Even, Eskimo; they had all lived there from the earliest times. Their traditional way of life had survived down the centuries, following their own trades and customs. Thousands of kilometres away from civilisation, this severe land belonged to them. It provided all they needed food, clothing, and shoes, thanks to its natural resources.

Foundation of GYLAG camps had turned it into the industrial region of the country and changed the lives of native people forever. Since that time, the peoples of the North had led a settled life. This would all change for them, Houses were constructed; small settlements and kolkhozes (collective farms) were founded. Local people continued to pursue their customary trade: breeding deer, fished, and hunted, but now they were under state control and were directed to fulfil the requirements, agreed with the Far North Construction Trust.

The Trust was interested in the development of agriculture; because of the need in food supply to the camps had increased. They started to master new kinds of activities in many places in order to increase the production of agricultural products. This way, cows and pigs were brought to all the kolkhozes situated in the territory of camps of Zyryanka, farms were constructed and animal husbandry was developed.

A camp "Rodchevo" was founded around a hundred kilometres away from Zyryanka, where new methods of growing vegetables in harsh conditions were developed. It was the first experience of growing potatoes, cabbage, and turnip under permafrost conditions on the open soil, and was able to grow good crops as summer was short but very hot. After the closing of camps so much work that had gone into growing the crops was left abandoned and never continued.

On the one hand – kolkhoz establishment, development of agriculture and local infrastructure improved the living conditions of the native people of the north-east of Siberia with time. But on the other hand – many camps were opened on the lands where the native people had lived, invading their way of life, and scarring their memories, making them witnesses to the shameful events in the history of the USSR.

With the beginning of World War II, the development of some Kolyma camps was suspended, because first of all fewer prisoners arrived during that period and secondly, all people from north-east of Siberia worked harder to help with the war effort. People from Kolyma made and donated warm clothes and sent them to help the war relief effort.

The construction of the Kolyma road gathered pace during the war, 720 kilometres of the road linking the village Khandyga was constructed by prisoners within two years; this was the last part which connected Magadan and Yakutia. As a result of this effort, Kolyma region got the roadway to the mainland by which goods for the front were transported.

In June 1942, an agreement between the USSR and USA was signed about giving aid under the "Lend-Lease" program by which the USA was obligated to supply combat and transport aircraft to the USSR for using them along the Western front. The agreement specified that American pilots would deliver planes to the military base of Fairbanks situated in Alaska, and soviet pilots would fly them to Siberia from there. The Alaska-Siberian air route was developed for that purpose.

The route started in Fairbanks, went over the unpopulated arctic territory of Chukchi Peninsula, Kolyma, Yakutia, continued over Eastern Siberia and the journey terminating in Krasnoyarsk, situated in the centre of Siberia. The distance from Fairbanks to Krasnoyarsk was more than six thousand kilometres. Twin-engine American bombers and transport aircraft couldn't cover such long distances and along the route there were several airfields, where aircraft could get repaired, fuelled, and a change pilots.

Our country was completely unready for the necessary infrastructure that would be needed; and The Far North Construction Trust had the task of starting the building of new military airfields immediately, and refurbishing the existing ones on the territory of the Chukchi Peninsula and Kolyma, the construction of three main military airfields and a few reserve ones situated along the route the aircraft would take. There were no airfields at that time on the Chukchi Peninsula; the place chosen for its construction was a small Eskimo village Uelkal, situated in the north-east of the peninsula.

The fast construction of the airfields was in the permafrost, where not only Kolyma prisoners but also local people, who understood the importance of the construction to help with the war effort, worked day and night. The airfields were constructed within several months and were operational by the autumn of 1942. The military airfield Uelkal was the first one, where the aircraft could land on territory within the Soviet Union and from there they were transported to the settlement of Seimchan, situated in the upper reaches of the Kolyma River, 400 kilometres away from Zyryanka.

The air route continued onwards to the city of Yakutsk, to Krasnoyarsk, which is situated in southern Siberia on the banks of the River Yenisei. There was a large military base there, from where the aircraft were redirected to the war front. We can only imagine now, under what extremes pilots had to work, they didn't even have proper charts to guide them, or dependable weather forecasts, because there weren't any weather stations at the northern airfields. In winter, under severe frosts of minus 50 degrees, the fog was so thick that it seemed that there was a wall in front of you and in summer the earth was covered with dense clouds and pilots flew blindly.

Nobody knows for sure, the human cost to the country during the continued war effort, many accidents occurred along this air route. Many pilots died in such places where their bodies were recovered, but so many aircraft were lost in remote and mountainous parts of the territory, and listed as missing in action. After the war, many years later, the remains of aircraft lost on the Alaska-Siberia air route, were discovered by local villagers who would erect monuments to honour these lost heroes.

The military airfields, constructed during the wartime for Alaska-Siberian air route, played a positive role in the development of the Kolyma region. There were a total of 16 main and reserve airfields, which were re-equipped into civil airports for local airlines to use. During the post-war period, thousands of young people came to the north-east of Siberia under a work contract, after getting a Komsomol voucher and an assignment from college and university. Little by little all the camps of Gulag were surrounded with villages, where the infrastructure was developed, apartment houses, schools, kindergartens, and hospitals were constructed.

In Zyryanka, after the WWII, development had continued at a fast pace. Due to the requirement of coal to fuel the growing industry and heat the local population more production was needed. The Construction Trust developed two main enterprises in the territory of Zyryanka: coalfield and a shipping river line.

On the open cast coalfields, where the camp for prisoners was situated, a village where miners could live was constructed just after the war. Newly recruited workers contracted to work at the coalfields started arriving, easing the shortage of labour needed to develop the coalfields.

The main problem was transportation, getting the coal from where it was mined, to where it was to be shipped from. As I said before, the distance between these two places was 65 kilometres.

Before the war, only two methods of transportation were used: first – across frozen rivers and swamps, by horse and cart, second – by small trucks filled with coal travelled along the temporary winter roads, leading to the port and loaded onto ships. Both were used only during the winter months but not in summer time.

That is why after WWII they started to construct a narrow-gauge railway, which would connect the river port to the open cast mine. The construction of the road started from both ends at once and continues towards each other. Additional temporary camps with dreadful conditions and accommodation were created along the road for the convenience of the workers.

Prisoners built the road through the taiga and swamps under severe frost conditions and intense heat. The tools they used, as usual only picks, spades and wheelbarrows. After that, wooden railway sleepers and railings were laid on prepared tracks. Gravel for filling the railway bed was taken from the riverbank of the Kolyma; railway sleepers were produced at a saw mill which was situated 2 kilometres away from Zyryanka. Railings, a locomotive and railcars were delivered on steamships.

Thanks to the backbreaking work of prisoners, the road was constructed within 3 years, and a steam locomotive, collected coal, stored on wooden platforms, ready to be loaded and delivered to the river port. Nobody can deny the fact that the largest number of prisoners died while constructing the roads in the Kolyma region, and the construction of the railway link to the Zyryanka opencast mine wasn't an exception. This very important project, which was constructed under intolerable conditions, literary on the bones of people, took the lives of the largest number of prisoners of Zyryanka camps.

When the construction of the railway finished and a year-round delivery of coal to the settlement was organized, it was necessary to expand the shipping line, and increase the infrastructure of the ports, to cope with the volume of coal being shipped. They also expanded the mooring facility and increased the storage area for coal on the banks of the river Yasachnaya. Also constructed were a two-storey administration office building for the shipping line, and across the river was a ship repair facility.

In Zyryanka, previously there were only 20 houses built, however with the influx of contract workers more houses were needed, a village with streets and apartment houses which had central heating started to be constructed around the camps; the plants and shops started to work, a hospital, a school and a kindergarten were constructed.

In 1947, a unique two- storeyed wooden building was constructed by the camp prisoners. It was a river transport workers' club, which was considered to be the largest wooden building in the north-east of Siberia. At that time it was an amazing building with carved decorations on a façade, an auditorium for 400 people, a balcony, a library and a ballroom.

A new airport was constructed, on the banks of the River Kolyma and from 1946, flights to Yakutsk started and this way linking the village of Zyryanka to the central parts of the country. From that time and even today, there are only two types of transport able to take you there and back by river travel or by aircraft.

Chapter 18

Learning the Past

In 1953 after Stalin's death, the government of the USSR passed a decree about an amnesty and all the prisoners with a term for serving their punishment of not more than 5 years were dismissed based on it: This constituted almost half of all the prisoners in camps at that time. People, who hated the camps, destroyed barracks, towers and left those horrible places as soon as possible. Hundreds of thousands of ruined lives and maimed souls – that was the memory that Stalin and his system of Gulags had left behind in history.

After the amnesty, when a large number of prisoners left the camps, regions of the far north were left short of workers. In order to correct this situation, new workers were invited for employment, specialists in different fields and workers, who wanted to help the country in the development the northern regions. Many young specialists, who had just graduated from the universities, had been assigned to jobs there.

In order to interest people to work and live under such extremes, the government of the Soviet Union adopted a resolution "About benefits for workers of the regions of Far North", which provided for north bonuses (10%) and a coefficient (8%) to a salary and a free vacation every 3 years. After working in those regions for 15 years people had pensions and other benefits. For those who worked under contracts, a record of work was counted two for one – that is a man after working for a year got a record of working for two years.

Since that time, salaries in the north- east of Siberia had become several times larger than in central regions, a good provision of industrial goods was established and it was prestigious to work there. Thousands of people went to those places, where there had been labour camps before, but by now they were well-organized villages and towns with well-developed infrastructure.

I'd like to explain that a lot of what I said in a previous article about political repressions, I found out in the middle of 1990s, after I had already left the north-east of Siberia. During the period of repressions and after Stalin's death, there wasn't any real information given to the citizens of the country.

In 1961, at the XXII Congress of Communist Party, an issue about the Stalin personality cult was examined, and after that his monuments were destroyed and everything that was named after him: towns, streets, enterprises, state farms etc., were renamed all over the territory of the Soviet Union.

But nothing was said about the system of camps and the number of prisoners, who went through those camps and nobody, knew the truth, and if somebody did know, they preferred to be silent.

As a matter of fact, this issue was simply closed and people tried not to talk about what had happened in the past, and forgot everything as soon as possible. The material about Stalin's repressions wasn't even included in the written history of the USSR, which was taught at schools throughout country, there's also no information about that in a Large Soviet Encyclopaedia, issued during the Soviet period of our country.

In 1962, a work *One day of Ivan Denisovich* about a writer, a publicist and a dissident Alexander Solzhenitsyn appeared and later in 1973 *An Archipelago Gulag*, where he told the truth about life in camps, because he was a prisoner there himself and served a jail sentence at Gulag camps. When the works of Solzhenitsyn were printed abroad, they won high praise and he became a Nobel Prize winner in literature. But in the Soviet Union, these works were only printed illegally and read privately. Of course my parents and I knew about Alexander Solzhenitsyn and his works, but being ordinary people we didn't read them.

That is why when I and my husband decided to go to Magadan for work, we knew a little about those places from an article in a magazine, where it was said that Magadan was a modern town on the seashore of the Sea of Okhotsk, which was constructed by the prisoners of Gulag and workers in different specialities were invited there for work. For me, a young lady, who wasn't connected to Stalin's repressions in any way, the words Kolyma and Gulag weren't of any special consequence.

But it happened so in my life that I not only came to Magadan which was a holding place and the gates to the Kolyma camps, but also had lived in a village of Zyryanka for 20 years, where until 1949 there had been the camps of the Gulag ; and which was constructed by prisoners during Stalin's repressions period.

When I first arrived, within a couple of hours, I found out about the previous history of the region and the Gulag camps, I was shocked and felt uneasy but then I calmed down.

Firstly – 22 years had passed since the closure of the camps in that village and the period of Stalin's repressions had already been consigned to history.

Secondly, "What's the difference where to work and live for 3 years," I thought. But it happened so that I liked everything about that place right away: the village, which became a home for me, ordinary kind people, who lived there. Since the very beginning, I had worked with good friendly people who accepted me as their own, and I had plenty of friends. Besides, natural resources of the North, good support and high salary hadn't let me go from this land for 20 years.

Nobody forced us to be in the north- east of Siberia, we were all free, but those who got here didn't hurry to go back home and many of them stayed there to live forever. Despite the severe arctic climate and quite a distance from the centre of the country, the life there was unusual and interesting. I've already told you that there was no information in the country about Stalin's repressions. In 1989 only, during the period of perestroika (restructuring) and glasnost (publicity) Mikhail Gorbachev allowed access to some of the archives of the Gulag.

Memorial of prisoners of Gylag in Zyryanka, 1986

He was the first one of all the leaders of the country, thanks to whom historians had the possibility to work with the material, which had been kept for many years in the archives classified as "Secret" and "Top Secret". Since that time, the information about Stalin's repressions in the country, statistical reports about the location of camps on the territory of the USSR and the number of prisoners who went through all that, had been constantly published.

Press and internet contained plenty of memoirs of ex-prisoners and people who served in camps and also literary works telling about those times. It would seem that now every person can find out the truth from this material. But up to now we don't know the whole truth and maybe we will never find it out, because some of the archives were destroyed and lost and the only thing which is left is to guess what happened back then. I don't use the specific data and don't name the numbers in my text consciously, because not everything which is written right now is the truth and it is still a disputable issue.

But thanks to the fact that I lived on that territory, where camps of the Gulag had been situated, I knew a lot about many of the events before that information appeared in the press after 1990s, and everything that I have written about the camps in Zyryanka is authoritative. Since the first days of being at this place I had constantly found out new facts about the camps and life of prisoners from the tales of locals and colleagues and friends, who had lived there for a long time.

I didn't need information from the archives for that, they saw by themselves many of the events and were a living witnesses of what was going on and I saw myself as well what was left after the camps had closed. I have never thought that I would write about it and have never been interested in this issue; it all just happened so in the process of living.

For example when friends showed me around the village and told me where and what was situated they always added – constructed by prisoners. A beautiful building of a club in the centre … and added at once – it was constructed in 1949 by prisoners; public bathhouse – they told everything about it and again added – constructed by prisoners. An apartment two-storeyed house on the bank of the river Yasachnaya remained in everybody's memory as a house where guards had lived.

By the time I arrived, there were enterprises, warehouses and even a kindergarten in some of the buildings, which belonged formerly to camps and were constructed on their territory.

I remember the first year when we arrived, those who wanted to work a night shift at the warehouses of a sales office, were invited in August when many of the shipments arrived, to help unload containers full of goods for the local population. I with my friends made some money on the side, because they paid cash right after the shift had ended. The job there wasn't hard and very interesting; we sorted out the trays with goods and put them on the shelves at the warehouse.

If we unloaded food, we could open the boxes and eat anything we wanted, but it was allowed only before the goods got to the warehouse, you couldn't take anything from the warehouse because they had already been checked registered. The very first day I paid attention to the warehouses of a sales office – six long one- storeyed houses completely the same were situated close to each other in a row.

Each building had the same big doors and windows high from the ground around 150 cm in width and 50 cm in height. When I said those warehouses were interesting I was told at once that those were ex-barracks of prisoners and there was a camp at that place. They were re-equipped of course, the floor was cemented and the bars from windows were taken away, but it was a fact of life and everybody in the village knew that.

I will never forget an accident that happened to me in taiga, when the whole of our staff from the centre of domestic service went to taiga to gather mushrooms. I can tell a lot about the mushrooms, because there are so many of them in taiga that there's no need to look for them and gather – they are almost everywhere and you just go into taiga and take as much as you wish. So, we were taken to the road which connected Zyryanka with a small settlement Ugolnoe, where they mined for coal, on the open truck.

From the road, we went down the earth fill and right away almost all women went into the depths of taiga. Frankly saying, I find my bearings on the ground very badly and I can easily get lost in any town, the more so in taiga, that is why I didn't go far in and started to gather mushrooms right along the road. I saw railings overgrown with grass but didn't pay attention to that, I just stepped over them and continued gathering.

One local woman stopped me "Don't take the mushrooms here, let's go further. Do you see those railings; this is an abandoned railway, which was constructed by prisoners. Many people died here, there are several cemeteries along this road," she said and started to tell me the details that she knew or heard of at that time.

"Stop telling me about that, you are scaring me," I answered and tried to move away from her. When my bags were full of mushrooms I decided to come back to the truck but didn't know which direction to go, the whole taiga was the same, there were no signs, and maybe there were some but I didn't pay attention to them because while gathering the mushrooms I looked only on the ground.

I started to go one way and then in the other direction and came upon the tilted fence with a barbed wire and a sign 'No-go zone'. After the tale of my colleague about the construction of the railway I understood that there had been a camp of prisoners, I felt scared and I tried to run away from there as fast as possible.

Not only me but also schoolchildren could come upon a demolished barracks, towers, barbed wire, signs with numbers of prisoners buried at cemeteries along the road, no name just a Gulag identity number scraped with nails. With time these graveside signs were washed away with water during spring floods and carried away into the river and it was harder to find the places of former cemeteries. Human bones were discovered out in the suburbs of the village during the construction of new apartment houses; all these reminders of those far-off horrible days.

There, I found out for the first time about Varlam Shalamov, a prose writer and poet, who had served a sentence as a political prisoner for 15 years since 1937, and had worked in the gold fields of Kolyma. As soon as a conversation dwelt on the history of the camps, I was told: "Read Varlam Shalamov if you don't believe us, everything is written there."

The life of Kolyma camps was really depicted there as it was, because he went through this horror himself and saw everything. Many locals had his works *Kolyma Tales*, and *Kolyma Notebooks* rewritten by hand and it was possible to get then if needed. But I read them only in the 1990s when they were published in our country, though they were published as far back as in 1970 abroad.

Many people who stayed there after the closure of camps lived in the village; those were mainly political ex-prisoners, guard, free-lance workers who worked during that period and locals. All of them were living witnesses, to the events as the period of repressions developed before their very eyes and they always could tell about it when the occasion offered. A local woman worked with me, whose husband was a political ex-prisoner; he was an educated and good man who worked as an engineer at one of the enterprises.

After the camps had been closed, he stayed on, married to her, and lived there for the rest of his life. There was also a girl in the same form as my son at school, whose father went through 17 transit places and labour camps, he worked at camps situated all over the territory of Kolyma and his last place was a camp in Zyryanka. He stayed there, constituted a family and lived in the village until he was 83 years old.

I'll also tell you about one more historical fact, there hadn't been any information about it for many years but I knew about it in 1972, only because I was lived there, where it happened. As I've already told you about the Alaska-Siberian air route, along which military aircrafts flew, under lend-lease agreement. The main airport of this air-route in Kolyma was in a village of Seimchan, 400 kilometres away from Zyryanka. But we had a reserve airfield and the air-route passed over our village and the mountains of Argaa-Taas, which are 120 kilometres away.

In 1972 they noticed metal from an aircraft reflecting in the sunlight from a helicopter while flying. When the helicopter landed, pieces of a crashed aircraft, Boeing-20, which was flying along the air-route in 1943, was found. This event became an important incident in the village, journalists, workers of a local history museum, and even school-children did prospecting work: they wrote letters to military agencies, archives and as a result they determined the cause of the accident and identified the dead pilots.

It came out that in June 1943 aircraft couldn't proceed in a flight over Kolyma from Seimchan to Yakutsk because of a thick fog and in order to define weather conditions an aircraft Boing-20 with a crew of three people was sent. After a while communications with the plane broke down, at that time, searches didn't get any results, they didn't find anything and the crew was considered to be missing.

After 30 years the aircraft was discovered accidently and thanks to its registration number, the cause of the crash was found out and the crew identified. After that they looked for the relatives of the dead pilots for several months; they lived in different parts of the country after they had moved but they were all gradually found!

Memorial dedicated to the crew in the crash, erected in Zyryanka 1973

In autumn 1973 a wife and a son of one pilot and the relatives of the second pilot came to the village, they visited the place in the mountains where the aircraft had gone down, and a memorial plaque was placed. Nobody was indifferent to what had happened in the past and every resident took part in the burial ceremony at the local cemetery, where a monument was erected. The relatives of the third pilot weren't at the ceremonial and only in 1988 did his two sons come to the village and visit their father's grave.

It was a historic event for the this place because many people who came from the central parts of the country including myself had never heard of the Alaska-Siberian air-route and about the aircrafts which had flown many years before. Up to the middle of 1990s this topic was closed, and only the fact that I lived where the events took place, allowed me to "touch" the history and find out a lot in those years.

One can write a lot about the period of Stalin's repressions and Gulag camps, but I think that it's time for me to end up with this topic because this book is about me and I wrote about those times, only because I had lived for a long time in those places, where all this happened. And now, before I tell you how my life had been going in the north-east of Siberia, I would like give to you more information about my previous personal life.

Chapter 19

Yakutia

For 20 years of my life I used to live in the village of Zyryanka, in the territory of Yakut Autonomous Republic or one can simply say in Yakutia, which is situated in the north-east of the Siberia. In order to explain better what the place is, I'll tell briefly about the USSR administrative division. It is well known that the state included 15 Union Republics, in which there lived more than 100 nationalities and ethnic groups, all of them differed from each other in respect of the area they occupied, national composition, language, traditions and customs of the local people.

Some Union Republics composed of Autonomous republics and as the USSR was the biggest country in the world, the territory of some autonomous republics was bigger than the territory of many independent countries in the world. Yakutia was the biggest Autonomous republic in the USSR, and occupied the territory of 3,850,000 square kilometres (1,101,000 square miles) and this means that it was 12.5 times bigger than Great Britain and 6 times bigger than Spain.

Despite being such a huge territory, the population of the republic only averaged one million people during the Soviet period. Yakutia is situated in 3 time-zones and the difference with Moscow time is between 6-8 hours. The biggest part of Yakutia is covered with mountains and taiga, which is dense forest consisting mainly of coniferous trees, which can endure the subarctic frosts. Further to the North the taiga gets thinner little by little and passes into forest-tundra and then into pure tundra where only grass and lichen grow, together with swamps and clumps of moss.

Tundra stretches all over the shore of the Arctic Ocean, which washes Yakutia from the North. All the territory of Yakutia is situated in a zone of permafrost where the soil has stayed frozen for centuries. During the summer period, a surface layer of the soil thaws out to a small depth – from a couple of centimetres in the North up to two metres in the south. In the region where I lived the soil thawed out in summer to a depth of 70 cm (27"), but in the mountains which were only 120 kilometres (75 miles) away from our village it had never thawed out.

Landscape of tundra in summer time

It might seem that life is impossible in such a climate, but people have lived and survived here for thousands of years adapting themselves to extreme conditions, living in isolated settlements all over the territory. The reason for modern development of the republic was the huge reserves of natural resources of the land. Here one can find almost all fuel, energy and mineral raw material resources known to mankind, but I'll list only the main ones – those are diamonds, gold, silver, uranium, oil, gas, coal, etc.

But the main wealth of Yakut land lies in its diamonds, deposits which cover a huge area of the republic. The deposits, known as the kimberlitic pipes "Udachnaya" (lucky one) and "Mir" (peace) are some of the biggest in the world and that is why Yakutia is called 'A diamond land'. Yakutia is an amazing and unusual region of North-Eastern Siberia, having unique natural phenomenon.

Almost the half of the territory is situated within the Arctic Circle and that is why Yakutia is the coldest settled region on our planet, and where air temperature during wintertime is much lower than at the North Pole. In the region of Oymyakon district of Yakutia, there is the coldest spot in the Northern hemisphere, where the temperature of the air in 1924 was minus 71.2 degrees Celsius (minus 95.5 F), but this fact was not officially confirmed, the official temperature is considered to be minus 67.8 degrees Celsius (minus 90 F).

Across this area the Kolyma Road passes, which connects Yakutsk and Magadan cities. It is difficult to imagine how, in such a record-breaking cold region, Gulag prisoners in the Stalin period constructed this road.

The second cold place of Yakutia is also the smallest town situated within the Polar Circle – Verkhoyansk, where only 1300 people live. During wintertime the temperature here also reaches the same level as in Oymyakon, and it is also claimed to be the coldest place in the northern hemisphere. It's interesting to note, that in both of those places, temperature in summer goes up to plus 36 degrees Celsius (96.8 F).

Scientists have proven that the whole territory of Yakutia turned into a zone of perpetual congelation as a result of a quick fall in temperature of the Earth more than 12 thousand years ago. There have been numerous finds of mammoth remains and other animal species that inhabited that land during those times. The majority of these finds occurred in the North of Yakutia and especially in the Kolyma and Indigirka river basins. Besides just the tusks and bones, whole well preserved animals have been found and with so many remains being found that the area has become known as the 'Mammoth graveyards'.

Although the remains of mammoths are well preserved in the permafrost, it's almost impossible to retrieve the remains without damaging them, because they are frozen in an icy shell. However, during opencast mining operations, when the top layer of earth is removed, the subsoils below thaw out little by little, and it is then possible to find and retrieve skeletons and even whole carcasses of mammoths with the remains of skin attached. For example, in the end of 1970s, a body of a seven-month old baby mammoth was found, that was preserved enough to become a museum exhibit.

In those places, where due to the changing of a water course and the consequential destruction of the steep river banks, there could be found bones and tusks of mammoths on the surface of the land. I remember when in 1989 I heard for the first time that some people from our village and others from neighbouring regions of Magadan oblast were looking for the tusks all over the banks of the rivers of Kolyma basin, and this during the 1990s became a full time business for many people in the area. Tusks and bones of mammoths were a valuable raw material for the crafting of souvenirs crafting and that is why they were delivered to Vladivostok city and sold there for dollars.

The capital of the Yakut Autonomous Republic is Yakutsk city, situated on the navigable river Lena – the biggest river of North-East Siberia, and which flows across the whole territory of Yakutia from the south to the north and falls into the Laptev Sea. The first settlements of people began in this area in 1632, and one developed gradually into Yakutsk city. When huge mineral deposits were discovered in the territory of Yakutia during the Soviet period, Yakutsk began to develop rapidly and turned into a modern city with developed infrastructure.

The city eventually became the cultural and scientific center of North-Eastern Siberia, where a Yakut State University, Institute of Permafrost Study, Siberian Department of the Academy of science and other different schools, libraries and theatres were established. Yakutsk is rightfully considered to be the biggest and the coldest city of the world, situated in the zone of perpetual congelation and it is hard to believe that all conditions needed for the normal life of people were created in such a severe climate.

Even during the severest frosts, the city lived its usual life, where business enterprises and establishments like hospitals, kindergartens, and schools worked normally, and people visited cinemas, dancing clubs, restaurants and museums at weekends. Despite the fact that half of the Yakutsk population was made up of people who came from different republics of the USSR, it still preserved its unique national peculiarity. Traditional customs of the local Yakut people were respected, preserved and honoured.

I visited Yakutsk for the first time in winter during 1973 and was amazed at everything I saw there, because life in that big city differed totally from life in my small village of Zyryanka. Even though I had lived for two years in Yakutia and was used to severe frosts, the feeling of coldness was much stronger in Yakutsk especially in the center of the city, which was lined with multi-storeyed buildings of concrete.

Even my warm clothes didn't keep me warm enough, because I spent more time in the open, standing at bus stops, etc., and even when the bus came it often seemed colder inside the bus than outside! That is why I always tried to go to the café, situated in front of the "Lena" hotel, where one could have some tea with cognac in order to warm oneself.

Winter in Yakytsk, the Lenina square in center of Yakytsk

When there were frosts below minus 50 degrees Celsius (minus 58 F), there was a thick fog and reduced visibility in the city, and it was hard to notice even streetlights or the headlights of the cars.

I often wondered how the buses, taxis and the other types of transport could drive in these streets under those conditions. Yakutsk, like any other city, had regions of the old city lined with one- and two- storeyed houses constructed from wood and with minimal foundations, without bathrooms or toilet facilities. Only such houses could stay undestroyed under the permafrost conditions, surviving the changes of soil levels, which thawed out and sank in summer and turned into ice and thrust up in winter.

It was only at the beginning of 1970s, that construction of multi-storeyed concrete buildings and apartment houses were undertaken, built according to new technology. This technology involved the use of reinforced concrete piles driven deep into the permafrost and thus immune from the thawing and freezing of conventional foundations. This way the houses were raised a couple of metres above the ground and season changing of soil didn't matter, because the piles were frozen at a depth lower than the level of the soil's thawing out.

Together with the new technology of house construction, there developed new methods of heating and sanitation. The heat and water pipes were also raised above the ground and wrapped in the heat insulation material that prevented freezing. Such technology allowed the constructing of multi-storeyed apartment houses, which by the end of 1980s lined the quarters of Yakutsk.

I knew Yakutsk well with time, because I had to visit it very often and during different seasons. Firstly, if we went on vacation we flew by plane from Zyryanka with a transfer at Yakutsk airport.

Secondly, for business reasons – there were higher Party Bodies, bodies of power, and also Offices of Administrations of the various departments and I often had to attend meetings, seminars, career development courses, etc. Despite the fact that the distance from Zyryanka to Yakutsk was more than 1200 km (750 miles), and the time of flight was 4 hours, it was a simple matter for us to fly to Yakutsk for a couple of days. I personally never missed an opportunity to go there, because I became close friends with some of my colleagues who worked in these higher organizations, and I loved meeting them and spending time with them.

Chapter 20

My Life in Siberia

There were 34 districts in Yakut Republic, each of which had its own specific part to play in the economic development of the country. Depending on population size, composition of the population and geography each region developed those to which it was most suited. Industries such as gold and coal mining, diamond, oil and gas recovery and other mining operations were developed in some district, and other district were engaged in agriculture.

I used to live in Verkhnekolymsky district (Upper Kolyma district), which is situated in the north-east of Yakutia. Although it is only one of the counties of Yakutia, its territory covered nearly 68 thousand square km that is three times bigger than Wales in Great Britain. The district is situated in the upper reaches of the Kolyma River, which is the biggest river in the north-east of Siberia with a length of 2000 kilometres. Its source is in the Magadan Region and flows for half its length through that region, and then it goes across the territory of Yakutia and falls into the East Siberian Sea of the Arctic Ocean.

The Northern part of the district is situated within the Arctic circle, and that is why during summertime there were polar days (white nights), when the sun didn't go down and during winter there were polar nights, when it was dark as if it was night even during daytime. Beside our district there are two more districts along the Kolyma River within the Arctic Circle with their administrative centres in Srednekolymsk town and Chersky village. Srednekolymsk is one of the oldest towns of Yakutia. It became a town in 1775, but since the middle of the 17th century it was a traditional place of exile for revolutionaries and political prisoner. In 1970, the population of the town was only around 2.5 thousand people.

Chersky village is the last center of population along the Kolyma River, with around 9 thousand people living there during the 1970s. Despite the distance from our village of Zyryanka to these centres of population, was a distance of between 300 to 700 kilometres (188 and 440 miles), they were our closest neighbours, and which we could get to only by air or on the Kolyma River when it was not frozen.

The Verkhnekolymsky district belongs to a group of industrial districts with the main occupation of coal mining. Actually, I've told you before that it is thanks to coal that this district was developed during the Stalinist purges. The administrative centre of the district was Zyryanka village, which situated on the confluence of the Yasachnaya River and the Kolyma River.

There were also five other small villages in the territory of Verkhnekolymsky district, which were distant from the center and differed from each other by their traditional way of life. Though the population of the district was only 10 thousand people in the 1970s there were more than 30 enterprises and organizations including a local hospital, four schools and seven kindergartens.

The biggest enterprise, which employed over five hundred people, was a Zyryanka strip mine, where mining was opencast. It was situated in a village which is 65 kilometres (40 miles) away from the administrative centre of Zyryanka. A road, by which coal was transported, started to be constructed by prisoners during the period of Stalinist purges and was finished only in 1975. What is interesting is that this 65 kilometer road was the only road in the district which functioned year-round and later became the route for a regular bus service.

Kolyma River Shipping Lines were of great importance for the district, the main task of which was to transport coal to the northern counties of Yakutia and Chukchi Peninsula. Our life in the truest sense of the world depended on this enterprise, because it was also responsible for keeping us supplied with industrial and consumer's goods as well as food provisions. I'd like to tell you more about the process of supply in detail, because this is a very interesting issue. I'll tell you from the beginning that the delivery of goods to the north-east of Siberia including our district was carried out in the same way as delivery of prisoners during Stalinist purges.

Of course, a lot of time had passed since those times and everything had changed, but shipping lines remained the same. All goods shipped to this region were sent by a Northern Sea Route, which started in Murmansk, which is on the shore of Barents Sea, and ended in Vladivostok, which is situated on the shore of the Sea of Japan. This Northern Sea Route goes across seven seas of the Arctic Ocean, three seas of the Pacific Ocean, but despite a huge distance is the shortest way between Murmansk and Vladivostok – which were the biggest seaports of the USSR.

During this long sea journey between these two main ports there were some intermediate ports, where goods were transferred from heavy sea-going ships to river-going vessels, on which they were delivered to corresponding destinations up the rivers. For example, to Yakutsk and Central districts of the republic, goods were shipped to Tiksi seaport which was on the shore of Arctic Laptev Sea on the mouth of Lena River. To Kolyma districts of Yakutia and our neighbouring villages, goods were delivered to the arctic sea port of Zeljony Mys (Green Cape), which was not far from the Kolyma River mouth on the coast of the East-Siberian Arctic Sea.

Delivery of freight was only carried out during summer navigation, when shipping channels were free of ice, and as summer was quite short here, it lasted between two and a half to four months. Before the development of heavy ice-breaking vessels, the seas of Arctic Ocean were navigable for an even shorter period, necessitating ships to spend a winter at an intermediate port until the next year, when ice broke. Only at the beginning of 1960s, a nuclear-powered ice-breaker *Lenin*, constructed in the USSR, began to work in Arctic.

It was the first ice-breaker in the world with a nuclear power plant, capable of piloting ships in the arctic seas of the Arctic Ocean for the time enabling the journey to be completed in one season. It worked for over 30 years breaking ice and leading freight convoys in those northern latitudes, which was so necessary for the isolated population of north-eastern regions of the country. It was eventually retired to the port of Murmansk where it is preserved as a working museum.

More than a million people lived in Yakutia, and they had to be provided with normal necessities of life, for work, and accommodation, supplied with equipment, industrial goods and provision. The development of the North-East Siberia was of utmost importance for the USSR and that is why the support and implementation of the supply of goods and services received top priority and was under strict control at all times. I came to Zyryanka in the middle of summer and at the time when the annual supply ship was due to arrive, all the people of the village were concerned about was when would the boat arrive and talked only on that topic. I only understood how vital this was for people after I had lived there for a while.

I can describe the activities that occurred throughout each year in a continuous cycle of preparation for each winter. The biggest part of freight was delivered by the river only once a year, estimating that this would be enough to keep everybody supplied with necessities until the next year. The time that the river Kolyma was navigable was the most intense and in order to make it successful, people prepared for it whole winter long. Preparation started immediately the river closed for next year's navigation by the repair and maintenance of the river boats and port facilities. These river boats were small self-propelled river vessels designed for different purposes: container ships, oil ships, dry cargo ship, tugboats, barges and vessels for repair works on a river during the time of navigation.

There was a transport enterprise in the district, which had at its disposal dump trucks, bulldozers and other machinery for coal transportation from places of coal mining to a river port and preparing for its transportation. Coal was being carried to the river all winter long, dumped on a high bank, and with the help of a bulldozer, formed embankments, which were huge by the beginning of navigation and after one the place was empty. Navigation on the Kolyma River lasted for three and a half months, during which self-propelled vessels went from the river port down the flow of the Kolyma River to Zeljony Mys (Green Cape) sea port loaded with coal, wood and other freight, and came back from there loaded with oil, construction materials, consumer goods and provision.

For the time of navigation self-propelled vessels went back and forth several times and the more trips they could manage, the more freight they could deliver. The villagers were well informed of the process of navigation, because many of those who worked at the river port told all the news to the members of their families. I personally found out many interesting things from my work colleagues, whose husbands were workers on these boats and dealt with delivering freights

It seems funny now, but we were the first ones in the village to know which self-propelled vessels were being loaded at the sea port, which were already near the village, what freight was being carried, etc. I found out from my colleagues that navigation, which was repeated from year to year, wasn't the same all the times and its process depended on many nuances. For example, it was considered to be good if everything went according to schedule, that is when the Kolyma River was completely free of ice right down to the seaport and the sea going ships arrived on time for the transhipment.

If everything worked exactly to time it would mean that all freights intended for our district would be delivered during the period of navigation. But if in the course of navigation, there were delays in loading the river boats due to weather conditions preventing the sea going ships arriving on time, or break downs while transporting freight, or other unpredictable situations, then they delivered only the goods they had time to and people of the district were left without some necessary goods till the next year.

So, if everything was fine, the river boats approached the village one by one, but those with provision were unloaded first and the cargo of provisions place in the district's sales office warehouse – an enterprise, which dealt with the distribution of those supplies.

Regardless of the type of goods delivered to the warehouse, a couple of days later they were on the shelves of the shops and since that moment the best time in life of the village began!

During the period of new goods arrival we couldn't work normally, we were on pins and needles and were looking forward to the end of a working day, to run quickly to the store and buy everything, and in the quantity that our salary allowed. The country was interested in further development of the north-east of Siberia and in order to make people stay in such extreme conditions, this region received a first-rate supply.

You can say that all the country worked for us, because we received the best provision and delicacies from all the Union republics of the USSR and the other countries.

126

River boats at work on Kolyma River

We were supplied with many products that were in very short supply and that the other regions of the country hadn't even ever seen. For example, we received the best wine, tiny pickles and cherry tomatoes in small jars from Bulgaria; 5 litre jars filled with assorted vegetables (tomatoes, cucumbers and pepper), liver pâté, cheese in little tins from Hungary; 5 kg tinned ham, salami sausages from Czechoslovakia; and different vegetable and fruit juices, purées, baby foods from Moldavia; sprats and the best canned fish from the Baltic republics, the best candies and even in boxes (which was a rarity) of a Moscow confectionary called 'Red October'.

But the main product, which we waited anxiously for, was potatoes and we bought these in large quantities, enough for the whole winter. This was necessary because the warehouses of the storage company weren't meant for keeping potatoes and other vegetables in winter and those products, by be necessity were sold to people as fast as possible. All the villagers bought their winter provisions by the box or case, much easier to store than a lot of single jars or cans. During my first year there I had little money and only a one-room bed-sit, approximately eight metres square which did not provide much space to store a full winter's supply of food.

I had to buy everything in small quantities, and in the middle of winter I was left without many of the staple foods, and ate only canned food, dried potato and dried onion, which I hated, till the next navigation. Later, when my husband's and my salaries became bigger and we were allocated our own flat, I bought so much food that the flat turned into a supply depot, where there were 5-6 cases of potato, a couple of sacks of vegetables and a couple of cases of various other products, which being in short supply, vanished from the stores very quickly.

The last river boat always delivered cabbages, and in order for it to be equitable distributed, it was divided among the enterprises depending on the

127

quantity of workers employed and the size of their families. For my three-member family I could take not more than two sacks, which were delivered straight to my home. Cabbage is a main food product in Russia, and is used for cooking of many dishes in everyday life. One could preserve cabbage for the whole winter by fermenting it in wooden barrels. I chopped it, and according to a recipe added some carrots, sugar, and kept it in a barrel for several days. When the cabbage was ready I put it into 3- litre jars and it was preserved for the whole winter, stored in an outside shed under freezing Siberian temperatures.

I've paid attention to the main products, which we stored for winter, on purpose; the other products delivered to our village during navigation were on offer for sale all winter long and only ran out by spring. But this didn't mean that we were constantly hungry, because all year long food was continually being delivered by cargo airplanes from Yakutsk and Vladivostok and was instantly delivered to the shops. This way we received some cheese, apples, oranges, tangerines, and even exotic, for our country, fruit like bananas, pineapples, and grapefruits, which I tasted here for the first time in my life.

We also received a special treat before the holidays, which were traditionally celebrated in the USSR – New Year's Eve, a women's day March 8th, May 1st and others. I remember in 1974, some instant coffee, oranges, tangerines, chocolate assortments in boxes of the highest quality, fruit jelly, etc., were delivered to Zyryanka by plane before the New Year's Eve. I bought so much of everything that I could hardly manage to bring all those goods home, and on arriving home put two big bags with tangerines on a table. My son ran to the table and dragged the bags off the table in order to see what was inside as soon as possible, and the tangerines scattered all over the kitchen.

I will never forgive my son's eyes and reaction – he was so impressed that he couldn't even express his excitement right away. A bit later when we began to gather tangerines together into a big box, he started asking from whom I had bought so many tangerines. "I bought them for us and you can eat as many as you want," I replied. "As many as I want?" He wondered. Before that, for four and a half years he had lived with my parents in Ukraine, where tangerines were sold only on the market. They cost a lot and that is why my mother bought him only two to three fruits at a time, and now suddenly, so many of them ...

Actually I grew up myself in the same miner's town in the 1950s to 60s and remembered from my childhood the same things as my son did. We had never had on offer anything like that, and tangerines were bought also by the individual fruit by our mother and only when we were ill. However, we did use them as a decoration for New Year's Eve, threading them and hanging them on a Christmas tree.

In principle, one could survive in Yakutia without the provisions that were delivered, the way native populations had survived here for thousands of years, breeding reindeers, horses, hunting and fishing. Nature gifted the land with richness of taiga, rivers and lakes, thousands of which are all over the territory.

Local people told us that they had never been hungry even during war times, they could not only provide themselves with food, clothing and shoes, but also produced enough to be able to contribute to the country's war effort.

When I lived there, I didn't even think about this self-sufficiency of the local people, and only some time later, remembering my life in Zyryanka, I understood that usage of local resources allowed us to live normally under such severe conditions and even made our life original, unusual and interesting. In fact, from the first day of arriving in these remote northern parts, I had to change my usual life from that which I had lived in Ukraine and accept the conditions under which people lived here. I eventually and with time adapted and accepted, not only the severe climate, but also to some of the traditional cuisine of Yakut people, where meat was the main product.

There were not only the usual types of meat such as beef and pork that I had been accustomed to, but also unusual foods that I had never even heard of. Reindeer farming and horse breeding were developed all over North Siberia, which is why venison was on offer all year round, which we generally ate. I didn't need to cook any special dishes of venison, because this meat was totally free of fat if a little dry. Venison was traditionally eaten boiled or fried with onion in butter.

Sometimes, for a change, I cooked foal meat, which we didn't like a lot, but ate. Besides horse and deer meat, I often ate the meat of wild animals which was not generally available in the shops; friends and colleagues who loved hunting often provided us with it. I loved moose or Eurasian elk meat the most, because it was not as dark and dry as venison and was much tastier. Once, at a party, we were treated with boiled bear meat, which I of course tasted, but I couldn't eat it due to its specific smell and taste.

Of course, we didn't only eat meat, because once a year we were supplied with necessary provision, but unfortunately, they often weren't enough for the whole year long. So, we were always glad when spring came, when frosts became milder, the sun was so bright that one couldn't look at it and even when the temperature was minus 25 degrees Celsius, the snow melted little by little and melt water dripped from the icicles hanging from the roofs of the houses.

However, spring, with all the joy of the return of better weather and longer days, was also the hardest time for us, as food delivered during the previous summer began to be used up. Another significant reason for the lack of food stuffs was because, with the increase in temperature, our landing strip which was on the bank of Kolyma River became unfit for the landing of cargo planes. We therefore, had to wait until August before fresh supplies could be shipped in down the River Kolyma.

Shops weren't empty of course, because they were still filled with the less popular foods which remained in the warehouse and we began to eat some pasta, dried onion and potato, which I hated by the way. There were pyramids consisting of tins of canned fish, sprats, cod liver and many other types of fish, but people were sick of them and wanted something else. The irony is that in the rest of USSR these products were in short supply and people would have been delighted to be able to buy them.

This was the period when the nature of Siberia and traditions of native people of Yakutia came to our help, because as soon as the river was free of ice there began wild game hunting. Every year thousands of different birds, swans, geese and ducks migrated for summer season to the North of Siberia, because there were plenty of forage and favourable conditions for breeding. The spring hunt usually started in May, and was an inseparable part of the native population's lifestyle, but for many of us, who had arrived from the other parts of the country, hunting was just a hobby.

Almost all grown-up men were the members of 'The hunting and fishing society', which gave them permission for hunting, and enabled them to buy guns and cartridges. The beginning of the hunting season was a very important period for people and its carrying out was well organized. An executive committee determined the duration of hunting season and people were informed about it in local newspaper and on the radio. No other social events were planned for that period, because it was mainly women and children who were left in the village. Cartridges and other necessary hunting gear were equally divided among the members of the society, and that is why all hunters became members of the Hunting and Fishing Societies at the start of the season.

My husband grew up in Ukraine and had never been involved in this type of activity, but he nonetheless went hunting a couple of times with his friends. I remember when he brought a couple of ducks and a goose from his first hunting trip, the goose was so big that when I was holding its neck near my chin its legs almost reached the floor. Jokingly he told me that he was lying in ambush waiting for the ducks to break cover, when suddenly this goose flew right in front of him and he shot it in fright. Sometimes when my husband was busy with his work and didn't go hunting, our friends and work colleagues brought us some ducks and geese, because it was a tradition to share game. Thanks to hunting and the presence of game in our diet, we easily survived spring with its food shortages.

However, the autumn hunting season was the most important, and this started in September and was a bit longer than the spring season. During this season local hunters – Yakuts – having broad experience, could shoot as many as three hundred ducks and geese. This was part of their traditional lifestyle and they preserved this game, meat of other animals and fish in basements, dug in the permafrost, where the temperature was below zero even during summertime. The basis of our diet in Yakutia was traditionally not only local meat, but also fish from the many lakes and rivers. Fishing started about June, when there was no ice on the rivers and lakes. The first kind of fish that started a fishing season was a carassius (Carp) – a small fish with big scales that we all loved, because it was incredibly tasty in the clean waters of the Yakutian lakes.

This type of fish wasn't stored for future use it had to be eaten fresh and that is why almost all people ate carassiuses at that time. They were everywhere: in the shops, cafeterias, they were sold right on the bank of the river, and some fishing-lovers, who had come back from fishing, gave it away for free. Our friends, who had boats and often fished, would bring a bucket of carassiuses and I would fry them all at once or stuffed them with rice and onion and bake in the oven with some sour cream. I always had a big plate of this fish on the table and we ate as much as we wanted and an odour of carassiuses filled my whole flat and it seemed that it penetrated to every single corner of the village at that time.

A bit later a small fish called a Siberian roach or retile was being fished. The Kolyma River and the lakes of the district were full of them. This kind of fish was eaten dry and in every back yard of the house in summer and in every flat in winter, Siberian roaches were hung on high wires using hooks. Siberian roach was the most popular beer fish, and that is why people who went on vacation from the village took bags full of it with them. My husband and I always took a suitcase full, when we visited our relatives, and in addition I always sent parcels containing Siberian roaches to my parents. Post services were very cheap and there were no limitations on the sending of goods, and that is why one could send ten kilogrammes of the fish for a couple of roubles to any place of the country.

Premium quality fish could also be found in the Kolyma River, one particular example was the stenodus nelma, many of which could be found closer to the mouth of the river. This was quite a big fish with white meat without bones. I remember once, during the first year of our life in Zyryanka, our neighbour called me and my husband to go outside – "Go and see what fish can be found in Kolyma River," they said. When we went outside we saw a huge nelma, which was lying on canvas spread on the ground and I think it was about my height. My husband, his eyes bulging, said, "If I saw such a fish in the river I would leave everything and run home in panic!" I helped our neighbours to cut the fish into pieces and put them into jars, sprinkling it with salt, and as a result we got seven three-litre jars, one of which they gave me.

There were so many different fish in the rivers and lakes that I could write a couple of pages about that, but I won't do that and will dwell on the most important and special delicacy of the North of Yakutia - sliced frozen fish. Only premium quality fish like broad whitefish, fished during sub glacial fishing, was used to make sliced frozen fish. People went to the river, usually in October when the river was already frozen, made holes in the ice and fished using fishing rods, but, in the places where the river hadn't been frozen yet it was fished using nets.

After the fish was taken out of water it was thrown on the ice immediately, where it froze in a moment and it was stored without defrosting in the sheds all winter long. When the fish was consumed it was brought into the house and it was given some time to defrost a little, because it was so frozen during severe frosts that if one knocked one fish on another, the sound was as if frozen logs were being knocked together.

A traditional Yakut knife

Only very solid and sharp Yakut's knives were used for sliced frozen fish with a sheath made of wood or deer's skin, these knives were made by local metal smiths.

All men were proud of their knives, showed them to each other and proclaiming that their knife was the best.

For the time that we lived in Yakutia we had several knives at home, but the best of them was gifted to us by our friend Vladimir, whose family we were friends with for many years. He worked as a smith at a local state farm and the knives that he made were the best ones in the district; it was one of his knives that we took to Ukraine with us in memory of those times. When the fish had defrosted a bit, it was skinned with a knife, and then sliced into very thin strips, which rolled up in spirals as they were sliced from the fish.

It was eaten right away, before it melted, and was dipped into a specially cooked sauce of tomato sauce, onion and black pepper. Sliced frozen fish was the best delicacy for us and it's impossible to describe its taste – fish was very delicate, of pink colour, smelled of a fresh cucumber and simply melted in your mouth. Everybody loved and ate sliced frozen fish, and there wasn't a single party without one because it was the best with vodka.

I'd like to tell you about the other properties of the land in which I lived. Those people, who had never been to the North of Siberia, believed that people there have the scurvy because of the lack of vitamins.

Even my parents used to think so, and warned me of that and told me that if needed they would send me some rose hips and the other dry berries and fruit.

However, thanks to some unique properties of North Siberia nobody suffered from the lack of vitamins. In fact it was just the opposite; I consider that I consumed no less vitamins than before.

There were always plenty of different mushrooms and berries in taiga during summertime, which could be gathered in unlimited quantities if one went to the trouble.

During the season, enterprises organised collective trips by truck into the taiga, people gathered mushrooms and berries in taiga situated along the road, and those who had motorboats gathered the same on the bank of the Kolyma River. As opposed to the other regions of the country, where people were walking in the forests and looking for the mushrooms all day long, we didn't have to spend time to look for them they were everywhere. We just went a couple of metres into taiga and gathered as much as we wanted, because there were places where mushrooms covered the soil like a carpet.

There were several types of mushrooms, but I loved suilluses the most and that is why I took only them. During the mushroom season I mainly ate mushrooms, using them in different variants, I even invented my own recipes to include them. I also preserved them for the rest of the year, I had jars with frozen marinated and fried mushrooms in my shed all winter long, and they were enough till the spring. Besides the mushrooms, the taiga was rich in a wide variety of berries, some of them, such as northern bilberry grew all around the village, and the others were all over taiga and we always had a rich choice of places in which to gather this natural bounty. Despite the fact that summer lasted only for two and a half months, I had time not only to eat different berries but also to store them for the whole winter long.

The most widespread berry in Yakutia was okhta, which was also called the Kolyma grape in our district because it resembled bunches of grapes, but was a bit smaller. In places there were whole plantations of it and as a rule red currants always grew nearby. Cranberries grew in almost any place in the taiga and we gathered it using special scoops with lengthwise holes in the end in the form of a comb. Using those scoops one could gather a lot of berries for a short period of time. These were also stored in sheds in small plywood barrels or cases. What was interesting about this fruit is, that cranberries never froze together and even during severe frosts they scattered like dried peas.

When we were collecting berries we usually went by boat with our friends for a whole day long and gathered a couple of buckets of each type of berry. After that we would light a campfire, fish and then cook some soup with the fish, which was called ukha and organize a picnic. I loved summer very much, because this was the time when we not only stored everything for winter but also spent our free time in the wild. It must be said that our village was surrounded with taiga, which could be a dangerous place as there were many wild animals roaming the taiga.

I can tell a lot of sad and funny incidents that happened to people out in the taiga. But I will tell only about an incident that happened to me personally, when I and my husband and our friends – Ivan and Tatiana were gathering some okhta and red currants about 15 kilometres away from the village up on the Kolyma River. Ivan grew up in these places and knew this area of the taiga very well and he persuaded us to go with him, because he knew of a place where a tributary joined the Kolyma River and good picking could be found. He said that few people knew about it and that is why no one went there.

When we were left alone on the steep bank of the tributary we took some buckets and climbed up the bank, where there really was a plantation of untouched berries. We had just started to gather it when Tatiana said – "Ivan, you told us that no one knows this place, but I have just seen a man who is gathering okhta here as well." Ivan laughed at first, and said that it was impossible, because there was only our boat moored there. But then he began to say that someone really had just gathered the berries there and that it would be better if we moved away from this place. He began to hurry us up and urged us to come down from the hill and get into the boat quickly.

His behaviour made me angry and I began to protest. Tatiana was screaming at her husband as well, and saying that it was useless to change the place, because that place was perfect. But as soon as the boat left the bank, Ivan pointed on the hillock with his hand and said – "And that is the man that gathered berries with us." Up there was a huge bear on his rear legs and he followed us with his eyes.

Of course we made fun of the incident remembering it after a while. "Why didn't you tell us from the very beginning?" Tatiana asked her husband. "I can only imagine how you would roll down the hillock out of fear," he said laughing.

Clothes and manufactured goods were delivered the same way as provisions during the annual navigation, and I was warned the moment I came to Zyryanka that one had to prepare for winter in summer. There was only one shop for manufactured goods in the village, and at the end of the navigation it was overloaded with different goods that were hard-to get in 1970s. Things that everybody else in the rest of the country could only dream about were available in this shop: women and men's sheepskin coats, mink hats and collars, warm mohair scarves, sheepskin fur-lined leather boots, golden jewellery, etc. Besides this there were many warm clothes backed with fur for everyday use, without which one wouldn't be able to survive the Kolyma winter.

When we arrived in Siberia and just started to work we had very little money to spend and why I bought only the most necessary winter clothing that I had enough money for. I bought a very warm and heavy beaver lambskin coat for my husband and fur hats for both of us, mittens lined with fur and some warm knitwear. My work colleagues warned me that I had to buy some warm clothing for future use because there would be frosts in winter below minus 50 degrees Celsius (minus 58 degrees F), but it was hard for me to imagine how cold this could be.

Our first winter was the hardest one for us, because as it turned out we weren't ready for it.

The winter coat that I brought from Ukraine and a beaver lamb hat didn't keep the warmth in at all and that is why I wore a big Russian shawl of goat's down all over my head, over the hat and my face, but it was still cold all the same.

I bought myself wellington boots two sizes bigger and wore them with two pairs of wool socks, but my feet were quickly frozen and in order to keep warm I didn't walk but ran. I inserted wool-mittens inside of the fur ones and hid my glasses in my pocket because they froze to my skin in a moment.

I couldn't get used for the first time covering my nose with a mitten because when the temperature is minus 50 degrees C and more one can easily suffer from frostbite. It was dangerous because you can't feel anything at first and find this out only when it's already too late.

It was a rule in Yakutia to tell a person passing by if his or her cheeks and nose or ears were white. As in such a case the person had to quickly rub their face with something woollen – a scarf or a mitten to avoid frostbite.

It was a commonplace for a teenager to suffer from frostbite and that is why my son's skin in those places always peeled in winter. Such clothes were made of local materials (different fur and animal skin) at the enterprise of consumer services where I used to work. It could be bought only in turn, but they made exceptions for the newcomers. Despite all these peculiarities, I and my husband kept our spirits up and learned to live in such unaccustomed conditions, as it was for us out of the question to go back home. From the experience of the other people who lived here, it was hard for everybody to get used to this life during the first years but with time they all felt at home and didn't want to leave that place.

It was the same for us after about a year because we began to dress like real northerners for the next winter and I understood at once that it can feel comfortable even in such a severe climate, if one wears traditional clothes like the northern people. That is why I could order a silver fox fur hat for myself which covered the whole head down to the neck and its ends came together on the chin, where laces made of fox tail were stitched. It was warm in such hats even during severe frosts, and that is why similar hats of different types of fur were worn by almost all the female population.

135

I also learned quite quickly how to sew men's hats from muskrat fur even preparing the skin myself by a traditional Yakut method. Firstly I damped the skin side with strong tea containing sugarless evaporated milk, and then I pummelled them by hand for quite a long time until they became soft and elastic. I sewed my first such hat for my husband. Muskrat fur was not expensive and readily available here because there were plenty of these animals in the lakes of Yakutia.

Many other men there wore hats of grey wolf, wolverine, or dogs' skins, but they were heavy and rough, that is why my husband never had one, always preferring muskrat fur. I also bought the traditional winter footwear of Yakutia – "mukluk", which were made of the lower leg portion of the reindeer skin. The nearest description of the "mukluk would be a form of Wellington boot, but these usually had a warm lining, were solid with thick felt and seemed almost impervious to the penetration of frost and feet did not feel cold even after long periods standing on the frozen ground.

My first silver fox fur hat in Siberia, 1972

Mukluks of deerskin were worn by most men, but my husband preferred boots made from the same material. Besides the deer skins, horse skins were also used for men's boots and mukluks; they were just as warm, but much rougher and heavier than those of deer skin. During the first years I wore a warm hooded fur coat trimmed with polar fox fur, which was called a 'covered fur coat'. Such coats were made of various skins with fur inside as a lining and the skin side covered with strong denim like fabric called kirza, which was of a black colour.

My son in his muskrat fur hat, which I made myself in 1973

Such winter clothes were not expensive, but very warm and that is why almost all the population wore them: men, women, and teenagers.

It should be said that in such an Arctic climate, one could only wear clothes of natural materials (fur, skin, wool etc.), because artificial materials couldn't stand up to the low temperatures, becoming brittle and stiff and even disintegrating, making walking and bending difficult.

I remember once, during frost of minus 56 degrees (minus degrees F?), I bought some food in the shop and put them into a bag of strong oilcloth fabric. The shop was only five minutes walking from my home, but as soon as I went outside the bag became brittle and when it touched my legs while walking, began to fall to pieces and food poured out onto the road. I had to pick everything up and carry them in my hands. Unable to cover my face, when I reached home my nose was almost frostbitten.

The traditional boots made from reindeer skin

In all the subsequent years of my life in Yakutia, I dressed well and had several natural fur-coats, several coats with fur collars and hats of different styles of mink, white and silver polar fox and red fox and sable.

Besides that I bought fur as presents for my parents and relatives of my husband and that is why my mother also had coats with different fur collars.

I always bought presents like musquash hats for my father and once I even presented him with boots of deerskin, but soled with artificial rubber, which he liked very much. My mother told me that when they were walking in the street wearing those clothes, people turned to look at them, paying special attention to my father's boots. We wore winter clothes all winter long, starting from the middle of October, when everything around froze and the rivers were covered with ice, up to the middle of April, when the frosts were still up to minus 25 degrees(minus 13 degrees F), but this was already the beginning of spring for us. Starting from April time one could change from winter clothes into the one lighter ones and show off a bit in a fabric coat, a hat with open ears and leather boots. The time we called 'spring', lasted for around a month and then temperatures rose quickly and the short and hot summer came.

Sewing skills, gained during school years and especially during my work at the regional consumer service enterprise, came in useful for my later life, because besides the clothes that we bought in the shop, I sewed many pieces of clothing for my family by myself. My friends used to joke with me that there was a non-waste industry in my family because I never threw away old clothes I altered and recycled them.

All the shirts of my husband, where collars had frayed, but otherwise looked well, I altered to fit my son. I sewed for myself, skirts from my husband's trousers which were made of high quality fabric, jackets out of coats and sundresses out of men's suits, etc. Clothes of big sizes, which were sold very cheaply in the reduced price shops, was a real catch for me; I chose such clothes that could be altered for the members of my family.

That is why even during those times when there was a total shortage of clothes in the country, I sometimes sewed trendy and unusual pieces of clothing. For example in 1985, I sewed windcheaters for me, my husband and my son out of reduced price raincoats. When we visited my friend's house in St. Petersburg, their first words when they saw us were as follows: "Why didn't you write and tell us that you have such trendy windcheaters on offer, I would have ordered some for us!"

Thanks to the fact that all kinds of fabrics were on offer all over the country and especially in Yakutia, that I was able to sew clothes for myself, which differed from those that were sold in the shops: business suits, all kinds of blouses, evening dresses, quilted jackets, berets and even handbags. I remember when I worked at the party's regional committee in 1988; two workers from the Moscow higher trade union organization came to visit us. It was my duty to meet them at the airport, settle them into a hotel and organize meetings at the various enterprises that they were expected to visit.

When I showed them the details of the arrangements I had made, after they had glanced at them, they put them aside and said, "We'll do that later, and now we would like to visit your shops and buy our wives the same Japanese coats like yours." I laughed and told them it was impossible because I sewed the coat by myself, but they couldn't believe it and laid the coat out on the table and began to examine and admire it. I really had sewed a quilted coat of Japanese fabric, a sort of waterproof nylon, which was very trendy at that time, and lined it with a winterized synthetic fabric.

At the end of 1980s, I even made for myself an astrakhan fur coat from 30 astrakhan fur collars that I bought. I worked in the evenings for more than a month, choosing and connecting the skins of the 30 collars by hand and as a result the fur coat turned out to be so beautiful that I couldn't believe that I did it by myself. My colleagues were simply awe struck when they saw me wearing it. They began to ask me to sew the same for them, offering me any sum of money for my work, knowing that I had previously made clothes for my friends. During the first years of life in Yakutia I really had earned a lot of extra money this way, but when I started to earn high salary I began to turn down the offer of this extra work.

Chapter 21

District Centre of Domestic Service

The enterprise where I worked dealt with the domestic needs of the local population producing all kinds of goods and services that were required for a normal life. It had several buildings situated in the village. There was an administration office in the main building and tailoring shops where they sewed women, men clothes, knitwear, fur-coats and fur-hats of real fur. In the other buildings there were: a clock workshop, a hairdresser's, a photo studio, dry-cleaner's and a shoe workshop, where western shoes were repaired and also made the traditional shoes of Northern people – warm high fur boots of deer fur.

The staff of our enterprise consisted of around hundred people and was multinational workforce. People of many different nationalities, worked there coming from all the Republics of the USSR as well as yakuts and other local people of Yakutia. In the hall of the main building there hung a big map of the USSR and each town from which workers had come to Yakutia was marked and with the help of a pin and a piece of red thread was linked to Zyryanka. I liked to look at this map, which was all red from all those threads and the whole country could be seen.

There were many people from Ukraine, especially miners from Donbass, because coal mining was being carried out and specialists in this sphere were needed. I was lucky to be the part of such good and friendly staff, where women of different ages and nationalities worked; they were all friendly, shared eagerly the secrets of sewing and helped each other in everything. We always had plenty of work. In 1970s tailoring shops were very popular in the country because there weren't any smart and different designed clothes in the shops as there are now.

Clothing factories of the country produced mainly standard designs and qualities. There was such an expression: "the product corresponds to standard requirements", which meant that it was sewed without regard for the peculiarities of a certain person's figure and that is why it did not fit everybody properly. Millions of coats, suits, dresses of the same colours were cut and sold all over the country. These clothes were not always of high quality and they were bought for everyday wearing.

It was believed that clothes in a socialist country should be simple and comfortable, and even in school our clothes must be simple and all look the same. So, in schools all over the country pupils had to wear a school uniform. Boys had grey woollen trousers and a tunic jacket with a belt and buckle topped off with a separate white cotton collar. Girls wore brown cashmere dresses with white cotton collars and cuffs attached, these collars and cuffs had to be changed every week. Every day, girls also wore black aprons and had black bows in their hair.

On special occasions these aprons and bows were changed into white and this was then called a full dress. At this time it was impossible to buy some smart and beautiful clothes or evening dress in the shops and this was an issue, generally speaking, neglected in the country. Many people didn't want to wear standard clothes; they preferred "bespoke tailoring", and tailoring shops offered this service.

People in these establishments made smart clothes of unusual fashion that fitted the purchasers figure and taste. A network of shops called "Textile" was established all over the country offering a big variety of fabrics of different types to fit any taste. In order to make it more convenient for customers, tailoring shops also stocked a range of textiles that clients could choose from; they ordered clothes and chose the fabrics in the same place.

Tailoring services were inexpensive, and this allowed women to have something new for each holiday, and for a long vacation they changed their whole wardrobe. When there was an order for 10-15 pieces of clothing for one person, it meant that this woman was going on vacation. Fashions designs were mainly taken from the magazines "Soviet woman" or "Village woman", which had them on the last pages. As soon as the new magazine was issued – there was a queue at once to order these fashions.

In a workshop where I worked, there was a bonus type of wage system. Everything was kept very simple – the more you sewed the more you earned. A skilled seamstress could usually sew 30-35 things per month. I did my best – I was able to design and sew my own creations and soon had plenty of personal clients. All my friends and colleagues asked me to make their orders, that is why I always had plenty of work to do and I earned well.

There were times in the year when we had the opportunity to participate in other activities which were organized by the Centre of Domestic Services.

These activities united staff and made life more interesting for everyone employed at the centre. For example, each season there was a fashion show to demonstrate the latest designs and colours.

Fashion shows were held at clubs, at big enterprises and sometimes even during the meeting of the Communist Party's District Committee.

For such occasions I sewed smart things and modelled them myself. I had a fine figure and liked demonstrating new fashions in clothes; even today I still enjoy wearing fashionable clothes.

Here I am at a fashion show contest, 1973

I could well have been a model, but my height being only 164cm, was too small to do this professionally as one had to be at least 170cm tall. However, on January 1973 I had the opportunity to take part in the Regional fashion show and contest which was held every year in Yakutsk. I was fortunate in being selected for this task as it was considered a great honour to represent our centre in this competition. I modelled and showed more than 20 items of clothing, all of which had been specially made for me by the workers in our centre. The collection consisted of a great variety of clothing, winter and summer clothes, an evening dress, casual clothes, national clothes and uniforms for work.

All 34 districts of Yakutia took part in this annual contest and it was very interesting to find out about the new trends in fashion and see what models other tailoring shops were making.

Our tailoring shop took the third place in the contest and we were awarded with a diploma and a valuable present – a special 'Over locking machine'. This trip was also especially delightful for me as it was my first visit to Yakutsk – the capital of Yakutia.

On another occasion there was a hairdressing contest. Hairdressers at the centre chose girls, who were willing to take part in the competition. Needless to say I was an eager participant as I had long straight fair hair and they made me a wonderful hairdo.

The competition winner had the title of "The best hairdresser of the year" conferred on them, and afterwards all the girls with the hairdos were photographed and an album made of these photos so that they could show potential customers what could be created for them.

I came to the contest wearing a skirt and jumper, but my hairdo required something special and I wanted to go home and change into something more suitable.

However, a friend of mine forced me to take off the sweater and threw her new coat, which had a silver fox fur collar, on my shoulders and it complemented my hair beautifully and looked very cute and unusual. This was my first and my most favourite photo made in Siberia.

The International Women's Day was a favourite holiday in my country, and which was celebrated each year on the 8th of March. On this day everything was for women – meetings were held, concerts, parties, different competitions at the enterprises and clubs. At all the schools and kindergartens there were concerts where children performed, congratulated their moms and teachers; men gave presents and flowers to all women at the enterprises and at home.

A competition for the best cake was always held on that day at the Centre of Domestic Service. Being that the majority of the workforce in this establishment was women, there were many cakes made. We showed all the cakes on the long table where we usually cut out the clothes, we showed all the cakes which we made and chose a winner. After that we usually took all the rest of the food brought from home and continued celebrating, to the Russian tradition: with champagne, vodka, songs and dances.

Once after such a celebration, I came home almost at midnight, and of course, I was drunk. I thought there would be a scene at home, but luckily my husband said that once a year on the 8th March women could do everything they wanted to.

When one of our staff was returning to their original home republic it was regarded as a special occasion by the whole staff. On this occasion a ceremonial meeting was held attended by a member of the district executive committee who spoke publicly how the person had worked and lived for all those years and thanked them for the work in the Yakutia and gave them a diploma and presents. Their name was then entered into the Honourable Book of the District Centre of domestic service. This was a book of memories of the best people who worked there. All the friends and close colleagues presented something to be remembered by, and after that the whole staff went to the restaurant together.

My photo for the hair style competition, 1972

This type of send-off was not only done at our centre, but was common in all organisations in the area. When I saw such a send-off for the first time I was amazed, as it was not commonplace in other soviet republics and regions of the country. It was a sign of the close camaraderie that those of us who worked in this inhospitable area felt. It was an emotional time for everybody when someone was about to leave. Many of the women would be crying as they wished the person leaving good luck in their new ventures. After that every time I thought of the moment I would leave I wanted to cry and thought that after such a send-off I wouldn't be able to leave those people and that place.

Chapter 22

Joining the Communist Party

Once, when I was working, I was invited to office of my boss - the director of the centre of domestic service. When I entered the office, there was an instructor from the communist party's district committee of ideology. She said that she wanted to talk to me and started to ask me whether there were any communists in my family and for how long I was going to live in the village. I told her that neither my Mother nor my Father was communists and that I liked the life at North Siberia very much and wasn't going to leave any time soon.

"Be ready. The next week there will be a party meeting and we'll recommend you to be the candidate for the membership at the communist party of the Soviet Union," She said. I was startled and started to tell her that I couldn't, that I was afraid, that I had lived here for only a year and was not ready for that. "Don't worry. You are active, energetic, you have authority with people and we think you deserve to be a communist," insisted she. I didn't know what to do, but I was afraid to refuse.

My husband was in a panic and displeased when I told him – "why do you need that? You are a woman and have to do your house duties and not the social work. Besides, I'm not a communist yet, and you want it first?" He exclaimed. "That is not normal!" – He finished. But it was too late for changing anything and I started to prepare for the meeting. According to the regulations of the Communist Party of Soviet Union, in order to become a candidate for the CPSU you had to have references from two communists, to learn, understand and agree to the regulations of the party.

I also had to be prepared for the questions concerning the political life of the country and answer various other questions. When I went to the meeting, I was worrying quite a lot, but everything went well. Two women, my colleagues, who had been members of the party for many years, gave me great references. Then I answered all the questions concerning the Regulations of the CPSU and the political situation in the country and the world. After that I became a candidate for the membership at the CPSU. It might be assumed, by many people, that all Russians are Communists, but this is not so.

That meant, that in a year I had to complete the probationary period and prove with my good work and behaviour that I really deserved to be a communist. If everything was satisfactory, in a year I could become a full member of the Communist Party of the Soviet Union. Only those people who are considered worthy and capable of contributing to the party and the country are "Invited" to become members of the Communist Party. So for me it was a real honour to be considered for membership, particularly, when in a couple of days after this meeting there was an article about me in the local newspaper *Soviet Kolyma*.

They wrote that I came from Ukraine to develop Siberia, that during the year that I had spent there I had earned the respect of the youth of the village. They also wrote that I had chosen the right way in my life by joining the Communist Party. I sent a copy of this article to my parents and also to a teacher from my college in Chernovtsy. My father replied with a letter in which he wrote that he was proud of me. My mother on the contrary didn't approve. She thought, like my husband that a woman should take care of her family and it was unnecessary for me to become a member of the Communist Party.

Actually I hadn't planned to join the communist party at this time and would never have asked about it myself. Maybe it was because I was only 23 years old and my adult life has just begun but, now when I was accepted as a candidate for the communist party, I felt very happy and I wanted to be a member as fast as possible.

The fact of joining the Party was a logical continuation of my previous life, because I lived in a Soviet country and had passed all its lower levels starting from school and was brought up in the spirit of patriotism. It was as they say "To be in the first ranks of the developers of communism."

The October children's pins

So, from the beginning of primary school I, like other pupil, was considered to be "Little Octobrists" – that meant the grandchildren of Vladimir Lenin.

That was a communist organization for young schoolchildren with their own creed, which I had to learn by heart and carried out in practice.

Also I was given little red badges in the shape of a star with the picture of Vladimir Lenin as a boy. These badges I attached to school the uniforms on the left side near my heart, and warning at all times. Pupils in our class were divided into special groups of 5 "Little Octobrists", this number selected because stars have 5 points. Every group had a leader selected from within the group. Every pupil wanted their group to be the best, and that's why they tried to study well, to do errands and to help each other in many things.

When I was in the 3rd grade in school, I together with my fellow pupils joined the Pioneer Organization and to mark this there was a celebration in our school. Everyone was wearing our special occasion uniform. We were lined up in ranks and senior pioneers held the banner of Soviet Union Pioneer Organization, whilst others played drums and bugle. Then we repeated after the teacher the words of the oath, promising to keep our red pioneer tie, to be excellent pupil, to set a good example in everything we did, to respect older people and help the younger ones, and to be the worthy citizens of our country.

After the oath the pupils of 7-th and 8-th grades tied the red pioneer ties on our necks and presented us with the pioneer pins. The pioneer ties were just a kind of kerchiefs made in the shape of a triangle and made of red satin or silk. The pioneer pins were in the shape of stars with the image of Vladimir Lenin and the inscription: "Always ready!" A teacher addressed us with the words – "Young pioneers! In the struggle for the ideas of the Soviet Union Communist Party be always Ready!" We all raised our right hand on the level of our foreheads and answered-

"Always ready!"

From that moment we became the pioneers, and to the sounds of drums and pioneer horns the pioneer banner was carried away. That was the established procedure of initiation, and which had always been carefully kept.

Becoming a pioneer was an important event in my life, and I had looked forward to it and was very proud of being accepted into the organization. I remember that day in November quite clearly; it was very cold, frosty and snowy, but in spite of this I didn't just walks, I ran home with my coat unfastened so that everyone could see my red tie.

148

The Pioneer's Pins

Being the pioneer was far more interesting for me than being just "October Children", may be because I was more adult than before. Our class had its pioneer leader who was a senior pupil and a Komsomol member, who instructed us and helped us to fulfil pioneer tasks. These tasks were to enable us to become useful members of society, and the first thing we were supposed to do was to study well, and the second was to help elderly people. The school had lists of such people who needed help.

Every pioneer group had its person who they regularly visited and took care of– went shopping, cleaned the house or did what they asked. It was a very honourable thing for me to help an elderly person in crossing a street or carrying a heavy bag as well as giving up my seat in a bus. After classes or on weekends we had waste metal and paper gathering and the best groups were rewarded with letters of commendation.

I remember we went round to different houses to ask if people had some metal or waste paper for us. They gave us broken irons or some other unserviceable metal things, old books, papers and magazines. Often we would find such items in the streets or behind the sheds. Once I even climbed a pit slag heap in search of these items, as these heaps were very old there was often a lot of metal scrap on it which I grabbed and carried off.

Most of all I liked the pioneer summer camps for children, which were held all over the country and in some beautiful places like river banks, forests or sea coasts. The camp vouchers were distributed free of charge or could be bought by parents at their place of work and could be afforded by everyone as these were not expensive. I spent time in several different camps and I enjoyed them all and had real fun during these trips.

We were arranged into divisions of 20-25 people and each division had its pioneer leader who was a Komsomol member. All the camps followed the same Pioneer Organization routines, in the morning we were woken up by a pioneer horn and did our morning exercises which was followed by a camp meeting where the flag of the Pioneer Organization was raised and only then would we have our breakfast.

After this we could participate in various activities, like hiking or enter different sporting competitions and participate in a contest for the best pioneer team/division. Not only did I have a rest and relaxation away from our usual home environment but also sang pioneer songs and learned how to dance or swim which were useful activities to promote good health.

A pioneer fire was a symbol of the Pioneer Organization and I have very special memories about this. Even that pioneer pin we wore on our right hand side had a picture of the fire. The anthem of the Pioneer Organization also started with the words about the pioneer fires.

"Lift up like the fires, blue nights,

We are the pioneers, children of workers.

A future age is coming,

"Be always ready!" – That's a pioneer call.

These pioneer fires were made in the evening or at night and were usually set in a clearing in the woods or on the sea shore depending on the location of the camp. We all sat around these fires until late into the night, playing games, singing songs, baking potatoes and listening to our pioneer leaders telling us interesting stories. The most famous was the International pioneer camp "Artek". It was situated in Crimea on the Black Sea coast.

Not only children from our country were allowed to attend but also those from other socialist countries under the influence of the USSR. This camp worked throughout the whole year, because of the warm weather in the Crimea, even in winter.

The camp vouchers were not sold but given to the schools to be awarded to the best pioneers and pupils for their good behaviour, excellent studies and other achievements. Sometimes the schools received only one voucher in few years and only the luckiest pupils could get it. Unfortunately I was not one of these!

Two years before I finished school, a very important thing happened in my life. I joined the Communist Union of Youth (Komsomol). The procedure for entering the Komsomol was more difficult than entering the Pioneer Organization.

The Komsomol's pins

Every pupil was accepted individually, but only after being interviewed by several members of the local ruling Komsomol party.

It was a serious interview which sought to determine your suitability to join such a prestigious organization as the Komsomol.

Not only were questions just asked to you at this interview, but questions were also put to members of your peer group who were asked to comment on your suitability to become a member of Komsomol.

To qualify as a member of this organization, it was necessary to study well, take an active part in social life, and to show exemplary behaviour. Only the best pupils according to their commitment would be accepted into Komsomol. Not everybody could make it into what was considered to be a very prestigious organization, but I wanted to be Komsomol member because it would be a great honour and responsibility for me.

It was a serious organization with its own statutes which had to be carefully studied and fulfilled. Breaking these rules was a reason for expulsion from Komsomol membership.

According to the Statute; I received a membership card and had to pay the required fee. I also had to attend Komsomol meetings which were held every month.

Out of 27 pupils in my class there were only 19 who joined the Komsomol organization. All the others either did not want to or were considered to be unworthy. I did not even doubt for a minute whether I wanted to join it or not. I wanted to join as soon as possible and to become a member of this organization which unites millions of the best young people in my country.

At the first meeting that I attended there were some social duties distributed, and I was chosen to be the editor of a discussion news sheet, which was displayed on a wall in the classroom. This broadsheet was to promote socialist ideals and ideology. I did this work with pleasure. I believe that the experience of work at those organizations was useful to me in the following days, and opened the way to an interesting life, and eventual full membership of the communist party.

So, the year passed quickly and I became a member of the Communist Party. This event changed my outlook on life, the thought that I was now a communist was always with me.

It didn't matter whether I simply walked in the street, worked or had a rest – I always remembered that I was not only a woman, but also a communist. I took this responsibility very seriously as I had to justify the party's trust in me.

I was proud to be a communist (My photo on this time, 1973)

Chapter 23

Komsomol experience in Siberia

Almost half of the workers at the centre of domestic service were young energetic, cheerful, and lively people and I found many friends at once. A Komsomol primary organization also functioned there, as well as at the other amenities of the village. It so happened that at the first meeting of the Komsomol that I attended, which was convened to hear reports and elect new officials, I was selected to be the new secretary of the primary Komsomol organization.

I was very surprised to be nominated and tried to explain that I was a newbie at the village and it would be hard for me to accept this position. However, my protestations were useless, nobody listened to me and all the Komsomol members voted for me. I was then congratulated by everyone present. When I arrived home and told my husband about it he immediately started laughing at me – "Why did you agree? You should have refused. Nobody wants to do that job, which is why they chose you!"

Ironically, several weeks later, a primary Komsomol organization was formed at the construction company where my husband worked, and they elected him to be a secretary as well! This resulted in both of us being involved in the same type of extra-curricular activities. On the one hand it was very honourable to do such important Komsomol assignments, but on the other hand it was a big social duty, because we were responsible for the work of Komsomol organizations at each of our organizations.

In the whole district there were more than a thousand Komsomol members in twenty primary Komsomol organizations, the work of which was coordinated by the District Committee of the Komsomol, and controlled by three secretaries assisted by a couple of clerical staff. The first secretary was a young man, who came from Moscow and had lived in our village; he enjoyed great prestige among young people. Every five years a plenary meeting was held and this was the highest authority of the district committees.

Primary Komsomol organizations reported on the work done for the previous five years at the Plenary and confirmed a plan of operation for the next five years. Secretaries and executive members of the District Committee, which was considered to be the highest authority of the district committee in the period between the Plenary, were elected there as well. This executive consisted of 12 people who were the best Komsomol members selected from different enterprises in the region. They weren't full-time employees of the committee and this was their social assignment.

In the north-east of Siberia the Komsomol organization paid more attention to its members, ensuring that they had many forms of social and educational work to keep them occupied. We didn't have time to get bored; we were always busy with some interesting work: sports competitions, excursions around the enterprises, public debate on different issues. One time there was a competition for the best primary Komsomol organization of the region, and we started to prepare for it by trying to think of something new to do. At first we wanted to create a dancing team, and I selected several girls and started to teach them.

However, it was clear after a couple of lessons that I had to give up on this idea because the girls had never danced before and it was hard for me to teach them. Then we decided to create a choir of six girls. The director of the centre gladly supported us, and she allocated money for a musician, who came to play his accordion twice a week and to teach us to sing.

I had known from school that I couldn't sing, but there was nothing else left to do. I was obligated to sing myself, if I didn't sing how I could awake anybody else's interest, so I just had to try. We must have succeeded quite well because we were invited to perform concerts at various clubs and other locations. In order to look more like a professional company we sewed ourselves dresses of cotton printed with flowers and called the company 'Daisy'. We simply chose this name because our first song was always about daisies. Later we made different costumes and sang other songs. Maybe we did not sing particularly well, but we were all young and attractive, and perhaps that is why we were so successful.

Singing group of Komsomol members Centre of Domestic Services, 1973

Komsomol community work days, when we worked for free, were frequently held. We usually worked on our days off – on a Saturday. In the Russian language we called these days "Subotnik" which is derived from a Russian word "Subota" which means Saturday. It was not only Komsomol members who worked on "Subotniks" but other employees also worked at this time. We performed mainly unskilled, but necessary work, such as cleaning out farm buildings or tidying up building sites. At certain times of the year we helped unload containers at the river port and transferred wares received to the warehouse. Once a year 22nd April, the Birthday of Vladimir Lenin, the USSR Lenin Communist 'subotnik' was held, and on which day the whole country worked for free.

According to the Komsomol organization's regulations, young Komsomol members were a part of the organization until they were 28 years old, even if they had already become members of the Communist party. This happened to me, becoming a full member of the Communist Party when I was 23. Not only did I have to carry out communist party's assignments, but at the same time I was still a Komsomol district committee member, and since the age of 26 a member of the executive of Komsomol district committee. It happened this way because of one very important event in my life which I will never forget.

It is well-known that during these years under the communist system a so called balanced development of the national economy was carried out. The USSR State Committee organised it, drawing up elaborate five-year plans, which were distributed among all the Soviet Republics, to every enterprises and to every worker. Everybody knew their five-year plan and tried to carry it out as soon as possible in order to be of benefit to the country. There were slogans everywhere about the carrying out of the plan ahead of schedule, such as –

'We will carry out and over fulfil a five-year plan under the direction of the Communist Party!'

'Let's carry out a five-year plan in four years!'

'The Five-year plan to be achieved in three years!'

There were originally thirteen five-year plans altogether and twelve of them were carried out with various degrees of success, the thirteenth wasn't completed because at the beginning of the thirteenth five-year plan the USSR collapsed. My work in the Siberia started in the period of the ninth five-year plan. As soon as I started working at the Centre of domestic service I was familiarized with my personal five-year plan detailing the amount of production I was expected to achieve and how much money this would generate for the company. I have already written that I tried to work hard and sewed very fast and achieved a good salary. I didn't pay much attention to my five-year plan because I knew that I would easily fulfil my quota.

In 1975 – X plenary session of the Komsomol district committee was held and I was invited to attend as usual. When I arrived the atmosphere seemed different and I felt that they treated me somehow differently and with some special attention. It was a complete surprise to me when I was elected to be a member of the presidium of the Plenary, meaning that I had to take my place on the stage overlooking the rest of the meeting. This only happened to the best 20 people in the Komsomol. The Plenary continued the whole day and I sat all the time on the panel on the stage facing the audience; I couldn't talk to anybody or relax until the end of the day, I became so tired and wanted this all to come to an end.

At the end of the Plenum they rewarded the best Komsomol members for a good job and active participation in social life. The first secretary of district committee made this announcement and said that he was very proud that two people in our region carried out the ninth five-year plan ahead of schedule.

For that they were to be awarded with gold and silver badges of the Central Committee of Komsomol of USSR. A golden badge was awarded to a man who worked as a bulldozer operator and carried out a five-year plan within three years.

The silver badge was awarded to me. I was so surprised that almost fell of the stage, I couldn't believe it! It turned out that I had carried out my five-tear plan in four years. Before I had chance to recover from my surprise they gave me a free tourist voucher for a holiday to Bulgaria and also elected me to become a member of the Bureau of Komsomol district committee. I can't even express how excited I was; I almost jumped for joy and was proud of myself and my country. When all our friends found out about this they congratulated me, my husband was also proud of me but he was a bit disappointed that they didn't give me a family voucher for both of us.

My silver badge, 1975

At that time it was very hard to go abroad even with a tourist voucher. Groups were made up according to the social structure. For example there was an unspoken rule that a group must contain 50 percent of workers, 20 percent of agricultural workers, and the remaining percentage of communists and komsomol members, etc. (I don't know exactly the percentage this was just an example.) Of course all the tourist's journeys were to socialistic countries only: Bulgaria, Poland, Yugoslavia, Czechoslovakia and Cuba.

There was a conversation with the tourists before they left, they were told how soviet tourists should behave abroad: we were forbidden to communicate with any foreigners we might meet there; to admire the country we were going to, but remembering that our country was the best in the world.

We had to stay together with the group and we must not walk alone on the streets. We were only allowed to take a small amount of currency with us which we might change for foreign currency. Each group had a leader or minder, who worked for the communist party and who took care of the tourists and watched the discipline.

I went to Bulgaria for 20 days as a part of a Komsomol group of 26 people, who were all from different parts of Yakutia. During that time we went along the seashore of the Black Sea, we enjoyed ourselves for 10 days at the international youth centre named after George Dimitrov, and then we visited many historical places and cities of Bulgaria. I was charmed with the country, with its beautiful nature, warm sea, interesting traditions and dances, wonderful cuisine, variety of wines, fruit, vegetables and especially the grapes.

I was very grateful for this award and it spurred me on to work even harder and as a consequence for many years after I regularly beat the five-year plan. In November 1977 the local newspaper the "Soviet Kolyma" published an article about me with my photo. It was the second time that an article had been published in this newspaper, the first was in 1973, when I joined the communist party which I did not keep, but I kept this newspaper and still have it to this day.

Article about me in newspaper the 'Soviet Kolyma', 1977

Chapter 24

Social life in the village of Zyryanka

My life in Yakutia was unusual and interesting from the very first day I arrived. I don't know why, but I think that even people there were different, ordinary, joyful, dedicated, energetic, and always ready to help each other in a tight situation. The village of Zyryanka was small, everybody knew each other and was on friendly terms; maybe it was the severe north land that united us and helped each other to survive under such extremities.

I was a very young woman when I came to this place, which was thousands of kilometres away from my home and I practically had to start my life from scratch. There was so much I didn't know and didn't understand, but I always had good and kind people by my side that took care of me, and gave me help and guidance. I felt that I had a family here and everybody loved me. The population of the village was around six thousand people, and that is why almost everybody knew each other, and when new people arrived they all tried to help them to settle down faster. The life there was special – almost nobody locked the doors of a house or a flat, and if they locked them they just put the key under the rug at the front door and everybody knew about that.

Money didn't mean so much here – they helped themselves to the full extent of the resources available for free – they could get some meat, wild ducks, geese and a bucket of fish or berries. There was very little crime, because a criminal couldn't hide anywhere. The taiga and swamps were thousands of kilometres around and you could leave the settlement only by aeroplane; there was no other way in or out.

Everybody was there in the public eye and lived as if part of one big family; some invisible force united all people and kept them there in that severe land. This wasn't just for the money, at first everybody came there to earn money faster for a decent life and then leave. But when you arrived there, almost at once you fell in love with this land and nobody hurried to leave it, and many people stayed there forever.

It often happened that after people had lived there for many years and then left to go back home, only to return again, back north to the land they loved, unable to settle anywhere else. Despite the fact that this place was far from the centre of the country and there was a severe climate and often uncomfortable living conditions, it was very interesting to live there. Of course, the main occupation for people there was their work, everybody worked there and there weren't any housewives as in other cities, around the country.

Besides this there were the special traditions of the region, and which were celebrated annually. People from all over the USSR were represented in this community and all took part in the social activities of the village, thereby helping to unite them. For example, once every two years there were amateur arts festivals and talent competitions, which were held at local clubs according to the schedule approved by the ideological department of the Communist party's district committee.

At these festivals the winners were chosen and awarded with diplomas and valuable prizes. Each enterprise, for example, local schools, hospitals, factories, prepared for the festivals beforehand; they wrote the program and did the performance themselves, and many of these organizations had very talented people working for them.

Rehearsals were usually held after work and on days off. Many people eagerly took part in it: they danced, sang, some of them made verses and read their poems. Those who didn't want to perform were forced to do it, they joked about that: "if you can't we'll teach you," "if you don't want to we'll force you." Those who couldn't and didn't want to do anything sang in a choir, which opened all the concerts. Villagers attended the concerts with pleasure, the halls and clubs were filled with people, and it was amazing.

Almost each concert included performances by people, the talents of whom nobody had even known before. For example everybody respected a head doctor of the local hospital, who was a very reserved, serious man of few words, but at the concert he showed himself to be exactly the opposite! – he performed comedies so that everybody roared with laughter; and of course they loved him even more from that moment on.

Speaking personally, there was no need to force me; I used every opportunity to take part in any concert performance. Of course, I always danced. A colleague of mine became my dancing partner. He worked at our centre of domestic services as a shoemaker, and was an ethnic gipsy who danced wonderfully. We danced together in many concerts and in 1974 we received the first prize for the gipsy dance performance!

The "sending off "of winter was a traditional street festivity for the village, it was held every year at the end of April. On that day in the morning leaflets were thrown about the village from a helicopter. They congratulated people with the ending of winter and invited them to the banks of the river Yasachnaia to take part in the celebrations on the occasion of the holiday.

A stage was constructed on the solid ice of the river, alongside which a high wooden pole had been frozen into the ice. On the top of this pole a prize was hung and was to be retrieved by any man who could climb this pole. A little further from the stage and on the ice, they made an effigy of winter, made from wood and straw. This would be ceremonial burnt, to signal the end of winter, during the course of the celebration.

I am in a dance performance, 1974

There were also stalls which sold hot pancakes, buns, sandwiches, sweets and drinks. The people, who by this time, were tired of the long and severe winter prepared with pleasure for this holiday. Local residents thought up the scenario for performance, rehearsed and made costumes.

The theme could be anything they wanted; favourite performances were usually short sketches from Russian fairy tales, where the players would wear pantomime costumes. Everybody gathered by the river at ten a.m., and the festival started. First of all a woman wearing the costume of winter went on the stage, she resisted and didn't want to leave, but was driven off by the shouting crowd and afterwards they burnt the effigy of winter.

After the departure of winter, spring arrived in a helicopter, in the form of a young beautiful girl wearing a long Russian sarafan (long dress without sleeves) of green colour, decorated with flowers and with a flower crown upon her head. She was to be the hostess of the concert. Upon her arrival the entertainment began, each group of performers is giving their best performance, after which a judgment of the performances was given and the winners chosen.

After the performances the festival continued, people danced, sang, and had picnics right on the ice (standing of course). Men took off their shoes, undressed to the waist and tried to climb the pole in order to take the present – that was the funniest show because it wasn't so easy to climb the pole.

After several attempts somebody usually managed to get the present eventually, which traditionally was a bottle of vodka and a snack to eat with it.

At the time of this festival frost was usually not so cold, about minus 10 degrees C, resulting in a partial thaw and everything started to melt and dripping down from the roofs, but the weather was unpredictable and very often the frosts would return.

I remember on one particular occasion when I took my son, he was very excited and tried together with the other children to drive Winter away as far as they could. However, the next day the weather turned nasty, it was snowy and there was a heavy frost. My son Alex told me, "Mummy, you see how sly the winter is, we drove her away yesterday and she ran away and the when everybody left the river she came back!"

However, the most important holiday in Yakutia was the traditional holiday of the Yakut people which was called Ysyakh. This holiday had its roots in ancient times and represented the approach of summer, warmth, sun and abundance. It was celebrated at the end of June all over the territory of Yakutia, when hot summer came after a long cold winter. This Ysyakh holiday was always celebrated in our region in a Yakut village called Verkhnekolymsk, which was situated 5 kilometres (3 miles) away from Zyryanka on the bank of the river Yasachnaia.

Verkhnekolymsk village is a most ancient and historical place, because the first settlement of people here began in the middle of the seventeenth century, when expeditions stopped there to spend winter, whilst exploring the north-east of Siberia.

In 1647, a stronghold was constructed here and it became a stockade town, and later a church was constructed, the bell for which was produced in central Russia, and under incredibly hard conditions was delivered to the stockade town. At the beginning of the Soviet period the church was destroyed, and what was left of it was reconstructed into an apartment house.

The Ysyakh holiday was celebrated on the bank of the river Yasachnaia, where many other people, who had come from the other villages, gathered as well as those from Zyryanka. This was a folk festival with concerts, contests, traditional people's games and Yakut sport competitions. According to tradition, guests at the holiday celebration were treated with Yakut national dishes, cooked by locals and also with a traditional drink called koumiss.

I tasted this drink for the first time in my life at one of these celebrations. Koumiss is a traditional Yakut fermented dairy product, traditionally made from mare's milk, and which according to the Yakut legend gives strength and improves health. Ysyakh was celebrated according to a traditional ritual, which had been preserved from the ancient times and was always ended with a dance in which all guest participated. All guests made a circle and by taking each other's hand moved slowly in the direction of the movement of the sun.

I would also like to tell you about the hay making at harvest time, which began in our region at the end of June, and lasted for around three weeks. Out in the Taiga there were plenty of meadows from which hay could be collected. They existed in small clearing in the taiga or on the dried swamps. Hay was used on farms for feeding cattle during wintertime; nature gave a short period of time when the hay was green, juicy and rich with necessary vitamins.

Soon after June it became increasingly hot, and hay lost its quality and faded in the sun. That is why at harvest time everybody abandoned all their other duties to gather in the hay. Depending on the size of the workforce, all the enterprises and organisations had a haying plan, which they had to follow. Some big enterprises discharged their workers from the main work, created teams and sent them to the meadows. Smaller enterprises simply closed for a couple of days and the whole staff went to make hay. On small patches men cut the hay with hand-scythes and women raked it up and made big haystacks throughout the day.

The haystacks were left until winter to freeze, then gathered by tractor and taken across the frozen swamps to the farms. The weather at that time of the year was usually quite warm, and whilst cutting the hay we were bitten by clouds of mosquitoes. We were given insect repellents which we spread all over our bodies and worked in the sunshine wearing our swimsuits in order to get tanned. While we were working 3-4 of us cooked food and at the end of the working day, there was a big dinner for everyone held in a glade. They always cooked some soup, local meat and fish straight from the lake.

The insect repellent we used during the day was oil-based and we were all tanned in the boiling sun and so dirty that it was hard to recognise each other. However, we always came back home happy and I loved to go to hayfields because the way of life was so interesting, and different from anything I had experienced before. I remember my first hayfield, we were taken by car along 12 kilometres of highway and then we had to walk into the depths of taiga across swamps where the water came out of the ground as we were walking.

After a couple of kilometres we were taken by boat across a small lake, and were left to walk a short distance to the dried swamp where the hayfield was. One would think that there's nothing special about it but when I came out of the boat and walked on the grass, there was around ten centimetres of water to paddle through, and everywhere around me and between my legs were running fish by the name of carasius (like a carp).

I won't deceive you; "running" is an appropriate word, because they were moving in a zigzag manner on their bellies from one lake to the other. I was so excited and surprised that my colleagues looked at me as though I had gone wild, then they started to explain and laugh at me. They had seen this amazing sight many times before and it was a nothing unusual for them.

Chapter 25

Our First Holiday

According to the "Agreement about work in the region North of Siberia", a first holiday was given after the first two years and only after a total of five years' service did one receive another holiday. Subsequent holidays were allowed every three years. These official holidays were fully paid, that is all workers got not only a holiday with pay, but also the cost of the journey to the place of their holiday. It was possible for a worker to take a holiday every year, but they had to pay the full cost of travel.

The duration of a holiday for a year was from 30 to 42 working days depending on the place of work and ones position within an organisation. It was more usual for people to take a holiday every three years which could be between 4-5 months. This length of holiday was fully paid and sometimes a family could receive 5-6 thousand roubles in holiday pay, and they usually took the whole sum with them. (Let me remind you that the salary at that time was 75-150 roubles per month).

I have already written that Yakutia is situated in the north-east of Siberia. It is not an island, but this is a remote territory of the continent of Asia, and for some reason when people were told that they were leaving Yakutia they referred to the fact that they were going to the continent. Maybe it was because you could get there only by air as if it was a desert island.

My husband and I received our first paid holiday in two years in 1973. Our holiday was nearly 3 months long and we received 3.5 thousand roubles in holiday pay for the two of us. We bought presents for all of our relatives and flew to Ukraine in Donetsk.

For the two years whilst we had been away I had missed my son and my parents terribly, so much that I couldn't wait to see them. We flew to Yakutsk on a small plane in around 4 hours. We then changed planes and flew for around another 12 hours to Moscow arriving in the morning.

I felt myself very tired, there being a time difference of eight hours from Zyryanka, but despite that we went to the centre of the city right away and went shopping. We were very conscious that we had a substantial amount of money and we were determined to spend some of it. We were in the biggest department stores in the country: State department store and Moscow shopping mall. There were so many products available for sale that we didn't know what to look at first. We bought two smart suits for my husband – a dark one and a light one, together with new shoes and shirts.

I bought for myself a nice fur coat, boots and couple of pairs of shoes. We also bought many clothes for our son. Then we went to the most famous food store of the country – A food store No 1 and there bought the most expensive cognac for my father, and many chocolates in boxes Being able to buy chocolates in boxes was a rarity, they could only be bought in big cities. In the rest of the country chocolates were sold by the weight or in paper bags. After our shopping we ate dinner in a restaurant and then returned to the airport.

After a two hours flight we were in Donetsk we took a taxi from the airport and went home. I had missed my parents and son so much that for the whole way home in the taxi I cried and couldn't believe that I was nearly home at last. Two years had passed since we went to Siberia looking for a better life. These first two years seemed to me to be the longest years in my life and I could not wait to see my son again, my parents, relatives and home grounds where I was born and where I spent my childhood.

After such a long absence, I began to perceive things differently, and even the landscapes with the waste banks of Donetsk that I had never loved before, suddenly became for me, friendly and familiar. It is hard to put into words the feeling I experienced – I literally felt with my skin that I was finally home and this was my land. Waves of childhood recollections, which passed very quickly, crowded in upon me, leaving aching memories of that time, but as we drove nearer to our house I had to return to reality. I had sent a telegram to my parents, and they knew exactly what time we would be arriving, so when we reached our home all three of them were standing on the balcony and were waiting for us.

I couldn't believe how big our son was. When we left him he was 2.5 years old and now he was 4.5. He had become estranged from us; he knew that Mommy and Daddy were supposed to come, but he did not immediately recognise us and hid behind grandmother's back. Mother laid the table. She cooked everything as usual: borsch, potatoes with meat and a salad. Everything was so tasty and remembered from childhood; it seemed to me that I had never eaten anything tastier.

Because of the time difference we were very jet lagged and had to retire to bed early. In the morning our son couldn't wait until we woke up, he came in several times to check if we were still sleeping.

At noon he came in and said loudly "Good morning Mother, good morning Father, it is time to wake up!" as he had been instructed by my mother and the he ran away. Then he came to my mom and said "Granny, mother slept for so long that her eyes got blue." Everybody laughed at me. I had been so tired the

165

night before that I forgot to wash away my make-up and blue mascara got smeared on my eyes.

After lunch we put out all the presents brought from Yakutia and showed everything we had bought in Moscow. My father got scared – "Where did you get so much money? Why did you spend so much?" and we were proud and happy that we could afford all we had bought. While I was living in Zyryanka I wrote home a lot about my life in Siberia, and sent photos; that's why they knew everything about us: how and where we lived, what we did.

They were fully informed about our life and that we lived well and were ready to take our son back with us. We were both very grateful to my parents for taking care of our son, and if it was not for their support and the money they had lent us we would never have gone to Siberia to live.

A week later we left my mother and father and went for a holiday to the Black sea. We stayed in the resort of Sochi which is situated in the West of Caucasus. The Caucasus is a territory situated between the Black and Caspian Seas and the main part of it is covered with the Caucasus Mountains. The highest peak in this area is Mount Elbrus, with a height of 5640 metres. The natural features of the Caucasus are wonderful and that is why the best sea and mountain resorts of the USSR were situated there.

In the 1970s holidays on the seashore were very popular, the special microclimate of the seashore, seawater and the boiling sun were considered to be healthy, especially for children. After rest and recuperation here kids seemed to get less sick during the rest of the year. At that time the General Secretary of CPSU was Leonid Brezhnev. The life in the country was calm and stable, the salaries weren't high, but it was enough to have a decent life. Everyone could afford to have a 10-15 days holiday by the sea. People usually did not stay in hotels, but would rent a small room in a pension, and eat at local cafés.

Holidays in the small villages located all over the seashore of Black Sea were especially cheap. During the summer time thousands of people from all the regions of the country went to the sea and the population of the resort places grew several times bigger. The resort towns had equipped beaches, but sometimes there weren't enough places for everybody. Due to the shortage of space, people tanned on the beach beds made of wooden laths or simply lay on blankets put closely to each other. In order to go into the sea you had to go very carefully so that not to step on people.

We had plenty of money so we decided to go to Sochi – the biggest and most famous resort on the Black Sea. The town is situated on the subtropical shores of the Black Sea and is protected with a backdrop of mountains giving it warm windless weather and a special microclimate. In its many parks there were what for us were exotic plants, palm trees and other flowering shrubs and this created special atmosphere of colour in the town. We rented a good room

166

not far from the sea, near the "Caucasus Riviera" Park and not only rested and relaxed, but also spent some time exploring and finding interesting places.

There was a summer theatre in the town, where famous singers, musicians and comedians performed and we didn't miss a single concert. We also visited the new Sochi circus pavilion which was constructed in 1971 and could contain around 2000 spectators. Every night we went to dine in different restaurants, but we especially liked the restaurant at the Seaport, where there were often dinners with Caucasus wine sampling!

We also bought a 4 day excursion tour and travelled along the seashore of Black sea from Sochi to the town Batumy which was a town in the republic of Georgia, as well as visiting many other towns along that coast. This trip was a delight for us giving us a glimpse of another world. Despite the fact that Sochi was just a 12 hours train ride away from Donetsk, there was such a tremendous difference in everything that we experienced that it seemed to us that we had arrived to a totally different world.

We discovered that in other republics of the USSR like the Caucuses there lived other people with their own interesting traditions and customs. I will never forget just how hospitable and wonderful the people of Caucasus were. During the trip we stayed for nights in small villages in the private houses of local people. They were not obliged to provide food, but they always invited us to join the family for dinner and offered us homemade wine and different traditional Caucasus dishes to try.

Each host praised his wine and if we liked it they gave us a bottle to take with us. Nobody even thought of money, everything was free according to the local traditions of hospitality. Caucasus is a land of plenty, not only has it the most beautiful landscapes but also an abundance of fruit, vegetables, meat and wine which attracted the tourists. We had a month holiday in Sochi and got so suntanned that when I looked in the mirror I could hardly recognize myself.

After our time in Sochi we continued our holiday with a visit to Chernovtsy so that we could see my husband's parents and our friends who lived there. Victor had many relatives and they all gathered to see us on the first day. It was very interesting for them to see us after the two years of life at Siberia. Victor's mother looked at us and the present we had given her and cried and said – "I thought I would never see you again."

During our visit we never had a day to ourselves. One day we visited someone, the next day friends came to visit us. Time passed fast and we soon had to prepare for the journey back to Siberia. However, before we departed, my husband invited our friends and some relatives to a prestigious restaurant for dinner. There were around 14 people and we spent a great time dancing and singing till 1 a.m. even though the restaurant had officially closed at 12 midnight. Live music is usually played in all the restaurants of Ukraine so that people can dance. For small amount of money it was possible to ask the musicians to play longer than normal.

When they brought the bill for the evening's entertainment, all men produced their wallets and began to give money in order to pay the bill, as men always do when a group gathers in a restaurant. My husband immediately stopped them saying- "There's no need, I'll pay by myself," and he put 150 roubles on the table. People earned from 70 to 140 roubles a month at that time in Ukraine.

It amazed everybody present that we had so much money and were able to spend it so freely. It prompted people to ask us questions about our lives in Siberia and ask whether they themselves should consider moving there. Nobody could believe that for two years we had managed to improve our lives, have a job and a flat and money to spend. Our friends who worked in Ukraine for a small wage either lived with parents or rented a flat.

"Come to us, we'll help you to settle in," said my husband. Everybody livened up and started to discuss the topic further.

(We didn't even think that the discussions we had over dinner during the last night of our holiday in Chernovtsy would actually lead to anything, but a month later Victor's relatives arrived in Zyryanka. Initially they lived with us in our small flat of 15 square metres, for about a year. Then they got their own flat and lived in the village for 3 years. During this time they managed to save enough money to move back to Chernovtsy and construct a house there, a house in which they still live today. This family came just to earn money for a house, and the money they earned at Kolyma for three years work, they would never be able to earn in Ukraine.

After a while another relative of my husband with a one and a half year-old son came to us. We accepted them and lived with them for nine months. It was a little bit harder to live with this family, because there were two children in the flat: our son and a small child, who cried at night and didn't let us sleep. They eventually got a flat not far from our house, and where they lived for 15 years before moving back to Ukraine. For all these years we have been great friends and they have always been grateful for all that we did for them.)

Our holiday finally finished in the middle of October and we had to travel back to our home in Siberia. It was 12 degrees above zero in Ukraine when we departed, in Zyryanka at that time the river had already frozen. Our son had always lived with his grandmother and had never travelled anywhere, and now he was about to start an adventure that would take him a long way from that which he had known. I was worried how he would manage to cope with the travelling and culture shock.

He had never flown before and eagerly ran to the first plane at Chernovtsy airport, because he wanted to fly on the plane as soon as possible. Even during the long flight from Moscow to Yakutsk he walked between rows of seats at first and then he slept. However, when we arrived at Yakutsk he asked –

"Where is our home? I want to get home faster!" "Our home is not here. We have to fly for four hours more on a small plane," I answered.

At this point in the journey he had had enough and started to play up. He didn't understand about the distance from Yakutsk to Zyryanka, to him it just meant another 4 hours on a plane and he refused point-blank to fly saying- "I'm sick of those planes. Take a taxi and let's drive home! I want to sleep!" While we were waiting for a plane in Yakutsk airport he fell asleep on our suitcase.

Chapter 26

The University of Law

When we returned to Zyryanka, it was minus 20 degrees, there was lots of snow but at least the sun was shining. The apartment was warm and cosy, my heart was high and calm and I felt that I had arrived back to my home. It was out of the question to go back to live in Ukraine, as having lived in Siberia for two years, I had fallen in love with this places, our village and the taiga and finally understood that I come there not just for the money but to live a good life.

To my surprise, my son quickly got used to the new conditions, and the next day I found him already playing in the street with some of the local children. Being afraid that he would feel cold, I had put a new fur coat on him (it was of a bigger size than he needed and so long that it reached the ground), a fur hat, felt boots and pulled a scarf up on his nose.

The coat and the hat were of brown fur and that is why he was just like a small bear and looked very funny. A week later, I managed to arrange for him to attend a local kindergarten, to where I had to take him in the morning and collect him in the evening after I finished work. And so the life went on ...

Everything seemed to be going well; however I was not satisfied with my social status and was constantly thinking about it. After I had become a member of the Communist Party, I wanted to be better and to do something special. I was aware that I was working as a seamstress only temporarily and in the future I would like to have a good job and earn higher wages.

Having some experience in life, I knew that I had to have a university degree and to be a member of the Communist Party, because in our country those were the two necessary conditions for promotion. Since I was already a member of the Communist Party, I had to study for a degree in another discipline, but I found it very difficult to decide what kind of profession I wanted to be in. I was afraid to make the same mistake in choosing a profession that I had made before, when I qualified as a Geodesic Engineer.

Some of my friends studied at different universities, all over the country, by correspondence courses. Studying by correspondence was very convenient for those who worked and already had families and Children. If one chose to study in this way it was necessary to travel several times a year to the university to hear lectures and pass the exams. This period are called "sessions" (examinations). The rest of the time students spent at home worked and studied on their own.

I started thinking of the fashion designer's profession once again. Moreover, I had worked in this sphere and had an advantage before entering the institute. I applied to the Moscow Institute of Technology of light industry, quickly received a letter, whereby they informed me that a fashion designer speciality could not be taken by a correspondence courses.

In its place they offered me the chance to study the speciality of processing engineer in clothing manufacture. They sent me a programme and details of the requirements for enrolling on these courses. I looked through the programme and found there were many modules connected to maths! "No! Maths again, I don't want that. I'm fed up with land surveying, where maths is essential," I thought and decided to enter the University of Law.

There wasn't any maths, but there were: history, philosophy, scientific communism, law and other subjects which I loved. The National correspondence institute of law was in Moscow, but had branches in many cities of the country. I could study in Moscow or somewhere closer to home, perhaps Magadan or Khabarovsk. I'd already been to Magadan. Now I wanted to see the Far East and chose Khabarovsk. In August I departed to Khabarovsk, to sit the admission examinations. I hadn't any advantages here, but I passed the exams very successfully, and was selected and entered the university.

A few days later we attended lectures on our subjects to get better acquainted with our future profession, were also given books, and a programme of study and then we left for home.

I had to study at home by myself and only returned to the University twice a year for examinations and lectures: in December and in May. This was to be my life for the next five years. I was happy that I'd chosen this university as I found it all very interesting. I listened to the lectures with such an interest that it seems to me I remember them even now. I liked my future profession.

When I came back home I immediately started to prepare for my winter exams. On the one hand it was easy for me to study. I understood everything and enjoyed the subjects I studied. On the other hand it was very hard work, because there was so little time. I worked the whole working day from 9 am till 6 pm five days a week.

Labour legislation of the USSR made no provision for part-time work. Everybody worked 8 hours a day. Besides my main job, I also had my social work, which I did after work and sometimes on weekends. My family took up much of my time as well. I had to spend time with my son, clean the flat and cook. I cooked every day.

At that time there were no pre prepared meals which could be bought from the shops; All the more this was Siberia and the idea of even buying food in packets did not exist. We had plenty of meat, fish and other main products which had to be prepared before it could be cooked and it took a lot of time. We often went to the cinema at weekends, to the parties, in summer; we went to taiga to gather mushrooms, in winter we skied.

All these demands on my time left little time to study during the day. That is why I studied at night. When my son and my husband fell asleep, I went to the kitchen and sat at the table, with my back leaning against the stove, this kept me warm, and I studied till 3 or 4 a.m. I didn't like just reading, I preferred to take notes – after reading the text and capturing the meaning of it, I put down the main points in a notebook.

Such a method of studying had two advantages. Firstly, when I wrote it down I remembered it better. Secondly, I had in my notebook all the topics from the book but in the shorter form. I had summaries of all the subjects.

At the university, when there was little time before the exams I could just look through the notes and I was ready. I didn't have to open books again.

Many students, however, didn't do any studying at home and only studied at the institute, when they came to take exams. Doing this it was almost impossible to get a good mark, because you couldn't study the whole programme in a couple of days.

Those students who did this were happy to get a 3 which is just a satisfactory mark. These students made fun of this saying – that it's an "International students' mark". In order to receive the degree you don't have to get more. I got a 3 very rarely, my marks were mostly 4 (well) and 5 (excellent).

Other students laughed at me and asked: "How many times did you read the book? Six or seven?" and I answered – "I didn't only read it seven times but also rewrote it one time!" Of course it was a joke. But many of students asked to read my summaries at the last minute before the exam and were grateful for the help.

There were 27 students in my group. Almost all of them worked in the police, courts, or in the public procurator's offices. There were also many military students. They all had an experience of working in this sphere and it was easier for them to study. I on the other hand had no experience and advantages, and tried to compensate it with a good studying.

I've already told you that I went to examinations twice a year. Examinations lasted for 22 days to a month, depending on the course. It meant that I didn't go to work and wasn't at home for two months a year. For this period they gave me educational leave without payment. This leave didn't influence my yearly holidays of 36 working days a year. It was only my family who suffered from my studying.

There being the additional expenses for the flight to Khabarovsk, rent for the room while the examinations and my food. My husband and son were left alone and it was hard for them. We missed each other. But how happy we all were when I came back home after the examinations with another victory and the bags full of presents and tasty, exotic foods.

Chapter 27

Finding My Way from Deadlock

The years of studying at the university were a happy period in my life, I loved to go for the exams and come back with another victory. I travelled to Khabarovsk for the exams twice a year; in December/January and in May/June, depending on the course. These times were the most uncomfortable for flights, due to the frosts in winter and floods in the spring. Thanks to that I had plenty of adventures, and lots of inconveniences connected to those trips. Sometimes the way home was much longer than usual, as I had to change my route depending on the weather and other circumstances.

I can't tell you everything that had happened to me during five years of studying, bit. I want to tell you about two of the most interesting, which occurred whilst travelling. For the winter exams I used to take a flight to Khabarovsk at the beginning of December and travel back home at the end of the month, before the New Year. At this time of year in Yakutia the hardest frosts occurred. All the winter long, when the temperature was minus 50 degrees Celsius aircraft could fly without any problems; but when the temperature dropped minus 53 degrees Celsius or lower, fog appeared and most flights were cancelled.

The weather in Yakutsk changes very quickly, sometimes the plane departed in fine weather, but during the six-hour flight the weather changed abruptly forcing the pilot to change direction and land at another airport. There were two airports in Yakutsk, the main one was situated four kilometres from the city centre, and the second one was 25 kilometres away from Yakutsk in a small village called Magan. It was really a "military aerodrome" opened during the Second World War to accept American transport aircraft, supplying provisions for the battlefront.

It was further from the city of Yakutsk, and in the countryside where there was less fog and besides which it had a good runway, more than three kilometres long said to be the longest soft-surface runway in the country. When the main Yakutsk airport was closed, planes landed at the military aerodrome, from where passengers were transferred to the main airport by bus. It was a torture for me because the buses weren't heated and the temperature inside them was the same as the outside. The trip was around an hour, but due to cold it seemed to be an eternity.

The building at the main airport in Yakutsk was not big and had no improvements. The toilet was heated, but it was outside far away from the airport building. You may have noticed that I often mention about toilets in Siberia, back then for me as a woman it was very important. To use a public toilet outside when the frosts were more that minus 50 degrees Celsius was not pleasant to say the least. Besides, you had to go there together with all your bags and heavy luggage which had to be carried by hand, as baggage with wheels were not available at that time. No one had ever even heard of wheeled travel bags in my country until USSR breakdown.

This main airport was very busy as it was from here that aircraft departed to all destinations throughout the country as well as to all the villages throughout Yakutia. If the flights were cancelled or delayed there were hundreds of people at the airport. It was impossible to find a seat or even find somewhere to stand! I remember the exams finished on 28th December and the next day I flew Khabarovsk to Yakutsk. Before departure I had sent a telegram to my husband and told him to meet me on 30th December off the flight from Yakutsk.

I had plenty of luggage with me as usual, having bought a Christmas Tree with new fashioned decorations, and an electric machine which made the Christmas Tree spin, an electric ice cream freezer and lots of different foods and many other interesting things for the New Year. I departed from Khabarovsk all right, but on arriving over Yakutsk the plane started to land then flew up again, on a second attempt at landing the plane flew up again; several attempts later the pilot still hadn't managed to land. We made circles over the city for around an hour; a flight attendant entered the cabin and said – "Don't worry, nothing serious has happened, due to hard frost and thick fog the plane can't land." Some women started to cry, others, trembling with fear, thought the aircraft was about to crash land!

It would be hard to describe the fear and panic on board the flight; I cried and trembled with fear myself. At last the plane abandoned the attempt to land altogether, flying on to land at the military aerodrome at Magan. The pilot entered the cabin apologizing to us, saying that the frost outside had caused difficulty with lowering the undercarriage. Thank God, we had eventually landed all right, I was so relieved to get off the aircraft, and I grabbed my luggage and ran to the waiting bus.

When I came to the main airport in Yakutsk I opened an entrance door to get in, but I couldn't enter; it was packed with people inside. Everyone was standing so close to each other, the entrance door was blocked; somehow I was pushed inside by the people following behind me. It was impossible to reach the information desk to ask about flights, I just listened to people passing the information to each other.

174

It turned out that there had been frosts of 55 degrees below zero, for several of days, and there had been no flights at all. However, on this particular day the weather was a bit warmer and at least something was happening. The check-in of airplanes to some villages in Yakutia had started, but apparently not to Zyryanka.

I elbowed my way through the crowd and I saw plenty of people from Zyryanka, who had been waiting for the flight for a couple of days. They told me that we wouldn't be getting home until New Year, because the passengers, who had tickets for the previous days, would be flying first.

I was shocked, what to do? I imagined how my husband and son would celebrate New Year without me; and what would I do here? Sit at the airport? Stand actually; there were no vacant seats. I was deep in thought … how else could I get home? How? There was no means of transport except to fly to Zyryanka, from Yakutsk, from Chersky or Magadan …

Hurray! There was a way! There is a Russian saying, "there's always a way out even when it seems to be a deadlock". I knew that there was only one flight a week, on Wednesday, from Magadan to Zyryanka. Today was Tuesday which meant that tomorrow there would be a flight.

'But if I missed that flight I'd have to wait until the following Wednesday,' I thought, but it didn't stop me. I made my way somehow to the ticket desk and asked whether there were tickets to Magadan. A ticket clerk replied – "There are. The flight is tonight. It'll arrive in Magadan tomorrow morning." "Are there tickets from Magadan to Zyryanka?" I asked. "I don't know such information," She replied.

There was no time for thinking and I made up my mind to take the risk. I cancelled my ticket from Yakutsk to Zyryanka and bought a new one – from Yakutsk to Zyryanka via Magadan. It cost almost twice as much; there were always tickets available for this flight as hardly anyone took this route to Zyryanka. The distance from Yakutsk to Zyryanka is 1250 km to the north-east, however I flew to the east, in the quite another direction from my place. The distance from Yakutsk to Magadan is about 2000 km and from there to Zyryanka a further 700 km. adding a further 1450 km to the trip.

When I arrived at Magadan the next morning, I found out at the information desk, that the flight was cancelled for that day, and was postponed until the following day. "Maybe you should stay in a hotel at the airport," the clerk suggested.

"Thank you," I said and turned away, I had no money at all, having spent nearly everything on presents for the family, and the rest spent on the tickets; I had only two roubles left in my purse, just enough for a bun and a cup of tea to last the whole day, I even had no money to call home and tell my husband where I was.

It had been five years since I first arrived in Magadan, with my husband, and a lot of changes for the better had been made since then and a new airport building had been constructed. There were two spacious waiting rooms with soft leather seats, two bars, and a hairdresser. Few people were sitting around, as most stayed at the airport hotel, which for much of the time had vacant rooms. What is most important – it was warm in the building and there were restrooms. I could stay here for a week; it was so comfortable, if I had the money of course.

The weather in Magadan was good; the climate was kinder, as the town was not far from the sea. When I arrived it was minus 12 degrees only, and it was snowing a little. After the frosts in Yakutsk it seemed to be warm and cosy. After thinking this I felt that it was a pity that when we first came here five years before we might have stayed instead of moving to Yakutia. Yet it wasn't to be, fate had sent us to another destination. I spoke to a girl, who was waiting for her flight to the small village of Provedenie, which is situated by the Bering Sea on the Chukchi Peninsula, this area being very close to Alaska.

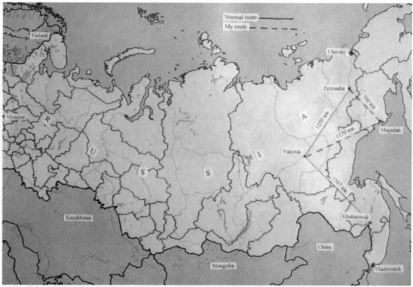

My route on a map

She studied at the teacher training institute of Magadan and had travelled here to take her exams. She told me a lot of interesting facts about this part of the USSR and how it was often isolated, due to frequent fogs that covered her village. Flights from this area were often postponed, once she had to wait for a flight for fourteen days!

'Oho! You can't mess around with the North, there are situations worse than mine, I'm not alone in suffering on the way,' I thought. We talked for the whole night until her flight was ready to go. In the morning, the flight to Zyryanka was delayed again because of the weather. It was 31st of December, and my good mood disappeared, thinking that I would never get back home for New Year.

The girl at the airport, gave me some money for a breakfast, I didn't know what to do, to buy something to eat, or to call my husband. It was likely that I'd celebrate New Year at the airport, when suddenly they announced check in for my flight, but after that announcement I still waited for a long time, eventually departing in the afternoon.

The plane was half-empty, there were only a few people travelling on New Year's Eve. All the passengers were in a good festive mood and all of them wanted to get home in time for New Year. During the flight the second pilot came into the cabin and talked to us, joked and congratulated us for New Year, he said that he was in radio contact with the airport at Zyryanka, and if anybody wanted to send a message to their home phone, he could pass the information on to the airport. I wrote to my husband a short message, to meet me at the airport and together with my home phone number gave it to the pilot.

My husband Victor met me, and later on that night, 31st December I was at home. My husband and son missed me so much that they followed me around the flat. They were so happy looking at all that I had brought, rushing about the flat to decorate the Christmas tree and lay the table ready for our celebration; in time for New Year.

Kolyma region – "Land of frost"

We laughed a lot when my husband told me that he didn't want to go the airport because of the frost, he thought that they called him by mistake, and asked – "Who will arrive? I'm not expecting anybody from Magadan. I'm waiting for my wife from Yakutsk. Maybe it's a mistake?" "We don't know, we were passed the information for you to meet the flight," they replied. Alex, our son started to insist and said to Victor – "Go to the airport, I know its Mum. Don't you know Mother, she can fly from everywhere."

After that my husband went to meet me. "Only you can do it this way!" he repeated, but he was really very glad, because many people from Yakutsk, couldn't reach home by New Year.

Chapter 28

My Adventure on my way back home
from Khabarovsk

There are people about whom they say – "She can't live without adventures." This concerns me, something unusual and interesting always happened to me. I used to tell these stories to my friends and we used to laugh; this was one such story that I will tell you about now. It happened when the exams finished at the institute at the beginning of May and I had to come back home immediately, because it was the time when the ice on the river Kolyma and its tributaries usually started to break up and float down the river in large chunks.

No one knew on what day exactly this thaw would start, everything depended on temperature. The warmer it was the earlier the floating started, it usually happened around 11-15th May. You know already that the airport was situated on the banks of the river and the runway was just a sand bar. When the ice floes started it raised the water level of the river and flooded the runway. In normal circumstance this could stop the planes from flying for perhaps, 7-10 days. However, if there were "ice holdups" the airport could be closed for a long time.

An ice holdup – was a piling up of ice on the river; this happens when the ice from the upper reaches of the river cracked and floated down, meeting the ice along the river where it was still frozen. It caused a difficult and dangerous situations because blocks of ice piled up and created dams. Water couldn't pass through them, and gathered there causing the river to burst its banks flooding the runway and the surrounding area. If this happened, a gang of men would be taken by helicopter to where the holdup was, and using explosives, blast away the ice, freeing up the river.

The force of nature is very strong, and sometimes it happened so quickly, with blocks of ice floating down the river with great force, sweeping and destroying everything in its path. Very often during the floating of ice down the river, large blocks were left marooned on the river bank and landing strip. Only after the flooding had subsided, could the ice blocks be broken up by the airport workers and pushed back into the water, and the river bank and runway repaired. If they didn't touch the blocks of ice they would remain solid for months, sometimes outside the village the blocks of ice were left and could take all summer to melt.

The landing strip of Zyryanka airport in spring flood.

My flight plan as usual was from Khabarovsk to Zyryanka via Yakutsk and when I left Khabarovsk the evening 9th May, I was hoping to get back home the next day for arriving in Zyryanka, before the runway was flooded. The flight from Khabarovsk to Yakutsk was good, arriving the next morning, after a six-hour flight. When I arrived, there were many fellow passengers from my village still at the airport, who were waiting for a flight to Zyryanka. They told me that up the river there was an "ice holdup" already, but in the village itself the river hadn't flooded yet.

Despite that, for the purpose of safety, the airport at Zyranka was closed for two days. The Yakusk airport control said they would send an aircraft as soon as they possibly could.

People started to panic, everybody knew that floating ice in the area of the village could start at any moment, and there would be a long wait to get back home.

The next morning they announced that the floating of ice started on the river Kolyma and Zyranka airport was now flooded and that planes could not fly for at least another week. The airport was becoming crowded as people

180

from other cities had arrived at Yakutsk airport, also wanting to take a flight to Zyryanka.

People were everywhere – they sat in the waiting room, on the steps, on the windowsills, near the walls. They simply sat or lay on the floor with a newspaper beneath; if somebody left their place to go to the bar or the restroom it was occupied right away. It was a nightmare being there. The conditions for passengers in transit were very poor. In Yakutsk and other airports, there were only mother-and-children restrooms set aside, where mothers with young children could stay and rest with their babies. Only women with children under 5 years old were allowed to use these rooms, and they had to show a health certificate before they could use these facilities.

Husbands and older children of the same family couldn't even go in there. Many women had to spend nights sitting in the general waiting room, because they had children of different ages and they couldn't occupy these rooms with a smaller child and leave the older outside alone. The airport bore no responsibility for the delays of flights and there were no compensation; there was a tradition of "Russian sluggish service" in the country, which really meant there was no service at all, and each passenger had to look after themselves.

There was a hotel at the airport of Yakutsk, but it was impossible to get a room there. Women with children were given priority at the hotel in the first place, and you could stay there for one night only. There were no family rooms at that time, just separate dormitories for men and women, if there was a family, the wife with children were taken to the hotel, and her husband stayed at the airport. Very seldom would there be vacant rooms in the morning, and only a few lucky people could get them, if they had been waiting there all night.

The city of Yakutsk was four kilometres away from the airport and had several hotels. At the main hotel 'Lena' there was always a sign 'No vacant rooms' at the registration desk. This sign was never taken away, as the hotel was always full. The other hotels in the city were owned by local companies and were reserved for their own workers. Such a situation existed with hotels in many cities and airports across the country. I strongly disapproved of the situation that existed and could never accept that ordinary people, who could pay for a hotel, had to suffer the indignity of sleeping on the floor in, such humiliating conditions.

More passengers to Zyryanka arrived, and I met a couple of my friends and it became a bit more cheerful; we took it in turns to rest on any seats we could find or just stood around the airport.

There was a bus from the airport to the town and we went there every morning, and caught the bus back each evening. We tried to use every opportunity to have a rest somewhere during the day, as we had no idea how long we would have to wait to get our flights. We went to the cinema during the day sometimes to watch a movie, or just to sleep, as it was more comfortable than the airport. Often we went to the hairdresser's to freshen up and rest there for as long as possible.

Then we had an idea to go the public baths, which was near the airport. Such baths were very popular in Yakutia as many people lived in old houses where there were no proper facilities. We liked the bath so much that we started to go there every day as we had lots of time on our hands. Eight days passed in this way, no flights and we were still living at the airport. On the ninth day they promised to give us some information regarding the state of things in Zyryanka, and we didn't go anywhere just waited to see what would happen next.

They announced that the runway at Zyryanka was still blocked, and no large aircraft like the Illusion IL-14, that worked this route, could land there. Maybe in a couple of days the airport would be able to accept only the smaller planes such as the Antonov AN-2. An alternative flight was offered on which we would have to fly to the village of Chersky, situated inside the Artic Circle, and where the airport was still open for the IL-14 aircraft to land. We could then wait for another smaller aircraft to take us on to Zyryanka, our final destination, but it was a bit of a gamble that we would then be able to get a flight to Zyryanka. There were only twelve vacant seats left on this flight and my friend and I didn't hesitate, as we raced to book the tickets for the flight.

The village of Chersky was the centre of the Low Kolyma region, and is situated at the mouth of the river Kolyma, only 70 km from the arctic coast of the North-East Sea. I had never been to Chersky or within the Polar circle before, and that's why I was glad to have a chance to visit this area. Nevertheless, it was May, and yet it was still so cold in Chersky, it seemed that I felt the closeness of the Arctic Ocean … Locals who arrived on this flight went home, leaving only the passengers at the airport who were supposed to fly on to Zyryanka. The terminal building of the airport wasn't big but it was warm and cosy, there was a hotel on the second floor as well, where we managed to get a room; there was also a small café on the first floor.

I didn't know how long I would have to wait, before I could fly home, but at least I was glad to get here safely and be staying in such good conditions, I could manage to wait here for a couple of days or even more. When I went to bed I thought – "I'll call my husband tomorrow and tell him I'm in Chersky already." The next morning a woman on duty, woke everybody up and asked us to go downstairs to the waiting room, where the director of the airport was waiting for us. He told us that maybe in a couple of days Zyryanka would be able to accept small aircraft and then we could continue our journey back home.

However, there was a chance to get home that very day, everybody just laughed and thought that he was joking. He continued to tell us that tonight an aircraft AN-14 would be flying to Zyryanka in order to test land on the new runway, the construction of which is not quite finished yet, but the runway is good for accepting this type of aircraft.

The main pilot being a distinguished pilot who had worked in the Artic North for many years and had vast experience of flying under extreme conditions. He had landed already on this runway, but without passengers. He warned us that the main pilot doesn't guarantee that he will land for sure, only that he would try.

The weather conditions are fine and he hoped that everything would be all right. However, if the weather changes or he can't land we would be returned to Chersky. Those who are willing to fly were invited to come at 8 p.m. He then left us to decide on what we would do.

We all knew that 9 kilometres away from the village of Zyryanka they were constructing a new airport. There was a big open place on a dried-up swamp and for two years a runway had been under construction. Gravel was delivered by truck from a quarry, which was situated on the river Kolyma. Thousands of tons of gravel were dumped on to the field during winter time and in spring when the thaw started, the gravel fell into the swamp; but the work continued as the building specialists thought that everything would be alright, and they just needed more gravel to fill up the swamp.

The plan was to construct a permanent year round normal runway. When construction was finished it would offer great advantages for the village. Firstly – there would be regular flights regardless of floating of ice and the floods, because the new airport was 9 kilometres away from the village and the river of Kolyma. Secondly – there was an opportunity to accept big cargo airplanes with goods and food at any time of the year. When the construction of the runway would be finished, and in what condition it was in at that moment, none of us knew of course.

An argument between passengers started, some men saying it would be impossible to land there, as the runway wasn't finished, others saying that the pilot knew what he was doing and wouldn't risk our lives if he couldn't land safely. The women stood and listened to them, not knowing quite what to say. There were 12 of us altogether – four women and eight men; I asked my friend – "Will you fly?" "No I'm afraid. I'd better wait," she replied. Actually I could also wait for a couple of days at the airport of Chersky because the conditions for the passengers here, compared to the airport at Yakutsk, were quite comfortable, but I had no doubts for a second; I wanted to get home, the sooner the better. I thought: "What do I lose? Fifty/fifty, either we land or come back, and what if we land!"

Seven people came to the departure gate: a young Yakut-girl, me and five men. After we had taken off, an unusual panorama could be seen. I could see the village of Chersky and the estuary of the river Kolyma, which was still covered with ice, which did not usually start to melt until the beginning of June.

I'd like to add that I had flown over different regions of Yakutia and each of them had a special and unique landscape. Here it was arctic tundra covered with snow – and quite a desolate landscape. While the flight was in progress, I looked out of the window constantly, although it was 9 p.m. the sun shone brightly, the sky was clear and so blue – this was the time of white nights.

In the North and Arctic regions of Yakutia white nights lasted from May until August. There were also white nights in Zyryanka, as the northern part of the district was within the Arctic Circle and the village of Zyryanka was not far below it. In this period the sun usually shone from 5 a.m. till midnight and at night it was as light as during the day. When we first moved to Zyryanka we couldn't sleep well, I curtained the windows with blankets and black tissue so that it was dark in the room, but it was still hard to sleep. People get used to everything and we soon got used to it as well.

The distance from Chersky to Zyryanka was 700 kilometres and our flight went over the basin of the Kolyma River from north to the south. During the flight the scenery changed constantly: at first there was only bare tundra covered with snow, and then gradually there started to appear poor vegetation – small bushes, sparse wood and some areas without snow. As the flight progressed, there appeared taiga (Siberian forest) and closer to Zyryanka there were rivers, interlaced lakes, snow in some places, but everything was mainly covered with water.

The whole flight was long, and I kept looking out of the window to take my mind off the obsessive thoughts about the how the pilot would land the plane. It would be a pity to return back to Chersky after all the problems I had faced trying to get there. Under normal conditions, the flight from Yakutsk to Zyryanka to the north-east was 1200 kilometres and a four hour flight. The roundabout route that I had to take hadn't been easy; I had flown from Yakutsk to Chersky which was 1920 kilometres to the North, and then another 700 kilometres more to Zyryanka in the south. If you count up the distance I had travelled it was 2620 kilometres which meant I had travelled an extra 1420 kilometres and taken ten days longer!

As the plane started its decent, I could see the houses and streets below. I sat and thought what my husband and son were doing at the very moment; it was nearly midnight and of course, they would be asleep, and didn't know that I was already here. I hadn't called my husband to tell him where I was and what I was going to do, I did not want to upset him because I didn't even know myself how everything would end up.

I had not been at home for more than a month and I missed them both so much, and I fancied that they could hardly wait to see me. There was my house, it seemed that I could reach out and touch it with my hand; it was so near yet so far away. I suddenly felt scared and pity for them and myself and started crying realizing that we might not land and have to fly all the way back.

The aircraft made several attempts at a landing approach, each time as it skimmed the makeshift runway the pilot changed his mind, and aborted the landing, going round again to make another approach. I began to feel certain that we would have to turn back to Chersky. I had flown many times before and knew well how the landing should go. At first the plane touches the runway with its wheels as if it trying the ground, then it settles on the ground and goes along the runway for a long time until it stops. This time everything was quite different; the plane seamed to simply fall out of the sky, hitting the ground with a bump and rocking from side to side.

This rough landing caused the wheels to break through the makeshift surface and the plane skidded along, with the gravel base of the runway flying right and left, I was paralyzed with fear. At last the plane finally came to a halt, but crosswise on the runway.

After the experience of such a landing, I couldn't feel any joy that I was at home; I was still shaking with fear. This place could hardly be called an airport, the runway still under construction and there wasn't anything on the field except a small building for the workers. There was nobody about while the plane was landing, but when it finally stopped people ran out of the building surprised to see us arrive and so spectacularly.

The pilot said, "Wait here, a bus is being sent here to collect and take us to the village." Everybody left the aircraft and walked around discussing how it had managed to land at all! At last the bus arrived with a woman on duty from the official airport of Zyryanka. She laughed and congratulated us – "You are the first passengers, who landed on this runway!" – she said.

It was night, and there was nobody on the streets, the settlement had fallen asleep, each passenger was given a lift direct to their own house. When I entered the building, I saw that the door to my flat was slightly open and could hear people talking. I was holding bags in both hands so I just pushed the door with my foot and entered the flat appearing in the doorway to the kitchen. There were three men sat at the kitchen table, my husband and two others. I knew one of them, and he worked at the airport. The second one was wearing a uniform and I had never seen him before. There were bottles of vodka, cognac, with some tinned food on the table and the kitchen was filled with smoke.

They were eating, drinking and smoking and they didn't even notice me coming in. When they saw me they stiffened in astonishment, it was quite funny to observe. "Why aren't you meeting me?" I asked Victor. He rushed to me and took the bags from my hands and kept asking, "Where did you come from?" I pointed to the ceiling and told him, "From the sky, I arrived on a plane." They all started to tell me that it was impossible; no plane had arrived from Yakutsk yet. The runway on the river Kolyma was still flooded.

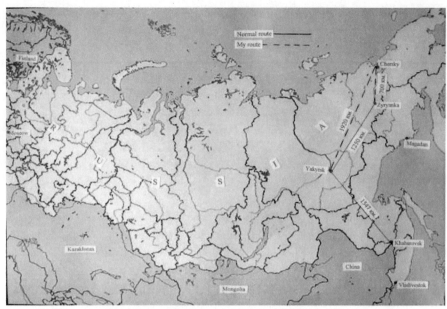

My route back home from Khabarovsk, 1976

"I didn't arrive from Yakutsk but from Chersky and the plane landed on the new runway which is 9 kilometres out of the river," I said. After those words they were amazed even more and started to explain to me that the runway wasn't ready yet and no plane has so far landed there. I was so tired from all my travels and had no desire to continue this conversation. "My plane did land! Anyway, what are you talking about? Look at me I'm at home and that is what is important," I said.

The next day I told my husband about everything and he scolded me for taking such a risk, saying, "You never think before you do something." It turned out that he had invited those people, in order to negotiate with them, to arrange that I would be on the first flight back from Yakutsk when the airport was re-opened.

Chapter 29

The Job at the Film Distribution Centre

After my third year of my five-year course at the university, I decided to look for the professional job. As a future lawyer I could work at the police, court, in the public prosecutor's office or in the notary's office. That's why I made an appointment with the Chairman of district Executive Committee, who was able to recommend me for any of these positions. I had never spoken to him, but he knew me due to my voluntary social work.

After listening to me he said, "Of course you need to change your job right away, but I don't think there are suitable vacancies for you right now but, let me think about it."

About a week later I got a call from the district Executive Committee, and they told me that the Chairman wanted to see me that day at 4 p.m. When I arrived at the appropriate building, he was waiting for me outside in his car. "Take a seat," he said.

"I've found a job for you. Maybe it's not quite what you wanted but it's better than sitting at the typewriter anyway. You'll be a director of the film distribution offices," I wondered 'what on earth is that?' He then explained, "The job is not hard and but interesting. The staff is good, and if you work as a director you'll get the experience of a manager – that will be useful for you in the future."

"Wow!" I was not expecting that, but thought he would offer me a professional job within the legal profession. I had no idea what film distribution was, I understood only that it was something connected to film industry. We eventually arrived at a small building that I had often passed before, but didn't know what was inside. When we entered the building, the workers of the film distribution office had already been waiting for us.

The chairman introduced me and said, "She's your new director. She doesn't have any experience in this sphere so you should help her get into the swing of things," then he told me, "I'll leave you here. Get to know each other and get down to business as soon as possible."

And then he left me to it! I looked round. This was a spacious place, to be more precise, a warehouse. There were shelves everywhere on which there stood cans of film. They stood in piles 7 to 10 pieces each. There was also a smaller warehouse where bigger metal cans were stored. I didn't know what they all were at this time. I was shocked.

There were around nine film distribution workers, who were mainly women. They could see that I felt confused and tried to calm me down: saying, "Don't worry. The job here is not so hard. We've been working here for a long time, we know everything that you have to do and will teach you." I felt even worse after these words. I was to be their boss, but I knew that I knew nothing at all about the jobs they did, how could I possibly be a director in charge of these people.

The next morning, on returning back to my previous place of work, I went to see my boss – director centre of domestic service and told her about everything that had happened on the previous day. Having had time to calm down and think more rationally I wasn't in a state of shock anymore, and as I explained my predicament, I was even able to laugh about the situation.

I asked her to call Chairman of the District Executive Committee, and tell him that I didn't want to work at the film distribution office. Thinking it was better to stay at the previous job and wait until something more suitable appeared. "Don't even think to refuse. He'll get angry with you and will never offer you anything else," she said.

I therefore, perhaps a little reluctantly, accepted the position as the director of the film distribution office. Eventually I found that the work was not as difficult as I had first imagined. I had my own separate office complete with a phone, a safe for documents and a huge bookcase for the advertising material.

The film distribution office worked by receiving new films from the Republican film distribution office in Yakutsk, which I then scheduled a timetable for the showing of these films throughout the region. An engineer also checked the quality of a film using special equipment, and if everything was normal or just in need of a small repair which he could carry out we sent the film to the cinemas. The ticket money paid by customers to watch the film at the cinema went back into the budget of the region and eventually enables more film to be acquired.

We were, therefore, interested in attracting as many people as possible to watch these film, so we placed advertisements for the movies in any place possible. The attendance depended very much on the good advertising. Cinemas were very popular during those years all over the country and when a particularly good film was advertised everybody wanted to watch it, sometimes even twice or more.

I can still remember very well some of those very popular movies, one was *Moscow Does Not Believe Your Tears*, and another was *Office Romance*. I had watched them both six times and could do it over and over again.

In the north-east of Siberia, especially in winter with the long dark nights, people had plenty of free time and eagerly visited cinemas and other entertainments, because we don't had TV on that time. One aspect of my work that I particularly loved was the advertising. I once got so carried away with my innovative ideas that I had troubles with a district committee party. There were many foreign movies in the warehouse so I decided to diversify the methods of work and think of something new. I decided that each week we would only show all movies from one foreign country.

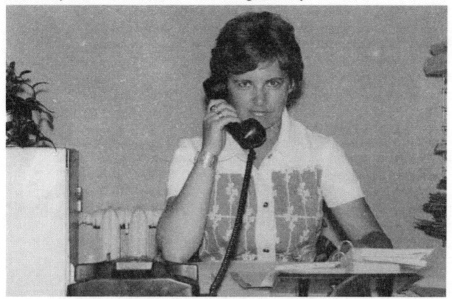

My working day at the Distribution Office, 1979

I planned to show every day during a week movies of a certain country. The first one at the central cinema was a week of Italian movies. After that there was supposed to be weeks of French, Indian movies and so on ... We advertised on posters in clubs and other areas and started to show these movies the next week. The first day was OK. The second day I was invited to attend the district committee by the ideology secretary. She was very strict and everybody was afraid of her.

I had no idea of why she wanted to see me, but because of her reputation I was afraid of meeting her. Immediately I came in she asked me, in a severe tone of voice, where I had received instructions to organise weeks of foreign movie shows. I answered that this was my idea to diversify the methods of work in our movie industry. "You must immediately take away all the advertisements and work properly. And for the future – all the methods of work must be approved in advance with the district committee of CPSU," she said.

I was upset. I had tried what I thought would be for the best and it turned out that I did everything wrong. After that I always scheduled the plan of movie shows for a month, and submitted it to the district committee for approval. From then on I worked under the control of the ideological department of district committee of CPSU. Even though this particular job was not my ultimate objective which was to have a position within the legal profession, I continued in this position for approximately two more years.

There was a particularly funny moment, when I had just passed the exam in judicial forensic science, when my lecturer asked me where I worked. He said, "I feel that you know the theory but you appear never to have seen what you're talking about." When I then told him where I worked he was surprised and started laughing. He said that for 30 years he had never had a student who worked in cinematography. He also said that in order to fully qualify, by law I had to find a professional job, otherwise I would have troubles.

I actually now liked my job in the film distribution office, and I did my job very fast had plenty of time to do social work. I was elected to be an assessor in the district national court, a freelance inspector of the committee of national control, a member of the bureau of district committee of Komsomol, and other ad hock commissions. I was always busy.

Chapter 30

Experience at the District Court

After the fourth year of studying at the University of Law, I went to the Chairman of the Executive Committee once again to ask for a professional job. Fortunately, my timing was good because at that particular time there was a vacancy for a judge at the District court. The current holder of the position was ill and was going to have an operation which would stop him working in this capacity for several months. It was, therefore, necessary to appoint somebody, who was suitably qualified, to undertake this roll during his absence. I was perfectly suited for the post of a judge, because I was a member of the communist party and preparing to graduate in criminal law with special emphasis on the judicial-investigatory qualification.

This gave me the right to try civil and criminal cases. I also had an advantage – I had been a peoples' assessor for a couple of years at the District court and had an experience of working at the court. (Peoples' assessors – were citizens, who were selected at the enterprises by an open show of hands for taking part in trying civil and criminal cases. All the cases at courts were tried by the judge and two peoples' assessors. According to the constitution of the USSR, the peoples' assessors were elected for a period of 2 years).

I worked at the regional court for 8 months. This job captured me totally. I loved the work, the legal process itself and the giving of judgments, etc. I came to work earlier than everybody else and after the working day was over I didn't want to go home. At first court sessions were hard for me to deal with as I was still really a student and only 30 years old. I initially felt shy before the people in the court, but soon I felt less self-conscious and began to relish the roll that I was playing in society without any problems.

However, my position brought other unexpected problems, like the one I experienced in my first trial. This was a criminal case involving a case of a theft of state property. A crane operator at the trade company, together with his colleague, while unloading a container at the port, stole a pallet of wine. They placed a pallet of wine outside the warehouse area, planning to collect all vines later. On the face of it this was a simple criminal case, but complicated, for me, by the fact that the accused man was a brother of my neighbour with whom I was on quite friendly terms.

This neighbour's husband also worked together with my husband at the construction company. My husband started to inquire whether the case was in the court already, what sentence the crane man could get and so on. Then he said- "Please see if you can do something in the court to make his term shorter, because we are neighbours and colleagues and I feel uneasy." My patience was at an end and we had a fight and I eventually told him – "Mind your own business! Nothing depends on me. There's a court session with three people involved and there's a law, based on which the sentence will be given. I'm not going to discuss my work at home!"

Later on my neighbour stopped me and started to ask me to help her brother. She said that she would visit me in the evening to talk about it. "You'd better not come to me, I won't even open the door," I said. The session took place and both men got a couple of years of imprisonment. After that my neighbour never greeted me again. I thought then, 'This village is small and everybody knows everybody else. If every time after the case I'll lose friends, I won't have any soon.'

On another occasion there was a case about the unlawful dismissal of a worker in the mine construction administration. The court resolved to re-establish the worker and to pay him indemnification for the damage caused, because there was an obvious infringement of the labour legislation on behalf of the administration.

A couple of weeks later there was a meeting of the District Committee of the Party. I don't remember now what particular topics were on the agenda, it was attended, among others, by the director of the mine construction administration. At the end of his speech he said,

"We have to improve the work of the recruiting system. Why was a young student appointed to be the judge, without education and experience? This has resulted in her making the wrong decision concerning the dismissal of a worker from our enterprise. We have sent an appeal to the Supreme Court of Yakut Republic."

It was as if somebody poured cold water on me. There were around 400 people in the room and everybody knew me, but was obviously unaware of the circumstances to which this man referred. My face went red and I was trembling and I didn't know what to do. However, I was lucky as at the end of the meeting a secretary of the District Committee asked as usual – "Has anybody got any questions or does anybody want to speak?"

I jumped up at once without even thinking and said, "I want to speak!" I explained briefly the point of the case and then, addressing the director of the mine construction administration, I said – "Yes, I am young, I don't have any experience and I haven't graduated from the university yet. But my decision was based on the law, and if you don't like the law it's not my fault! It is good that you have appealed to the Supreme Court as it can decide whether I tried the case right or wrong."

After the meeting a couple of people congratulated me and said that it was a brave thing to do, to oppose him. Then a friend of mine from the District Committee of the Party told me that I would have troubles. "You are 'nobody' for now, and he is a respected man, a director of a big enterprise, a member of the District Committee of the Party. You would have been better off if you had not said anything. You'll never work now at the court and won't get a good job," she said.

I was very disappointed, I felt miserable and I didn't want to believe what she had said. Soon there came the judgement concerning the appeal. There were no remarks regarding the case and the court decision was confirmed. This was my victory, but my friend was proved right. When the next elections were held for the post of peoples' assessor at the District court, my candidature was crossed off the list without any explanations.

The following year after I had fully graduated, the Supreme Court of Yakut Republic placed me on the list of reserves for judgeship. Two years later I received the letter from this Court, asking me if I would agree to be a candidate for the post of a judge in a Court in the other district of Yakutia. I refused, because I had by that time a good job, a new flat and I didn't want to move any were.

Chapter 31

Work at a Committee of Popular Control

I successfully graduated from the University with a degree in Criminal Law. To achieve this, at the end of my course I had to take examinations in five subjects. My marks in four subjects achieved an "excellent" grading and in the other a "good" grade. Because I had chosen as my speciality at the university the course of "judicial-prosecutors-investigatory" I could now choose to work either at a court, a prosecutors' office or at an investigative body. After the exams I was invited for an interview by the University Chancellor.

He told me, that there were four places on the postgraduate course that year for the best students, and he thought, that the one in the speciality of 'Theory of country and law', would perfectly suit me. Postgraduate studies lasted for 5 years, and all the exams would have to be taken in Moscow. If I successfully completed this course of study I would be awarded a PhD, and become a Doctor of law. The chancellor gave me until the next day to think this over. If I had agreed the institute would have assigned me for studying.

I was so amazed. Oh God! The theory of country and law was my favourite subject. On the exams of this subject I always got an excellent mark. I had studied all the main works of V. Lenin and K. Marks. I adored studying and would gladly undertake postgraduate studying. This opened up the possibility of a successful future for me, but what about my family? I called my husband on the phone and told him everything.

He didn't even want to listen to me. "First of all I'm sick of your trips for exams for five years and constant spending of money. Second of all – if you become the doctor of law, I will be nobody beside you. Come home fast. I and our son are missing you!" He said.

I understood that without his support it was impossible for me to continue with my studies, I had to choose between my family and my career. At this time in my life and throughout my whole life my family took precedent over everything, and that is why I let go any thoughts of postgraduate studies and went home to my family.

In the four month after graduating the institute, the chairman of a district committee for the popular control, offered me a position of an inspector. This was a prestigious position, and the salary was big – 160 roubles per month plus north bonuses. I eagerly agreed, because I had already done this job for several years, but on a voluntary basis and knew it well. The Popular Control at the Soviet Union was a system of bodies, acting with the authority of laws, passed in 1979.

The main body in the country was the Committee of Popular Control of USSR, to which the committees of the republics, cities and regions were subordinate. In the village of Zyryanka there was a district committee, which consisted of two regular members of the staff: a chairman (my boss), an instructor (me), and 11 members of the committee; all of them were elected to become members and worked on a voluntary basis. This was a controlling body, which checked the fulfilment of resolutions made by the party and government, a production plan, socialist property protection and labour discipline. In order to do this job, at all the enterprises and organizations, groups of popular control were elected, which included 6-10 people; they carried out on the spot checks.

For the people included in these groups, this was a social assignment. Once a month a meeting at the committee were held, where different issues were discussed. Bodies of popular control had extensive rights, and when they detected serious violations and dangerous practices, they had the right to stop the work of an enterprise, to suspend directors from office or to punish the guilty with a fine or a reprimand.

I worked as an inspector for five years from 1980 till 1985 and during that time there were many changes in both social and political life in the country. During this five-year period, the country was governed by four General Secretaries of the CPSU Central Committee, three of them died whilst in power. My labour activity and independent life began under the reign of Leonid Brezhnev. He had been a leader for 18 years and at that time there was a peaceful political climate in the country; the living standards of the citizens were raised, more consumer goods and food were produced, and what was most important of all, the prices for all these were stable.

Also people were able to save more and nobody was afraid that money could devalue suddenly, or the banks not allow the withdrawal of their saving. But this was only my opinion, an ordinary woman who studied, worked and took care of her family. Many years on, historians would call this period a "No-growth Period", maybe that is true, they would know better, but people lived not too badly, especially in comparison with what happened later.

Of course, in the last years of his incumbency as a General Secretary, Leonid Brezhnev's authority eroded, and no matter what he did everything was criticized and drew ridicule. People laughed when Brezhnev was decorated with Stars of Soviet Union Hero (he had 5 of them), when he wrote and published his memoirs: *The small land Rebirth* and *Virgin land*. I was forced to read those books only because I, together with my colleagues, took tests on them.

The changes happened only after his death. I remember in November 1982, late in the evening, all the members of the party's districts committee were gathered for an extraordinary meeting and it was announced that Leonid Brezhnev had died (he was 76). The secretary of the district committee and some women cried (it was supposed to be this way), the rest were simply silent, and after the meeting they joked and laughed.

Working day at the Committee of Popular Control, 1983

After that we were all were forced to design mourning portraits and make wreaths, which we had to deliver to the enterprises, organizations and schools in the morning. A period of mourning lasting two days was declared in the country, entertaining broadcast and telecast was cancelled and only dirge music was playing.

People hoped that at that moment the leader of the country would be a younger more energetic man, but Yuriy Andropov was elected, who was 68 years old. Being an ex-chairman of KGB, he started his activities by the establishment of a better order in the country, sometimes by the use of force, which stirred up discontent among people. Special consideration was given to the issues of socialist property protection, anti-corruption drive and the enforcement of labour discipline. Controlling committees had never had so much work as under the reign of Yuriy Andropov.

Frankly, I was sorry that I worked as a committee's inspector; sometimes I was even ashamed to accomplish my duties. It seemed that at that moment in time the people of the whole country turned out to be thieves, violators of labour discipline and shirkers. For example, peoples' inspectors were forced to stand at the entrance of an enterprise before work began in the morning and tick what time each worker came to work. If somebody was late even for a couple of minutes, they experienced big problems, all the way up to dismissal.

During working hours, inspectors went to the shops, cinemas, hairdressers and many other public places, checking documents and putting down on a list the names of all people, who were and perhaps, those who should not be, including schoolchildren, and then those list were sent to the enterprises and schools for an investigation and taking any corrective measures.

We also checked documents and stock in commercial establishment i.e. shops seeking out corrupt practices that had become endemic over the years and was looked upon as normal and traditional. Words incomprehensible for people from the other countries were in daily use. There were such words and phrases as deficit, string-pulling, hiding goods under the counter and black door. There was always a shortage of manufactured goods for people in the Soviet Union. From my very own childhood I can't remember a single incident where we went to the shop and bought what we wanted, there were always items missing or products in short supply and there wasn't a big choice.

Factories and plants worked according to a plan and produced goods of only approved range, that is why there wasn't any competition between the enterprises and the design just didn't matter, what was important was that there was a needed quantity and presence on the stalls of the shops. For example, if you bought red boots and wanted to buy a red handbag to match, it was useless to try to find it.

You could never find it, because there were only black and brown ones at the shops, there wouldn't be any other colours. TVs, fridges, vacuum cleaners and other household appliances were hard-to-get things at different times, and there were only 2-3 trade names, which were popular, and people still remember them.

Many goods were always in short supply. Cars, in particular, had a long waiting list and were always distributed according to the waiting lists which existed at every factory and mine, or occasionally they were raffled.

My father worked at a good mine, and had money for a car, but he remained on the waiting list for a long time. I remember when my sister and I were children, my father dreamt of buying any model of car. The only choice at this time was between the Pobeda and Moskvich, but only 1-2 cars a year were allocated for coal miners on the waiting lists. The list at my father's mine was so long that we grew up and he still didn't have a car.

Furniture, especially imported, was also always in deficit and in order to buy it you also had to be added to a waiting list at the shop concerned and wait for many years. Additions to the list were made rarely and, only on certain days each year, and there were huge queues at these times. At any time of the year people stood for a couple of days and nights in the queues, because usually at night there was a roll call (to check who was on site) and if a person was absent he/she was eliminated from the queue, and therefore did not get put on the list in the shop.

Other manufactured goods and food, which were in short supply could only be bought by wangling – which meant that those goods which couldn't be bought freely at shops could only be bought by people who had relatives or friends who worked at the shops. Sometimes goods didn't even arrive to the shops, they were sold by the backstairs right from the warehouse and the money was given to the shops. Those people who had such profitable connections lived well, and it was very prestigious to have such a connection.

This meant that those with connections could buy things that others simply could not e.g. any goods or food in short supply, to place their children in the institute, get a good job, buy air or railway tickets when there were holidays, and also the tickets to a cinema and a theatre. All this was done illicitly and secretly and it was impossible to prove anything.

For example, when I entered a shop, there were home-produced shoes at the stalls, at the same time a shop assistant took imported shoes from under the counter, where he hid them and sold it to his friend. Goods were often wrapped in paper, that is why you couldn't see what was there, but you could easily guess according to the price of the goods when the person paid for it.

All people knew about these violations, they often protested and made complaints, that is why in order to avoid it people, who wanted to buy the goods in short supply entered the shops not through the main entrance but through the back door (through the exit of the shop to the yard from the other side of the building), so that nobody could see what they bought.

Yuri Andropov, when he came to power, committed the people's inspectors to intensify the work in the elimination of the existing violations in this sector of commerce. We created groups with the power to visit shops and check for goods hidden under the counter and force the shopkeeper to lay them to the storefront, also check for the presence of goods at the warehouses and demanded that they be sent to the shops for sale right away. Inspectors had the right to keep an eye on the back door and check the goods carried out of it by third persons.

At the same time, managers of some shops and warehouses were convicted for serious violations and corruption in the central parts of the country. This unpleasant work stopped after February 1984 following the death of Yuri Andropov. He had been a leader of the country for less than a year and a half, and for such a short period of time that his activities showed few if any positive results, on the contrary, the life in the country became worse.

Konstantin Chernenko was next elected to be the General Secretary of the CPSU Central Committee, but he was elderly, too, and died the year after he had been elected. It was part of my responsibilities to hold meetings in factories with the primary group of popular control, and I was constantly asked: "Why are they always electing old people with health problems to hold such a responsible position?" What could I say? I also didn't understand what was happening in my country and why we elected such elderly leaders.

After the death of Chernenko living standards became even worse; people, however, didn't know the real reason for this and they thought it to be a temporary phenomenon. There was a calm and stable period in the country during the Brezhnev era, nobody was afraid of the future and it seemed that it would always be like that. We had been persuaded since childhood that the USSR was the richest country and the best one in the world, which we believed.

For years, we had only been given information which the Communist Party thought we needed to know, and which was not always true. It was why the people didn't understand what was indeed happening in the country and hoped that when a new General Secretary was appointed everything would fall into place and our life would be the same as it had been earlier.

When Mikhail Gorbachev was elected to be the General Secretary of the CPSU Central Committee in March 1985, we all were happy and proud to have at last a young (54 years old), competent, energetic and purposeful person as head of the state. Earlier, when previous secretaries had made speeches, they just read their reports from notes repeating the same things, over and over again, and as a result many people turned off their TVs. However, when Mikhail Gorbachev made a speech on TV everybody tuned in and listened with great interest. They would then discuss his speech with each other and talk about its implications.

For the first time he talked straight out about existing problems, about negative phenomena that had happened in the country, which couldn't be concealed from the people anymore and there was no point in hiding it. He talked about irreversible changes that had happened in the country over the last years and that it would never be the same as it was before. In order to help the country out of the situation, Mikhail Gorbachev offered to make radical changes in the political life of the country, he elaborated a program of using new forms of economic and social development leading to raise living standards for the people.

He said the things that we wanted to hear and we trusted him and hoped for a better life in the future. The first activity of reform that Mikhail Gorbachev began with was a campaign to reduce alcohol consumption, as he believed it was one of the main negative phenomena preventing the reorganization of society. It is no secret that Russians aren't good at drinking, as they don't know when to stop. From time immemorial it has been a Russian tradition to drink until the moment they fell under the table. We could see that in the movies and read about it in books.

In contrast to other countries, where they drink a glass of wine during supper just for the pleasure of it, our people regarded alcohol to be a solution of all problems – get drunk, forget about everything and there's an end of it. Instead of intensifying explanatory and educational work on the subject, a special emphasis was laid on drinking prohibition. Prices for vodka and the other alcohol drinks were multiplied up many times and restrictions placed on the sale of it in all the shops, cafes and other public places. The result was that alcohol could only be bought at special liquor shops, which were situated farther from the city Centre, and which worked only from 2 p.m. till 7 p.m. and were closed on weekends.

Besides, coupons (permission tickets for buying some foods or goods) were introduced in order to limit spirit purchases. Every grown up began to receive coupons which allowed them to buy 1 bottle of vodka and 2 bottles of wine per month.

It was expected that the measures taken would entail inconvenience in buying spirits and force alcoholics to drink less. People lined up at the shops that sold alcohol from the very early morning, because spirits were delivered then but in limited quantities and shops ran out of it before they closed. That is why a person could stand in a queue a whole day long and go away without buying anything.

At that time, my main job, as an inspector of the committee for popular control, was to organise groups of people to do anti- alcoholism work. Earlier we had just revealed violators of labour discipline, but now we had to contend with workers and alcoholics that formed the large queues outside the liquor stores.

Groups of 3 to 5 inspectors would visit such facilities as restaurants, cafes and especially liquor shops. Sometimes they just made lists of people who stood there in the queue and sent these to their factories or offices. We also checked that the regulation opening hours were being observed. There was only one liquor shop in my village, but the village population wasn't big and at the end of the month people could get the spirits that their coupons entitled them to.

It was a problem to buy spirits in the central cities of the country, many people couldn't as they were ashamed of standing in queues at such shops during working hours, but at weekends the shops were closed. Measures taken in the country entailed inconveniences and changed the life of normal people, but they had little effect on alcoholics.

I remember being in Moscow that time and while driving in the city I saw a huge queue, mainly of men, at a shop. They screamed, abused and pushed each other, it seemed that the shop was taken by storm and I was greatly surprised when I found out that spirits were being sold there. But it was not only the queues which made people's lives uncomfortable, more importantly it was the methods the government used to conduct a non-drinking campaign.

It was generally supported by most of the population, but nobody really expected the methods which were chosen to actually solve the problem. So, was the decision made to reduce the quantity of alcohol produced by reducing the areas of vineyards. It was simple logic for them – What is wine made of? It is made of grapes – that is why they decided to wipe out vineyards. If there are no grapes, there won't be any wine! Hundreds of thousands of hectares of quality vines were uprooted in Moldavia, in the Crimea and in all the southern regions of the country, where they were traditionally engaged in wine production.

In order to survive many distilleries began to produce alcohol- free drinks, but others simply closed down. Thousands of people, for whom wine-making had been their life's work, lost their jobs and any hope for the future.

At the same time as the anti-alcohol campaign, sobriety clubs and societies were created all over the country and people flocked to join them, having given up drinking alcohol.

It became very prestigious to have alcohol-free weddings, birthdays, proms and other arrangements. Both me and my husband joined one of these societies, an imperative for me to do so as I was a party member and as an inspector of popular control were expected to lead by example. However, I still received an allocation of alcohol coupons, but what should I to do with these coupons?

Together with my husband we received an allowance to buy 2 bottles of vodka and 4 bottles of wine each month; we didn't buy so much alcohol earlier and now in order not to waste the coupons we had to buy it! So from the one side we were agitated to be total abstainers and from the other side all the conditions were created to drink. Of course, I swapped spirits coupons for the other coupons (to buy sugar, butter and etc.), so did many other people.

The end result was that the people who drank before continued to drink and normal people were afraid of public censure and stopped drinking altogether. Spirits sale control entailed some other negative phenomena. Everywhere, especially in the rural areas, people began to produce home-distilled vodka (called "samogon"), using not only sugar for the purpose, but candies, fruit, etc., as well.

Alcoholics even bought cheap cologne from the shops and other alcohol containing products, including industrial alcohol which often led to mass poisoning. Thereby, the anti-alcohol campaign had incurred displeasure of many people even before it gave any successful results. I personally found the experience of working in the campaign to reduce alcohol consumption distasteful and I took no pleasure in it.

Chapter 32

Beginning of my Work at the Communist Party Committee

I like my job at the district committee of popular control and I didn't want to change it, but fate decreed its own way. In October 1986, I was instructed to visit the party's district committee and to meet its first secretary. I didn't know what the problem was and I was worried that I had done something wrong.

After the main preliminaries of introduction and enquires about my family and my work, she immediately got down to the main purpose of the meeting. She said, "The communist party's district committee believes that you have been an inspector of the popular control committee for far too long, and you can do a more important job. We think that you'll be able to cope with duties of an instructor of an organizational department. "

I wasn't ready for that, and started to excuse myself, because I knew how strict was the party's discipline at the district committee and how hard it was to work there. Despite this she stood her own ground: "You are a communist party member and you have to be amenable to party discipline, if the district committee believes that you belong here you can't refuse. So begin work on Monday, we have a meeting at 8:30 a.m., so don't be late," she said.

I rushed out of the office, and didn't know what to do, and decided to tell everything to my husband at first. After he had listened to me, he started to scream at me, "You have got what you wanted, you've graduated the institute, joined the party and you madly love social work that is why they are taking you there! So go and work!"

On Monday, I put on my best suit and went to my new job, of course I had been to this office many times, and everybody knew me, but despite this I felt uncomfortable because this time I was there as an official worker. All women, who worked there, were wearing business suits and high-heeled shoes. It was beautiful in the building, there were pot plants everywhere, and there were red carpets with green stripes on the edges in the corridors and offices.

District Committee of Communist Party of Zyryanka, 1987

The district committee was situated in a two- storeyed building, one of the first stone constructions in the village. On the ground floor was an assembly hall, a conference hall, library and three offices, where the district committee of Komsomol was situated, the first floor was fully occupied with a district committee of the CPSU.

In the Party committee there were three secretaries, departments of organization, ideological and general departments, and a department of party's accounting at the district committee. Like I say, it was a surprise for me when the Secretary at the district party committee had asked me, no, ordered me to work at the District Committee, but I received another more unpleasant surprise on my first day at work – I was commissioned to supervise an agricultural sector of the region. This meant that I had to know well all about the workings at the District state farms, to help them and be responsible for their working.

I was shocked and tried to explain to the secretary that I had had no agricultural education, had never lived in an agricultural village and it was just not my scene! But it was useless. My protestations were ignored and I went back to my office and burst into tears, but my colleague calmed me down: "Why are you so upset? There are no agricultural specialists at the district committee so what's the difference who is going to supervise it. Work gradually, and do everything you can and that's all you can do."

But I couldn't work "gradually". It was my temperament that if I was given a task, I had to carry out with my full commitment, and that is why I took this all very seriously. It seemed to me that the state of things at the state farms were going to depend directly on me, and I rushed to explore the issues of development of agriculture in the region.

So, I started to visit different farms of District state farms because I was a responsible for all aspects of agriculture in my district. Sometimes I went alone; sometimes together with the secretary of primary party organisation of state farms which was born in this village and knew practically everybody and almost everything about the farms. I on the other hand, had no experience at all, and she helped me by sharing her knowledge, and I'm thankful to her for that. Many of the places I had to visit were away from the main centres of population and this meant staying away for a couple of days or more at a time.

The living conditions in some the places where I had to stay on those trips weren't the best ones, and it was especially hard in winter when temperatures were very low. There were no hotels in the villages and I stayed (sometimes alone) in the buildings of the rural council house. There were no conveniences or central heating, there were only stoves heated with firewood. It as warm while you were stoking, but as soon as the firewood burnt down it was terribly cold and I had to wake up all the time during the night and put some more firewood into the stove.

Nevertheless, I am happy that life gave me a chance, not only to look into the work of agriculture, but also to find out a lot of new and interesting experiences for myself. During those trips I saw under what conditions local people lived and worked. I also took part in many national holidays and understood the traditions of the indigenous people of Yakutia. And now I would like to tell a little bit about it.

All agriculture in the region was under the control of one large central state farm, with smaller outlying farms (There weren't any private farms or farmers at that time in the country). This central state farm was in a village which was situated 5 kilometres away from Zyryanka. The subsidiary farms were situated from 5 to 130 kilometres from the centre, and different types of agriculture were carried on at the outlying farms.

Two of these outlying farms were dairy farms, breeding cattle for dairy production. Animal breeding had been developed since the foundation of Gulags, when the first bull and two cows were delivered there on a steamboat, together with the prisoners. The first farm was established in a Verkhnekolymsky village and provided people with milk. During the period of my work in 1985 the state farms had only one modern farm building, the others were of older construction and had poor conditions in which to work, this made life very hard for employees, especially in winter.

I felt pity for the dairymaids when I saw them milking cows by hand twice a day and lugging buckets and the heavy milk cans by themselves. They did the rest of work by hand as well: breaking up bales of hay, feeding cows, and cleaning dung from the barns. The cows that were kept were of a special breed which could endure the heavy frosts in Yakutia. There was no heating in the farm buildings and it was only due to the presence of animals that it was a bit warmer inside then outside.

During the summer time cows were let out to feed on the plentiful taiga grasses. Despite such poor conditions milk yields were good and the best cows produced about 2000 litres a year. This enabled the people of the region to be fully provided with fresh dairy products throughout the year. Fresh milk, butter, cream and sour cream were always on offer and as the fat content was very high the products were always very tasty.

Besides the dairy farms there were also several stud farms which dealt with horse breeding. The horses that were bred were of a type of horse that was peculiar to Yakutia. They were very solid but not particularly tall and could endure the frosts up to minus 50 degrees. The horses were bred both for meat and for work on the state farms. These stud farms were usually situated in the taiga and on the river or lake banks and could only be reached by a helicopter. I only once visited one of these farms and fortunately it was in summer. I was accompanied on this visit by two of my colleagues, and we all flew there by helicopter.

We brought some food, fresh papers and magazines, and delivered a lecture about perestroika and how our region would be affected and then held a question and answer session. Horse breeders were happy to see everybody who came to visit them, and who would listen to their problems. They were pleased to show us how they lived, and treated us with their usual dinner of boiled horse meat, fish and tinned food. On this particular farm only seven people were employed. They all lived in one big house which was heated by a firewood-burning stove. There were not even basic facilities in this house; even water was taken in buckets straight from the lake.

They ate mainly horse meat, tinned food and some other products which were brought to them by visitors like us. They had no TV only a radio. It was the indigenous Yakuts and Yukagirs who worked there, and they were used to such a remote life away from civilization. They loved their work, many spending their whole lives in such places and rarely venturing to the central village. Many of them didn't have families and had never been on holidays away from their region. I don't think that any other Russians or people of other nationalities would work and live under such extremes.

The Fur trade was another very profitable activity for the state farms and was particularly suited to this area as it was a traditional ancient trade of the indigenous people of the North. Not everybody could do this, and not everybody could understand the secrets of hunting. You had to be borne a hunter. This profession required such special features of character as courage, powers of endurance, and sensitivity to the nature of the taiga. A hunter also had to have robust health, a keen eye and a firm hand. Hunting was a solo occupation and hunters never went to the taiga in groups. A hunter went there alone and had to defend himself in a dangerous situation.

The Siberian taiga was rich in both flora and fauna. There were plenty of sables, red foxes, polar foxes, beaver, squirrels, and other animals with good fur, produced as a protection from the extreme cold. The hunting season was in winter when the animals had the best and most beautiful fur. Hunters always prepared well for their expeditions into the taiga, not only taking such things as big knives, guns and bullets, but everything needed to survive a Siberian winter.

One essential requirement was special hunting skis. These were short and wide and on the bottom of which was attached fur from a deer's bottom leg. Such skies slid forward well and didn't slide backward on the hill. All hunters had signal rockets with them, essential in case of an accident or other emergency out in the taiga. Such rockets could then be seen by a plane or helicopter and immediate assistance could be given.

Hunters travelled into the taiga by dog sleigh and could disappear for weeks or even months, depending on how successful the hunt had been. They could venture out on hunting trips several times during the season and a good hunter could bring back around 1200 skins in a season.

Sable fur was the most expensive, but only considered to be of high quality if it wasn't damaged. A sable is not a big animal and you had to be very skilled to get a skin of high quality.

During the summer time, hunters trapped muskrats in the lakes. There were thousands of lakes in Taiga and everyone was inhabited by these animals. In order to see them one did not have to travel very far into the taiga. One time I was with my colleague in the village of Arylakh, which was 120 kilometres from Zyryanka, when we found a small lake full of muskrats in the suburbs of the village.

They weren't afraid of us because we didn't touch them and they swam near the shore, sat on the hummocks and logs and gazed at us. That was fun. Another common animal in this region of Siberia was the wolf. This, too, was hunted for its fur, particularly during the non-hunting season when other animals did not produce good fur. Once again I happened to be in the village of Arylakh and was due to meet the chairman of the rural council house. He wasn't at his office when I arrived and so I decided to venture out and look for him. People outside told me that he was in a nearby workshop, where they processed fur.

This workshop was situated in a very old one- storeyed house constructed in Yakut style – not high, but with a dome-shaped roof in the centre of which there stuck out a pipe from the stove. Surrounding this building was a small fenced yard. It was winter time and very cold so I ran quickly along the path and barged straight away into the workshop. The smell inside was so horrific that I immediately almost choked and vomited. Due to the difference in temperatures inside from that outside, my glasses misted up straight away and I couldn't see anything for a moment or two.

After I had removed them from my face and cleaned them I saw a group of women in the workshop who were cleaning fat and meat from the skin of animals. They removed the upper layer of fat from the skin with a knife and wiped it on a rug, which they had on their knees. Across the ceiling wires were stretched and from which hung hooks in rows on which skins were attached. The stripped carcasses were piled up in the corner.

After seeing, and taking all this in, I couldn't stay there a minute longer and rushed out of the building into the yard. Although I had not noticed them when I had walked towards this building, outside in the yard, stacked like firewood were the frozen bodies of wolves waiting to be processed. I still don't know why I hadn't seen them before, but after witnessing all that I had seen in the workshop and then in the yard it was too much for me and I was in a completely shocked state.

I covered my face with my hands and was running back towards the rural council house when the chairman caught up with me and started to calm me down. I couldn't calm down for a long time, I was all shivering and I was in low spirits. I couldn't get over how women could do this job and stay there for the whole day. He asked me why on earth had I gone to that place, telling me it's too much for my nerves and please don't go back there again.

Looking back, this now seems a rather funny experience and I can laugh about it, but at the time it was quite a shocking experience and a taste of real Yakut life. Fur was called "soft gold" because it was a big the part of the wealth production of the county. The best fur was despatched to the rest of the USSR and some exported for foreign currency. The lesser grade of fur was given to the factories of the region for the production of clothing for the local population.

The job of a hunter was very hard and dangerous. Some of them went away and never came back; maybe a fatal accident or they just froze to death in the taiga, who knows? They were face to face with nature on a daily basis and accepted the risks and lifestyle. Professional hunters, could in a season, bring back furs valued at many thousands of roubles, but their salary wasn't high.

A hunter earned the same as the other people, who worked on a state farm. There were no bonuses for a very good season's hunting.

In 1953 they brought 27 silver foxes into the district and this formed the basis for the fur farms that were established in the district. It was also part of my remit to visit the farms which bred animals for furs, not only silver fox but also, polar fox and mink. These animals were kept in small cages made of metal lath, and stood in rows on the wooden shelves which were readily accessible.

There was only one animal to a cage but a farm could have 300 to 800 animals. The work at these fur farms was very hard; workers had to be outside in the cold of winter and in the heat of summer. They had to protect and treat the animals against illnesses, clean the cages and feed and water them. Feed consisted of low-grade fish and the wastes of meat left from butchering, this they had to process before feeding the animals on time.

The better they took care of animals the higher quality of fur they got. To grow the total number of animals and raise young animals was the hardest job to do. Unbelievable some of these animals could be terribly picky when choosing a mate and it was often necessary to present up to a dozen females for selection before the males would mate with one.

Reindeer herding was another very profitable occupation in these northern lands and it did not require a lot of capital. In the mountains of Arga-Taas, which were situated 130 kilometres away from Zyryanka, there lived natives of the north-east of Siberia – "Evens". Reindeer breeding was their traditional trade and was centred on one small village. The reindeer, of course, ran more or less wild over the range of hills, but the herders and their families lived in houses in this particular village.

Besides houses there was also an office, a warehouse, a bath and a club, where they showed narrow-film movies. Although their homes were in Arga-Taas the children of the village boarded at a school in Zyryanka during the school year. Reindeer breeders took care of themselves and took everything that Yakut nature gave them: stored firewood for heating their houses in winter, hunted, gathered mushrooms and berries, sewed traditional clothes of furs.

The profession of a reindeer breeder was passed on from one generation to another. Children of reindeer breeders would take over the herds from their parents. If they said about a person that he "comes from a family of reindeer breeders" it was considered very honourable.

Around ten thousand reindeer were pastured in the mountain valleys and remained there throughout the year and were only brought back to the village, and corralled in special enclosures, made of wood, for counting and vaccination. Once a year, usually in February-March there was an annual slaughter or harvest of reindeer. Marksmen from the village flew by a helicopter to the reindeer herds in the mountains.

When they found a herd of deer, they chased it and shot at them from the helicopter. The bodies of reindeer were then collected and delivered by helicopter to the reindeer breeders' village, where they were butchered and the meat was sorted from fur and the proceeds of this despatched for distribution by the central state farm.

At the end of this annual cull, it was traditional in this village to have a festival and holiday to celebrate a successful season. It was usually held at the beginning of April, and everybody from Zyryanka dreamed of getting there at least once in a lifetime. It was not possible for everybody to be able to get there because only a limited number of people could be taken there by helicopters or small AN-2 planes. Those who usually attended were mainly the workers of district committee and executive committee, the chairmen of state farm and public organizations.

Entertainers were also transported in to add to the ambience of the festival and celebration. I was lucky, as I was able to attend one of these festivals, together with my husband. I was included on the list of guests because I was in charge of the district agriculture, and my husband was invited because he was in charge of the construction company, which constructed houses for the state farm. The mountains of Agra-Taas were situated 130 kilometres away from Zyryanka and when it was sunny and cloudless you could see them from the village.

Their height is between 1300-1500 metres and even in summer they were snow-capped, and when I flew over them I saw a fascinating panorama from the plane. It took only 40 minutes on the plane an AN-2 and we arrived into a totally different world. The temperature, even in April, was minus 20 degrees, the sky was clear and cloudless, the sun shone brightly and the snow was dazzling white. The reindeer breeders met all guests in their traditional costumes and led them to the club, where an official reception was held.

The Director of the central state farm presented the financial results from the year activities gave a summing up of the work done for the year. He would then announce the winner of the competition for "The best team of reindeer breeders," and award prizes.

Then outside there was another competition between the reindeer breeders. This showed their skills in how they worked with deer: the fastest ways to corral them, the best ways to stop a running deer with a help of a rope etc. The winner received the accolade of 'The best reindeer breeder of the year.'

After these official speeches and activities all the guests were invited to eat at an outdoor feast. A couple of metres from the village there was an open cast coal-cliff. The entire cliff was made of coal which glistened in the sun. It would be possible to simply hack pieces of coal straight from this cliff, and I thought about my father, who for his whole life worked extracting coal from deep underground. He would have been amazed to see all this coal just for the taking.

The table for lunch set by a cliff face of solid coal, 1988

There was a big long wooden table, set at the foot of this mountain of coal, with benches covered with deer fur for us to sit on. There was a variety of different types of Siberian meat: boiled venison, foal meat, wild goose, duck, and fish of different types: salted, dried and raw sliced frozen fish. The special delicacies were boiled deer's tongue, heart, liver and kidneys, and of course, lots of vodka and wine. There were traditional Yakut deserts called kerchik which was an ancient Yakut creation.

It was made from whisking double cream until the cream became dense. Then they added fox berries and put it on a tray in small pieces and froze it. In such a pleasant atmosphere, in the fresh air everything tasted much better than at home. Fresh boiled meat smelled so good us I loved venison and foal meat. But most of all I liked boiled deer tongues. They are small, much smaller than beef ones but they are very delicate and tasty.

After the dinner, we returned to the club where there was a concert and later a sale of the articles of traditional Yakut art: beaded high fur boots (shoes of deer's fur), mittens, bags, souvenirs and women's jewellery (necklaces and earrings) – everything was made of deer's skin.

After that guests wore the traditional costumes of the reindeer breeders and were then photographed with reindeer breeders as a memento of the occasion. That was the best event I took part in while living in the Yakytia and made a lasting impression on me and I still think very fondly of that occasion.

Chapter 33

My Job During Restructuring

I think I was lucky because I started to work for party bodies during the period of the *Restructuring*, when Mikhail Gorbachev was a General Secretary of the CPSU. I can explain what this new word meant in this way: it was a program according to which radical changes in all fields of the Soviet country and society were carried out. In the course of the Restructuring there appeared some new terms: *Glasnost, Acceleration, Demikratizatsiya* (democratization) and slogans which later became the symbol of that time.

It was considered that a necessary condition of the Restructuring was *Glasnost* that is every citizen had the possibility to know the truth about the things that were going on in the country and to express one's opinion on any issue.

It was natural that the responsibility for the course of the Restructuring be assigned to the workers of the party bodies and that is why the style of their work changed. I could tell what was going on in our country by the example of work carried out by our regional committee of the Communist party, in which I worked.

For example, during the period of Glasnost under the slogan *"The Party must be closer to people"* I began to visit, more often, the enterprises which I supervised, to assist their managers in solving different questions and to be present at all the opened party meetings. Despite the fact that there was Glasnost and freedom of speech in the country, a majority of the communists, accustomed to strict discipline, were concerned about the responsibility and expressed their opinions warily, as they had done before.

Those workers who were not members of the communist party weren't afraid of anything and that is why they criticized openly all the leaders of the country and especially blamed the communists for all the mistakes that had been made. This hadn't happened earlier and it was hard and not very pleasant for me, as a communist and committee member, to be present at these meetings.

During the period of *Demikratizatsiya* (democratization) of society the first sign of the development of democracy was an evaluation of managers of commercial enterprises, who had been appointed to their post according to a recommendation of the party bodies. Earlier such managers had only been responsible and reported to the higher communist bodies, but now they must report on their work to their own staff, which also had the right to remove a manager from work and choose another one by open voting.

These changes in personnel policy also took place at the party bodies as well, where every worker was scrutinized and examined to ensure each person was qualified to hold their position in the organization. The professional standards, to which members of the nomenclature bureaucratic establishment (Bureaucratic rank) were held to, were particularly high. This way a new Soviet party top bureaucracy was approved, and according to which the lives of many people, who worked in the system, changed at a later date.

What was the Soviet party nomenclature or top bureaucracy? This was a list of positions for which suitable people were approved according to the recommendations of only senior party bodies. The list contained the names of top bureaucracy officials who worked at that moment and a list of people who were recommended to replace them in case of necessity. For example, I worked at that time in the position of an instructor of organizational department and this position wasn't included in the list of nomenclature, but while approving the new top bureaucracy I got to the reserves for the position of General department chief.

After that I became a privileged functionary and my life began to change noticeably for the better. Immediately after appointment the new privileged functionaries received an assignment to attend further education facilities. One went to the Higher Party School. It was very prestigious to study there, but capacity was limited and it was quite hard to gain entry, which is why I and my colleagues were assigned to the Marxism-Leninism University opened under the Yakut Party Regional Committee.

I studied in the department of party-economics for active functionaries, studying Marxism-Leninism philosophy, CPSU economic policy, social psychology and the other subjects which I liked.

I studied with pleasure and graduated from the University with honours, passing all the tests with excellent marks.

Right after graduating from the University changes in personnel took place at the regional committee and according to the party top bureaucracy list I was appointed to be a General department chief of the CPSU regional committee.

This was a great promotion for me and I was very glad to have this new job, because I enjoyed all aspects of my duties in this position: to work with documents (including the secret ones), with a party archive, organizing meetings, and to deal with general issues of the party regional committee. My salary was quite high and I had a separate office with a secret safe (access to which I was the only one who was permitted out of all the workers at the regional committee) and what was the most important I wasn't in charge of agriculture anymore.

This all seemed to be perfect, but it wasn't very convenient to have a status of a privileged functionary. Though the Soviet party privileged functionary posts had always existed in the country, and as I said before, this was just a list of positions for which the workers were approved according to the recommendations of the party bodies, but people never liked members of bureaucratic establishment, considering them to be a privileged class.

Especially during the period of glasnost people openly expressed their discontent and demanded the abolition of high-ranking positions and pressed for incumbents to be shorn of their benefits and privileges. When I began to work at the district committee I found out that there really were some benefits and privileges at the party bodies. In this way the Administration of affairs of the CPSU Central Committee, which was called the 4th administration, had a network of bureaucratic hospitals with good equipment and qualified medical staff.

The Regional Committees had their hotels in each districts city and every party official could stay in one after he had shown his certificate. There also were sanatoriums of the Communist Party Central Committee, where workers of three categories rested and improved their health: the Party, Komsomol and KGB (Committee for State Security) bodies.

But, maybe higher Party bodies had even more benefits but I didn't know anything about that. We worked the same way as everybody else did for a salary, received treatment at a local hospital, but all the same people thought it to be unfair that the Party workers had the things the other categories of workers didn't and demanded equality of rights in everything.

It's even funny now to remember those times when such ordinary things like staying at a hotel for a night or receiving treatment at a sanatorium were considered to be a privilege. I personally took advantage of those two "privileges" because there weren't any other benefits at our Party district committee. Firstly, I didn't spend nights at airports anymore and when I was in Yakutsk I always stayed at a single room of a hotel of the regional party committee. Secondly, when I had health problems I had an opportunity to rest and receive treatment at the sanatoriums of the Communist Party Central Committee.

My work at the district committee during the period of restructuring was very intense and nervous because qualifying standards were high. I personally was responsible for preparing and running different events, after which I became exhausted and had terrible headaches.

My working day began by taking various pills and this regime started to impede on my work. One day my boss saw some pills on my table and asked me what was going on.

When I told him everything he said: "You must receive treatment, you are young yet and you'll probably work at the Party bodies for a long time, and the

Party needs healthy people. So take a sanatorium voucher, go improve your health and have a rest." I was surprised that he personally had offered me a trip to a sanatorium.

Before that I had worked at other organizations where vouchers were given to old people mainly, those who suffered from chronic diseases. Generally speaking, issues of health improvement were paid a good deal of attention in our country; trade-union organizations which functioned at all the enterprises, state farm, organizations and schools dealt with it.

Soviet trade unions were some of the most mass social organizations in the Soviet Union, and practically every person, after graduating from school and entering a technical secondary school or the institute or work became a member of a trade-union organization. This organization implemented the party's policy, helped to execute a programme of social development, and raised cultural and material standards.

It dealt with all the important issues of social life of people starting from birth until the last days of life: creation of safe working conditions, target execution control, the raising of the cultural standards of people, accommodation distribution, and the protection of rights of workers, birth, disability and pension benefits.

Trade-union organizations paid special attention to preventive measures and health improvement of workers, they dealt with the distribution of vouchers to pioneer camps, tourist bases, holiday centres, boarding houses, and sanatoriums that belonged to them. In 1919, Vladimir Lenin signed a Decree "About the creation of resorts all over the country" and from that moment they started to construct health-improving establishments all over the territory of the Soviet Union where mineral water springs and mud with curative properties were found.

In the 1970s to 80s thousands of sanatoriums functioned in the country, where millions of people had holidays and took treatment. Receiving treatment at sanatoriums became very popular and affordable for every working person; vouchers were not expensive and workers paid around 30 % of their cost. You could say that for many people it became a tradition to receive treatment at sanatoriums and it was hard to find a person who hadn't ever been to a sanatorium.

Those who were there once usually wanted to go there again. Apart from trade-union organizations' sanatoriums, there were also sanatoriums that belonged to different offices, and only people who worked there could have holidays there. For example, my father received treatment several times at sanatoriums that belonged to the Ministry of coal industry. All the sanatoriums specialized in the treatment of some main diseases.

Depending on the disposition and medical resources, they were subdivided into sanatoriums for digestive organs treatment, orthopaedic, respiratory organs, vascular and nervous systems treatment etc. So, I liked the idea about a sanatorium, moreover my son had already graduated from school so I was free and could go whenever I wanted to. I called right away to the voucher-selling department of Yakut Regional Communist Party Committee and I was offered a voucher starting December 3rd to a sanatorium of the CPSU Central Committee "Gorny vozdukh (Mountain air)" in a town Zheleznovodsk, which is situated on the territory of North Caucasus.

My husband wasn't against my visit; I had enough money at this time to be able to have a rest and improve my health. But to my surprise I didn't need to spend much money, I couldn't believe that I had to pay only 20% of the total cost of the voucher and got a medical benefit of 200 roubles. Besides that I also received a paid a round-trip ticket so that was I could improve my health almost for free.

I was very pleased about this and before this I had had no idea those workers of district regional committee had such good benefits. When I went to a secretary to sign my holiday application, he made me even more pleased by telling me that I could also stay for a couple of days at Hotel Russia in Moscow because I was working at the system of the Party bodies. "You need to make a reservation at the Communist Party Central Committee in the Kremlin. Don't be afraid of anything, go there safely at any time of the day, but take your certificate with you," he said.

A plane from Yakutsk to Moscow (Domodedovo airport) arrived late at night and when I arrived in the centre of the town it was around midnight. Of course, I wanted to stay at the hotel, but couldn't believe this to be true and quite frankly I was afraid of going into the Kremlin, particularly at this time of night. I thought – should I go right now or should I wait till morning?

But remembering what the secretary told me I decided to go. I approached the Kremlin and saw the entrance which I needed, and by which stood two soldiers – an armed guard! When I got closer, a soldier met me halfway and asked me what I wanted.

I replied that I needed a reservation to the hotel 'Russia', he then checked my certificate and led me to the reception room of the Communist Party Central Committee, which was situated on the ground floor of the Kremlin.

I entered a big hall, where an officer of the day was sitting at a table; there was also a staircase which led to the first floor at the bottom of which stood an armed guard. The officer of the day checked my certificate and said – "Pick up the receiver of this phone and tell the person who answers what you need." As soon as I picked up the receiver I was immediately asked where I came from and was I alone or with family and for how many days I was going to stay in Moscow.

After I had answered all the questions I was asked to wait for a couple of minutes. Ten minutes later I was given a reservation to the hotel 'Russia', which was situated at Red Square, right opposite the Kremlin and all I needed to do was to cross the square. It was the biggest and the most comfortable hotel in the country and was kind of a symbol of the Soviet Union. I was lodged on the sixth floor in a single-suite, but I didn't get a good look at it as I went straight to bed, because it was past midnight and I was exhausted after the flight.

In the morning I was woken up by a chime of bells (of a clock on the Spasskaya Tower of the Moscow Kremlin, according to which they synchronized Moscow time all over the country).

I approached the window and saw the Moscow panorama, which caught my breath. The window was big from the ceiling down to the floor, and from the sixth floor I could see clearly the promenade by the Moscow River which was situated not far from the hotel.

In front of me there was the Kremlin and the panorama of the centre of the capital city.

I'd been standing for a long time at the window enjoying Moscow and thought: 'How great it is that I live in such a great country and have everything an ordinary woman can dream of: a good job, money, an opportunity to travel and staying at such a hotel.'

I decided to spend two days in Moscow and see the places of interest of the city, but firstly I needed to have breakfast. Entering the hotel cafeteria I was taken aback by what I saw – there before me were the best food and delicacies one could think of: boiled and steamed flesh of sturgeon, smoked and steamed salmon, sausages and cheese of all kinds, sandwiches with black and red caviar, beer of different kinds in small bottles and even in cans (I had never seen such beer, because beer was sold only by the glass at that time).

And all this was at the time when all over the country there were shortages in food supply. Guest staying in this hotel was very important; I think they were people's deputies and Party workers of the Communist Parties of the other Republics. Some of them were from Central Asia and the Caucasus, I recognized them due to their accent and there were also foreigners

Beside such people I felt uneasy and only took the same food they did: some coffee and a sandwich, but after I had grown bolder I went to the cafeteria a couple of times and bought everything I wanted.

Exactly just how big the hotel was I understood when I began to search for a hairdresser's and was walking along a corridor for 15 minutes. When I was tired of walking I asked a woman on duty where the hairdresser's was.

The woman on duty replied that I was heading the wrong way and I needed to continue walking which eventually would bring me full circle to the hairdressers, but I lost hope of getting there and went back to my room.

Identity card of '"Russia'" Hotel, 1987

It was very beautiful in the hotel, Kremlin rugs were laid in all the corridors, there were huge carpets in the halls, flowers in big boxes, huge paintings with Moscow views were on the walls.

I visited all the central shops in two days, but what is more important I visited the Tretyakov Gallery, that I had dreamt of visiting for a long time, but had no opportunity of visiting before. I spend, I guess, a couple of hours and got an unforgettable impression from this visit.

After that, every time when I went to Moscow I stayed at the hotel 'Russia'. Once I was there with my husband and he was very proud of that. And my relatives and friends from Ukraine didn't believe that I had been there

217

until I showed them a business card of the hotel. It was hard for ordinary people to believe, because it was impossible to get in there without a reservation and identification as a worker of the communist party department.

Many years have passed since that time and the hotel has been demolished. They decided that such a big building held no architectural value and shouldn't be situated in the centre of Moscow beside the Kremlin and the other historical and architectural monuments of Russia. The hotel doesn't exist anymore but the memory about it and that wonderful period in my life will stay with me forever...

Chapter 34

Spa Sanatorium of the CPSU Central Committee

After spending two days in Moscow I continued my trip to the town Minvody – which is situated in the foothills of North of Caucasus in the south-east of the European part of the USSR.

The town Minvody is the centre of the biggest and the most famous spa area 'Caucasus mineral water'. At the beginning of 19th century, a mineral water spring was discovered there and people from all over the country have come there to cure different illnesses since that time.

The resort area includes 4 resort-towns: Kislovodsk, Zheleznovodsk, Esentuki and Pyatigorsk, in these four towns there were situated approximately 130 sanatoriums and around a million people a year took treatment there. The sanatorium 'Mountain air' is situated in Zheleznovodsk, which is located at the foot of the mountain Zheleznaya, which gave the name to the town. It appeared at first sight that the sanatorium was situated in a nice three-story building. At the entrance to the property, there was a gate and you could get inside only if you had a voucher or sanatorium book.

The sanatorium book was given to every patient and it contained full information about a person: surname, a room where they lived, illness diagnosis and a set of manipulations prescribed. This book was jokingly called "a passport of a holidaymaker." When I entered the entrance hall of the sanatorium, it seemed to me that I come to a palace, it was huge: two storeys in height and the walls and floor were finished with white marble.

A staircase leading to the first floor was also made of the same marble; the ceiling was decorated with huge crystal chandelier. There were also beautiful rugs and exotic palm-trees in big decorative boxes all over the building. There was good quality furniture and curtains in the rooms, together with upholster armchairs and the blankets on the beds were of the same colour and made of velvet. I couldn't believe that after the modest living conditions in North Siberia that I would live in such a luxury for 24 days!

I was lodged in a double room and I lived there together with a woman who came from the city of Novosibirsk (the centre of Siberia). She was around ten years older than me; she had worked for a long time at the communist party department and came to such sanatoriums every year. I was lucky because she turned out to be a very interesting person, she told me a lot about Central Siberia and the best spa treatment resorts in the country.

Besides this woman with whom I shared a room, I met many friends there during the time of my stay, and we congregated together at meal times and during other free periods. They were very interesting people of different ages, and nationalities from several other republics and different parts of the Soviet Union, but the things that united us all were common interests, a love for life and the desire to enjoy it.

I have already said that when I saw the building for the first time, it seemed to me that it was three storeys high, but it was designed very interestingly, and it actually had eight storeys. The building was partly set into the side of mount "Zheleznaya" and due to the difference in height you came in first from the town side on the fourth floor instead of the ground floor.

This sanatorium was a huge medical complex, which consisted of several accommodation blocks, a clinic where examinations were held, a medical building where people took different treatments. There was also a gym, swimming pool, cinema, dancing hall, library, and two dining rooms. All newcomers completed a medical examination, and depending on the diagnosis of an illness, doctor prescribed medical treatments including mineral baths, massage, and underwater massage, exercise therapy, electric manipulations, magnetic and laser therapy, mud treatment, etc.

But the most important possession of the resort was mineral water – natural springs, which were situated under the ground at the depth of 700 or more metres and which delivered water to the surface in a special drinking building which was situated in a central area of the spa resort.

There were four types of mineral water in Zheleznovodsk, each of them had its own mineral composition and was prescribed by a doctor depending on patient's disease.

I drank mineral water three times a day 30 minutes before meals – in composition it's almost the same as the water at the resort in Karlovy Vary in Check Republic.

We got three meals a day at the sanatorium, according to a dietary menu, which was prescribed by a doctor to every person depending on a patient's disease. (There were 15 types of menu in general.)

There was a strict daily order at the sanatorium, there were usually morning exercises and breakfast and then all the patients took their treatment procedures. We had some free time after lunch and I would meet with my friends and we usually went for a walk to a wood, a park or went for excursions all over the territory of North Caucasus.

The nature of this wonderful land fascinated me and I've visited the most interesting places: canyons, waterfalls, and a Blue Lake with thermal springs.

Three times a week there were dances, the other days, there were concerts and a cinema. The dancing hall was very beautiful. It was very big with a cathedral ceiling through two floors and under which hung huge crystal chandeliers in the shape of balls, which spun and sparkled with many- coloured lights. On one side of the hall, there was a spiral staircase, which led to the first floor of the hall where an orchestra played good modern and folk music.

There were always many people at the dances, and it was a great fun, everybody danced from 8 p.m. till 11 p.m., only people from my country could dance so fast and energetically. Doctors used to make fun of it: "Patients are sick only before lunch; there aren't any sick people in the afternoon or at the dances." Thanks to treatment procedures, and resort life, my headache had gone in 10 days and I rushed up and down the stairs and didn't use an elevator.

The 24 days of my holiday flew by very quickly and I went home saying goodbye to my friends with tears in my eyes. After that we corresponded with each other for a long time. I really liked taking treatment at the sanatorium; I enjoyed the procedures and an active and interesting holiday. I have to say that, my trip to the resort including two days at the hotel 'Russia' in Moscow, was the best time I ever had in that period of my life.

Since that moment on I used every opportunity to improve my health and spent my holidays at sanatoriums and during my time working at the regional committee I travelled to different spa resorts all over my country: to Almaty city (Kazakhstan), to Nalchic town and Kislovodsk (Caucasus), to the Far East, etc. They were all situated in different republics of the country and differed from each other by climate, nature, local traditions and therapeutic qualities of mineral water.

I won't describe all those places, but I would like to tell about one of them – a spa resort at Shmakovka and only because it is situated in an amazing and unique region of the Far East – the most distant territory of the USSR. There, in the far south- east, is the Primorsky Krai region, which borders with China, North Korea and is about 1000 kilometres (650 miles) from Japan. The Primorsky Krai is the only place in the country, where the monsoon climate prevails, but with minor frosts in winter and hot summer, during which the monsoon winds bring the biggest quantity of rainfall.

In the valley of the Ussuri River, which is the biggest river in the area, the Ussuriysky taiga – boreal forests, occupy the most part of the territory. Right there, in the central part of Primorsky Krai, in the territory of Ussuriysky taiga and on the banks of the Ussuri River, the spa resort Shmakovka is situated, famous for its mineral water, which possesses unique therapeutic qualities.

The sanatorium of the CPSU Central Committee, where I spent my holiday, still preserved its original name 'A sanatorium of 50 years of October Revolution'. The conditions in the sanatorium were the same as in the other sanatoriums of the same type so I won't describe them, but will tell in detail about this remarkable and unique region of my country.

I had been there twice and in different seasons, and on both occasions took the opportunity to take many exploratory excursions and that is why I have a full notion of its climate, weather, nature, interesting and unusual places, which I could only experience in this area.

In my winter visit which took place in February and March, there were minor frosts and much snow, and at the beginning of March the temperature wasn't lower than minus 5 Celsius.

It was never really windy there and the light fluffy snow which was falling just covered the trees and bushes, creating charming fairy-tale views. There was a sanatorium ski depot and from which I often went skiing.

The sanatorium itself was situated on a small hill and it was convenient to ski downhill from there to the Ussuri River. Also at the sanatorium was as skating-rink where I tried to skate for the first time. Despite being 40 years old, and with a help of my friends, even made some progress, managing to stay upright for minutes at a time! My second visit took place in the middle of summer during the monsoon season.

I soon understood exactly what was meant by the monsoon season. I had a feeling that I was constantly in a steam room, because due to high humidity my hair and body were constantly damp. During such weather I spent all my spare time at the river Ussuri swimming, boating or just walking. It was here that I saw many interesting and unusual things for the first time in my life. For example, in order to actually get to the Ussuri River I had to travel down from the hill and when I reached the river bank I found it was covered by tall grass.

One would think what is unusual about it? But when I got there for the first time, I was impressed by this particular grass! It was tall, very tall, as high as a man, there were paths through this grass beaten by other walkers, but neither these paths nor the people on them could be seen from the hill because the grass was so tall. I was afraid of going there alone, and that is why I always went together with my friends, because we passed through the grass as if through a thin tunnel, where one couldn't see anybody in the distance and an approaching person showed up all of a sudden in front of us.

We often boated on the Ussuri River and I could not help but admire the picturesque Ussuriysky taiga with its unusual trees with curved trunks, fanciful bushes and other vegetation trailing down to the river, and making some places impassable. A few kilometres away from the resort, there was a sign on the river, which warned people not to proceed further along the river, because there began a Soviet-Chinese Border, which went along the Ussuri River for more than 260 kilometres (163 miles).

The lakes of Ussuriysky taiga are unique in the country being the only ones in which the lotus flowers grow, and which are especially plentiful on Lake Khanka, which is not far from the resort and which is also the biggest lake in the Far East. The borderline between Soviet Russia and China dissected this lake, two thirds of which belonged to the USSR and one third to China.

Much of the flora and fauna of the Ussuriysky taiga is unique because during the last ice age, glaciers did not reach as far south as this and that is why some flora and fauna of the subtropics were preserved here. When visiting the Ussuriysky taiga – it's hard to figure out exactly in what part of the globe you are, because Ussuriysky taiga is a continuation of the Siberian taiga and that is why flora and fauna of taiga and subtropics are mixed up here.

Thousands of unique and rare plants and animals survive in this territory and which are listed in the USSR Red Book of protected species. One special plant from this area is the ginseng, which they call "a root of life".

One particular animal that survives in the Ussuriysky taiga is the Amur Tiger, the so called "Siberian Tiger". This being the heaviest and largest tiger in the world, but with a misleading name and should be more correctly known as Amur tiger. The name "Siberian tiger" is misleading, because people think, quite wrongly, that Siberian tigers dwell in Siberia. There even is a tiger depicted on the map of the central part Siberia, which is marked out as the territory of Russia on a geographical map of the world.

In fact there had never been tigers in Siberian taiga and the only place where they dwell is the Far East. This type of tiger got its "Siberian" name because it is capable of surviving in conditions of snowy frosty winters, which exist in this area. So lotus, ginseng, and Siberian tiger are the symbols of Primorsky Krai and are depicted on the flags and emblems of many towns of that region. Besides the flora and fauna, there are many historic towns in Primorsky Krai, each of which is striking with its history and places of interest.

This is why, my impressions from visiting Vladivostok, which is an administrative centre of Primorsky Krai, will always be in my memory.

Vladivostok is situated on the seashore of the Sea of Japan and is considered to be the biggest Russian city and port on the Pacific Coast. I had dreamt of going to Vladivostok for a long time, but I never had the opportunity, because the town had been closed for 30 years and in order to get there a citizen of the USSR had to have a special permission.

Only in 1988, during the period of glasnost, was Vladivostok opened for entry by the Soviet citizens and it was still closed to foreigners up to 1992. So, at the beginning of 1989, when I was choosing a place for improving my health again, I chose the Shmakovka Spa Resort, and not because it is famous for its therapeutic water but also because I wanted to see those mysterious places and visit Vladivostok.

After I had arrived at the sanatorium, I bought a two-day bus excursion to Vladivostok, which was situated over 300 kilometres to the south of the resort. After we had been travelling for several hours and at about dusk, I felt myself tired and sleepy but then the bus driver suddenly switched on a tape-recorder with the recording of a song about Vladivostok. This song, was sung by a well-loved singer called Alla Pugacheva, and was very popular at that time and I thought that the driver was inviting us to sing along with it, as we had sung other songs.

But within a couple of minutes the bus stopped and a panorama of Vladivostok city by night was opened up in front of us and which was breathtakingly beautiful, it was so beautiful that tears began to fall from my eyes. The bus stopped on the brow of a hill and one could see the lights of the whole city Vladivostok spread out beneath us together with the Gold Horn Bay, where the docks were situated.

I couldn't believe that my dream had come true at last, and that I was in the city, which was such a mystery for many people, and due to its distance from the central regions of the country, was out-of-reach for most. For two days we visited various interesting locations in the city, the river port, a museum on a submarine named C-56, and visited many other historical places in the city. Most of all I remembered an excursion to a railway station, during which a guide told me about the history of the construction of the Great Siberian Railway and some interesting facts about it.

Quite frankly, before visiting Vladivostok, I had known very little about the Great Siberian Railway and wasn't much interested in it, although one summer in 1986 I had even used it to get from Novosibirsk city to Omsk, where I had my cooperative flat. I didn't attach any particular importance to this railway journey back then, and it was just an ordinary train journey for me, and one on which I only spent a couple of hours.

During this short trip, however, I was amazed by the fact that there were many citizens of China on the train, and who one by one went to wash themselves in the toilet with their nice terry towels on their shoulders, while we Russians all used the towels which were a part of the bedclothes set, which was standard issue on trains.

I was struck by the fact that the construction of the Great Siberian Railway lasted for more than 25 years and was finished in 1916, a year before the beginning of the Russian Revolution.

It's interesting to note that at the ceremony on the occasion of the beginning of construction of the railway, which was held in Vladivostok in

1891, Prince Nikolai Alexandrovich, a future tsar of Russia, Nikolai II was in attendance.

The construction of the Great Siberian Railway continued during the Soviet period as well, when branches from the main line were constructed all over the territory and even abroad into China and Mongolia.

This way the Great Siberian Railway travels almost the whole length of the country becoming the longest railway in the world. The length of the main railway line from Moscow to Vladivostok is 9298 kilometres (5810 miles) and passengers taking this route are travel for 7 days. And, of course, I couldn't miss an opportunity, whilst in Vladivostok, to visit one of the local markets, which were famous all over the country.

I'd heard a lot about them from the stories told by my work colleagues, but what I saw exceeded all my expectations. At this time at the end of 1980s, when there was a total shortage of consumer's goods, there was everything that one might want and even more. I felt myself as if I had arrived at a totally different world – the world of wonders; one could buy there freely everything one wanted. Almost all the goods there were imported by seamen from Japan, China, etc.

I bought many amazing things for myself and my family: sneakers, jumpers, jeans (the most hard-to-get thing!), Japanese dresses and many other things for which I had money, and I felt terribly sorry that I had taken so little money with me.

I had admired the Far East since 1970s, when I studied at the University of Law in Khabarovsk, but after that last trip to Primorsky Krai and a visit to Vladivostok, the most pleasant recollections about this amazing region are left in my memory.

Chapter 35

What Glasnost Gave Us

In order to give you a better idea of the way Glasnost changed our lives, I need to tell you, first of all, about the way we had lived before the period of Restructuring and Glasnost. So, since the moment the USSR was formed, ideological work had been carried out by the communist party and the issues of propaganda and agitation were under their control. Only the Party decided what people needed to know and what was unnecessary for them to know, that is why some periods of our history were taboo, and many historical facts were concealed.

These concerned the period of Stalin's repressions, the starvation in the country during 1930-33 years, the war in Afghanistan, the Chernobyl nuclear power plant accident and the other incidents that took place in the country and took the lives of thousands of Soviet people. In the USSR the means of distributing propaganda such as the daily press, radio, TV, and books were under the control of all-union and departmental committees of the communist party.

Besides the fact that some topics weren't published at all, every single article in a newspaper, a magazine, a radio broadcast and TV-programmes were checked and corrected at the pleasure of members of the committee. Many works of Soviet and nonconformist writers, which, in the committee members' judgment "disagreed with the party's ideology and were directed towards an undermining of the Soviet government," had been under a ban for a long-long time, although the works presented the reality of life in the country.

Listening to the radio broadcastings of the BBC and Voice of America was prohibited, but despite that some people listened to them regularly, and knew what was going on in the country earlier than the media announced it. All the central newspapers and magazines published articles about the state of affairs in our country, and the countries of the socialist camp. We got very little information about life in the capitalist countries, and even if there were some articles published about them they were generally negative.

This was so that we could compare their "unbearable" life with our life and be happy that we lived in the best country in the world. Here is a verse from one of the popular patriotic songs which had been familiar to everybody since childhood:

Broad My Dear Country Is
Containing many fields and woods and rivers
Don't know if another one exists
Where man can breathe so freely

And that is true, we really didn't know anything about the other countries because had no opportunity to find out anything about them. Even those people who were abroad by the nature of their occupation or on the tourist trips couldn't tell the truth because when they left the country they had to give a written undertaking not to admire what they had seen after their arrival.

I personally had never been to the capitalist countries, but I had been to Bulgaria twice – the first time was in 1976 when I had a tourist voucher, and the second time in 1989 I vacationed in the Sandansky Spa resort which is situated in the south-west of Bulgaria. Our countries were on friendly terms and people used to joke that it wasn't a foreign country at all – that it was one of our republics, everything was the same there as in the USSR.

Yes, Bulgaria was one of the countries of a socialist camp and life of those people resembled ours, but it wasn't quite the same. Except for the sightseeing, I, being a woman, was interested in how people lived there, and I saw that there was always plenty of foodstuff and consumer goods. It was especially evident in 1989 when the shelves at our shops were empty. That is why I think everybody had something to say after going abroad, but we preferred to keep quiet.

The spheres of intellectual life such as theatre, cinema, music, art, etc., were supervised, and had to reflect only the positive aspects of life in the country, and were aimed at the education of the population in a spirit of communist morality. It was prohibited to mention topics like repressions against people, international problems, drug addiction, prostitution and sex. After movies had been checked, the parts which members of the committee didn't like had to be cut out or remade, and some of the movies were simply banned. When the lyrics of songs, stand-up comedy scripts and repertory concerts were checked, preference was given to those acts which contained patriotic material.

Any item of western culture such as movies, music, or fiction was also interdicted as well. I have to say that we could get some entertainment from abroad, but after all kinds of checks that it didn't contain any information about real life abroad we did not have much choice; we watched what they showed us. For example, cinemas showed mainly French and Italian comedies or movies made according the works of classics. There were many Indian

227

melodramas; all people cried together while watching them. It is funny to remember it now, but I always took a handkerchief with me when I went to watch such a movie, because I had to cry.

I liked foreign pop music very much, which was broadcasted on the radio and TV and some of the singers and pop-bands came to us with concerts. A generation from the 1970-80s remembers popular Italian singers: Robertino Loreti, Toto Cutugno, Adriano Celentano; French singers: Joe Dassin, Mireille Mathieu; pop-bands: Abba (Switzerland), Boney M (Germany), The Beatles (Great Britain). The Beatles, though, had been banned in our country for a long time and only at the beginning of 1970s did we get an opportunity to listen to some of their songs.

But all the same, the western world was closed for us officially, and everything that could be sneaked across the border (forbidden fiction, magazines, movies, rock-music, and clothes) was considered to be contraband and criminals were given appropriate penalties. It was the way we lived, we had been trained to be orderly and to keep up traditions and decorum that had been developed over the years since childhood, and were happy. We knew for sure what we could do and what was forbidden, but at the time of Restructuring everything began to change in leaps and bounds.

Glasnost brought so much that was new and unusual to our lives that it was hard to understand it all. Despite the fact that Mikhail Gorbachev used to speak about the necessity of "new ways of thinking" in the country, for the majority of ordinary people it was hard to conceive and accept what was going on and some of them didn't want to. During the period of Restructuring and Glasnost, as my mother used to say, "The bottom was knocked out of the world," and she was right in some way.

In the course of changes that took place in the country, supervision by the bodies of propaganda and agitation was reduced. A resolution "About Glasnost" was adopted in July 1988 at the 19th All-union conference of the CPSU, censorship was all but abolished. Since that moment on, something unbelievable had been going on in the country, under a slogan "We don't have anything to conceal from people," and we were frothed up with all the information, which had been concealed during the previous years.

After Mikhail Gorbachev had allowed access to secret archives, mass media began to talk over tragic periods of the history of the country, using newly discovered facts, proved by documents and statistical data. It wasn't even possible to talk about it earlier and that is why we knew nothing of it. At that moment, when we found out the scale of the past events, people were shocked again, and began to consider political repressions a crime against the nation; they began to demand a restoration of justice and penalty for those who were guilty.

So far as the events took place long ago there weren't any – so the communist party was blamed for it. After getting their liberty, the media began to use new forms of work, unknown for us earlier. For example, there appeared live radio and TV programmes, where the burning issues of the day which people cared about were discussed. New programmes like "The projector of Restructuring" and "Glance", which reflected the course of restructuring, its positive and negative sides were very popular.

There were live broadcastings of The Peoples Deputies' sessions as well as CPSU Congresses and Conferences. Peoples' politicking was on the rise, everybody wanted to listen to and watch what was going on as it was actually happening and not after it was edited to just show what the party wanted. For the first time for many years party bodies began to work openly, involving people of the country to the process of restructuring as well.

Press bodies began to publish works of Soviet and foreign writers which had been forbidden before. For the first time Oleksander Solzhenitsyn's work "Archipelago Gulag" and Boris Pasternak's novel "Doctor Zhivago", which were well-known abroad and out-of-reach for soviet people, were published.

Cinemas began to show the movies, which had been banned earlier and of which we had no knowledge. A sign on the posters 'Movies which were forbidden earlier' attracted viewers, but very often after viewing them we didn't find anything that could give cause for banning them for so many years.

There also appeared new movies where the earlier forbidden topics were revealed. We watched a movie about Stalin's repressions with a heavy heart; it was called *The cold summer of 53rd*. There were the other ones as well such as *A collapse* about the accident at the Chernobyl nuclear plant, *Two steps to silence* about the war in Afghanistan etc., which reflected truthful events of those periods. Glasnost and liberty of speech entering our lives changed the Soviet ideology, our minds, ideals and universal values.

When a film about prostitution *An inter-girl*, about a prostitute servicing foreigners; *Small Vera* about sex, were viewed for the first time, they caused mixed reactions in people, because we had not been used to talking about these topics earlier and it had been considered that there was no prostitution or drug addiction in our country. Here's an interesting fact: the word "sex" entered into our vocabulary only during the period of Glasnost, and it was associated with the word "pornography" as there was no pornography, therefore, there wasn't any sex as well.

There was sex, of course, but it was called in a different way in everyday life: "to make love" or "to sleep with each other"; and called "sexual intercourse" in medicine. There were also many swear words, which were used to talk about close relationships between a man and a woman. There were very many more events in the country which caused joy and perplexity at the same time, but there wasn't time enough to reconsider it all and we just accepted everything as it was.

I was really shocked when a ban on everything that arrived from Western countries ended. As the saying goes, Glasnost opened a "Window to the West" and everything which had been out-of-reach for almost 70 years began to arrive in the country, like information about the life in the capitalist countries, western culture, and imported goods from the West. While telling you about this period I'll always have to repeat a phrase "For the first time".

So, foreign series (soap operas) were shown on TV screens for the first time, we had had no idea of those before. The first ones were *The slave girl Izaura* (Brazil), *The rich also cry* (Mexico) as well as the series from USA which were shown later *Dynasty* and *Santa Barbara*, they became a sensation and made a revolution in our minds. Viewing TV-series distracted us from everyday life with its problems, and we got to a totally different world for a couple of minutes, with its culture and traditions.

When I talked over the series with my friends and colleagues we admired everything we saw there: their lifestyles, houses, cars, behaviour, and the clothes they wore. Unfortunately we hadn't anything like that at that time it was simply out-of-reach for us.

Commercials appeared for the first time on TV, which we took very seriously and trusted everything we were shown. For example, the first McDonalds restaurant in the USSR, which was opened in 1990 in Moscow, was widely advertised and in this period of total shortage of food and empty shelves in the shops we got an opportunity to eat the same way as abroad with an unusual system of service and incredibly tasty food.

Thousands of people went to the restaurant during the day and that is why one had to stand for an hour or more in a queue in order to get served. Sometimes Police even kept order of the queue.

I often passed through Moscow and due to long queues I couldn't get to the restaurant and it was not until ten years later that I managed to eat at a McDonalds opened in Kiev in 1997, where there were no queues of course. I was not sure whether it was worth waiting ten years for, but at least it was something different to the standard fare served in Ukraine at that time.

A German fashion magazine "Burda" appeared in our country for the first time as well, where patterns were attached which could be changed to different sizes. This was unbelievable for us! Using those patterns, even the women who had no experience began to sew clothes for themselves. It was good that we had plenty of good and various fabrics to sew from even in the period of Restructuring.

For me personally, the appearance of the magazine was a big event, because I had sewn for all my life and made patterns myself.

Though I had experience and imagination, the magazine "Burda" was of great help for me in sewing clothes. I used to sew everything for myself: coats, jackets, business suits, and bags and I was always dressed up better than others and thought I had everything.

At about this time a friend brought to me at work a German magazine which she brought with her after acquiring it during a vacation in Moscow. "Here's an interesting magazine from Germany, she said, "I will let you have it until tomorrow only, because many other people want to see it as well. Please don't give it to anybody else, as it was brought from abroad illegally." The magazine was very heavy (more than 500 pages) and in German.

I couldn't read a word from it, because I didn't know German. At first I thought it to be a fashion magazine, but after I began to turn over the pages I realized it was something else, because there were several parts: clothes, furniture, curtains, dishes, electrical devices etc. of course, I couldn't work anymore that day– I locked the doors of my office and was paging through the magazine till the end of the working day. I admired the beautiful, fashionable, elegant clothes, and noted that everything was chosen to match in all the different colours.

And what curtains! Those were art actually. It was hard even to imagine such furniture, carpets, dishes, electrical devises which I saw there. It would be better if I hadn't seen the magazine at all, because after I had seen it, my furniture, clothes which I considered to be beautiful seemed to me to be drab and insignificant. At that moment I felt miserable and unhappy and I wanted to cry.

My friend took the magazine from me in the morning, and in reply to my question told me that it was a list of items that could be chosen and ordered in the magazine. "Look, there are pages at the end of the magazine which can be filled in and sent by post to the address, and the items will be delivered to your home," she explained. "I would order everything they have here!" I exclaimed, and got even more depressed.

At the same time as "Glasnost" was being introduced, customs supervision was reduced for the first time and private individuals were allowed to bring goods from abroad up to a certain amount of money. And there appeared imported goods at once in the country from different foreign countries, especially Japanese and Korean TVs and tape recorders made by Sony, JVC, and Panasonic etc. Japanese electrical devices were delivered to out village from Vladivostok and were distributed among the enterprises. Of course not everybody was lucky enough to buy some of those, but those who did, invited friends afterwards to have a look them.

In the central regions of the country, imported electrical devices were sold freely in the commission shops, and despite the fact they cost very much they were in heavy demand and were bought up quickly. I personally bought in 1989 a Japanese Sony tape recorder for my son in St. Petersburg, which cost 2000 roubles. It wasn't a big amount of money for me because my salary in the North was 1000 roubles per month plus that of my husband, but where did people get the money when average salary was 80-150 roubles per month.

It was a mystery for me. I think money must have been saved up because there had been a shortage of goods before and there hadn't been much to buy during earlier times.

A real revolution took place in the country when the first video tape recorders were imported to the country; they changed not only our consciousness but also introduced a lot of new horizons into our lives. Their appearance brought video-movies from abroad which were forbidden previously. Here video theatres began to open all over the country by leaps and bounds. Any small rooms that could contain 50-100 people were used for the purpose. They were everywhere: in the basements of apartment houses, in the clubs, in the temporary buildings constructed for the purpose.

There were video theatres even in the airports and train-stations, where passengers could view a movie while waiting for their transport. Signboards "Video theatre" and "Video club" attracted very many viewers like a magnet, especially youth and teenagers. All the movies were translated into the Russian language in low quality with usually only one voice, but with the low quality it was often impossible to make out the text, but no one complained. It was more important for us to see what was on the screen than to hear.

Pornographic movies were sneaked across the border along with the video films, but only people who had video tape recorders could watch them. Friends would gather at the house of someone with a recorder and watched pornographic movies together. In the beginning men and women watched separately, because it was embarrassing to watch it for the first time together.

I think that everybody was shocked after viewing a porn-film for the first time and many of them were embarrassed even to admit that they had already seen such movies. Soon porn-movies spread all over the country very quickly, and they were shown at video theatres during late-night shows, although they were banned officially. Special commissions were created which checked the repertoire and had right to close the video theatres if they found porno movies. Later they were allowed to be shown officially at nightclubs, which were opened all over the country as well.

One more very important event which changed our lives forever took place during the period of Glasnost. For the first time in the existence of the USSR, we were allowed to go abroad! It was hard to believe, but since 1987 any citizen, if one wanted to, could get a foreign passport and go freely abroad. This was an incredible event for us and a proof that changes for the better on rights and freedoms were really taking place in the USSR.

Since that moment Visa and Registration Offices, which executed foreign passports, visas and invitations for foreign citizens, were opened all over the country. There were huge queues at these Visa and Registration Offices, which worked the same way the queues for carpets and furniture had done, that is with a roll call during night time.

A stir was caused also by the fact that people were allowed to import and export consumer goods while crossing the border, which was the main reason for many mass trips abroad. In order to get a visa one had to have an invitation from a private person of a country one wanted to go to.

People who live near the borders of Poland, Hungary, Bulgaria, Romania, Finland and Norway began to go to those countries regularly in order to export their goods for sale and import from there other goods or foreign currency.

There was a shortage of consumer goods in the country at that time and a coupon system for the main types of food was introduced, many of which were home-produced, these products were unpopular among population but they filled the shelves of the stores.

As soon as the borders were opened, people began to export almost everything; they even took everything they could from their own homes, sheds and attics: old things, the dishes, tools, nails, home appliances, bulbs, notebooks, ballpoint pens, spare parts of cars, and even homemade products. Because these goods were cheaper than those in the other countries – they were sold there like hot cakes and brought profit for the people involved, but the mass export of goods wrecked the country's economy even more and led to the situation were shops were empty and their shelves were covered with paper in order not to be dusted.

I found out about the trips abroad for the first time in 1989, from my husband's relatives in Chernovtsy, when I visited them on my way back from holiday. They had travelled to Poland together with their friends on a regular basis for two years and during that time they had earned dollars and brought many stylish and beautiful clothes for all the members of their family. I understood that I had failed to keep pace with them while living in Yakutia because no one had a foreign passport in our village, and no one made such commercial trips. "If you have a foreign passport, we can take you with us," they promised.

After I arrived back home I went to a police station right away, where they issued Soviet passports and asked about a foreign one, but without any hope of getting one. Luckily, it was very easy to get the foreign passport in our village. All the needed documents were sent to a Visa and Registration Office in Yakutsk and in 10 days they sent me a passport. I was so happy, that I wanted to share this with some of my friends. On my way home I met a work colleague and showed her my passport and told her that I could go abroad anytime I wanted.

She was amazed at that, looked at me distrustfully, picked at it for a while and gave it back to me. "Are you serious? Don't show it to anyone nor talk about this," she said and went quickly on her way. I understood the difference among people who lived in the main centres and those who lived in such distant villages like ours, who continued to be afraid of everything and accepted the changes that took place in the country with misgiving during the period of Glasnost and Restructuring.

During the period of glasnost attitudes to religion were changed, too. Before, the USSR was an anti-religious state, where religion was officially prohibited, it was considered to be incompatible with the soviet ideology and the party's policy, which was pursued in the country. In the period of revolution and formation of the new Soviet state, they tried to eradicate religion and a special persecution was aimed at the Russian Orthodox Church. Crosses and domes were flung down, the buildings of the church were destroyed, even those which were of historical value, all over the country in big cities and small villages.

Thousands of churches and cloisters that escaped destruction were closed and handed over at command of local authorities together with their property, who used them their own way.

In this connection, the buildings of the church were reconstructed according to different needs: clubs, libraries, museums, warehouses, hospitals, plants, kindergartens, flats. For example, there is a Roman Catholic Church in the centre of Chernovtsy which is of historic value and was used as an archive during the soviet period.

Several years ago I was at an excursion in one of the small towns of Lvov Oblast (Western Ukraine), where we were shown a cloister, where there was a military hospital, a warehouse for keeping agricultural products, and even a stable in different periods of history. Antireligious propaganda was introduced by the communist party.

They used a slogan which was known all over the country "Religion is the opium of the people" and that is why school and party were separated from church. When I studied at school we were all regarded to be atheists and we were entered to Octobrists and Pioneers, without asking for our personal approval.

All the religious traditions, customs, holidays were regarded to be the survivals of the past and were condemned by the society, even the tradition of christening a child. Of course many people continued to keep up traditions and christened children secretly. All the members of our family were christened in a church and when my son was born my mother took him to a small village church which was far from our town to christen him. Of course I wasn't against this but I didn't take part in the business and didn't tell anyone about this.

A church wedding ceremony was also regarded to be a survival of the past and I don't remember a single event, when some of my relatives or friends did it. Elderly people, especially those who lived in villages, were more religious. They kept up the religious traditions and had icons at their homes, which hung in the corner of the room. Even the holidays like Easter weren't celebrated. In the central part of the country, especially in the villages, people backed Paskha (sweet cakes eaten at Easter), and elderly people went to the church for a ceremony.

I remember when I was a child my grandmother always brought us Paskha and painted eggs and it was a great joy for us, but since she was gone neither I nor my mother have done it.

One would think that a generation of soviet people who grew up in such conditions was really supposed to be atheists. But this wasn't so, because everybody treated religion in their own way. My parents advised me not to engage in controversy with anybody about the question whether there is God or not, to trust or not to trust in God.

It was interesting that we asked God for help when we were ill or got to some hard-to-solve situation. Even at school and high school one could hear students whispering "God save me", "God help me". No one taught us to say those things, but almost everybody did, because we all were orthodox believers and we were born with faith in God in our souls and no one could take it from us. As a result of reforms that took place in the period of restructuring in the USSR, people got their liberty and many rights which had been limited earlier and since that moment the attitude to religion has fundamentally changed.

There began a renaissance of religion, which developed quickly because people were trying to recover lost ground as soon as possible. Churches and cloisters were used according to their intended purpose, the destructed ones were rebuilt, and the construction of the new ones began everywhere in towns and especially in villages, many of which were constructed by means of people who lives in the territory. There appeared pious literature at once: prayer books, orthodox calendars, many different icons, candles and other stuff which could be bought in churches.

Christening of children became necessary and even grown up people who hadn't been christened earlier went through the ceremony. Church wedding ceremony took on special significance and became a symbol of love and God's blessing of the family and that is why not only the newly married couples but also those who had lived together for many years got married in church. Centuries-old traditions and customs of the Russian people came back: the ceremony of Easter celebration, services on religious holidays, which we hadn't even known before.

Many people, as well as myself, hadn't been to church before that and didn't know what to do there, where to put candles, how to cross ourselves correctly and we had to learn how to do this. There appeared a special attitude to church after the USSR breakdown when people survived a hard period in their lives. After they had lost everything: a country, faith in authorities, faith in the party, job, money, hopes for better life, people came to church. This is the way human beings live, they have to trust somebody and have faith in something and at that moment God was the only one to go with their hopes for rescue and help to.

Chapter 36

The Reforms of International Foreign

Policy

A reform of the political system was considered to be the main direction to start the restructuring, because during the existence of the USSR some problems had accumulated and it was impossible to move forward without solving these. There was a great deal of work ahead in changing international relations, foreign military policy, and political system inside of the country. In order to understand what the political climate had been like earlier you would have to look at the terms which had been used in the USSR: "Cold War", "Iron Curtain", "armament race", "nuclear war", "testing of nuclear weapons", etc.

Those were words used in the media while discussing the political issues and were buzz words for the population, and were also the topics discussed between colleagues and relatives. The idea that our country was in danger from the capitalist countries and that there was the possibility of attack at any moment had been instilled in us since childhood. A course in civil defense was introduced at all the primary schools and we were taught how to use the gas masks and other protection facilities and how to render first aid to injured people. We were trained to be ready in case of a military attack and be able to protect both our Motherland and ourselves.

The more serious topics connected to nuclear and chemical weapons were studied at the institutions of secondary and higher education at "Military science" lessons. Civil defence stations were organized in every town, this course of action involved all the grown up population and even the housewives. I remember that several times somebody from the local building-utilities administrator office (ZhEK) came to our house and tried to force my mother to study in a group of housewives, but she didn't go there.

The "Iron curtain" fell during the period of restructuring and glasnost and since that time truthful information about western countries had been opened and we understood that in most of the cases what we had been told about threats from the West was propaganda and the situation was stirred up artificially. It was becoming clear that the foreign policy which had been pursued in the USSR had outlived its usefulness and it couldn't continue the same way anymore.

This promoted the fact that as a result of a political reform, implemented in a period of restructuring, the foreign policy course was changed from that of opposing the capitalist countries' ideologies to one of understanding and cooperation. In this policy Mikhail Gorbachev called it a "New way of thinking" and deciding the issues which were of great importance not only to our country but to the whole world. He was the first one of all the general secretaries of the CPSU that managed to stop, at least for a while, the armaments race on which a great piece of the annual state budget was spent.

This spending by the military was used for the purposes of creating and testing of nuclear weapons and not for the rise of living standards of people.

For the purpose of prevention of nuclear war Mikhail Gorbachev in 1985 declared unilaterally, a moratorium on nuclear testing in the USSR, and later made statements about a full liquidation of nuclear weapons in the whole world. In order to solve different political issues, Mikhail Gorbachev organized regular meetings with the leaders of capitalist countries – Ronald Reagan, George Bush, Margaret Thatcher etc.

This was the time when our life was full of changes and these events happened for the first time. This way we found out for the first time the truth about the life in capitalist countries and saw their leaders, some of them during their visits to the USSR. We couldn't even imagine, before the restructuring, that the leaders of capitalist countries, which had constituted a menace for us, would pay a friendly visit to our country.

The prime minister of Great Britain, Margaret Thatcher, impressed us the most; she visited our country twice during the period of restructuring. First of all we were amazed at the fact that a woman could be a leader of a capitalist country. At this time I worked at the district committee of the communist party and many of my colleagues tried to dress and look exactly as Margaret Thatcher did. I personally admired the way she behaved, spoke and was elegantly dressed with taste. At that time we knew very little about Great Britain and could judge this country only by Margaret Thatcher.

From the very beginning of his time in office, Mikhail Gorbachev had raised the question about the ending of the war in Afghanistan, which had taken the lives of thousands of soldiers many of which were 18-20 years old. There was still Conscription Law in the USSR at this time, and all young men aged 18 were called up to serve in the Soviet Army, practically kids who had just graduated from secondary school.

As a rule they had taken military training for 6 months and were sent straight to Afghanistan afterwards. This had lasted for 10 years (since 1979 till 1989) and the quantity of soldiers who had died there over this period had been concealed from us, but there were many thousands of them for sure. I think that it would be hard to find on the map at least one town where they had not buried soldiers, who had died in Afghanistan. Every mother who had a growing up son was worrying about the possibility of him being sent to fight in Afghanistan.

When my son graduated from a secondary school in 1987 and was preparing for the recruitment into the army I couldn't sleep at night and asked God to save my son. Soon my son got call-up papers with the date and time of his departure and together with other men from the area was scheduled to depart from the local airport at Zaranka to Yakutsk where there was a centre which allocated them to other military regions of the country.

The procedure of seeing off to the army in Yakutia was much simpler than in Ukraine, maybe because the situation there was different or maybe people just began to treat many events and traditions differently during the time of restructuring. We organized a small party at our house one day before the departure and invited only close friends of ourselves and those of my son. The next day we came to the airport where there were the other men due for call-up: classmates of my son and his school friends.

I thought that there would be an official departure as was usual, with congratulations and wishes of a military commissar, but there wasn't anything like that. A military commissar came a couple minutes before the departure of the plane apparently just to check that all who were due for call up were present. He counted them, twelve all together, and ordered them to get on the plane. Everything happened so fast that I didn't have any time to say anything special to my son, to wish him anything or to cry; I just hugged him quickly and he ran to the plane.

After the plane had taken off and became hidden behind the clouds, together with my husband I went home, we were both exhausted and couldn't even discuss the topic. That was it, I thought, my son was taken from me and would be sent to Afghanistan and I would never see him again. He could be ordered to serve in some other place, but the worse scenario was in my mind. I was waiting to hear at least something from my son.

Within a couple of days he wrote that he was in Yakutsk at the centre of placement and from where he and his group would be sent off to a paratrooper school, from where soldiers would be sent to Afghanistan or Mongolia after 6 months of studying. There was not another message from him for a month and one can imagine what I went through while I was waiting for the next letter. He wrote in his next letter that they had been kept in Yakutsk for a long time, because they were waiting for further instructions.

When these instructions finally arrived they were orders to send them to serve as airborne troops in Chita region, which was situated in the south-east part of Siberia and bordered with China and Mongolia. The distance from Moscow to Chita is more than 6000 km and from our village of Zyryanka is around 3300km. His actual posting was at Bezrechnaya Military area which was several kilometres away from the meeting point of the borders of three countries: Russia, China and Mongolia.

There is an extremely hard continental climate at that place, the summers are hot and a winter brings 40 degrees of frost and strong winds. During the first year of our son's service he contracted hepatitis and during the practice parachute jumps he got kidney infection and was hospitalised. We immediately made arrangements to travel to our son's base to help him if needed. His military unit was situated in a small village where there were very few local people and mostly families of military men lived there.

That is why there was a school, a library, a kindergarten, a small shop and some other buildings. When I saw my son it was hard to recognize him because I sent a normal strong man to the army and at that moment I saw an ill and a very thin soldier, as they say "all horn and hide". My husband and I settled into a guest house for the four days during which we were allowed to stay and which was situated not far from the hospital. The living conditions here were bad and despite the fact that it was late autumn and very cold there was no heating and we both couldn't sleep very well because of the cold.

During this time we visited our son every day and brought him and all the other soldiers that were with him in the ward some home-cooked meals that we had brought from home together with any other necessities that were available from the small local shops. On my return I had very bad memories about visiting this military unit and the hospital because after I had seen the conditions in which my son had to serve, I began to worry even more than I did before.

I didn't know how people managed to lived there and what they ate because there wasn't anything except candies and out of date biscuits in the shop. I was very glad to leave that place and never have to go there. Soon the service conditions of my son became better, because after leaving the hospital he was sent to the road-construction forces in the central part of Russia, not far from Moscow, where he served for another year.

I found out later that the fate of our son had already been decided whilst he was still in the Yakutsk placement centre as a decision about military withdrawal from Afghanistan was adopted at this time, and that is why my son was sent to serve in those other places. This way, thanks to Mikhail Gorbachev and the foreign international policy reform, my son served his two years in the army and came back home unhurt.

After the ending of the war in Afghanistan, there began a Soviet troop pullout from all the republics of the socialist camp: Mongolia, Czechoslovakia, GDR, Poland, Hungary, etc. It is known that Soviet troops had been in those countries for external defence purposes and maintenance of order since the ending of the World War II.

The restructuring in the USSR and the ending of confrontation between the Eastern and Western countries, as well as the extension of political rights and freedom in the countries of socialist camp led to the situation when further deployment of the troops in these countries lost its point. This restructuring in the USSR stirred up almost all the Eastern European countries, where socialist way of development was imposed by force.

These Eastern European countries were given the opportunity to decide a political system for themselves, and they, one by one, abandoned socialist regimes and stripped the communist governments of power. In particular the political changes in Germany, which resulted in the destruction of the Berlin Wall, resonated around the world. This construction, built in 1961, divided the city of Berlin and Germany into two countries: the Federal Republic of Germany was in its western part and German Democratic Republic was in the eastern one.

The Berlin Wall had been guarded by frontier troops for many years and the citizens of Germany who lived on both sides couldn't visit their relatives and friends and had no right to travel between the two countries. For all those years, Germans had sought reunification of their country, but it only became possible after the changes in the international policy of the USSR and European Socialist countries. You have to hand it to Mikhail Gorbachev who didn't interfere with the events that took place in Germany and showed sympathetic understanding of the wishes of its citizens. So after 28 years, in November 1989, the Berlin Wall was destroyed and Germany became a single state a year afterwards.

In this way, the restructuring of foreign policy in the USSR and the events which took place in this connection in the other communist countries led to a break-up of the socialist camp and adoption of capitalist executive system by the countries of Eastern Europe. Mikhail Gorbachev's efforts, in the normalisation of international relations, prevention of the threat of nuclear war, and the introduction of rights and freedom, were appreciated by the international community and in 1990 he was awarded with a Nobel Peace Prize.

Chapter 37

The Economic Reforms During

Restructuring

Many people thought that problems in the socio-economic development of the USSR arose after the ending of Brezhnev Era, that is, after his death in 1982. It was then that Golden times in the country finished and living standards began to worsen quickly, but, in my opinion, the process had started earlier.

At least, consumer goods provision became worse, notably in 1980, during the time of staging the Moscow Olympic Games and immediately after it. In the central cities, such as Moscow, St. Petersburg etc., everything was as before, but in the other regions of the country, products which could have been bought easily earlier were in short supply. We connected the changes in the country for the worse with the costs for staging of the Olympic Games and believed that everything would come back to normal soon.

But since that moment the situation in the country worsened steadily, and it was not to return to the way it had been earlier. Nothing changed for the better in the first years of General Secretary Mikhail Gorbachev's work of restructuring the country. On the contrary, shortage of many industrial goods and food had grown and it garnered people's unrest and panic.

People had money, but they couldn't buy what they needed, that is why they hunted through the shops and bought everything they could get just in case: thinking, 'What if it would be even worse tomorrow?' At that time I visited my parents and they had a cupboard full of matches, soap, light bulbs and the other small electrical goods, as well as foods, some flour, rice, tea, and biscuits, etc. They went to Donetsk in order to buy things, because supplies in their small mining town were so bad.

It was a bit easier for the rural population because they were farmers, they kept cows, pigs, chickens; they also grew vegetables and fruit. There were farm markets everywhere, that are farmers markets, but everything was bought up very quickly and the prices were much higher than in shops. Of course, we weren't hungry or undressed and we had enough money, but in order to maintain a normal family life, one needed to search for different sources for the necessities of life and throw much energy and time into the business of shopping.

This meant that people's lives became very busy, with little time for leisure activities. Instead of having a rest after work and staying a bit more at home, people went hundreds of kilometres away to the central cities and bought as much food as they could take with them. Sale restrictions were implemented in big cities in order to stop food outflow. For example: one person, irrespective of his/her family structure, could buy only 1 kg of flour and sugar and 500 grammes of sausages, butter, cheese etc.

That is why people stood in queues several consecutive times and went there with children, if that was possible, so that they, too, could queue separately and buy the same. Sometimes they persuaded a passing child with no connection to them to stand in the queue and help to buy something in exchange for some ice-cream or 100 gr of candies.

Sale restriction rules didn't function for a long time, because in spite of the rules products were bought up very fast and there weren't enough of them. There were empty shelves in many of the shops, and they were covered with paper in order not to become dusty.

In order to provide people with food, rationing by coupons was introduced; these were issued once a month, the quantity of coupons depending on the number of family members.

Some other methods for goods distribution were also used. In my village for example, coupons were raffled. When goods in short supply were delivered to a warehouse a number were allocated to each office or factory in the village where members of staff drew lots to be able to purchase one of the items. One person for example may have drawn a lot to purchase an iron, another person to buy bedclothes, etc. I remember when I jumped for joy when I took out a coupon to buy an electric cooker with an oven called 'Mechta' (a dream) – which was very popular at that time in the country and which was really a dream for any woman.

All over the country big queues could be seen, people formed long queues, often many hundreds of people long, especially in big cities just to put their name on a waiting list, so that they could buy a particular item when it was received into stock. Big queues formed, particularly at the shops where you could buy carpets, furniture, TVs and the other electrical devices. There were only certain times when the lists were open and only at these fixed times (2-3 days only), could people sign up to buy a certain item at this shop.

On the advertised dates for the opening of the lists to purchase, and as the queues began to form, another list was started to list the order in which people could enter the shop to put their name on the official list to purchase.

People could sign up on the first-come-first-served basis only, that is why rain or shine (even when it was frosty in winter), and people could stand there all day and all night. Family members usually changed with each other: some stood there during daytime and others at night. Names on the first list which entitled a person to enter the shop, when it was their turn, to put their name on the official list were checked at random intervals by the holder of the first list who was usually at the head of the queue.

These roll calls were often at night, and if someone was absent at the moment of a roll call he/she was simply stricken off the list, and therefore, could not then enter the shop and put their name on the official list to purchase. When the period ended for signing one's name on the official waiting list, the shop sent an official numbered notification for buying an item. Because the waiting list was long and the arrivals were limited, many people had to wait several years for the opportunity to buy.

Once I stood in such a queue, when there was a signing up for buying carpets and fur-coats in my village. There had always been a shortage of carpets. People used to hang carpets on the walls and that was a symbol of wealth. If you wanted to tell how good a family lived you could say, "Carpets are hanging all over the place."

Even here in the North, where the provision was quite good, it was almost impossible to buy a carpet, and after I had lived there for 15 years I had on my wall only an imitation of a carpet. Under extreme climate conditions, a fur-coat was a must-have, because only a fur-coat of genuine fur could keep you warm in severe frosts. Fur-coats were usually available for sale in our village of course, but during the period of restructuring they became in short supply.

Because such circumstances hadn't happened before in the village, people were excited and the event was broadcast on the radio and as this was considered an important function in my village, a committee was formed for the purpose of creating the waiting lists. This committee included not only workers from the shops, but also from the Council House. All the shops in the village were small and this necessitated the signing up for goods to be held at the gym.

Each family could get only one carpet and a woman only one fur-coat, that is why a signing up was conducted only according to passports. The population of the village was around six thousand, I don't know how many families this consisted at that moment in the village, but in my opinion every single villager came there, because everybody could use an extra carpet or fur-coat.

I remember it was the end of April, the temperature outside was above-zero and at night it was 10 degrees C below zero. Only a couple of people at one time were let into the gym, the others were standing in the stadium, which was situated in front of the gym. My husband flatly refused to take part in this arrangement, and I spent Saturday and Sunday alone in the queue, where I stood at night as well, because there were roll calls twice a night.

Between the roll calls I ran home to eat and warm myself for a while. I will never forget those two days that I spent in the queue. It is unpleasant for me even today to remember how people quarrelled and screamed at each other, everybody wanted to move forward by any means. It was humiliating for me, I was chilled to the bone and felt thoroughly miserable, but I wanted a carpet badly and *I* had to endure everything. In two years I bought the first carpet in my life and was exceedingly happy with it. I waited for five years to buy another fur-coat, but I left the North without getting one from this list.

I remember, we had been taught since school that a capitalist system was bad, because it was based on private property, exploitation of working people and appropriation of profit by individuals. There was a well-known term – "a rotting capitalism", that is, it had no future and it was doomed to failure. Only a country with developed socialism, a plan-based economy, a social ownership of means of production and a uniform distribution of incomes could ensure a socio-economic development of a society and satisfy the needs of working people.

But as events turned out everything happened vice-versa.

The socialist system, the very cornerstone and foundation of the country's economic development was failing to meet the needs and aspirations of the people and was in obvious need of radical reform. A transformation to a more market based economy in which supply and demand were more in line. In fact, an economy based on competition and freedom for individuals to be more self-supporting and able to develop ideas and private enterprises and profit from such endeavours. This was deemed to be necessary in order to save the country.

That is, during the period of Restructuring, the capitalist system's principles of development of economics were gradually being introduced. The first step in this direction was taken in November 1986, when a Law of the USSR "About an individual labour" was passed according to which the citizens were allowed to produce different goods for sale off duty and to provide paid services. The situation in the country forced it to replenish the market with consumer goods somehow.

People gladly accepted the law, because it had never been allowed earlier. Before the restructuring, producing home-made goods had been considered to be illegal and criminal.

After receiving permission for self-employment, many people began to sew clothes and shoes, to knit and to make souvenirs and to pay set taxes.

Goods made by private individuals appeared in markets at once, and those goods were in quite high demand. Everything that appeared in the market was bought up, because people produced goods according to their own tastes and designs, and these goods differed from those standard ones made at state-run enterprises which people were tired of.

This was now official policy, unlike my own early sewing work in Siberia which was strictly un-official and not sanctioned by the state. Many people became self-employed, not only in order to earn extra money, but also because some types of activity were traditional for them. For example local people of Yakutia produced hunting knives, fur-clothes, and souvenirs made of deer leather. Some regions of Western Ukraine specialized in making clothes of sheepskin fur, wooden souvenirs, traditional embroidered clothes, and amber paintings. Wedding dresses, flowers and candles were made in some villages of Chernovtsy region.

After receiving permission for self-employment from the government, people were eager to do any job which could bring extra earnings. Many people illegally and without registration began to make and sell home-made wine, compote, buns, cutlets and other types of food. In resort towns, where there were many holidaymakers, locals laid out on stalls, right in the streets in front of their houses, everything they could cook for sale.

In the markets, at the railway stations, in the trains and other public places, people were walking and selling hand-made bijouterie, vegetables, fruit and all kinds of food. During these hard times, everything was selling like hot cakes.

During 1987 – 1990 several laws were passed which were aimed at an initiation of radical changes and economic reforms. As is well known, before that, enterprises in the country had worked according to five-year governmental plans, and had produced goods according to an assortment approved by superior offices. The new laws abandoned central planning and allowed enterprises to choose by themselves what and how much to produce, how to sell it and how to divide the income.

That is, the enterprises became self-supporting and more independent. Since that moment, state enterprises stopped producing cheap planned goods and began to produce profitable goods which lead to breach of automatic procurement, dissolution of treaties among the enterprises and slowing of the economy. The laws which were passed one after another not only expanded the rights of the state-run enterprises, but also introduced progressive forms of market relations into the economy, which hadn't been used before in the country.

The law "About cooperation in the USSR" for example, passed at that time initiated the development of cooperatives, which were independent economic players and worked on the basis of official Charters. Introduction of cooperatives not only changed the economy, but also changed the lives of many citizens of the country forever, as well as mine. For the first time people got a right of choice – to work at the state-run enterprise (as they always did) or to found their own cooperative enterprises and work in a totally new way.

According to the law, cooperatives got a complete liberty in choosing a sphere of activity, in the creation of their own resource base, in the conclusion of contracts and in the distribution of profits. Cooperatives worked on the basis of Charters where their activities were defined. The Charters were discussed at the meetings of all the members of a cooperative and after that were approved by a majority vote.

With the beginning of private enterprise their evident advantages could be easily seen: people worked there with pleasure, disregarding the time, being their own bosses, which gave them an opportunity to get a good profit and high salary. This was all very contagious and favoured the swift founding of cooperatives in different fields: public services, commerce, construction, public catering, etc.

Several cooperatives appeared even in our small Northern village of Zyryanka, and the first one was a cooperative producing sausages. Though we had plenty of meat, sausages had been delivered to us from the central regions of the country. From that moment on, the cooperative supplied people with home-produced sausages, and it was very important for us, especially during the last years of Restructuring, when there was a complete shortage of food.

There was also a trade cooperative, which delivered imported consumer goods from Vladivostok by planes: tape-recorders, TVs, washing machines and other electronic devices. Of course this wasn't enough, but it was better than nothing. The workers of the social club founded a cooperative rendering services in organizing weddings, anniversaries, parties and other festive events. It was very popular because it was a tradition for us to celebrate all such events at a restaurant.

The idea of founding a cooperative was discussed everywhere – I discussed it at work with colleagues and at home with my husband. He advised me to leave my work at the party's district committee, because it wasn't prestigious to work there anymore, and to found a fashionable women's-wear sewing cooperative. Having quite a lot of experience in the field and many friends who liked my style of sewing, I would have had a great success.

But I liked my work and I couldn't leave it just like that, moreover I had a very good salary by that time. My husband then said, "If you don't want to have your own business, I will found a cooperative myself." A couple of weeks later he told me that he was going to start working at a construction cooperative, which he was going to found together with his friend on an equal basis. I was glad for him, because working as a chief superintendent engineer he used to have problems with the supply of materials, bureaucracy and the development of his team.

He didn't like to visit different meetings, commissions, and other arrangements held by district and executive committees, though it was his duty as a chief of the enterprise. He was a production worker by nature and liked to come down from generalities to particulars. The main activities of their cooperative, provided by the Charters, were manufacturing and construction of accommodation, logging and stocking of construction materials as well as other services. "Other services" meant that everything profitable and not interfering with the Soviet law was allowed.

At the beginning of its functioning, the cooperative bought a licence for processing salmon caviar (red caviar) in the Magadan region in order to earn money for creating a resource base. My husband went there with a team of workers in order to organize work and then to come back, but later he called to tell me that stocking of caviar was a crucial business and he had to stay there with his team till the end of the season.

There wasn't a single man in the cooperative that had any caviar processing experience that is why he hired locals – experts in the business. They rented a motor boat and other necessary equipment. He had been there for almost two months and I worried about him because I had no idea of the conditions he lived in.

At last he called me and told me he was in the village of Zyryanka already. "We brought a plane full of caviar with us, most of it in barrels and part of it in cans. How much of it do you want me to bring home? Until the moment we send it for sale I can take two of the three-litre jars home, will it fit into the fridge?" He asked. I almost jumped for joy. "Of course it will!" I answered. He brought not only two of the three-litre jars of caviar, but also plenty of canned fish and smoked-fish of different kinds.

I worried about him for nothing, because he looked as if he came back from a resort – he was tanned and had gained weight. Then he told me a lot about a fishing village and the people who lived there, about high and low tides of the gulf, where they were and about the way caviar was processed.

Of course, I had never heard about it before, and it was very interesting for me to find out, especially about the method of caviar processing.

When the salmon was caught, caviar was taken out of it, and small quantities of it was wrapped in gauze and dipped in bowls with salt water (brine). 5-10 minutes later it was taken out and hung for the water to drip out, and after that the caviar was ready.

"How interesting it was there! No wonder you didn't want to come back home!" I joked.

The red caviar (salmon roe) – the best Russian food

There were food shortages at that time so caviar was the mainstay of our diet. I only went to buy some fresh bread and butter for sandwiches. Caviar is a symbol of plenty in my country, and the most expensive delicacy.

I remember in the middle of 1970s, when I studied at the university in Khabarovsk, caviar was sold in shops by weight, and it was very cheap – 20 roubles per kilo. People came to the shops with their dishes (a jar or a cup) and bought as much as they wanted. In the villages situated on the shores of the River Amur, locals produced it by themselves and sold it for 10 roubles per kilogram.

I could also buy some caviar tinned in cans of 140 gr. They were sold in the fish-shops called "The Ocean" in Khabarovsk and Vladivostok, there was often a long queue though and you could buy only two cans at time. Suddenly, thanks to the cooperative, we had an opportunity to eat as much caviar as we wanted, a once in a lifetime experience. They say that Russians eat caviar with pancakes. I lived in the country and have never heard of it. Actually Russians ate it with a spoon or made sandwiches with butter and bread.

Of course processing and selling of caviar was a temporary business, because the cooperatives its main activity was accommodation construction. At first the cooperative constructed accommodation in the village for its workers and for sale, the wood for the purpose was logged 180km. away from the village of Zyryanka. Then a branch in Krasnodarsky Kray was opened, which was situated in the south of Russia and bordered with the republics of Caucasus.

With the opening of this branch, the cooperative began to develop very swiftly, and got a licence for logging in Siberia, in the region of a town called Yst-Kut, which was located on the Lena river of Irkutsk Region, where a team of loggers was sent. My husband began to deal with organizing wood procurement, and the arrangements for delivering it to Krasnodarsky Kray.

Since that moment, I almost hadn't seen him at home – he used to be with his team in Yst-Kut when they logged, and then escorted wood while travelling by rail from Siberia to North Caucasus and this was more or less constant for more than one year. Sometimes he came back to the cooperative on business and managed to visit me at home, but he always went away again.

When he went to work at the cooperative he dreamt of working for himself and earning more money, he achieved this, but he didn't have a normal life, because he wasn't the only one who worked this way, being inconsiderate of time and family, because the main purpose of the cooperative was now the expansion of production and income.

Thanks to the development of cooperative movements and the introduction of new forms of working, the quantity of housing cooperatives grew during this period, and this had a great influence on our family. Of course, the far bigger part of the housing stock in the USSR was public housing, which was available to all citizens for a nominal or token rent. Every person, in turn, could get a state-owned flat according to the place of residence or work.

During the twenty years of work in Siberia my family changed flats three times and improved our living conditions each time, and all the flats were given us for just a token rent. However, we had planned to go back to Ukraine soon and we needed a flat there. According to Northern benefits citizens had an opportunity to get a cooperative flat in the central regions of the country, before ending work in the north.

Such flats were constructed by using the money which people invested before the beginning of construction, and then paying the whole sum for 15-20 years, and after that the flat passed into their ownership. It was a similar scheme to that which building societies operated in the West. It was prestigious and safe to own a cooperative flat, because one could sell or exchange it at any time, but it was very hard to get one.

Due to the huge demand for this type of accommodation, there existed long queues that moved very slowly and one had to wait for at least a couple of years before being successful, and even then people didn't have the right to choose the exact location of the flat. Of course, in order for people living in the north to go back to their original home area, they often had to accept a flat in a different area and hope that they could then exchange it for a flat in the area in which they wished to live.

If they insisted on waiting for a flat in a particular area they would have to wait a long time and then may not be allocated a flat in the area they wanted after all. For example, my husband and I dreamt of going back to Chernovtsy, but when in 1987 it was our turn we were offered a flat in Omsk city which was in the centre of Siberia. We had no connections to that city and we had no intentions of living there, nevertheless we agreed to take the flat, hoping to exchange it later for the one in Chernovtsy or at least in any other city in Ukraine.

Chapter 38

The Restructuring of the USSR Political

System

I was very proud to work at the party regional committee during such an interesting period of the country's history, to take direct part in the processes of society's renovation, and this job became a sense of my life. This was the time of the beginning of the Restructuring, when new programmes and reforms aimed at society's reorganization were approved, and I hoped that thanks to them, that the situation in the country would get better.

But it turned out to be not so easy to put the intended measures into practice, because any adopted regulation which extended the rights and freedom of individual led to mass meetings, demonstrations and unrest. All this happened because during the time of the existence of the Soviet Union many questions had been solved by force and dictate, paying no regard to people's opinion, and as soon as glasnost and freedom of speech appeared everything that people had accumulated within themselves for so many years began to struggle its way outside.

For example, we thought that the issue of inter-ethnic relations in our country had been solved long ago, and that is why attention wasn't focused on this issue, and wasn't talked about. But life showed that this wasn't so because during different periods of the existence of the Soviet Union the rights and political liberties of many nations and even republics had been infringed. The issue of inter-ethnic relations began with the Baltic republics: Estonia, Latvia and Lithuania, which declared that in 1939 they were joined to the USSR illegally and against will of their people based on Molotov-Ribbentrop Pact.

Mass public demonstrations, involving thousands of people who demanded to cancel the Pact and restore national independence began in those republics. This gave the impulse for a worsening of inter-ethnic relations all over the country. Almost every republic regarded its political rights infringed upon and began to make different demands including independence. National and territorial conflicts in Georgia, Armenia, Azerbaijan, Moldavia and some republics of Central Asia led to mass unrest, disorder and armed conflicts.

Fierce ethnic struggles between nationalities in Abkhazia, Chechnya, Nagorny Karabakh and Fergana lasted for a long time and entailed numerous human losses.

The problems concerning the fortunes of deported peoples who were sent for permanent residence to sparsely populated areas of Central Asia and Far East by force without any possibility of return during the period of formation of the Soviet Union and during the time of the Second World War resulted in political aggravation. Repressed peoples (Crimean Tatars, Germans, Chechens, Jews and others) began to demand justice and reconsideration of the issue concerning their forced deportation and returning to their historical homeland …

The situation was worsened by the fact that an economic crisis increased swiftly in all the republics which led to food and goods shortages and the republics began to blame the central government. They considered it to be unable to rule a state and to get it out of the situation that had arisen. This led to the fact that all the Soviet republics one by one adopted a declaration about state sovereignty. This meant that since that moment they had gained political and economic liberty, though they were still a part of the Union.

Taking up their lead many autonomous republics and even districts adopted sovereignty. Yakut Autonomous Republic where I lived adopted sovereignty as well and gained the right to be in charge of its rich natural resources and this had a positive impact on its subsequent economic development. It was expected that there would be two state languages in future: Russian and Yakut; and that is why we all began to study the Yakut language at the courses organized under the regional committee.

I couldn't believe that national relations had worsened to such an extent that it could lead to the disintegration of the state at a later date. There were 15 national republics which differed from each other in their religion, culture and traditions, but before the period of the restructuring we saw the country as one single state where there were no borders and where one could move freely all over its territory. I travelled around the country a lot; I had been to different republics in the Caucasus, Central Asia and didn't feel any hostility in relation to me.

On the contrary, people who lived there were very hospitable, took care of me and tried to show all the best they had: places of interest, traditions, national cuisine etc. Nationality didn't matter at all – I can assert that on the basis of my own experience, because I lived in a small village, where people from different ends of the country and different republics came to and we all lived in a friendly manner. We were more interested in where the person came from and not in his/her nationality. We had very good friends, who had come to Siberia from Armenia and South Ossetia, to whom we had been close with friends for many years.

Unlike the central regions of the USSR, it was quiet during those hard and obscure times in our village which was thousands kilometres away from the centre and was lost in the taiga. We found out about the events which took place in the country from the newspapers, radio- and TV-news and from the instructions that were sent to our regional committee by higher bodies. But all the same, I was terribly worried for the future of my country and my family because the events that were taking place led to greater tensions in the relationship among the republics.

It was very important for me because my parents and relatives lived in Ukraine and we were going to go back there in the near future. Of course any aggravation of national relations adversely affected the carrying out of the reforms, and besides that there constantly appeared other unforeseen events, which added chaos to the process of the restructuring. It turned out that the more rights and personal freedoms people got the more disturbances there were. For example, after the republics had received the right to self-determination, they one by one adopted sovereignty.

The moment a decree was passed allowing meetings and demonstration to take place there was a wave of street procession of many thousands in all the republics of the Caucasus as well as in Kazakhstan, Uzbekistan that led to disturbances which led to loss of life and deployment of troops.

Immediately after receiving the right to strike, there were mass strikes of miners, bus drivers and other categories of workers, all over the country. Due to this, the process of the restructuring went out of control and that is why they had to act by trial and error.

Carrying out of the reforms of the restructuring was further constrained as well because of political divisions and confrontations, which led to confusion in solving the political issues which had worsened by the end of the restructuring. The real paradox took place with the USSR communist party. It is a fact that the restructuring in the country began on CPSU General Secretary Mikhail Gorbachev's initiative, and took place under the leadership of the communist party.

The intentions of the communist party were quite positive – to create a normal life for people and give them, at last, the rights and freedoms, upon which they had been infringed and of which they had dreamed for many years and expected this to be received with gratitude and the approval of the people. But everything happened quite the other way – since the very beginning of the restructuring and especially with the appearance of glasnost, the CPSU authority was eroding by leaps and bounds.

By telling the truth, the party bodies hoped for the confidence and support of people, but when people understood that they had been deceived for years, they began to blame the communist party for everything. They discussed it the following logical way – if all the tragic events that had taken place in the country took place during the Soviet period and under the guidance of and by approbation of the party, but were kept secret from us, do we really need such a party?

The standard slogans about the role of the communist party which had existed for years lost their sense. Most people in the country began to doubt the correctness of the policy conducted, stopped trusting the communist party and demanded to remove it from authority. Meetings and demonstrations of many thousands of people took place all over the country, where they demanded the cancellation of the 6th article of the Constitution of the USSR, according to which the CPSU was the only party in the country and was its governing and guiding force.

Many Republics, after adoption of sovereignty, suppressed the activity of the CPSU on their territories and began to set up other political bodies, which led to mass resignations of members from the communist party. I remember, at the beginning of the restructuring when a resolution of the Central Committee of the CPSU "About measures to combat drinking and alcoholism" was being discussed by my local committee in Zyryanka, one of the members of this regional committee mounted a strong criticism of it and said that the resolution would never be supported by the people.

At that time - it was incredible that someone would criticise the decision of a superior body in this way. It was then decided that his dissention involving the communist party's instruction was going to be considered at a closed sitting of the local committee Bureau. After he had found out about this decision he brought his party-membership card and put it on the table of the first secretary of the regional committee and told him that he was voluntarily going to resign from the Communist party.

This was an extraordinary event for the regional committee and this case was quickly hushed up without publishing it. No one could think at that moment that only a few years afterwards the communist party would lose its authority to such an extent that resigning from it would be an ordinary thing. It was obvious that the communist party's influence was weakening and they had to take immediate action for the enhancement of the role of the Soviets in the political life of the country.

According to the Constitution, the USSR was a socialist state where authority belonged to the Congress of People's Deputies, that was its political basis. That is why one could see all over the country the following slogans: 'All authority to Soviets!', but practically the Soviets only wielded executive authority and acted under the guidance of the communist party.

The political reforms, which were carried out under perestroika devolved power and authority to the individual soviets, turning the Soviets onto the real authority, but before this could be implemented there was a need to change the principles of the electoral system. From the very beginning of the foundation of the country, elections of deputies had been carried out as a formality, because in every region there was only one people's deputy candidate, recommended by the party bodies.

As a result, it was easy to adopt any resolution offered to deputies at sessions of the Soviets of all levels, because they always voted approval. Free elections for alternative deputies, involving extensive discussions, were held for the first time in the history of the USSR in 1989. Thanks to which, representatives of public organisations, members with no party affiliations and people with different political views were elected to become people's deputies.

This led to differences of opinions of the deputies at the 1st Congress of People's Deputies of the USSR, which was shown live on central TV. Millions of Soviet people watched carefully the course of events, trying not to miss a single sitting, because due to the differences of opinions of different deputies, there flared up discussions which determined the future of the country. Some deputies stuck to the old policy, believing that the restructuring must be continued, but that the old governmental system and the communist party must be preserved.

Others thought it was better to cancel everything which had been in place before and to create some new bodies of authority and take on market relations based on private property. A speech by academician Andrey Sakharov, who had been banished into exile to Gorky city as a nonconformist and could only return back to Moscow during the restructuring, aroused special interest. He was elected to be a people's deputy of the USSR as a result of an election according to the new electoral system and from the very beginning he opposed the party's monopoly of authority.

The 1st Congress of People's Deputies was of historical importance, because the Supreme Soviet of the Soviet Union was formed at it – a new supreme body of political power and Mikhail Gorbachev was elected to be its chairman.

Since that moment, the power in the country belonged to the Soviets; in this way throughout the country, including at my District council, a new bodies were formed. Under this reorganization a new organization department was established and I was offered the post to head up this department. At this time I didn't expect to be offered a promotion to a more senior position, although I had been thinking about changing my job for some time.

By this time I had worked at the regional committee for about five years and I liked very much the job at first, but I hadn't been fully satisfied with it for some time past, because it was getting harder and harder to work as time went on. I didn't like being present at meetings of a team and listening to charges facing the communist party for all its previous faults. It was hard for me to deny any of those things discussed because they were generally known facts and I just had to pay lip service to these words, still being a loyal party member.

After the meeting, people with whom I was on good terms used to ask me: "Do you really believe in things you've said at the meeting?" At that time one did not need to be afraid of saying the wrong thing, so I replied to them in a friendly manner: "The things I've said are the opinions of party bodies, my opinions differ from theirs and unfortunately I can't tell you about them." Of course we said all this in a joking manner and laughed, but I took it personally and I felt awkward with them.

I asked myself a question again and again, "Why should I feel awkward with these people for things which are beyond my influence and some of which happened even long before my birth?" I was probably not the only one who had such feelings, because there was an increasing turnover of employees at the regional committee. Four first secretaries, two second ones and all the heads of departments had changed for the period of the restructuring at the regional committee.

It was obvious that the communist party wouldn't be able to hold its positions, and that is why some changes in the functions of the regional committee together with manpower cuts were planned. This all disturbed the normal work, because we didn't know what to expect in the future. At that time, I would gladly leave to do my professional work as a lawyer within the legal profession, but I couldn't leave just like that – I had to wait for an opportunity and when I was offered a chance to move to a regional Soviet I agreed right away.

As it turned out I left in time, because the communist party found itself to be in such a critical position, that it couldn't practically carry out its functions. In order to handle this and stop an increasing tension in the country an extraordinary 3rd Congress of People's Deputies was called, which did the thing they hadn't dared to do for a long time.

It revoked the 6th article of the Constitution, which gave the communist party sole authority and power, leaving the communist party with only the same power as other political parties, which had been already created all over the country. Besides, this The Congress changed fundamentally the political system of the country, ratified the position of a President in the country and elected Mikhail Gorbachev to be the first. Right after that, presidential elections took place in all the Union and Autonomous Republics.

I was very worried about the future of the communist party and quite frankly it was very hard for me to accept what had happened. Though I no longer actually worked at the party bodies anymore I was still a communist and would never contemplate withdrawing from the party on my own, because all my life was connected to it. So, as soon as the communist party lost its previous status, a multi-party system was created in the country and many other political parties with different views appeared, including nationalistic ones which fought for the independence of their republics and secession from the USSR.

It was very important to make the right decision at that time, because it determined the fortune of every republic and the fortunes of the country as a whole, with its population of 280 million people. That is why, for the first time in the history of the country and in order to know the opinion of all the population; a nationwide referendum took place on 17th March 1991.

Some republics such as Lithuania, Estonia, Latvia, Georgia, Moldavia, and Armenia refused to take part in the referendum because they had already taken an independent resolution about their sovereignty. People of the other republics voted for preservation of the USSR with a majority of between 70% to 90%. This way, the referendum showed that despite the events that had taken place in the country, people were interested in preserving the nation.

Despite that, nationalist parties continued to use any opportunity and occasion to persuade people against a central authority and promoted to them the idea of the necessity for the secession of the republics. Unfortunately, there were plenty of occasions for them to do this.

For example, there was a currency reform in the USSR at the end of January 1991, and the Prime Minister Valentin Pavlov took the lead in it, he thought that 50-rouble and 100-rouble notes issued in 1961 should be called in and exchanged for smaller ones.

As a financier he had proof that fake money from abroad was arriving in the country in these denominations and also that quantities of money earned illegally were being stored in people's homes rather than in official financial institutions. We were informed about the proposed reform on TV at 9 p.m., when all the branches of the savings bank were closed and told it would take effect the next day at 8 a.m.; we then had only three days in which we could only be allowed to exchange a sum equal to a month's salary for each person.

Those who wanted to exchange a bigger sum had to apply to special commissions during these three days, who would then examine the request for about two months before giving a decision as to whether the exchange could take place. His exchange raised such a panic that some people stood outside the branches of the savings bank for a whole night and by the morning huge queues had gathered everywhere.

There was a commotion in the country and no one worked normally because those who had 50-rouble and 100-rouble notes stood in queues at the branches of the savings bank for whole days.

There was only one branch of the savings bank in our village, but there wasn't any queue at it because it was 50 degrees Celsius below zero outside at that time. This branch was small and with so many people inside it that one had to return several times to gain access inside. Fortunately, I had no big notes and I wasn't in those queues for exchange, but I spent a couple of days trying to withdraw 500 roubles from my account.

The thing was that together with the exchange they limited a sum which one could withdraw from one's account – 500 roubles only per month for a person, the rest of the money in deposits were frozen. Many people had accounts in several branches of the savings bank and not necessarily in the same town, but as only one withdrawal of 500 roubles was allowed, a record of withdrawals were put into passports so as to avoid multiple withdrawals. Of course, every person wanted to withdraw as much as they could, as soon as they could, because they didn't know what would happen the next day.

This way after the reform, there were constantly huge queues at the branches of the savings bank and sometimes they turned into meetings, where people expressed dissatisfaction with the actions of the party and the government. As a result of the Pavlov reform many people lost their money: some of them didn't exchange notes in time, some of them didn't apply to the large amount exchange commission, other who did apply did not receive permission, because their money was considered to be illegally earned, and instead of exchanging the money they launched an investigation into those who had applied.

Before people had time to fully recover from this currency reform, another initiative was launched. Two months later in the beginning of April 1991 another reform was carried out as a result of which state consumer prices were three times increased.

This time all the population of the USSR suffered, because people's purchasing power and living standards dipped down. It's hard to convey the condition of people who felt themselves deceived robbed and grown poor in one day.

Many people considered that the government had been duplicitous; because two weeks before these reforms started the Minister of Finance Valentin Pavlov had publicly stated that no reforms of the financial system were planned. I personally was lucky and my family survived the reform calmly, because in 1990 we paid fully for a cooperative flat, spending all our savings on it.

The money that was left devalued certainly, but this didn't influence our material standing, because at that time my husband and I had good salaries. But for millions of people the reform had tragic results. For example, good friends of ours – the family of Valentina and Vladimir, they had lived in our village for 23 years and had saved enough money for a house, they were planning in July 1991 to buy a private house in central Russia because they wanted to move there for permanent residence. A house cost 25-30 thousand roubles in 1990, and they counted on the sum and were even ready to pay a little bit more with due regard to inflation. But they couldn't get their plans implemented, because after the April reform of 1991 the prices for the houses multiplied up many times. Because of this they had to live and work in the village many years more and could only go back home some 15 years afterwards. It was especially hard for pensioners who lost the money they had saved for all their lives.

My parents lived in Ukraine, where due to smaller salaries people didn't have large amounts deposited at the branches of the savings bank, but due to the reform they lost even that money.

My father (stepfather) had a high salary because he worked at a mine and over time he had saved for a car – about 4 thousand roubles – that was exactly how much a car cost. Despite having been on the waiting list for a several years he did not see any prospect of being able to buy a car any time soon and removed his name from the waiting list.

Since that time his money had been on deposit at the savings bank earning interest, as they say "for one's old age". After the last reform, when accounts were eventually released, father went to a branch of the savings bank, withdrew all the money from his account and bought himself a pair of Czech leather boots of good quality with real lamb's wool lining inside. He had tried them on before, and liked them a lot, but he didn't dare to buy them because they were very expensive.

Although he bought the boots he had coveted he came back home sad and told my mother: "I never thought that the money that I had saved for so many years for a car would only be enough for a pair of boots today. I bought them to have at least a memory about my money, because after the next reform that money will be enough for nothing." I knew my father very well he had never said bad things about the leaders of the country and always tried to justify their actions. At that time I think he refused to understand what was happening, and by buying the boots he expressed his dissatisfaction and protest.

So, the currency reforms which were carried out were aimed at the stabilization of the financial situation in the country. Trying to eliminate corruption and to stop profiteering and fraudulent gains, but they led to exasperation with the political situation in all the republics. People considered themselves to be deceived, defrauded and had grown poor through the fault of the USSR government and the Prime Minister Valentin Pavlov.

I think this was the one of main reasons that led soon to the separation of the republics and disintegration of a single state.

Chapter 39

My Last Vacation

After the republics had announced their sovereignty, there began a migration of population from one republic to another. At the beginning of 1991, my husband and I decided that after 20 years of work in Siberia it was time for us to go back to Ukraine, but where to? For this move we already had our flat, but we were not happy with the place where the flat was. The idea of exchanging our apartment in the centre of Siberia to one in Ukraine was utopian from the very beginning, because Ukraine had been a very prestigious place to live in previously.

The mild climate, beautiful nature, fertile soil for growing fruit and vegetables contributed to the fact that many people, who worked in Siberia and in the North of the country dreamt of receiving a pension and living in Ukraine. So one would think that no one would ever want to leave Ukraine (especially Chernovtsy) and move to Siberia. It was hardly likely, but we didn't give up hope and advertised for 3 years in the local papers of Omsk and Chernovsy about an exchange, but there wasn't any result.

Despite this fact, we decided to sell our flat in Omsk the following year and go back to Ukraine and try to buy another flat in Chernovtsy. But suddenly, in May 1991 we received a letter from a woman who lived in Anadyr (the biggest town, situated in the North of Chukchi Region – the most distant territory of the USSR, which is divided from Alaska by the Bering Sea only). This woman had worked in the Chukchi Region and had received a cooperative flat in Chernovtsy, though she was from Omsk.

She had never lived in Ukraine and had no intention of moving there, particularly now, when events were taking place in Ukraine which meant it could become independent at any moment. We were very happy with the fact that fate had made such a present for us, a year before our planned departure, we thought that everything was under control and according to plan. I was in charge of the flat exchange because my husband was busy with logging for a cooperative in the south of Siberia at that moment.

I had to go to Omsk urgently to retrieve the documents for our flat and then to go to Chernovtsy where the woman from Anadyr would wait for me with the documents to her flat. All the documents we would have to give to the

Chernovtsy city executive committee and wait for a month for the final solution of the exchange. By that time I was entitled to take a vacation for up to ten weeks, but this was too long for the flat exchange so I decided to use my last vacation efficiently. I began to think how to plan the vacation in order to do everything I wanted.

First of all I had to fly to Omsk, where I would need a week for exchange of documents, then I needed a month in Chernovtsy. I wanted to go to Poland while in Chernovtsy because I had a foreign passport. I wouldn't go there by myself of course but my husband's relatives were going there on August 15th and agreed to take me with them. I still had some free time and I decided to take a voucher to the sanatorium of Shmakovka, which was situated not far from Vladivostok.

This sanatorium belongs to the Central Committee of the Communist Party, and I had been there already two years before and I wanted to have a rest there for at least one more time. This was the last opportunity in my life for such a visit and I decided to use it because I understood that I would never ever be in Siberia again after I moved. I received a voucher for 24 days without any problems, maybe because people didn't think about vacations in those hard times.

At first it was hard to think about how to plan the vacation in a better way and do everything and be back home in time. I wrote down everything on a piece of paper and went to the airport to buy tickets. Siberian people travelled all around the country and it wasn't any surprise that I was flying off again, but a ticket clerk admired me for my intention to visit so many places of the country for such a short period of time after she had had a look at my list.

When I also told her that the list didn't include Poland which I wanted to visit August 15th she began to laugh as she was issuing my tickets. So, I bought some tickets from Zyryanka to Omsk (with a transfer in Yakutsk), from Omsk to Chernovtsy (with a transfer in Moscow), from Chernovtsy to Khabarovsk (with a transfer in Moscow), and back: from Khabarovsk to Chernovtsy (with a transfer in Moscow), from Chernovtsy to Zyryanka (with a transfer in Moscow and in Yakutsk). Despite the fact that I was going to cross the country back and forth for four times I paid for everything around 1000 roubles and it was my monthly salary.

The flat exchange went well and we had a cooperative flat in Chernovtsy! I couldn't believe that my dream had come true. The flat was on the fourth floor of a new nine-story block of flats, which was situated on the central street of the town. It was far from the town centre but it was easy to get there by public transport. The relatives of my husband began to help me to settle in immediately so that I could live in Chernovtsy and wasn't forced to go to their village every day, which was 30 kilometres away from the town.

Thanks to them I had a bedside table, a folding bed with a mattress, a pan where I boiled some tea and a TV. This was a very heavy black and white old tube TV but I could watch the news and soap operas which were popular at that time. After I had settled a little I began to go shopping in search of the home-made goods needed for selling in Poland, but the shops were empty in the literal sense of the word. Since the ending of 1980s, when goods were allowed to be exported abroad, people had exported everything, I think in the chase for dollars, which was one of the reasons for the commodity deficiency, because the peak and a phenomenon of empty shelves had happened to be at that time.

I brought some things with me from Siberia to sell but this wasn't enough. Of course, I wanted to export as many goods as I could and bring dollars back, because almost all the population of the Western Ukraine did such business and had dollars and I hadn't even held a dollar note in my hands being a wild Siberian! So I couldn't buy anything in Chernovtsy but I hoped to buy something in Khabarovsk. I will never forget a funny accident that happened to me when I was leaving for the sanatorium.

When I was leaving my flat holding a suitcase, a next-door neighbour saw me and asked, "What has happened to make you come back home so quickly? You said you had a long vacation." I was in a hurry and didn't have much time for talking so I answered her question, "I am not going home, I am going to the sanatorium for 24 days and will come back after that." But she continued to ask questions: "And what is the sanatorium – Truskavets?" (Truskavets is a popular sanatorium which is in the west of Ukraine).

"No, Vladivostok," I answered. She almost fell off the stairs for surprise and it was funny to watch her astonished face – "Where to?" Of course it was unbelievable for her that I was a few kilometres away from the western border of the country and I was going to the sanatorium which was situated a few kilometres away from its eastern border meaning I had to cross the whole country from west to east over 10 thousand kilometres.

I was laughing along all my way, remembering the conversation and I thought about the difference between people who lived in the central part of the country and those who lived in the North of Siberia. It was a routine matter for us to go to any place of the Union while many citizens of Ukraine had never been anywhere else except Odessa and the Crimea. Some of them didn't go anywhere at all even to Moscow.

After I had arrived in Khabarovsk I went to the central department store and was very surprised, because there were many different cheap home-made goods of high quality, which weren't in demand in our country. I began to buy, as they say, one and all: flashlights, lighters for gas cookers, enamel cups, men's pyjamas, undershirts, woman's old-fashioned underwear, cotton robes, combs, house slippers, pens, pencils, etc. After I had bought two full bags of the stuff, I went to the post office which was situated not far from the department store and sent the goods to the address of my relatives in Chernovtsy.

This way I sent around 18 parcels and exhausted I went to the sanatorium, which was situated between Khabarovsk and Vladivostok, by train. I enjoyed every moment of my vacation forgetting about everything in the whole world because I understood that I would never come back there. But everything good ends quickly and I had to go back to real life. When I came back to Chernovtsy the parcels had already been delivered to my relatives' place and after they were opened they began to admire what I had purchased.

I had to go halves with them in goods because for the time of my absence they made a visa to Poland for me and bought a ticket. There were eight of us going to Poland; seven of them had repeatedly visited Poland to trade and only I was a trade virgin. We departed from Chernovtsy August 15th by a through train to Peremyshl, which was situated in the territory of Poland on the border with Ukraine.

I was surprised with the fact that tickets were sold in a day coach, where one could only sit, even though the journey included a whole night. I had never travelled by a day coach before and began to express my indignation at this fact. My friends then began to tell me about the events that took place when people were allowed to go abroad for the first time. The quantity of people who wanted to go was several times bigger that a train could seat, people who didn't have tickets broke the windows of the train and got in through these.

So at those times trains travelled to Poland with broken windows. When our train arrived, there were so many people that I was afraid that they would break the windows again. Of course windows weren't broken anymore, but the train was taken by storm – those who were stronger went ahead, pushing away the others. Luckily a man from our company secured a place for me.

I was going for the first time and I didn't know what was waiting for me, and thought of nothing, but the others were worrying because of crossing the border, remembering unpleasant stories which had happened to them or their friends and they didn't sleep for the whole night long because of that. The train was stopped at the border for checking the passports and visas. Maybe because I going abroad for first time he looked into my passport and began to find faults and ask questions: "Who sent an invitation to you from Poland? Name the person and tell me where he lives," etc. – I couldn't answer a single question because the visa had been made without me while I was in the sanatorium. I knew that we were going to the market in Krakow and were going to stay at a place of one friend but I had no idea what her name was and even forgot the name of the town where we were going to out of fear. My friends, with whom I travelled, began to defend me, explaining to the border guard that I was going for the first time and it was hard for me to remember all this, but he still took my passport and went along the coach.

I was terrified at the thought that I was going to be put off the train right there. A relative of mine went away and came back a couple of minutes later with my passport and told me that he had negotiated with the border guard and he allowed me to go farther. After the passports had been checked, customs officers entered our coach and began to check all our things, opening every

262

bag, but they didn't pay attention to most things because they were looking for vodka.

The thing was that according to customs procedures, one could take 1 litre of vodka (2 bottles), but almost everyone tried to smuggle more, because vodka was a quick-selling product and brought a good profit.

People duly put two bottles of vodka in almost every bag on top of their contents, but hid others in the bottom of the bag. Because of that, everything was thrown out of bags and there was noise and panic: some people cried, some begged not to have their vodka taken away, but all the same all the excess vodka was confiscated by customs officers and put into boxes and taken away. I had no excess vodka with me but I had 200 Russian roubles, which I wanted to exchange for dollars and was worried that they would be found and those would be taken away as well.

I had never thought that I would be so shocked while crossing the border, but this wasn't the ending of my sorrows. In Peremyshl we had to change to a Polish electric train and go on it to Krakow. When it arrived, chaos and crush began and I couldn't understand anything. It turned out that more people arrived from Ukraine than the electric train could carry, but despite that everybody tried to travel farther into the country on it in order to be in time for the market the following day.

When I was pushed into the coach, I couldn't make a single step, because the whole compartment and the corridor was full of people and bags, and in order to go further you had to get over the piles of bags. 'How can one reach a toilet which is in the other end of the coach in such conditions?' this was the first thing I thought of. I couldn't go further than the entrance to the carriage I stood there for a couple of hours, but it was very hot and crowded there, so I and another woman went to the space between the couplings of two carriages.

It was better there, but the flexible flooring of aluminium sheets were spinning in different directions every time the train turned and I thought that my bags would fall under the wheels.

Thank God everything ended up well and we got to Krakow and went to the market right away. I felt myself very tired both emotionally and physically after such a trip and thought how hard people worked to get their dollars for which we had all come.

I began to sell goods at the prices that my relatives had written down for me on a piece of paper, because I didn't know the prices and the rouble-to-zloty exchange rate at first. A queue formed near me and I temporarily forgot about my tiredness and I sold almost half of everything that I had brought, during that day. I then went to exchange my zlotys for some dollars.

I thought that goods had sold so fast because the prices were low, but when I began to buy dollars I was surprised that I had earned so much money. Everything that I had bought for kopecks, I sold there for dollars and was so elated that I totally forgot about my tiredness. It was already dark by the time we reached the place where it had been arranged for us to stay the night. All of us (8 people) were accommodated in one room, in which there were two armchairs and a small sofa.

I was given the sofa, two others were sleeping sitting in the armchairs and the rest had to sleep right on the floor on which, fortunately for them, there was a carpet. Early the following morning, at around five, we went to the market again and it was the same way for the next two days. When I had finally sold everything, and now had the dollars that I came for, I began to think about buying some presents and clothes for my family, because I was warned right away that I had to buy something for the money because of the restrictions on the export of dollars from Poland.

You could export goods from Poland, but it was prohibited to export dollars, so those who didn't have any goods were checked very carefully and any dollars found were confiscated. The people who lived in Chernovtsy bought Polish food: two-litre Pepsi-Cola bottles, Fanta, Lemonade, crackers, unusual candies and other types of food, the like of which I had never seen in my life. My family was in Siberia so I took only those things that I could take with me to the plane.

There were so many trendy clothes at the market that I was taken aback and didn't know what to buy, because I wanted to buy everything. Jeans, jeans skirts, sweaters, jackets, and other clothes were so attractive, bright and unusual that I couldn't take my eyes off them.

So I bought some pretty clothes for all members of my family with all the zlotys that I had not exchanged for dollars. Despite the fact that it had been a stressful experience and I had an awful lot to carry, I was happy, imagining how glad my children and my husband would be with such presents and proud that I had earned 300 dollars.

Chapter 40

The USSR Breakdown

After we had finished business in Krakow, we went to Peremyshl by train on 19th August 1991. Peremyshl is a Polish city on the border of Poland and Ukraine; here it was necessary to change trains and to go on to Chernovtsy. We were travelling at night and there were enough places to sleep, but I couldn't sleep because I was worrying that customs officers would find and confiscate my dollars which I had earned so hard ... As soon as I entered the building of the Peremyshl train station I understood at once that something had happened, unusually for this time there were many people around and they were all discussing something very animatedly.

At first I thought that the train was delayed and got upset because I might have to wait for a long time. However friends from Chernovtsy came up to us and explained that civil war had started in USSR. Information was very vague, but in essence what he told me was that Mikhail Gorbachev had been arrested and was out of power, and that there were tanks in Moscow. I panicked so hard that I didn't know what to do.

First of all, I refused to completely trust this information, but understood at the same time that with the events that had taken place in the country before, anything was possible. Secondly, I worried about what would happen to my family, who at that time were scattered all over the country: I was in Poland, my husband was in Siberia, my son and his family were in Yakytia, and my parents were in Donetsk in Ukraine.

I was scared not only for myself, but for all my family as well. Such a situation as I found myself in at this time had only been shown in movies such as *About the war* and I couldn't even imagine that something similar was happening to me. All the passengers in the station wanted to get back home as soon as possible, and looked eagerly at the screen showing train departure times.

The Poles who were at the station made fun of us: "Where are you going? There's war in your country and here it is peaceful and calm, stay with us! "To our great joy, the tickets were still being sold as normal to all who wanted them and the train continued to depart according to the time table. There was usually a customs examination of all luggage on the border of Ukraine, but this time customs officers only checked our passports, they were probably shocked as well and had no time for us.

We arrived in Chernovtsy at night, and all was calm in the town, but the next day from early morning, meetings began in the central squares and near the building of the CPSU district committee. Here many people gathered waving banners and flags. The flags were divided – half was yellow and the other half was blue. Many people with the same slogans and flags were walking down the streets to the centre of the city. After I had joined them I came to the Soviet square and began to listen to what people were speaking about.

I hadn't lived in Ukraine permanently, and was only here for a week, that is why I knew very little about the state of affairs here. For example, I had a question at once: "What are those flags about? I have never seen them before?" however, the people who were standing beside me quickly explained to me that a yellow-blue flag was a flag of the *RUKH Party* (which is translated into English as *movement* party) (national Ukrainian democratic movement).

Of course I knew that the Rukh party was established in 1989 in Ukraine, but it was new for me that it had its own flag.

Besides the yellow-blue flags, there were many posters which called people not to obey the slogans of SCSE (State Committee for the State of Emergency) which most people considered an illegal organization, nor to accept the actions of the communist party as credible, but that they should fight for an independent Ukraine. All those who came to the meeting were given leaflets on which were printed specific economic statistics.

Those figures, like the quantity of steel produced, coal mining production and the amount of agricultural production helped to prove that if Ukraine seceded from the USSR the population would live no worse than in developed countries of Europe like Germany, Austria, Spain, etc. When I arrived back at my flat I switched on the TV hoping to find out the details of what was going on in the country, but they only showed the ballet at the Bolshoi Theatre.

The uncertainty was the worst thing that could happen in such a situation, I felt devastated and wanted to go back to Zyryanka as soon as possible and run away from the nightmare. The next day it was unbearable for me to stay at home, and for most of the day I just walked around the town, stopping at places where meetings took place. I didn't take part in them, but just listened to what the speakers said.

Everyone was discussing the same event: that there was a coup in the country through the fault of the Communist party, but no one knew the details because there wasn't any information for the first few days. Then the State of Emergency was announced on the radio and a night curfew was introduced in Moscow. This piece of news dealt the final blow to me, because I had to fly to

Yakutsk via Moscow. "What should I do next?" I thought, and understood at the same time that I had to calm down and wait until something changed.

I scolded myself for going to Poland in an attempt to buy some nice clothes for all my family and earn some dollars – at that moment, all that didn't make any sense and I didn't want any clothes or dollars anymore. In the course of time we finally found out from the TV what had taken place. It transpired that a State Committee for the State of Emergency (SCSE) was established on 19th August, consisting of people from the communist party of the USSR and the Soviet Government: the Prime Minister, the Minister of Defense, the President of KGB, the Secretary of the Interior and others amongst its members.

The chairman of the SCSE was a Vice-President of the USSR Gennady Yanaev. The committee was created on the pretense that Mikhail Gorbachev as the President of the USSR wasn't up to his responsibilities, and the country was on the edge of a breakdown, the SCSE tried to seize power in the country by force while Mikhail Gorbachev was having a rest at his Dacha, which was situated in the village of Foros in the Crimea.

According to the decree of the committee the Dacha had been under armed guard since 19th August and Mikhail Gorbachev was politically impotent. All the laws passed during the period of restructuring were cancelled by the committee, the activities of political parties and the work of publishing houses of the central newspapers was stopped. The traffic was blocked in the centre of Moscow and armoured troops entered the streets.

When the TV started to show what was going on in Moscow I understood that situation in the country was unpredictable and dangerous. Tanks and other military hardware flooded all the central streets and the square in front of the Union Soviet house of the Russian Soviet Federative Republic "The White house". Thousands of people gathered in the centre of Moscow defending the Union Soviet House and they were willing to do anything to protect it.

The President of the Russian Federation, Boris Yeltsin, was at the head of national opposition, and he signed a decree "About the illegal actions of the SCSE" and read it out at a meeting in front of the Union Soviet House. Boris Yeltsin was hoping to get the support of people and was trying to stop the coup which had just started, and his statement to the nation played an important role in those tragic days. People did everything they could, but unfortunately they weren't able to prevent bloodshed.

On 21st August while patrolling in the neighbouring territory around the Union Soviet House, a convoy of armoured troop carriers encountered a group of people who blocked the street with buses and tried to stop the military men. The situation became more complicated when three people died in the course of the army trying to proceed, but as a result of these actions and being afraid of drawing the country into a civil war the army refused to use further force against people.

The next day mourning was declared in the country, and a new wave of meetings and demonstrations washed across all the republics at which people condemned the illegal actions of the committee and impeached the credibility of the CPSU. The plan of the SCSE to seize power by force failed because people didn't support it and the army returned to barracks giving the streets of Moscow back to civilians, and the members of the committee were arrested.

After this Mikhail Gorbachev came back to Moscow and on 23rd August as President of the USSR he took part in the work of a session of Supreme Council of the RSFSR which was broadcast live on TV. The actions of the SCSE were condemned at this session, and then something unpredictable happened – Live at the session, and in presence of Mikhail Gorbachev and other participants, Boris Yeltsin, who was only President of the Russian Federation, signed a decree about the shutdown of the communist party within the Russian Federation and gave orders to seal the buildings of the party's bodies, which were situated on his territory.

What a surprise, a session meeting of the Supreme Council of RSFSR being broadcast on TV, I couldn't believe my eyes when I saw what was going on there. It just seemed impossible and incredible to me; one person can't take such decisions even if he is a president!

I was protesting in my mind and knew that this action contradicted the regulations of the Communist Party. The following day, on August 24th, Mikhail Gorbachev resigned responsibility as general secretary of the Communist party USSR and stopped its activities.

This piece of news stunned me even more than a coup attempt because I was hoping that this whole thing would end and everything would be as it had been before. This, however, as Mikhail Gorbachev used to say himself, "was of irreversible character." Of course, the events that took place in the country during the previous years had already brought down the authority of the Communist party, and after the abrogation of the 6th article of the USSR Constitution it hadn't been the one and only party of government, but it still existed!

For millions of soviet people the Communist party had been their sense of life and a lifework for almost 70 years – it was almost something sacred, and it was destroyed just like that with the stroke of the pen. I had been a member of the party for 19 years myself, and trusted that its activity was aimed at the welfare and development of our people and country, and at that moment I had a feeling that I had been betrayed.

Before I had even fully comprehended the changes and come to terms with everything that had happened, on the same day Ukrainian TV broadcasted that the Supreme Council of Ukrainian SSR passed a document about declaration of independence of Ukraine. In this way, since August 24th 1991, Ukraine became an independent and sovereign country. To confirm this decision of the Council it was also announced that a referendum would be held on 1st December 1991.

This was a long-expected day for the Ukrainian people, but this piece of news dealt the final blow to me, and quite frankly, I didn't know what to think about it. I understood very well that as an independent state, Ukraine would have its own laws, a constitution, money, and would establish borders, etc. What would happen with us, with our flat? If we decided to stay in Siberia we would live in the territory of The Russian Federation, and that would be another country.

In the morning when I found out that all the airports in the country were working as normal I decided to go back home immediately. While I was travelling to Zyryanka I talked to people on the plane and in the other public places and was surprised that the events that had taken place in the country had impacted on people in many different ways. Some people were as shocked as I was, but there were others who were glad because of what had happened and talked openly about it.

It was very noisy in the airports of Moscow and Yakutsk, one could see groups of men discussing the events that had taken place in excited and angry tones and were near to violence, some of them were happy that the country fell apart, and admired Boris Yeltsin, who abolished the Communist Party, some taking the opposite view. Soon after Ukraine, several of the other republics (Belarus, Moldova, Azerbaijan, Kirgizia, Tajikistan, etc.) one after the other declared their independence and it seemed that the country was falling apart about my ears.

Events showed that the changes that had taken place in the country during the period of restructuring had steadily led the republics to consider the possibility of independence and the August events just quickened the process. During my journey my heart was heavy with different thoughts. Only two months before I was going on a vacation and going into a sanatorium, exchanging my flat, and going to Poland and then returning back home.

Everything happened as I planned it, but some unpredictable events had happened at the same time: the coup attempt, the breakdown of the country, and the abolition of the Communist Party. It turns out that I went for vacation in one era and came back home in the totally different one. All the way home I was thinking of what should I do in the situation, and in the end I decided to move urgently to Chernovtsy which seemed the right decision in the circumstances.

When I arrived back home I called my husband in Ust Kut and asked him to come to Zyryanka as soon as possible. I told him, "We need to figure out what to do with our future life." He didn't understand what I meant, but I didn't start to explain to him on the phone and said that we would talk when he arrived home. I then went to the store to obtain some carton boxes in order to pack things for container transportation.

While I was returning from the store I met my friend Valentina, she was very glad that I had returned from vacation and asked me why I needed the boxes. I told her that I was going to pack my things for a container transportation and that I was going to move to Ukraine. "Are you kidding? Why haven't you told me about this before?" She exclaimed. "Because I didn't know about it myself before," I answered, and began to tell her about everything that had happened to me and why I had made this decision.

After she had understood that my intentions were serious she began to cry and tried to persuade me to think this over once again and take this decision after further discussion with my husband. Before this chance meeting I had planned everything emotionlessly and only at that moment did I understand that I was going to leave the village forever, a place where I had spent twenty years of my life, had many friends and where I had been happy. I felt ill at ease and began to cry as well.

A lot had changed in the village, as well as in the country, during the period I spent on vacation. The building housing the offices of the local branch of the Communist Party was sealed and all the workers had lost their jobs. Some specialists were instantly appointed to different government departments' in Yakutsk. The rest of them tried to find any job they could, which was quite hard to do. When I handed in my resignation, it was accepted by the chairman of the district council who was startled at first, but then I think he was glad, because I made a position vacant and he could hire someone else.

The events that had taken place in the country caused panic in the people of the village. People who came to Siberia from different parts of the Russian Federation didn't worry a lot because they could go back home at any moment. However, those who were from the other republics planned mainly to go back home as soon as possible. My husband came home in a couple of days and was surprised at seeing me so stressed. He had rationalized the momentous events that had recently happened and told me to stop panicking.

"We cannot change the things that have happened, but we have exchanged the flat in Chernovtsy for nothing and we might have a problem with this. The thing is we can't move to Ukraine because I'm going to get a flat in Kuban, in the town where our branch of the cooperative is situated," he said. I then understood that I had felt panic for my country and my family, and that I looked at things in a different way from my husband and my friends in Zyryanka.

People's perspective of events is often different depending on where are they at the moment of such events. Watching the events on TV at home on the sofa is one thing, but seeing and being part of the same events live is totally different. The words of my husband were to me as much as a surprise as snow falling in summer, and I began to remind him that we had always wanted to go back to Chernovtsy, especially after we had found a way to exchange flats. He, however, didn't even want to listen to me, and began to persuade me that it would be better for our family to move to Kuban.

His cooperative was already constructing housings for sale to its workers. The first houses were almost ready and one of these had already been assigned to my husband. He continued: "Do you understand that we have an opportunity to get a flat, the place where I'm going to live and to work? We can give the flat in Ukraine to our son, let him move to Chernovtsy and live there, he was born there and it is his motherland."

When he saw that I was continuing to pack my things in the box, he tried to stop me, and told me that we could stay during the winter in Zyryanka, as there was no reason for moving in a hurry and we could leave in spring the following year. But nothing could stop me and I said: "No! I can see no sense in staying here for winter; we need to change our life right now. Moreover you work in Kuban and are going to live there and are not going to come back here. I'm tired of everything and I haven't seen lilac blossom for twenty years!"

Indeed, we had lived for a full 20 years in Yakytia, had earned a northern pension, a flat and some money. Furthermore, I didn't like my job in the council house and I didn't like life in the village anymore, which had become uninteresting to me. I had the feeling that a certain period of my life had finished and I had to move on to the another, that is why I was ready to go anywhere – if not to Chernovtsy or to Kuban at least.

In the end my husband persuaded me to move to Kuban and live there by myself for a short time, whilst he was working in Siberia. I finally relented, thinking, "What's the difference, I'm here alone and I will be there alone as well. It might even be more interesting there, it's the North Caucasus and there's a spa not far from Kuban which I have already visited several times." We gathered all our possessions together, and put them in a five-ton container, drove it to the river port for transportation to our house in Kuban.

We then departed in different directions: I went to Kuban, where the new accommodation was waiting for me and my husband went to Siberia where he continued to work, whilst our son stayed in Zyryanka to live with his family. I have already written about the way people who had worked for many years at the place were given a moving send off from the village.

If I had left Zyryanka about a year ago, it would have been very hard for me to say goodbye, but now everything had changed and people didn't care about each other, everybody was busy with their own lives and businesses and thoughts about what to do next. That is why I only said goodbye to my closest friends and departed to meet my new life.

Chapter 41

Attempting to set up in Kuban

I went alone into unknown future, repeating to myself one popular Russian proverb: "Every cloud has a silver lining", hoping that this would improve my mood. When I finally arrived in Kuban I stayed at the house of our friends, who used to work with my husband at a construction organization in Zyryanka, we had both been friends with his family for a long time. The Caucasus was his motherland, and that is why he and his family came back there two years earlier.

It was this friend who has suggested the founding of a branch of the cooperative there, and who later became its chairman. It was good that we had real friends in the place where we were going to live and I wouldn't feel so lonely. They began to praise Kuban to just like my husband did, and started to tell me about the town, about a wonderful local climate, favourable to growing fruit and vegetables.

I listened to all this in silence, and was looking forward to what would happen next, because while I was travelling here nothing of any significance had captured my attention. Our new home was situated in a small town in Kuban, the town itself was small and resembled a village, and most of the buildings consisted of one-storey private houses. It was situated in the Krasnodar Territory, which is situated on the North Caucasus and borders with the republic of Caucasus.

The Krasnodar Territory is also called "Kuban" - because the river Kuban flows through its territory, and is one of the biggest rivers of the Northern Caucasus, and which eventually flows into the Sea of Azov. Resulting in the place we were supposed to live being called by different names: the Northern Caucasus, Krasnodar Territory and Kuban – which are all in fact the same place.

The next day they began to show me our new house, which was situated in the suburbs several streets away from their own house. As yet there were no streets or asphalt roads, and the houses were constructed straight in the fields where corn was growing. Some more new streets, and asphalt roads were to be constructed and utility services connected, but as yet this was still not done.

This way they planned to connect the new estate to the town. The first three houses were semidetached houses and were now ready for occupation; one of them was to be ours. The house wasn't bad consisting of a veranda, a hall, a kitchen, a living-room and two small bedrooms. The bathroom and toilet weren't quite ready yet and there wasn't even any water in the house!

I made the round of all the rooms, looked out of all the windows and didn't see anything accept the corn! However, from the window in the kitchen I saw a road which was not too far from the house and a cowshed on the hill. "Oh my God, where have I come to, how am I going to live here?" I thought. If we hadn't sent the container full of our possessions here, I would have left the place immediately, but at that moment I had to stay there despite my reservations and disappointment.

Our friend saw my facial expression and began to calm me down – "Don't worry, you'll get used to it with time and get accustomed to the place and we'll help you." All the six houses belonged to the cooperative, but some people who acquired these houses continued to live in Siberia.

A family of pensioners, who arrived there about a month before, lived in the neighbouring house. It could be seen that they had settled down already: curtains were hanging on the windows and young trees were planted near the house and in the garden.

I was supposed to live in our house alone, because our other neighbours weren't planning on moving anytime soon, and the other four houses were empty. It was in those six houses amongst the corn, having only one of neighbor, I was supposed to start my new life. In order not to bother my friends, I decided to go to Chernovtsy and stay there until the container came. During the period of my absence my husband returned on business for a few days and was very angry with me when he found out that I wasn't there.

After about six weeks I came back, received the container and unloaded all the things into the house, and found out that it was very scary to live there alone. After the Soviet Union broke down, there began chaos and unrest in the country, criminal activity increased, and the situation became even more unstable in the Caucasus. Although the Chechen Republic was 450 km away from us, everything that happened there reached us as well.

I was seeing refugees in the town; many of them had children, who went from house to house begging for help. Amongst the different kinds of crimes there were many incidents of burglary. There were adverts in the local newspapers which advised people not to leave houses unattended; it was also advised to close ventilator windows when leaving the house, because robbers pulled out things from the house through them.

They robbed even ordinary houses, and I had plenty of things that were valuable at this time in our house: a carpet, fur-coats, furs, cut-glass ware and other expensive things that we collected while living in the Yakytia. I listened to every single rustle in fright, and sometimes I even took an axe, and put it beside me near my bed, in order to protect myself in case of an attack. The streets in the town were lit only in the centre, and there were no light in the suburbs amongst the private houses.

The nights in Kuban are very dark, and you couldn't see anything without light: not the streets nor the roads and one could orientate oneself only with the help of the light from the windows of the houses. I came there in autumn, and it was raining all the time, the road became soft and you could walk on it only wearing rubber boots. If I wanted to buy something from the shops I had to walk two kilometres to the centre of the town and back, in the mud, wearing my rubber boots, because there were no buses.

I didn't enjoy the process. "What a land of plenty! Why on earth have I come here, I'd be better living in Zyryanka, and it was so convenient and comfortable there," I used to curse myself inwardly. Of course my friends supported me and helped me a lot and my neighbour considered it to be their responsibility to teach me how to live there. At one point a neighbour came to my house and told me to look out of the window as there was a spare piece of land between our properties and the road.

He wanted us all to move the fence to the road and thereby increase the size of our gardens, which would enable us all to grow more vegetables. I refused flatly to do this, because I didn't even want to deal with the existing garden and he wanted me to create even more of it! After that he called me lazy bones and he went to move the fence himself, so that lands of future neighbours weren't wasted.

The next time he rolled a metallic wheelbarrow up to my house – a small one with one wheel. "Do you see that cowshed, there's plenty of manure. You must collect some of it and spread it on your garden for fertilizer before it's wintertime," he said. I imagined myself wearing rubber boots and wheeling the manure. As a professional lady I had never been involved in this kind of activity and had no affinity or any wish to become involved in such.

Even the thought of becoming involved in this activity made me feel miserable and sad and sorry that my life had come to this, and I decided to go to Chernovtsy again, at least for a while. I wanted to give my valuables to my neighbours for safe keeping in case of robbery, but I had many of them and neighbours wouldn't be able to take all of them. I considered my carpet one of the most valuable things I possessed and took this to my neighbors.

After that I curtained the windows, took all the furs I brought from Siberia, locked the house and went to Chernovtsy. There was a town called Armavir about 15 kilometres away from us, where there was a railway station on the junction of the North/South lines and East/West lines. Both the trains bound for the North – for Russia, Ukraine and the South of Caucasus passed through the station.

That is why it was convenient to go by train, although the journey was quite long. One had to travel to Kiev for 17 hours at first, and then spend the whole day there and then go on to Chernovtsy which was 14 hours more. I used to travel the same route in the previous years, during the Soviet period, when I went on holiday to the Black Sea, and it was fine, and the journey didn't seem so long. Now that there was such chaos and mess in the country it was unbearable and very dangerous to travel by train.

All the trains from different places of Caucasus bound for Kiev (Adler - Kiev, Baku – Kiev and others) were crowded with refugees from Caucasus. Tickets were available for sale to anyone, but without reserving a seat, and on such long journeys people weren't able to lie down even in the sleeping cars, they were sitting on lower and even upper (second) sleeping berths all the way. Only those who were lucky to occupy the third luggage berth under the very ceiling could lie down and sleep.

All the carriages were full of people and luggage; there were many refugees from Chechnya, who were simply standing in the corridors of the trains with trunks, bags and children. Robbery was a routine matter in those trains and some people did whatever they liked with perfect impunity. Men drank vodka, cursed and fought and the conductors – for their own safety – preferred not to interfere.

I was sitting on the lower sleeping berth holding a bag; I put a backpack with the furs on the third luggage berth between somebody else's luggage when we were stopped at the city of Rostov-on-Don (situated in the south of Russia on the river called Don) where some Don Cossacks entered a carriage at the station.

This Russian region was traditionally a homeland of the Cossacks, where since the middle of 16th century their army and settlements had been created for the sake of the defence of the Russian state, and where they lived according to their laws and traditions. It had lost its popularity during the Soviet period, but in the beginning of 1990's the rebirth of the Cossacks began again. I was travelling in the autumn of 1991 and at that time a peace-keeping Cossack ward was formed – they wore their traditional uniform, patrolled the streets of the city train stations and checked trains.

When a check-up in the carriage began, they began to check passports and luggage underneath the lower sleeping berths on a selective basis, and then they began to drag down the luggage from the upper berths. When they apparently got tired of this they began to point with a stick at a pieces of luggage on the third luggage berth and asked whose things those were and what exactly was in them. My backpack was soft and I told them that it was full of my clothes.

During the whole process I was trembling so hard that I almost fainted. I imagined to myself what would have happened if they had found inside this pack my sable fur, muskrat and several pieces of silver fox fur, which I had collected for several years and which I was going to sew into a fur-coat for myself. Some of the passengers, men mostly, were forced to open their suitcases and bags, and if someone refused to cooperate, Cossacks opened the luggage by themselves and made those who refused get off the train.

When I told my husband about it he scolded me and repeated the same thing over and over: "Stay at home and try to grow vegetables, you shouldn't travel because it is dangerous right now and accidents will happen." Of course, I didn't listen to my husband and nothing could stop me. Every time he went to Siberia I took my carpet to my neighbour's place and went to Chernovtsy. However, he was right, a bit later an unpleasant accident happened to me when I was coming back to Kuban on a train from Kiev to Armavir. Not many people were going in that direction, back to where things were unsettled.

The moment we were passing through the territory of southern Russia I was sitting in a compartment carriage by the window, with a towel on my knees, and a cup of tea in my hands. Suddenly, I heard a dreadful crash and the cup fell from my hands. Everything happened so fast that I didn't understand anything at first, but then after I had revived myself, I saw blood dripping on the towel from my face, although I didn't feel any pain. A woman, who shared the compartment carriage with me was sitting on the opposite side of the carriage and holding a child, she was staring at me and screaming.

That started a panic and all the passengers gathered round our compartment. Then a conductor came and began to calm us down, "Calm down please, nothing serious has happened. Such things often happen, windows are constantly being knocked out and we can't do anything about it." It turned out that teenagers had hurled stones at the train and one potato-sized stone knocked out our window, and then knocked the cup from my hands, and rebounded against the doors hitting the woman's leg.

Window glass was strewn all over the compartment; small pieces of glass had scratched my face and the woman's hands. The conductor brought an old mattress and plugged the window with it. We went all the way to our station this way. I was thinking of the accident the whole way through; the stone flew so close to my temple, it could have easily killed me …

Despite everything that had happened I continued to travel to Chernovtsy because I realized very soon that life in Kuban wasn't for me and I would never feel at home. I yearned for Ukraine, because it was much more interesting, and it seemed to me that life was in full swing there and I longed to go there. I had kept up with the events in the country and especially in Ukraine, in order not to miss the opportunity to come back in case of necessity.

On 1st December 1991 a national referendum in Ukraine was held as planned. There was only one question in a ballot paper: "Do you confirm the Act of independence of Ukraine," and you had to tick "Yes" or "No". It had been obvious even before the referendum that most people would vote for the independence, because there had been good propaganda in Ukraine and people were eager to establish an independent and separate country.

The presidential election was held on the same day. I had been in Chernovtsy a month before the event and though there were several candidates for the presidency, but it seemed to me that only two of them stood any real chance of being elected: the chairman of Regional Council of the city of Lvov - Viacheslav Chornovil; and the chairman of Supreme Council of Ukrainian SSR - Leonid Kravchuk.

At least this was how it appeared to me, because only those two candidates were discussed among our relatives and friends who expressed their opinions, and sometimes they argued about this so fervently and passionately. They argued because the referendum and the presidential election were vital issues for them. Most of the people said they were going to vote for Leonid Kravchuk, because "He is one of us and we know him well."

That was true, Leonid Kravchuk was well known in Chernovtsy, because in 1960- 1970s he lived in Chernovtsy and worked as a teacher at a financial technical college. Following this he also worked as a lecturer and head of a department of propaganda and agitation at the Chernovtsy district committee of the communist party of Ukraine. He stood for President as a member of no party, because the communist party of Ukraine collapsed after the declaration of independence of Ukraine on 24th August 1991.

Despite the fact that he was no longer a member of the communist party some people were unhappy with the fact that he had been a communist for a long time and worked at different levels of the party bodies of Ukraine and had been a member of the Central Committee of the Communist Party of the Soviet Union. Some people preferred that candidature of Viacheslav Chornovil for the position because he had been fighting for the independence and freedom of Ukraine all his life and they thought this more appropriate for a presidential candidate.

Indeed, the biography of Viacheslav Chornovil was unusual; he had been a journalist since he was young, at different press organisations, and he had expressed his political views which often contradicted the state ones. Viacheslav Chornovil was elected to be a People's Deputy of Ukraine during the years of Restructuring, and took part in the creation of the Rukh party (The People's Movement of Ukraine) and worked as a chairman of the Regional Council of the town Lvov (a town situated in the west of Ukraine 70 kilometres away from the Polish border).

So 1st December 1991 was a very important day for Ukraine because it changed the fate of the country and its citizens forever. There wasn't a single indifferent person on this day, people showed a high political awareness and as a result around 90 % of the population who cast their vote voted for the independence of Ukraine and more than 61% of people gave their votes for Leonid Kravchuk.

An old dream of Ukrainian people came true – Ukraine became a free and independent state, and Leonid Kavchuk became its first president. All the republics of the Soviet Union at different times throughout 1991 declared their independence, and elected their presidents, and therefore, no longer formed part of the USSR.

The Soviet Union, which had contained 15 republics, broke down as a country and evolved into independent countries, but in fact it continued to exist formally. Mikhail Gorbachev was a president of a non-existing country at that moment and had no influence on the events that took place in any of the former constituents of the USSR. Such a situation in the former USSR couldn't last for any length of time and a reorganization of the political system was needed, the preparation for which was already under way, but it was taking too much time.

Therefore, a decisive step was taken by three independent countries: the Russian Federation, Ukraine and republic of Belarus. The Russian president Boris Yeltsin, the Ukrainian president Leonid Kravchuk and the president of the supreme council of the republic of Belarus Stanislav Shushkevych, on 8th December 1991 signed an agreement about the foundation of the Commonwealth of Independent States (CIS).

The signing took place in a governmental residence, which was situated in the territory of Belovezhskaya Pushcha (a forest) in the Republic of Belarus. This agreement united only three countries at the time of signing, but the other countries joined them over time. Mikhail Gorbachev was forced to vacate his position as the president of the USSR on 25th December 1991, because the country had ceased to exist.

My husband and I saw in the new year of 1992 in Kuban, together with our friends. Everything was as usual: at 10 p.m., according to Moscow time, we drank vodka and saw out the old 1991, a year which had been full of historical events and would go down in history as a year separating the two eras of our country: the era of socialism, and a new era perhaps of capitalism.

This year changed the fate of our country and the fate of every person who lived in the USSR, destroying their usual life and dividing it into two parts: the life before 1991 and the life after it. At 12 p.m., we saw the New 1992 year in to the Moscow chimes and the clatter of glasses full of Soviet champagne and congratulated each other in a traditional way: "Have a happy New Year! Have new happiness!"

Which happiness? Everything had fallen apart. We had no idea of what was coming and how to deal with it – in front were only uncertainty, confusion and fear for the future…

Chapter 42

Experience of First Business

My son continued to live in Zyryanka and to work at the plant producing slag stone. He called me just after New Year and said: "Mother, I'm tired; the work is very hard and not very interesting." He continued, "Many of my friends have their own business and I have an idea – to start a trade business. I'm thinking of buying clothes in the Chernovtsy market and selling them in Yakutia, maybe later I'll open my own store in Zyryanka."

I was startled and replied, "You can't do this alone; you have no experience and money for buying goods. However, if you want to, we can work together, as I don't have anything to do here in Kuban and I have money." I was very glad when he agreed, because it gave me an opportunity to come back to Siberia and have something to do. The next day I took my carpet to my neighbour's place and went to Chernovtsy.

There had always been a small market in Chernovtsy selling clothing, where, as a student at the end of the nineteen sixties, I bought imported clothes from Poland and Romania. Since the end of the 1980s, when the free importing of goods from abroad was allowed, the area of the market began to broaden swiftly until at the beginning of 1992 it became the biggest and the most famous market, not only in Ukraine, but in Russia as well.

The market developed swiftly; at first the goods were laid out on the ground on a rubber sheet, and then later they were sold in cars and minibuses. Although officially the market began to work from 8 a.m., the cars were already lining up in a long queue at 2-3 a.m. In time, the market was divided into the wholesale and retail parts. In the wholesale part of the market, goods were bought for the cheaper price being in bulk and usually taken away in sacks for sale all over Ukraine, Russia and Moldavia.

You already know that in the last years of the USSR's existence, the shelves in the shops were empty, and when at last fashionable clothes were imported from abroad, people would buy almost anything in order to be fashionably dressed. The market was piled up with the clothes from Turkey, which were not of a very high quality, but they were beautiful, bright and fashionable. From the first days I remember there were pullovers with BOSS printed on the chest.

They were cheap, and all over country people started to wear them, as thousands of them were brought to the market and sold quite cheaply. Everyone, from children to elderly men and women, wore such pullovers in Chernovtsy. It was funny to see an elderly woman from rural areas wearing a national bukovinian skirt together with the "BOSS" pullover.

We, as a new family business, firstly bought some of these pullovers for a small amount of money, and then my son took them to Zyryanka. Three days later he called me and told me that everything was bought up in a matter of a couple of hours, because no one had even seen such pullovers and they all wanted to buy one. He said, "Mother if only we could deliver a thousand of such pullovers here and even more get to sell them all." "Yes, that would be great, but we can't deliver so much," I answered.

The next time we bought three sacks of pullovers and departed to Yakutsk via St. Petersburg, because there weren't any flights to Yakutsk via Moscow. We stayed for a night at my friend's place in St. Petersburg. She was from this city, but she had lived in Zyryanka for many years and had come back home before the disintegration of the USSR. She had lost her job, like so many other people when the break up happened and now she had a small-scale retailing business: once a month she went by train to a town which was situated almost 500km away from St. Petersburg, where she bought cotton dressing gowns at a clothing factory.

She sold them standing at an underground railway station, even during wintertime in the cold, and making just 1 dollar profit on each gown. She usually managed to sell 200 dressing gowns per month which brought her 200 dollars and which was enough for her to survive.

My friend had an experience in business and gave us several pieces of good advice: firstly, not to buy cheap things in sacks, but to buy more expensive items, which would be easier to transport and the profit from one expensive thing would be the same as from several cheap ones; secondly, not to buy goods in Chernovtsy, but to buy goods in St. Petersburg instead, which would save time and reduce ticket costs. I liked her advice and I offered her the opportunity to work with us, to which she happily agreed.

In St Petersburg, at this time, the commission shops contained many expensive and high quality goods which were imported, especially from Finland. She knew the city well and it wasn't hard for us to visit all the shops in the centre in a couple of days and buy the goods we needed. We were buying expensive women's suits, coats, and quilted coats, from morning to night, also shoes and everything that could easily be sold in Siberia, including cosmetics, key rings, ballpoint pens and even chewing gums.

At first we sold goods to the commission shops in Yakutsk, who bought them gladly because there weren't such fine goods as I brought into the town. I increased prices two or three times and even then everything was bought up in a matter of a couple of days and the profit was quite good. In a week, after gathering money from the shops I with my son would travel back to St.

Petersburg to buy new goods. We worked this way for about two months and then everything went even better.

During our visits to Yakutsk we stayed at a departmental hotel, which belonged to the construction company where my husband had worked. Although he had gone to work at a cooperative, everybody still knew him well, and always offered us a room at any time. Workers from construction sites in many Northern villages of Yakutia who had lost their jobs, were now in the retailing business as well, and they also stayed at the same hotel. Many of them had opened their own shops and came to Yakutia for goods.

When they found out what I did, they started to buy direct from ourselves right in the hotel. Since that moment it was much easier for us to work, I stopped going from store to store in winter temperatures of minus 50 degree frost, and sold all the goods right in the hotel within a couple of hours. I could increase the number of our trips to St Petersburg, but because there were only two flights a week, on Tuesdays and on Fridays we just had to wait until the next available flight.

The amount of money increased with every trip, and so we transported more and more goods, but it wasn't enough all the same and they still asked for more. I began to buy air tickets for a whole month in advance for both myself and my son and we started to travel regularly almost to a timetable, departing to St. Petersburg with money on Tuesdays and back to Yakutsk with goods on Fridays. In this way we flew across almost the whole country twice a week, traveling the distance of 8000 km, and coping with a six-hour time difference each way.

Every single detail was considered and there weren't any problems in this work, except one – "What to do with the money?" Not a question that often arises in the capitalist west and now that I am writing about it, the question "What to do with the money?" seems a ridiculous one to me. But at that incomprehensible time in the country we failed to see the joke, we had to think of how to save the money in Yakutsk, how to avoid an unexpected currency reform and how to transport it across the whole country.

The fact was that not only workers at the hotel, but other visitors knew that after I had sold the goods I had a lot of money with me because the hotel was small and the information was spread in a moment. I didn't feel safe and listened to every sound and rustle, and couldn't sleep at night for the fear of being robbed. It was almost impossible to hide money in the hotel room and I couldn't carry it with me whenever I left the hotel. An idea suddenly came to me.

There was a small shed behind the hotel and some pipes were lying near it covered with snow. Because of heavy frosts around -50 degrees and a thick fog, visibility was very poor around this shed, and besides no one ever went there. I put all the money into a plastic bag and put it into a pipe and covered it with snow, where it laid until my departure. Because of the hyperinflation and currency instability it was dangerous to keep money for any length of time and I could lose it all at any moment.

After a currency reform had been introduced in January 1991, effectively devaluing the rouble, with many people losing all their savings, absolutely anything could happen. There was a rumour that another reform would be introduced very soon, but no one knew when exactly it would happen and people who had their own businesses were always afraid of what it might entail. It could easily happen that I departed from Yakutsk with a big amount of money and arrive to St. Petersburg with a just couple of roubles.

At this time, and as a result of inflation, prices for the goods were very high, but buyers usually paid with small notes of 10 or 25 roubles, consequently I could gather a plastic bag full of money very quick and easily. I couldn't exchange this amount for big notes in a bank without arousing suspicion and awkward questions, so I had to transport the money just like that across the whole country.

When I was departing I was afraid to put the money into my luggage, which I checked-in at the airport, and it was dangerous to carry it in my hand baggage as well – everything was examined closely. That is why I literally put bundles of money round myself, pushing them into a wide rubber belt around my waist as well as in my knickers and down my stockings!

I could sometimes hardly walk just waddle! I wore my largest fur coat and hat and tried to play the part of a little old lady. While checking at the airport, my son went first without any money, because young men were checked thoroughly. I followed as best I could, full of trepidation in case I was stopped and searched.

I couldn't take the coat off even on the plane because then everything would be obvious. After a 12 hour flight, wearing a long fur coat and high fur boots, I was very tired and hated the money. When I got to St. Petersburg and came to my friend's flat, the first thing I did was run into the bathroom in order to divest myself of all this money and came out holding a plastic bag full of money. Hurray!

Then began the most pleasant part of the whole business: I emptied the bag onto the sofa and we counted the cash, estimating the profit and divided everything into three equal parts: for myself, my son and my friend. Everyone was happy and satisfied; in the morning after getting up very early, we were shopping again. It lasted for three months like that, and then people's purchasing power reduced abruptly, because salaries weren't paid on time and there were limitations on the amount of currency which people could withdraw from personal bank accounts at the savings banks.

It turned out that people had money, but they couldn't use it. Besides that, business in the country developed very swiftly, and everyone who lost his/her job started a retail business at once, because it was the easiest thing to do. Such a business was called "Buy-Sell" as a joke, everyone did the same: we bought from one another and sold to each other and there appeared more and more competitors.

In Yakutsk I met two of my ex colleagues from Zyryanka, who worked at the district committee of Komsomol with me before the USSR breakup. After its abolition they began to sell electrical devices – they transported tape-recorders, video-recorders and other radio equipment in containers from Moscow. They advised me straight away that if I did not increase the amount of stock I was bringing to Siberia, competitors would overtake me and I would eventually lose my business.

Of course, I got upset after the conversation, but I understood myself that I was reaching a deadlock and we decided to reorganize our work. My son went to Zyryanka so that we could open a store there, it was easier for him to do this because all the papers contained his name, and I continued to transport stock by air to Zyranka. The shop was opened very quickly, the premises were rented and I delivered goods there only a couple of times, but the venture did not get any further because salaries weren't paid and people had no money to buy anything.

In order to get rid of the goods faster we made a list and gave goods to our friends on trust. Since that moment I understood that we had to wrap up this enterprise, moreover my husband had disapproved of the business, not having wanted me to undertake any business and now he insisted on the closure of this business. In his opinion I had to develop a home, redo the flat, face-lift it, do the housework, etc. For five months the flat had been empty because he continued to work in Siberia, transporting the logs to Kuban.

During that time we saw each other only twice in the hotel, when he came to Yakutsk on business. However, I was very tired after this intense period of activity, both emotionally and physically and realized that I really wasn't up to continuing. After I had consulted my friend we decided to close the business; but what to do with the money? It was a bad idea to keep it and we had to buy something for this cash or convert it into dollars.

My friend told me at once that she would buy a new flat and some furniture with her share of the money, she had dreamt of it for a long time. I also wanted to buy some new furniture because we had only the old stuff we brought from Yakutia. It would be difficult for me to buy new furniture in St. Petersburg for delivery to another distant town because I was not a resident of St. Petersburg, and the rules only allowed the transfer of household items when you moved residence from one town to another, and had the documentation to prove it.

Moreover, the size of the furniture would necessitate a container all to itself and have to be sent by the official railway transport. That is why I decided to convert all the money into dollars. There weren't any official exchange offices in the country at that time and individuals had to do it illegally. Any exchange operations were illegal in the Soviet Union and individuals doing this were held criminally liable.

After the country breakup, currency exchange supervision by the law-enforcement authorities was reduced, and very often the police didn't pay any attention to it. Those people engaged in the unofficial business of exchanging money stood in the markets, at the shops, near subways and other public places pretending they were advertising or selling something, but everybody knew that they dealt with changing of currency.

I was told that the best time for exchange was evening when the shops were closed and there were no police about. The first time I tried to exchange some roubles, my friend's husband drove me and my son to the centre of the city at eight p.m. I decided to convert money in parts and firstly I took money for buying 400 dollars. When we arrived at the place I saw a couple of young men, who stood behind the store and pretended to be talking to each other, but as soon as we approached them they came toward us and asked how many dollars we needed.

I answered 400 and they moved aside to count money and came to us then pulling money from under their arms, where they kept it, counted it again in our presence. There were exactly 400 dollars rolled up into a tube and bound with a rubber band. We all saw that. I counted off the needed amount in roubles and gave them. They pulled out dollars from under the arm and went immediately round the side of the house saying that they were afraid of police.

We were afraid of the police as well and came back to the car quickly and drove off. I pulled out the dollars that were rolled up into a tube in order to straighten them out, and when I took the rubber band off I saw there were only four one-dollar notes. I screamed in surprise and said that we had been cheated. Everyone was shocked, and we drove back to the store, but there was no one there, of course. When we came back my friend asked us, "Why do you look so sad, haven't you exchanged the money?

Did you drive for nothing?" "We've exchanged," I answered, and told her about everything. She began to scold her husband, saying that he lived in the city and knew about such incidents, and that he should have told us beforehand to be careful with what we took. After that incident, the question of money exchange was no longer considered. My son asked me to give him his share of the money and he would go back home to Zyryanka.

I persuaded him, however, that money should be spent quickly or it would be lost, and it would be better if I bought furniture for myself and him. "And how will you transport it?" asked my friend. "I will," I answered. The next day my son departed for home, and I went to the railway station to the department of freight service. I was told in the ticket office the same that my friend had told me, "You can transport your own things if you have documents, but if you want you can talk to the chief of transportation who deals with containers, maybe he can help you."

I went out of the station and went to the area where workers were loading and unloading the containers, and found the chief of transportation and explained to him what I wanted. After he had listened to me he told me he could do everything; take the furniture from the stores in his truck; send it wherever I wanted; and without any papers! "How much does this cost?" I asked carefully. "Six thousand roubles," he said without thinking.

I even jumped for joy – six thousand? Six thousand altogether and the problem would be solved! This wasn't a big sum for me and I went home satisfied. Together with my friend, we immediately began to plan the buying of our furniture. This turned out to be not a simple matter. We visited all the furniture shops and exhibitions that were in the city. At that time cooperatives began to produce their own beautiful furniture according to their own designs, some of them only started to work and organized exhibitions for market research purposes.

The most beautiful furniture was at these exhibitions, but it couldn't be bought there. The particular items that we liked and wanted to buy could only be ordered, we would then have to wait for it to be produced by the factory. This did not serve my purpose, as it was dangerous to keep cash for so long because of the possible future currency reform and I wanted to go home as soon as possible.

At that time you could do everything if you had money, so we paid sellers more than the price required and bought the demonstration stock, negotiating to collect the furniture in a couple of days. We bought a large volume of furniture because it was all so beautiful, and I had never seen such wonderful items before. For example, I bought myself a piece of upholstered furniture as if it was from the king's palace; beautifully designed, upholstered with golden velvet and a wall unit with a spinning bar.

In general, I bought two bedroom suites, two kitchen suits, and two wall suits and two upholstered suits for the hall. This was enough to furnish two flats –both my son's and my own; moreover I didn't spend all our money and had a bit left over for emergencies. At this time, as I have already told you before, people weren't being paid their salaries and there was a shortage of cash in the country. When I paid 20 – 30 thousand roubles for each suit it attracted attention.

It was especially funny when we together with friends bought three bedroom suits. They were freely available, and we came straight to the salesman and asked, "How much is the suit?" "26 thousand roubles," he answered. "We'd like to purchase three whole suites," I said. He stared at me and thought I was joking. "Three?" He asked again. "Yes – isn't it possible to buy three of them?" I asked "It is possible, but it will cost you 78 thousand roubles!" "Fine, write us out a check please," I insisted.

When we started paying the cashier, she stared at us as well, and when we were leaving the store she leaned out of the window and watched us leaving for a while. After I had noticed that I laughed, but a friend pulled me by the sleeve out of the shop. "Let's get out of here fast, before they call for the police and start asking us where we got the money from," she whispered. In the end I bought everything I wanted, and I went with all the checks for the furniture to the chief of container transportation.

Despite the fact that the shops were in different parts of the city, I went with the chief and driver in the truck to all of them and transported the furniture to the station, where the workers in my presence loaded it into two containers. One of them I sent to Kuban, and the other one with my son's furniture to Chernovtsy. The chief took my ID and went away to process documents, which he brought back to me for signing after a while.

After I had signed the papers, I gave him money for the transportation of the containers, together with an extra six thousand roubles for his work. I kept copies of the documentation for the transport and went home. "That was all, a big task was accomplished: we earned money, bought some furniture and sent it home. Now I can relax and have a rest," I repeated mentally.

But the further I was from the station the more I worried and different thought struck me: "What if he cheated me? Anything can happen, I don't know the man, I didn't go to the ticket office with him and I didn't watch him processing the documents. Maybe he made fake documents and sent the furniture who knows where or maybe he unloaded the containers the moment I left?"

My friend had doubts from the very beginning and told me I could lose all the money it had been so hard earning. Maybe it is our Russian nature – even if something good is going on, we are afraid of being glad, waiting for the worse. In the end, I came back to Kuban bearing the brunt of these doubts …

When I arrived back to Kuban, my husband was waiting for me at home, and indicated to me that he was very dissatisfied with the fact that I was running my own business and hadn't been at home for around five months. I was waiting him to compliment me for earning so much money and buying the new furniture, but he was indifferent to this and told me in no uncertain terms: "You'd better do some housework; I'm ashamed in front of the neighbour's that we haven't planted anything in our garden. And we could buy some furniture eventually, with time, anyway."

I was disappointed and upset at this resentment, and began to realize that this might be the beginning of the end of our marriage. The cooperative's license for wood harvesting in Siberia had expired and my husband was now working in Kuban permanently.

All the locals farmed, and he thought I should become part of this community, that is why he was going to bring me some chickens for breeding, and which was supposed to keep me at home. We had lived apart for almost a year – he had been to Siberia and I had been to St. Petersburg, Yakutsk, Ukraine, and the expectation for our future life had changed. We ceased understanding each other and it seemed to me that I was talking to a stranger.

I tried to persuade him to move to Chernovtsy, because it was dangerous to live here, I wasn't going to farm and I just didn't like it here, after all! We quarrelled a great deal and it all ended up with a divorce after 24 years of married life together. The fact that we didn't have any young children or any financial claims on each other made the divorce a quick deal. I took my belongings with me and moved to Chernovtsy.

Chapter 43

Moving to Ukraine

I had not been to Ukraine for more than eight months and much had changed there during that time. It was a difficult period in Ukrainian history, when the former good life had already been destroyed and the new one was just beginning to emerge. It was a time of muddle and chaos in all the spheres of activity. When I previously visited Ukraine, and stayed only for a short time, I did not fully understand the local situation because it was equally hard in all the former republics after the USSR breakdown.

When I decided to move back permanently to Chernovtsy I was most attracted by the fact that I would live in a big city, where it was a lot more interesting than in Kuban. Now, after I had realized the reality of the situation, I felt a wave of panic and a thought that I wouldn't survive suddenly struck me. But there was no one else but me to blame – I alone chose Ukraine for my future life and Chernovtsy to be my home, and I had to settle down there.

I had never thought that in my own country, where I grew up and was born, I would feel like a stranger. However, whatever official body I dealt with, I was disappointed. For example, when I was getting my passport address changed to that of my new apartment in Chernovtsy, a clerk in the passport office, while signing the documents, commented on Russia and its president, Boris Yeltsin, "Are you from Russia? Your authorities are no longer in power here as well as your Boris Yeltsin! And why have you come here, you'd better stay in your Russia!"

I began to make excuses and say that I was a Ukrainian, that I had lived and worked in Siberia temporarily and now I had come back home. To this he replied, "A Ukrainian? What are you talking about – you do not even speak the Ukrainian language!" I was uncomfortable with this conversation, and I felt bad for no other reason than he was right.

I was born in the east of Ukraine in a family that spoke Russian; I studied at a Russian school, where I learned the Ukrainian language, but I never actually needed to speak it, and consequently lost some of the fluency of the language although I understood it when it was spoken to me, and twenty years speaking Russian in Siberia had further dulled my ability in the language.

When, years earlier, while studying at Chernovtsy College where teaching was in Russian, I had begun to understand Ukrainian language well only because most of the students there spoke Ukrainian. Actually it wasn't necessary to study Ukrainian, because when Ukraine was a member of the USSR Russian was the state language as well as Ukrainian.

Since the moment of declaration of independence in Ukraine, Ukrainian language had become the only state language and all the business correspondence in the offices was in Ukrainian. The Russian language became a foreign one, and it was driven out of everyday life as well as everything else that reminded people of the soviet period in the history of Ukraine. Even streets and squares which were named after Lenin, Russian writers and military leaders were renamed. The TV programmes were in Ukrainian and even the well-liked movies, shot during the Soviet Period, were shown with a Ukrainian translation.

I understood that due to my poor knowledge of the Ukrainian language I had no chances of getting a good job here, although I could have worked at any institution with my education and experience. I think that even if I had known Ukrainian well, I would have been rejected anyway because, firstly, I had arrived from Russia and, secondly, I had been a communist in the past and I had worked for the party.

Such people were not in favour; and anything from Russia or the communist party was blamed for everything bad that was happening at that moment. Nevertheless, I was going to go to the Job Centre and try to find a job in order not to stay at home anymore. When I told a neighbour of mine about my intention she laughed at me and stopped me – "Are you crazy, people go there in order not to get a job but to claim for unemployment benefits, because it is even ridiculous to try to find a job at these times. Look what is happening around you and how many local people are unemployed now!"

So I was on the wrong side of 40 and at this age I found myself out of my depth. For the whole my life, I had been a patriot of my country, I had studied, had worked in extreme conditions and had hoped that the best was to be in the future, and what had I at that moment? I was useless, nobody knew who I was or what I was, and I had to collect my thoughts and decide what to do in order to survive.

Today I remember that period of my life and wonder how I could stand everything that happened to me. Of course, for many people who lived in Ukraine at that time, this period was also a hard one. They survived the USSR break-down, lost their jobs, money, usual life, but they continued to live in the same country, at their homes, among their friends and relatives.

I lost everything at one time in comparison with them: my country the USSR, the party, my job, family, friends and after I had moved to Ukraine from Siberia I found myself in a totally different country, where I had to start my life again. Frankly saying, the more I went into the situation which existed in the country the harder it was for me to accept and understand the situation I found myself in.

Because when people voted for the independence of Ukraine they hoped for the better life and couldn't even suppose that unemployment, lack of money and uncertainty in the future were waiting for them. It is well-known that the economics in the USSR during the Soviet period was an integration of Economic ties between all the republics.

Since the moment Ukraine gained its independence, this had all been ruined and some time and new reforms were needed in order to regenerate the economy, this had not yet happened in 1992. This resulted in the two biggest factories in Chernovtsy not being able to continue their steady and smooth work because of the rupture of the production contracts with the productions from the other republics' factories.

The system of necessary raw material provision for the majority of local plants and factories was troubled. Many of those were closed all over the region. This led to worker displacement and mass unemployment, which had never happened earlier. In order to survive these hard times and to keep productions running, many enterprises changed the specialization of production. Using materials and equipment which they had in stock, they began to produce different types of popular consumer goods: knives, locks, gas lighters, spades, etc.

The enterprises had no money and it was not considered good form to ask for a salary and could even lead to dismissal. People had to work for free for a couple of months and even a year just to preserve their jobs. In order to solve the problem somehow, the enterprises gave people goods they produced instead of their salary.

They received sets of enameled pans, toys for children, plastic goods, buckets, etc., equal to the value of their salaries. The workers of distilleries even received vodka instead of their salary. Workers of course, tried to sell those goods or exchange for food. At that time, people were standing along the roads throughout Ukraine selling cheaply everything they had got instead of their salaries. Those who lived not far from the railways took the goods to the railway stations and sold them for next to nothing.

At that time, hundreds of unemployed people had only one chance to survive – to go into business. Of course some people had done this since the end of 1980s when there appeared an opportunity to bring goods from abroad. But at that time almost all of them had a job and this trade just brought them some extra earnings. Since 1992 the country had turned into a market: they were selling anything and everything they could, set up a stall wherever there was space to stand.

For example in Chernovtsy prior to 1992, there was only one clothing market which was situated outside the town and there were several grocery markets in the town itself. When I came back it was hard to recognize the town – there were unregulated markets all over the town, where they sold not only groceries but different goods as well. Besides that, people from villages sold food laid out on newspapers and rubber sheets right on the pavements.

Small stalls sprouted like mushrooms after the summer rains, in the centre of the town, at all the bus and tram stops and other crowded places. These stalls generated good profits because goods were bought quickly at all prices. It might be reasonable to question, where the money came from under such economic conditions. The answer was very simple: those people who were trading or had some other business had enough money.

Everyone sold something and bought something from each other. In this was way nearly the whole population was drawn into trade of one kind or another, which inevitably led to different levels of trade and society. A wholesale trade was the most prestigious and profitable one, but it needed serious investments, which many people didn't have. That is why the next level included people who bought from the wholesalers and sold at retail market stall level.

Pensioners and poor people had no money for buying goods and carried out some small trades at pavement level which allowed them to live one day at a time. They took mainly food for sale – bananas, chocolate, cakes, chewing gums and small goods for everyday life, e.g. ballpoint pens, adhesive tape, lighters, notebooks, socks, stockings.

There was an old lady in our apartment block, who lived on the money she earned from selling bananas during the day, a box of which she bought in the market every morning and rolled it on a cart from there to the centre of the town.

There was a total mess with money in Ukraine. Despite the fact that the first Ukrainian currency "coupon-karbovanetzs" been introduced. Soviet Roubles, German Marks and American Dollars were used as well. In the shops, you could pay for the goods using roubles but you had to show the amount of coupons of the same worth, which was very inconvenient for sellers and buyers. All my savings were in roubles at that time and when I ran out of coupons I couldn't buy anything at the shops and had to go to the markets.

The markets were the only place where one could buy things using roubles or any other foreign currency without having coupons. Actually roubles and dollars were in favour at the markets and they didn't want to take coupon-karbovanetzs, because this was considered to be a temporary currency and because of the bad quality of paper, coupon- karbovanetzs quickly became unfit for use.

Due to the economic crisis at the beginning of 1990s the prices for food and goods weren't under any control by the government and began to increase and change almost every day. Smart people and those who did business understood that all that happened due to the devaluation of Ukrainian currency and tried to exchange it for dollars. But pensioners and other ordinary people who didn't know about this lost their small amounts of money faster than they could spend them.

Everything happened rapidly and if a loaf of bread cost 20 hryvnias one day it could cost several times more the next day and people discovered with amazement that their salary or pension, paid each month, was only enough to last for several days. Low income people like – pensioners, the unemployed and others became so poor that they had to find different means of survival, methods which had been considered to be indecent before.

People were standing reaching out their hands begging for help everywhere in the streets and underground passages, near the churches, shops and markets. It was especially hard to see among those beggars women holding newborn babies and old ladies who used to be refined, judged by their appearance, who now averted their eyes diffidently while begging for a piece of bread.

Due to devaluation of Ukrainian national currency there appeared a hyperinflation in which prices rose ten, hundreds, thousands times and up to millions. According to the prices new notes were printed with zeros added and the old notes were just thrown away because you couldn't buy anything for them. I'll give you an instance to make it clearer: before the USSR breakdown I had paid 12 thousand roubles while exchanging my cooperative flat in Chernovtsy, which was its full price.

Two years later it cost a million and a house of our relatives in the countryside cost two millions coupon-karbovanetzs. A year later we had several million denomination notes in our wallets and we bought food for them and used to joke that we all became millionaires at last.

The hyperinflation lasted up to 1996 and the situation stabilized when hryvnias were introduced, which is a Ukrainian national currency today. It was a crisis for those people who had money which they had saved for their whole lives and kept at the branches of the savings bank, because after the USSR breakdown money on deposits in Russia and Ukraine was frozen.

Once a month people could withdraw a small amount of money from their accounts, but due to the rush there were long queues at the branches of savings bank and many people didn't have time to take out that money. In fact, money on deposits cheapened completely due to the quick rise of prices and money reforms. I personally didn't have any money on deposit at the branches of the savings bank of Ukraine, but I lost money because changing my residency by moving from one republic i.e. Russia to another i.e. Ukraine.

All who lived in Yakutia and went for a vocation to the central parts of the country used to take letters of credit for a certain amount of money (3-5 thousands) in order not to take so much money with them. You could withdraw money at any branch of the savings bank in the territory of the USSR in case of need. In 1989 I opened an account at the branch of the savings bank not far from the Domodedovo airport in Moscow and deposited 6 thousands roubles.

I did it for convenience because I always flew on vacation via Moscow and could withdraw from the account any money that I needed. Two years later in 1991 as a result of Pavlov reform the account was frozen and since that moment on I could only withdraw only 500 roubles at any one time while flying via Moscow.

After moving to Ukraine for permanent residence I didn't go to Moscow at all, it was a different country. This way I lost my money, for which I could buy a car at that time. Thousands of other people also lost their savings, which they had saved for the whole of their lives, while moving from one republic to another.

Chapter 44

Trying a New Business

By the autumn of the same year my son with his family had moved to Chernovtsy to take up permanent residence and we began to live together in my flat. His decision to return to Ukraine was forced because he was planning to live in Zyryanka for at least two more years. But life circumstances were such that he had to decide in which country he was going to live in the future, Ukraine or Russia.

The fact was that Ukraine as well as all the other newly formed independent states had closed its borders, and if he did not come back to Chernovtsy in time he would only be able to return later as a foreigner, and it would take several years to restore his citizenship. At that time, a mass outflow of population from the regions of the extreme north and north-east of Siberia had begun where most people had lived only because of the high salaries and availability of life's essentials.

After the USSR breakdown there was a crisis in supply there as well as everywhere else and there was no point in staying and people came back home. When my son arrived we started thinking about our future life; what could we do in this situation in Ukraine. Because our previous business in Yakutia took much energy and strength, I didn't want to go into business once again.

But this time there wasn't any alternative like going into trade business like many other people in Chernovtsy did. We decided to allocate duties this way: Since I was the only one who had a foreign passport I would go to Turkey and import goods. Then my son and my daughter-in-law would import the goods to Yakutia, because it would be easier to sell such goods there.

I agreed to go into a family business and couldn't even imagine what hardships and disappointments were waiting for me in the future. Tourist agencies which organized trips to Turkey, Poland and other countries of Europe began their work in the town at that time. Those trips were tourist ones but people used the opportunity to get abroad to import goods for sale.

So I bought a tour for four days to Istanbul and began to prepare for the trip. First of all I had to exchange roubles for dollars, which I would use to pay for the goods in Turkey. It was almost impossible to do this in Chernovtsy, because there weren't any official exchange offices at that time, and you could do this only with a help of speculators in foreign currency who dealt only with customers they knew.

That is why I urgently went to St. Petersburg where I bought 700 dollars within a couple of days, supposing these would be enough for the first trip to Turkey. After I had settled up all my affairs I had to come back home as soon as possible. I decided not to wait for the through train and to go to Lvov which is about 70 km over the border from Poland and here change train to Chernovtsy.

There weren't any tickets for a sleeping-car and I had to use a day coach. Every person in my country knows how hard it is to go in such a coach, especially for a long distance and at night.

All the way to Lvov I was sitting squeezed by people and their belongings, passengers got off and the new ones arrived at the stations and there wasn't any chance to lay down at least for a minute or to have something to eat and we were not even served with any tea which is the norm on a Russian train. The train arrived at five a.m. into Lvov and I ran right away to the ticket office to buy a ticket to Chernovtsy. It was so crowded at the train station that there wasn't any place to sit or stand and it seemed that the station was humming with a thousand voices.

It was impossible to understand which ticket office sold tickets for the direction I needed and there wasn't anybody to ask about it, everyone was busy with their own business and didn't answer any questions. There was a long queue at the ticket office, a crowd actually; people just do not queue, surrounding the ticket office from all the sides, all pressing and pushing each other and quarrelling. I began to feel terrible after a night of my trip in the train: I had no strength, my head was spinning and I was thirsty.

I went round the station to buy something to eat, but all the cafés started their work at 8 a.m.

After I had stood for an hour or more on my feet, I felt that I was going to faint and grasped the sleeve of a man who was standing in front of me. He saw my condition, took me outside and left me at the wall: "Stay here in the fresh air, you'll feel better and I'm going back inside so as not to miss our turn in the queue," he said and went away ...

When I opened my eyes I couldn't understand anything: why am I sitting on the cold cement porch of the station, who are those people surrounding me and looking at me as if they have seen a ghost? I'm holding a small bottle of vodka in one hand and someone's bloodied handkerchief in the other hand with my broken glasses lying next to me. I felt that my face was hurt badly: I couldn't talk or even open my mouth because I felt that my teeth inside my mouth were broken as well.

It would appear that after I had been left alone outside the railway station I had fallen over quite heavily, hitting the concrete porch face down. After a while a nurse came to me and took me to the first-aid post of the station. I must say she did the best she could to help me: she measured my blood pressure right away and gave me some pills. "I'll call for the ambulance and will send you to the hospital because you won't be able to get to Chernovtsy in such a condition.

You're in a critical state, the pressure is 70/40, there's a very small pulse, your front teeth are knocked out and your lower lip is hurt and badly split," she said. "What are you talking about, I can't go to the hospital, I'm leaving for Turkey tomorrow," I refused. And this was the truth, I had to get back home faster, because, firstly, a bus to Istanbul was leaving the next morning and, secondly, I had 700 dollars in my belt and I was worried what would happen to them if I went to the hospital.

When I returned to the queue, the man who had taken me outside looked at me and understood everything at once; he began to ask the people in front to allow me to buy a ticket without waiting. But nobody budged nor even look at me – they didn't care, everybody thought only of him/herself. Then the man began to scream, pushed in and bought a ticket for me. I was so grateful to him and I regret that I never knew his name and will be eternally grateful for what he did.

My son met me at the station and when he saw my bruised and battered faced he was startled and began asking me about what had happened. He thought I had been beaten and robbed while was trying to exchange the money. I couldn't talk and just gave him the dollars and told him to take me to the hospital as soon as possible. A regional hospital is in the centre of the town and is quite big; there are separate buildings for different departments.

We didn't know what kind of doctor I needed and we entered the first building we saw. It was half-empty for some reason and we walked along a long corridor and couldn't find anybody. Then my son went by himself and brought a young man, who turned out to be a student of a medical institute and who was undergoing practical training there. After he had had a look at me, the student apologized to me and said: "I don't know what to do with you. Come here tomorrow when there's a doctor because his shift is over now and he has gone home and it is not allowed to send for him except for in an emergency."

After a good deal of persuasion he at last agreed to suture up my lip and handed us a list of what we needed to buy in the pharmacy. I was dumbfounded at this because such things had never happened in earlier times. But everything had changed and medicine was in the same crisis as the whole country. Though medical aid was supposed to be free, in reality we had to pay for everything and bring everything we needed for treatment with us: some alcohol to clean, cotton wool, bandages, syringes, pills and even a plaster cast if you had a broken bone.

In order not to waste time my son gave 20 dollars to the student and he went somewhere quickly. We were waiting for him for half an hour, until he came back with a handful of cotton wool, alcohol, a needle and a thread around 30 centimetres long. "This is everything I could find, but there is no anesthesia medicine, shall we suture you up without one?" He asked joyfully. After we had looked at each other I replied: "Do it anyway you want, but faster please."

The following morning I came to the bus station on time holding a bottle of water with a drinking straw in it so that I could drink. I don't even want to describe how terribly ill I felt, but despite this I got to the market in Istanbul all right and was stunned with the variety of goods there and the low prices for them. It was my first time at such a market and I spend a lot of time choosing and asking the prices, trying to buy as much as possible not only for resale but for home and presents for the family.

The other people on the bus who had been in the business for a long time had already completed their purchases and accepted the goods packed in big bags without even checking them.

When the "tourists" took their goods outside the market to await departure I couldn't believe that all those things could possibly be loaded onto the bus and leave room for all the people. But the bus drivers were skilled and experienced: at first they loaded the luggage space to the full, and then they made us take our places in the passenger compartment and then piled the rest of the baggage up to the roof of the bus.

I was scared even to think that in such conditions I was going to travel for 36 hours. The way home was long enough, we had to cross the borders, to get through the customs and cross the territory of four countries: Turkey, Bulgaria, Romania and Ukraine. It was very hot inside the bus during the journey, it was hard to breathe and bags weighed upon me so hard that I couldn't even move or change the posture.

When the bus stopped for a service or while crossing the border, they pulled out the goods at first and then all the passengers went out – and in this way we continued all the way home. I couldn't wait for the end of this torture and during the last few hours when we were approaching the border of Ukraine I was so tired that I couldn't even talk and I just sobbed.

All the goods I brought from Turkey we sold in Yakutia, but during the time taken to transport the goods there, the value of the dollar increased, but lack of this information in Yakutia we didn't get the profit we hoped for. This way the business which we started in Ukraine was a total disappointment. I had no strength nor had I any desire to continue the trips abroad and I stopped taking part in this.

Chapter 45

Activity for Survival

So, I couldn't just sit without anything to do so I take the decision to try the trade business in St. Petersburg again this time in my own but different way. I began to buy goods and take it to commission shops in St. Petersburg for sale. I bought Ukrainian folk art works mainly, e.g. souvenirs, embroidered table napkins, carved wood and boxes. But due to the problems with the transportation of goods, I had to give up this trade.

The hard fact was that there was a through train from Chernovtsy to St. Petersburg which went across four countries: Belorussia, Lithuania, Latvia and Estonia. Those were the republics of one country in the soviet period and hence there had been no problems earlier. A couple of years after the breakdown of the USSR and formation of the independent states, all the countries had gradually closed their borders, limiting the import and export of goods.

Customs Officers examined carefully all the luggage of the passengers entering and leaving these new countries, they sometimes even opened the covering of the train compartment, because people hid some illegal goods under the covering and tried to sneaked them across the border. I understood that a trade business wasn't for me anymore and I tried to find some other type of business, but I couldn't think of anything suitable. For more than a month I was sitting at home doing nothing, and then the problem was resolved unexpectedly.

Though markets and shops were overloaded with clothes, there was something missing. For example, I couldn't find a beret with a peak so I sewed one for myself. It was autumn and cold and I thought – 'If I need such a beret, there might be some women who need one, too.' I began to buy some cashmere fabric and to sew fashionable berets with peaks and made matching scarves using the same fabric. From that moment on I was always busy: after I had bought the fabric I started to make as many berets as I could, starting at 6 a.m. and ending at midnight. The following day I took them to the commission shops.

I extended my sewing repertoire with time, and began to sew curtains; kitchen sets (a tablecloth, placemats, aprons, mittens and tea cosies) all according to my own design. All of these were colourful and cheap, and people bought them eagerly. Then, by chance, I found a shop which was called 'Do it yourself'. Here one could buy different leftovers from factory production: clothing accessories, lace, thread, and off cuts of fabrics, etc.

This was a great find for me! I bought everything very cheaply there, because nobody needed those waste ends. I began to sew panelled skirts, hats, and children's sundresses using these materials and sold them very cheaply. Of course, there wasn't any profit from this work I was just trying to occupy myself. I stopped doing this after three months because the markets were becoming overloaded with the same type of Chinese and Turkish made goods and my goods weren't interesting for customers anymore.

I remember when I was a teenager and had just graduated my dressmaking courses, my mother told me – "this profession will definitely be of use to you and even in the hardest times of your life you won't be left without a piece of bread." Of course, I had always lived well, having subsequently studied engineering and qualified as a lawyer, but in these hard times, I needed my experience and skills at sewing to survive.

When a friend of mine, whose name was Tania, asked me to make a new skirt for her I agreed right away, having no idea that this was the beginning of my new business. When I had completed the skirt I took it to show Tania at her place of work. She was employed as a nurse at a local children's clinic. She liked the skirt very much and she began to try it on and show it to her colleagues. Her colleagues, who were mainly women, all liked what I had created and asked me to undertake the task of sewing something for them.

I immediately began to take their orders and left for home with several days' worth of work. The clinic was a five-story building with a large staff the majority of whom were women, so besides the ladies on Tania's floor there were many other potential customers and word soon spread throughout the clinic about the new dressmaker.

Over the course of the next two years I took every order, sewed new pieces of clothes, altered old ones, and everyone was grateful for my work. I made many new friends and acquaintances over this time. This was important for me because all my close friends made over the previous twenty years, and who were spiritually close to me, remained in Yakutia.

When I came to Chernovtsy I found myself as if in a vacuum, and it was hard for me to regain my equilibrium, because I had very few friends and my husband's relatives, who lived in the village, had a totally different outlook on life as well as interests. In the beginning of the 1990s in Ukraine a plethora of network and pyramid marketing companies which had been totally unknown before began to appear.

This new and apparently interesting type of business involved thousands of unemployed people at once. The first companies dealt mainly with the selling of slimming additives, vitamins and cosmetics. When a friend of mine began to persuade me to distribute "Oriflame" cosmetics I was skeptical about this and refused. I couldn't imagine how I would go in the streets and offer people my goods! And who would buy them!

Later, however, I went to a product presentation by an American company called "Neways" and was impressed with what I heard and saw there! The moment I entered, I liked the business atmosphere in the hall, the talk about network marketing, the staff of the company and the different products. For me, I was particularly impressed by the business speak and use in the conversation of the new, and unknown, words, such as: presentation, manager, distributor, network marketing, and price-list, all words that were obviously in everyday parlance in the west, but completely alien to me.

I believed and understood that I had a real opportunity to do an interesting business and concluded a contract with the company right away prepared me for my new business very seriously: placed an advertisement at a local newspaper, printed some nice business cards, assembled information and some samples of goods for presentation and made a business plan. I was self-confident, I had no doubts about my potential and I knew for sure to whom I would sell the products of the company to.

With some of my previous confidence restored I focused on my personal grooming, bringing out my best business suit, a new hairstyle and makeup. Wearing this outfit and a very high pair of heels and holding my husband's real leather document case I boarded the local trolley bus to travel to my first business meeting. Something most unusual then happened, on the crowded bus a man actually got up and offered me his seat! This had not happened to me for a very long time.

I felt elated and full of confidence and believed that I had arrived at last! I chose for my first business presentation the Children's Clinic, where they knew me well and trusted my every word. I made a successful presentation and made the first of many sales to the clinic staff. With my experience of work at the party bodies I could hold presentations of products by myself and persuade people that it was necessary to buy the vitamins.

I now considered myself to be a successful businesswoman and once, when I was going past the University, I saw a sign on the building "Business women's club" and confidently went in to find out more about this club for "Business Women". The manager of the club was Anna, and I discussed with here the possibility of mutual work. She was receptive to my ideas and among other things agreed that I could hold business presentations at the club.

I met many businesswomen at the club, Elena in particular, who was also a distributor at several different companies and had an office at her home. This woman turned out to be an extraordinary person and we became good friends. I earned quite good money for that time and spent some of money to buy the vitamins for myself and my family. After I had taken the vitamins for several years I received evidence that they are efficient and today I still buy the vitamins of this company.

Later some of this activity became very difficult to continue, because my husband returned to Chernovtsy and we began to live together as a family which also included my son and his family. Altogether we were a household of five people and the housework took almost all of my free time. There were constant interruptions in the provision of food and in order to provide for my family I was busy whole days long.

I woke up very early and at 7 a.m. I stood in the queue at the Dairy, though it opened at 8 a.m. and milk was delivered at 9 a.m. Dairy products were in limited supply and not everyone could be supplied and if they didn't reserve a place in the queue in time they could come back home with nothing. The seller usually announced how many milk cans had been delivered and people could figure out whether they had a chance of being able to buy something, and those who realized they stood no chance of making a purchase left the queue in order not to stand for nothing.

People usually bought three litres of milk which was poured into an enamelled can because it cost less to buy milk this way. There were very many older people in the queue because bread and milk was a main food for pensioners who had no money for some other types of products. Many of them never bought any meat or sausages because their pension was only enough for a "Soup set" (a set of bones without meat) with which they cooked some soup or borsch for themselves.

Bananas were bought by the singly and it was a luxury for a pensioner to buy one. There were huge queues at all the food shops and many people we went to the markets where there was better availability. You've got to hand it to the people, who lived in the countryside, if they had land enough to keep a few pigs, etc., or a large garden with vegetables they took everything they could for sale in the town.

I had to stand at the oven from morning till evening in order to feed my family three times a day, like all women in my country I cooked using only fresh products – meat, fish and vegetables which I peeled and cut by myself. Beside that my parents from Donetsk came to us on a visit and stayed at our place for a month. They liked to stay at our place very much and would like to have stayed longer but they had to go back because it was hard for seven people to live in one flat even if it was only temporarily.

There was a tradition in Ukraine to stock food by means of bottling during June till October, at the season of fruit and vegetables ripening. I didn't do this when I lived in Yakutia because we kept all food frozen, but as soon as I moved to Chernovtsy I had to master the skills.

My husband liked very much to have plenty of everything in stock so I preserved 200 litres of fruit-stew, which I bottled in the 3- litre jars, tens of jars of all kinds of vegetable salads, marinated tomatoes, pepper, pickles, tomato paste and jams.

I hated that season as I had to work till late at night because if I started something I had to finish it. The process of bottling was a long one, because you had to wash and cut-up the fruit and vegetable and put everything into the glass jars of different size, fill the jars up with brine which was prepared beforehand and then sterilize them for 40-60 minutes by double boiling them. After that I had to quickly cover the jars with lids while they were still hot and seal them quickly using special sealing equipment.

If one did everything correctly, bottled food could be preserved in the cellars for several years. It was great for those who had their own vegetable and fruit gardens, they had everything ready and free. I bought everything at the market and brought it home in buckets by myself mostly because all the other members of the family were busy with the business and all the housework was my duty.

Chapter 46

Husband's Return to Chernovtsy and

New Flat

In spring 1993, my ex-husband called me unexpectedly and told me that he wanted to move to Chernovtsy for permanent residence. In order not to lose a house in Kuban he asked me to find an apartment of equal worth for exchange. I was listening to him in amazement because he was telling me word for word what I had told him right before my leaving for Chernovtsy.

At that moment he didn't want to listen to me and only after he had lived for a couple of years in Kuban did he believe I was right in my decision to move to Chernovtsy. He told me that when he was in the town of Armavir he accidentally got caught in crossfire between two criminal groups. Apparently when he was crossing a square near the train station, two cars stopped on opposite sides of the road and people began to shoot at each other from the open windows. In order to save himself he lay down on the ground and stayed there until the moment the two cars departed.

He told me "I feel remote from my family and relatives here. It is hard and dangerous to live here, I'm constantly on edge after what has happened to me and I have decided to come back home." I reminded him that it was not much better here, that it was hard to live and our son and I were unemployed and were doing anything in order to survive. He answered me that he had experience of work and that he would try to create a family cooperative in Chernovtsy.

Quite frankly, I was very glad that he was coming back home and thought maybe we could live together again, because during those hard times it was very hard for me to be alone both emotionally and physically. The next day I went to the central market where agents, who dealt with selling and exchange of housing, gathered. I didn't expect that I would find a family very quickly who wanted to exchange a house in Chernovtsy for one in Russia and particularly in Kuban.

However, I soon found a family wanting to do just that. The interesting fact was that they had also lived in the North of Siberia in Magadan Region for a long time. After the USSR breakdown, this family came back to Chernovtsy, and now they no longer wished to live in Ukraine, but wanted to return to Russia and would have no objection if it was Kuban. We were very glad to meet each other and couldn't talk enough to each other at first, forgetting about the flats.

We remembered our former happy lives in those cold and distant places, shared our plans for the future and I had the feeling that I met dear and close to me people. Their flat was smaller than the house in Kuban and had only one bedroom, but it was situated in a good solid house, which was built during the Romanian period in the 1920s and was considered to be a part of an old historical stock.

The house had only four flats: two on the ground floor and two on the first floor and every flat had a lot of land in the garden which was situated around the house. But the main merit of the house was that it was situated in the most prestigious part of the town, only 200 metres away from the famous Chernovtsy University.

The documents had been completed for a month and I had made friends with Maxim and Valentina and was even sorry that they were leaving Chernovtsy, because we could be good friends. But when the procedure of housing exchange was over they moved to Kuban. I went there also because I wanted to make sure they liked our house and to help Victor to pack his bags.

The family which moved to Kuban was of pensionable age and they had dreamt of owning a house with a garden. That is why they were extremely glad and satisfied with everything, especially with the big garden where they were planning to grow vegetables. Before our departure we had laid a big table and invited our other friends and neighbours.

We were celebrating the arrival of a new family to Kuban and our homecoming to Chernovtsy. Maxim and Valentina were very grateful to us, because they got not only a house of their dreams but also our old friends with whom they are still friends to this day.

After we had come back to Chernovtsy, I gave my cooperative flat to my son and together with my ex-husband I began to live in the new flat. But after we had lived there for a little while, we understood that the flat was too small and inconvenient for us because it had intercommunicating rooms and one bedroom only. The area of the flat didn't allow us to place the furniture I had bought in St. Petersburg. That is why we decided not to hurry to redecorate the flat, but to try and exchange it for a bigger one.

When our neighbours from upstairs found out about our plans to move to a larger property they offered us the opportunity to move to their bigger flat, asking for two small flats in exchange, because they wanted to live apart from their daughter. It would, therefore, require us to find and buy another small flat to complete the exchange. When Victor and I saw our neighbour's flat we were impressed because the flat had 120 square metres of living area and three big rooms.

The height of the ceiling was 3.6 metres, the windows were big and that is why the flat was very light. We decided that we would like to move there as soon as possible, no matter what it would take. We had to buy a one-room flat in another district of the town, so that our neighbours' daughter could live separately from her parents. Our neighbours could then move to our existing flat on the ground floor.

We managed to find another flat without too much difficulty and the exchange was completed without undue delay. I was extremely happy with our new apartment, and we got down to work right away, hiring a couple of tradesmen to carry out redecoration. I had always dreamt of an unusual flat where each room would be of different colour and with a moulded and decorated ceiling. The kitchen would be fully fitted and in a brown tone with sconces on the walls and a big family table.

It proved to be very hard to make my dream come true, because at that time there was a lack of construction materials and coordinating accessories. It was impossible to choose matching wall tiles and paint which matched together with the limited choice of plumbing components. Although my husband was a builder, I had a richer imagination than he did and in order to stick to a design we had to use the materials that were available, together with a little improvisation.

For example, I used some brown plastic statuettes, designed for furniture decoration, for modelling the ceiling. I took a white metallic covering of the water heater to an auto body shop and somehow persuaded the workers to paint it beige with car paint. After the refurbishment was over, all the rooms were furnished with the furniture from St. Petersburg. I sewed the curtains for the windows and the blankets for the beds myself using a German mail order catalogue for inspiration and the whole flat turned out to be very beautiful and modern.

The biggest room was a living-room and it was 32 square metres in area and there was a double door out to the balcony where I planted some flowers. Our house was situated on a hill and there were wonderful views over the town from the balcony, which was especially nice in the evening when the town was all in lights. The summer nights in Ukraine are warm and I liked to stand on the balcony for hours looking at the view and just daydreaming.

I liked the kitchen the most, the window of which looked out on the garden and I could look there while I was having dinner. The garden was especially nice in spring when the fruit trees were blooming and they were all white as if covered with a veil. Under the kitchen window grew a big cherry tree which was old and had many transplanted branches for different varieties of cherries: white red and black.

At home in my flat on my 50th anniversary, 1998

When I opened the window I could reach the branches and pick some cherries. Our flat was unlike others because it had old fireplaces in two rooms faced with Romanian tiles and even though these tiles were of the same age as the house itself, they were still preserved in their original condition. We were very proud of these fireplaces because it wasn't traditional for our country to have these, and they did not exist in any modern flats or houses. They were only in the old houses which were constructed before the Soviet times.

There was one more peculiarity about the flat, which was of great importance to me as a woman. There was a high-quality stone staircase which started from the entrance on the ground floor and led to the first floor and the attic. The doors to the attic were in my flat so the whole attic (more than 150 square metres) belonged to me. There were windows in the attic and after I had tidied it up you could even furnish it and make one more room to live in, but I used it as a closet and dried my linen there. We finished the refurbishment in 1994 and gave a house-warming party right away, because according to a Russian tradition, moving to a new flat is a great event in life which should be celebrated. In fact, my family celebrated not only a new home but also a homecoming after many years of life in Yakutia. That is why we invited all our relatives, neighbours, friends, and students of the same year that studied with us at college, some 40 people in all.

In Ukraine a celebration never takes the format of a buffet. It is always in the form of a sit down meal. Guests usually come for a long time and have to be seated at the table. We borrowed some tables from our neighbours in order to seat all the guests and made one huge table where everyone could be seated. The house-warming party started at 2 p.m. and finished at midnight and during all that time I served up different dishes, drinks and alcohol.

Everybody admired our flat: the refurbishment, design, and especially the furniture, and despite the fact that I was very tired of all the preparations for the festive occasion I felt very happy. It seemed to me that my life was settled at last, I lived in a wonderful flat in a town of my dreams, my son was beside me and our life would be better from now on. But it only "seemed" to me, because there was the hardest period of my life ahead with its failures, disappointments and losses.

Chapter 47

Beginning of Family Business

My husband's idea when he moved to Chernovtsy was to found a cooperative and involve relatives and friends in it, in order to work with, as he used to say, "My people", whom he could trust. But nobody was interested in this because people were afraid of risk during the period of economic chaos in Ukraine.

Many people preferred to survive the hard times being content with what they had. They decided that they would hold on to their existing jobs, even though they didn't get a salary for months. We didn't want to trade in the market on principle and that is why we began to look for some other business. We considered all the possible variants of private business: auto service, apartment remodelling, bakery, café, European imported cars, trade, but we couldn't choose any of them.

We didn't have any money to fund a company requiring investments, because all the money was spent on buying and refurbishing the flat. The idea of a business connected with trips abroad was dismissed, because I was the only one who had a foreign passport and you had to spend much energy, nerves and time to get one. So we couldn't think of anything better than trade.

But in order not to stand in the market we decided, like many others, to take apples to Moscow and sell them there wholesale. Such business was very popular at that time because of the nature and weather of the Bukovina Region producing many agricultural crops and the enterprise of the people who lived there.

Local villagers have always lived off the land and in the regions near Moldavia they did farming and market gardening. During those hard times people took for sale everything they could grow, meat, sausages, vegetables and fruit. They took these products mainly to Moscow and other towns of Russia, because there was a big demand for food and the prices were much higher than in Ukraine.

They travelled by truck, train or car or any means they could. To start the business we hired a small truck, and then my son and my husband drove around the villages for a couple of days buying apples. People were happy to sell them at any price because it had been a good growing season and they didn't know what to do with all the apples produced, and some had even started to dig them into the ground.

So, after they had loaded a five-ton truck with apples, they drove to Moscow which was 1500 kilometres away from Chernovtsy. On this their first trip I was extremely worried, particularly after a couple of days when I had not heard from them. Of course, there were no mobile phones in those days. At last, they came back in six days alive and well and brought some money.

They then explained all that had happened to them whilst they had been away. I have already told you that after the collapse of the USSR, it was dangerous to go on the roads, especially at night and for a long distance, because of the growth of the crime rate. Cars, trucks and buses which transported goods from abroad were often robbed.

Of course, I heard about such things, but I didn't think that this could happen to my son and my husband. Apparently whilst they were traveling along a motorway at night not far from Moscow, a wheel was punctured. As soon as my son stopped the truck a car approached them, and four young men came out of it. Whilst my son was busy with the wheel they surrounded my husband and began to demand money, threatening him with guns.

It was good that my husband used to work in Siberia with different types of people as well as prisoners and he knew how to talk to them. "You came to us for nothing, guys. We are taking the apples to Moscow and we won't have any money before we sell them. You'd better come to us on our way back home. And now you can have some apples if you want, I've got a truck full," he joked.

They didn't trust him: they went to the back of the truck, opened the doors and looked inside, they checked the cab and then demanded a wallet from my husband where they found 50 dollars and some Ukrainian coupons. After that they got angry, took the dollars called my husband different names and went away. Of course my husband had taken some more money and before the departure he had hidden it inside the seat under the covering and because of the poor light at night the criminals hadn't found any money while they were searching the cab.

When they arrived in Moscow they decided to stop at the first market they found on their way in, and try to sell the apples quickly if the prices would be suitable. But a surprise was waiting for them – as soon as they entered the territory of the market several people came to them and asked where the apples were from and told my husband where to go to get unloaded.

When the people named the price for apples, my husband and my son refused to sell them and wanted to go to the other market. But no such luck! The workers at the market speaking in belligerent tones explained to them that if they wouldn't unload where they had been told and wouldn't accept the price named, they would leave the market with nothing.

There was nothing to do but to get unloaded and take the money and leave the place as soon as possible. As they found out later all the markets in

Moscow were controlled by certain groups of people who set the price, controlled everything and everything depended on them. This was the first and very hard trip, which took those six days on the road and a drive of 3000 kilometres, all of which was driven by my son, because my husband had never driven a car and had no driving license.

On their way back home they stopped several times because of the truck breaking down and rested at night in safe places in order to go during daytime along the Russian roads. Of course they came back home very tired and told us they would never ever go to Moscow again. But then after they had come around they counted up the money and it turned out that the trip paid for itself and even brought some profit.

I didn't want to let them go again but they went to the same market several times and only when there was a frost outside and apples began to freeze slightly did they stop the business. We bought a new car by the summer and began to trade Turkish chocolate wholesale, which we bought at the Chernovtsy market. At first we sold it in different cities of Ukraine, but then we found a wholesale buyer in Kiev and began to take the chocolate to him only.

After two months this business had to stop because the chocolate was bad quality and lost its marketable condition whilst being transported. For the next year, my son lived on his own wits and he made friends with people of his own age who didn't know what to do with their lives and rushed from one business to another just like he did.

Some of them after they had tried several types of business chose to trade in Turkish goods. My son and his wife decided to follow their example, because they also considered this type of business to be the easiest and the most reliable one. But first of all they had to get a foreign passport which was vital to carry out this trade at that time.

The Ukrainian Visa and Registration Offices issued passports and any Ukrainian citizen could get a passport after he/she had tendered the necessary documents and paid a due fee. But in order even to get inside the building of the Office you had to stand in a queue for a couple of days. Due to the volume of people wanting passports, there was always a large crowd around the building in which the Office was situated waiting to enter, both during the day and at night.

Because of this the people in the queues made a list and called the roll at night, in the same way they had done during the period of restructuring in the USSR. Nevertheless, my son and his wife overcame these difficulties and eventually got their passports. These passports gave them an opportunity to do business involving trips abroad. They then began to bring clothes from Turkey in their car and sell them at the Chernovtsy market.

In order to start the business they needed money and they borrowed the needed amount at interest. Both my husband and I knew about this, but we didn't worry about it because many people did the same, especially those young ones who had no start-up capital. Almost all the population in Chernovtsy was divided in two categories: those who borrowed and those who lent.

Those people that lent the money had obtained their capital from the trade that they had previously carried out in Poland and who had saved up dollars during the good profitable times of trade in Poland before the collapse of the USSR. At first the loans were unsecured, which was a great risk for those who lent, because if a business failed, people weren't able to get their money back. That is why big sums of money were eventually only lent against the security of a flat or a car.

Chapter 48

Abroad to Work...

Thank God I was an optimist, and that I had never had depression in my life, because I react in a different way to stress. Every time, when I found myself in a deadlocked situation, I started acting with new strength and energy and I was ready to turn the whole world upside down in order to change my life for the better. Maybe not all of my solutions were the right ones and sometimes I went from one extreme to the other, but I've never given up.

In the beginning of 1990s, in Chernovtsy, different agencies and companies were being opened. These were private enterprises which provided all kinds of different services. Anyone could open an agency. You just had to process documents provided by the law, to conduct clerical work and to pay taxes. To conduct these businesses, flats that were situated on the ground floors and in the basements of the houses were bought all over the city, but particularly in the centre.

Agencies needed rooms and offered people any amount of money to obtain a good location. Thanks to that many people who had lived in basements for all their lives had an opportunity at that moment to move into better apartments. The old flats were renovated, windows were made into the doors to provide a proper entrance, above which they hung a sign and outdoor advertising.

Those people who started a business without any initial capital with which to purchase a property, rented offices for a set period of time. Agencies opened one after the other and every day there appeared the new ones: 'A travel bureau', 'Job placement abroad', 'A dating agency', etc. Job placement agencies were especially popular at that time. There was a colourful show of advertising in the city like 'Job abroad'.

Hundreds of people, who wanted to go somewhere to earn money, always crowded near them. People were promised to have a good job, a fine salary in the countries with which the agencies supposedly had job placement agreements. In reality, though, there weren't any agreements between Ukraine and the other countries at that time, and so there couldn't even be any job placement agreements or any other types of agreements between the agencies and other countries.

Ukraine was passing many of the more important laws at that moment being a newly formed independent state. Many issues were just at the stage of consideration, and weren't even legislatively settled. Laws involving employment and foreign working were not yet in existence. This led to the uncontrolled working of these agencies and frankly to the cheating of prospective employees.

In fact people were sent abroad illegally. It was usually done with a tourist visa, issued for a trip of between 7-15 days. When such "tourists" got to the country abroad, they stayed there and worked illegally. It was good if someone from the agency met them abroad and helped them to find a job, but it so often happened that no one waited there for them, and thousands of illegal immigrants with overdue visas in their passports were wandering in Europe looking for a job.

They found one after a while and stayed abroad for a long time and some of them forever. It is ridiculous now to remember those times, and it is hard to believe how naïve we were. Even I, being a literate person, trusted and believed everything I was told by the agencies because it was what I wanted to hear. It was a hard period of my life, and in the period of confusion and despair, I was desperate to find a way out in order to improve my situation.

From that moment I thought that everything could be possible: a new country, new laws, a new life and it didn't even cross my mind that I could be cheated. After 20 years of working in the Siberia, the idea of working abroad seemed attractive for me and the only way out of the hard situation: 'What's the difference? We've worked in the Siberia and now we'll work abroad. Moreover, they offer us a contract job for a set period of time, so we can work for a while, earn some money and come back home,' I thought.

Once I found an advertisement in a newspaper, "A job in America", where a job placement agency offered a contract job on a fish-processing factory-ship off the coast of Alaska. I liked very much the idea of working in Alaska and I literally ran to the agency in order to find out the details. The agency was situated in 'Hotel Kiev', where it rented two rooms. Very many people crowded in the hall as well as in the street outside, because only one person at time was allowed to have an interview.

When it was my turn I entered the office. It was all very official: photos of Alaska on the walls, 'The activity of the agency certificate' with several official- looking stamps, there were also two desks with computers on them (which were a rarity for that time). The workers of the agency were very friendly, a manager told me that people who had already worked there were satisfied, the work was hard, but the salary was good.

Everything seemed to be official and true; I was given a form and a list of documents, which I had to prepare and notarize, which were needed for the conclusion of an employment contract. It was also necessary to attach a health certificate to the documents with the results of different medical tests, including an AIDS test. I brought the documents home and we began to discuss with my family what to do.

The contract that was to be concluded after a year and during that time you had to work on a fish-processing factory-ship and live there. The delivery of workers to the destination and back was supposed to be paid by the company and the salary was three thousand dollars per month. However each person was expected to pay an initial sum of 400 dollars as an agency fee and further payments to the agency would be deducted from salary each month.

The offer of the agency was very tempting, and after a long discussion we decided that my son and his wife were the first ones to go there, and I with my husband and a granddaughter would stay at home. Then in a year, when they came back, I with my husband would go. So – go ahead! My son and daughter-in-law gathered all the documents, underwent all the tests, passed the interview in the office and after that were invited to conclude the employment contract.

While signing the contract they paid the advance of 400 dollars each. The contracts were processed with apparent legal formality, and on the letterheads it included the addresses, phone numbers and stamps of an American company and our agency, in English and in Ukrainian and didn't give rise to any doubts. We had to prepare quickly because the first part of worker were supposed to be sent two weeks after signing the contracts.

I went to the market and bought warm clothes for my son and daughter-in-law (for myself and my husband as well): very thick wool socks, warm hats, pullovers, warm gaiters, and other things which were needed for work in such severe conditions. After we had fully prepared we began to wait for a phone-call from the agency, expected in two weeks' time, but after three weeks when no one called us I decided to go back myself and find out what was going on.

There were very many people near the hotel and they argued about something. I went past them and went to the second floor, where the office had been earlier, but there wasn't one anymore. I went downstairs and asked a woman on duty about the agency. "Why are you all coming here? The agency rented a room for a month only. And now they are gone. So don't come here anymore – I'm tired of you all!" – She protested.

I went outside and listened to what people were talking about in the crowd and understood that we all were victims of fraudsters. They took money from us and disappeared. Where to? No one knew; the phone numbers and addresses in the contracts were fake ones. All the people began to make police statements. The police promised to find everything out, but no one did anything about it and the fraudsters weren't found.

Each lost 400 dollars plus the money for medical tests, certificates and the services of the notary. Many people borrowed money for the trip from friends or relatives at interest and were even in a worse situation than the others. I was shocked and didn't even want to go back home anticipating a big scandal there. My husband blamed me for everything because it was all my idea and because

314

of that we had a big fight. He began to scream: "I won't go anywhere! Here's my Motherland, I should live here and I keep a business here!"

But despite the fact that we had lost our money the idea of working abroad didn't leave me, because everyone talked only about that. Newspapers and magazines called "Zagranitsa (foreign countries)", "Emigratsyja (emigration)", "Nashtsa granitsej (our people abroad)" appeared at that time, where there were a lot of interesting information about life in the other countries, procedures of legal job placement, and emigration laws. Some newspapers devoted every issue to a certain country, for example one month was devoted to Canada, the other one to Australia, etc.

I gathered all the newspapers, made files and studied the information in which I was interested. I have to say that newspapers didn't promote emigration they just provided information for people who wanted to emigrate, that is why there were often articles about the problems waiting for emigrants and about the negative points of living abroad.

On the one hand it was a great help for those who wanted to go abroad, because after a person had studied the information he/she could make the right decision of where to go or not to go at all. But on the other hand, after I had read everything: bad and good, and hoping for the better I wanted to run away from the problems at home and go somewhere with an unknown life and new impressions.

Since that moment I had a favourite phrase: "I don't know what is waiting for me abroad but I know for sure what is waiting for me here." While I was studying the information many people using the services of tourist agencies went to Greece, Italy, Portugal, Spain, Czech republish and worked there illegally. I didn't accept that possibility from the very beginning for some reason, and wanted to go abroad legally as a normal person.

Once, walking down the street I saw an advertisement in the window 'Emigration to Australia' and without thinking I went into the office in order to find out the details. It was explained to me there that the agency that dealt with it was actually situated in Kiev, and this was only a branch, where the workers provided help in processing the documents. They would, however, help me prepare documents needed for emigration to Australia and arrange a meeting with an Australian lawyer in Kiev when he arrived in the country in four months' time.

If the interview went well, he would take all the applicants to Australia and would process all the documents for permanent residence there. All the services including the flight would cost 5 thousand dollars. It was then that I had second thoughts, and said that I would like to go there to work first, and then if I liked staying there I would move there on a permanent basis. They started to persuade me that it would be better to have a permanent residence from the very beginning, because it gave the opportunity to get benefits and to find a better job.

"It is fine. I'll consult with my family and will come back to you tomorrow," I said. On my way home I was considering a plan, how to do everything better. I decided mentally to go there alone and earn some money, send it to my husband and then he would be able to join me the same way. Then I would probably bring my kids there. From the one word "Australia" my head was spinning.

I had read a lot about the country for some time before that, and had never even thought that I would be offered a real opportunity to live and work in the country, and all I needed was 5 thousand dollars! I was ready to borrow the sum or to sell something, but not just "something" I was ready to sell everything I had to move to Australia. OK, but, how was I supposed to tell the family about it at home? I probably looked so dumb that as soon as I got home my son asked me "What news have you got for us this time? Tell us where we are going."

"How do you know that I have something to tell you?" I asked, and began to tell them about everything. I had to persuade my husband for a long time, before he agreed. I prepared all the needed documents in a couple of days and took them to the agency and paid an advance of 1300 dollars. I had to prepare for departure and I went to the market again. For this time I bought a couple of light T-shirts, some other summer clothes and a nice bonnet.

While walking through the aisles, I met a friend of mine who was selling leather jackets. "Come here, she invited me "look what a beautiful jacket I'm selling for half price, only because it is not the season right now." "I don't need one! I'm going to Australia and it is hot there!" – I answered enjoying myself and walked on further. In three months I got a call from Kiev, they told me the date, when I had to come for an interview with a lawyer from Australia and I was glad to hear that.

"This time I wasn't cheated," I thought. When I went to the Kiev agency, the lawyer had already been there and was talking to the workers in the office. Though I was told from the very beginning that English wasn't necessary, I was worried all the same that I wouldn't pass the interview. But the lawyer turned out to be a Russian emigrant and talked in Russian to us. Several people including two families with children were waiting for the interview beside me.

When I entered the lawyer's room, all my documents and an agreement that I had to sign were laying in front of him on the table. He told me at the start, "So, I hope you know the conditions, so let's get down to the business right away." I answered that I was told the main points but I didn't know when and how we were going to go there. He then he started to explain to me that after the signing of the agreement I would come to Kiev on a certain day and then together with him I would fly to Germany and then to Australia.

On arrival in Australia he would try to achieve a refugee status for us and would help us to stay in the country, then after three years I would get an Australian passport. I couldn't listen to him anymore "A refugee status? I don't want to do it like that, I was promised legal emigration!" – I screamed.

"There is only one way to go to the country and I have just told you about it, there is no other way. If you agree, then sign the papers, send the money within 7 days and be ready for the departure. I will pick you up in 10 days," and he offered me an agreement.

I saw that he was getting nervous and quickly read the text. I stopped at the last paragraph which said that I was supposed to transfer 10 thousand dollars to the account of an Australian agency within seven days, the paragraph contained the number of the account. Everything went dark before my eyes – "Ten thousand? I was told five thousand!" – I exclaimed.

The lawyer then invited an agency staff member into the office and asked him why the client wasn't ready for the interview. The worker answered addressing himself to me –

"Everything is correct, madam, you pay us five thousand for our services and you pay ten thousand to the Australian agency."

"So I have to pay 15 thousand in total? Why didn't you tell me that earlier?" I protested.

"I don't know, we explained everything to you from the very beginning, you must have misunderstood us," he answered with perfect calm.

Then I started to ask the lawyer to allow me to pay the ten thousand dollars when I started working in Australia. He refused point-blank and told me in a higher pitch of voice: "You move to such a country for only 15 thousand dollars!" I understood that there was no sense to continue the conversation and left the room. I couldn't pay so much money even if I wanted to.

Firstly, I hadn't any; secondly, I lived in a family and I was dependant on my husband and kids because we had a common business. So that time I lost 1300 dollars which I had paid in advance, because I had refused to take the journey and the agency denied that it was not their fault I could not afford the extra money demanded. At this time such sharp practices were not of any real interest to the police and I just had to accept such a loss.

Chapter 49

The Family Business at the Market

For a whole year, my son had lived his own life and he made friends with people of his own age who didn't know what to do with their lives and rushed from one business to another just like he did. Some of them after they had tried several types of business chose to trade in Turkish goods. My son and his wife decided to follow their example, because they also considered this type of business to be the easiest and the most reliable one.

But first of all they had to get a foreign passport which was vital to carry out this trade at that time. The Ukrainian Visa and Registration Offices issued passports and any Ukrainian citizen could get a passport after he/she had tendered the necessary documents and paid a due fee. But in order even to get inside the building of the Office you had to stand in a queue for a couple of days.

Due to the volume of people wanting passports, there was always a large crowd around the building in which the Office was situated waiting to enter, both during the day and at night.

Because of this the people in the queues made a list and called the roll at night, in the same way they had done during the period of restructuring in the USSR. Nevertheless, my son and his wife overcame these difficulties and eventually got their passports.

These passports gave them an opportunity to do business involving trips abroad. They then began to bring clothes from Turkey in their car and sell them at the Chernovtsy market. In order to start the business they needed money and they borrowed the needed amount at interest. Both my husband and I knew about this, but we didn't worry about it because many people did the same, especially those young ones who had no start-up capital.

Almost all the population in Chernovtsy was divided in two categories: those who borrowed and those who lent. Those people who lent the money had obtained their capital from the trade that they had previously carried out in Poland and had saved up dollars during the good profitable times of trade in Poland before the collapse the USSR.

At first the loans were unsecured, which was a great risk for those who lent, because if a business failed, people weren't able to get their money back. That is why big sums of money were eventually only lent against the security of a flat or a car. For a year, our son had worked at the market and had told us that everything was OK. On the surface everything appeared to be satisfactory so we kept out of his business.

It was totally unexpected, when my son's business collapsed and my son was left without his flat which was repossessed to pay his debts. It turned out that due to the unprofitability of his business there was a constant shortage of money and he borrowed a bigger amount of money against his flat. This was a terrible shock for both him and for us. The flat for which we had worked so hard for many years in Siberia, our son managed to lose in the single year of his business.

From that moment the life of my family changed completely, all our reservations were abandoned and we, as I used to say, "Went over to a warlike situation." We didn't discuss whether we would like to trade at the market or not, because there weren't any other alternatives.

This time my husband decided to approach the trade business seriously and took control of it. The market in Chernovotsy mainly sold clothes, but since the middle of 1995 many people began to bring food from Poland and the market was divided into two main areas one for clothes and one for food stuffs. Consequently, with the clothes angle having been worked for a long time it was well-organized, but the food trade was just in its infancy and not as well organized.

Food Trading was established right in the middle of an open field and carried out in tents or from the back of a lorry. When starting the business we rented two vehicles: a minibus, which we used to bring food from Poland and a lorry, from which we used to sell the food at the market.

Both my husband and I had originally been very embarrassed at the thought of trading in a market and when we were eventually forced, by circumstances to take up this activity, we became even more embarrassed. Sometimes when we saw our friends at the market we even hid inside the body of the lorry or pretended that we were buying something and not selling.

After I had worked at the market and got accustomed to the situation, I was amazed with the atmosphere at the market – the market had a life of its own with its own unwritten laws and customs and joys and failures. The most amazing thing was that this life united people from different levels of society, of different education and professions, and through similar circumstances forced them to do this type of business.

Lawyers, engineers, doctors, University professors and students – they were all standing in one row. Our trade-neighbours were: a helicopter pilot, an electronics engineer, a Chernovtsy University chemistry lecturer, an economist from a big enterprise, and a gynaecologist amongst others, all who had filled prestigious positions and had good jobs before the USSR breakdown.

I stopped being embarrassed and began to work as everybody else did joining the ranks of thousands of people, who suffered during the period of changes. During this time of economic crisis, the market was the only enterprise in Chernovtsy which worked steadily, which broadened its area, improved its infrastructure and brought the main part of taxes to the local treasury.

It employed thousands, and every person could find a business opportunity there: one brought goods, the other one unloaded it and sold it; there were also those who acted as porters moving goods on small carts or barrows, and those who were walking in the aisles selling hot tea and coffee from thermos flasks, hot food and other snacks.

Everybody got quickly acquainted with each other, knew everything about each other's business, and despite the competition even helped each other, because each of us could find ourselves in a difficult situation. The so-called "wholesale night markets" will always remain in people's memory. Even now, when I think back to those times, I can't believe how hard we worked.

We went to the market every Monday morning and returned every Tuesday evening, irrespective of whether it was winter or summer, cold or hot. We just became zombies – we used to work to a frazzle in order to sell everything and get back home faster. It was especially unbearable during wintertime, when the frost was up to 20 degrees below zero and lower. No clothes could help, because we were standing in one place and just packing customers' orders into the boxes.

We wrapped ourselves up to the eyes during snowfalls and snowstorms, cut our gloves leaving half of the fingers uncovered so that it was easier to work and count money while receiving payment for goods … The light was bad and we used flashlights and candles at night while settling accounts with the customers. We always drank some hot tea and coffee that people were selling at the market, in order to warm ourselves.

Sometimes we took our car with us and left it behind our lorry, and when we were absolutely frozen to a standstill we went into the car by turns and started the engine to provide a little warmth and have a few minutes rest before going back to work. It was just the opposite in the hot summer months we didn't have any protection from the heat, and worked wearing only shorts and T-shirts. By the end of summer we were tanned as if just back from a tropical holiday.

The Wholesale market in Chernovtsy brought people from all over the country such was the size and reputation of this market. People came from as far away as the Crimea, Donetsk and other cities of Eastern Ukraine; they came on specially chartered buses running the distance of 1000 and more kilometres. In time we had some wholesale customers, who only bought goods from us, and who allowed us to sell almost everything we had brought with us, during those "wholesale night markets".

People snatched away everything in the truest sense of the word: sunflower oil, margarine, mayonnaise, herring, tartar sauce, paste, canned food, waffles, cookies, yogurts, juices, lemonade and Pepsi-Cola in big bottles. Everything was in colourful wrapping, it looked attractive and many of the items that we brought were seen by people for the first time because such goods weren't yet produced in Ukraine.

We had a good income for the first time in several years, and despite the fact that the work was very hard we were happy to find our business successful. However, life is unpredictable, and things constantly change, and not always for the better. Just as we "found our feet" within a couple of years other markets like ours appeared in the other regions of Ukraine and the quantity of wholesale customers became smaller and smaller and with time the night markets passed into history.

At first we even felt joy at the demise of the night market, because it was much easier to work during the daytime, but after the abolition of the night markets other problems in our business began to appear. Despite the fact that there weren't many wholesale customers, the quantity of Polish food sellers grew swiftly, which led to severe competition and reduction in the prices we could charge.

The only way to compensate for this was to increase the volume of sales in order to maintain a similar income and this required additional capital. We began to borrow some money at interest, but it never seemed enough and we had to borrow more and more which made us dependent on other people. Borrowing money, especially during times of unstable economic position and inflation is not a good thing to do, because the laws regulating this field changed constantly and we didn't know what to expect.

I would have preferred to have a business that allowed us to work using only our own money, but nobody listened to me because my husband was in charge of the business and he only consulted our son. "That is not a women's business, keep out of this," he told me, because business was considered to be men's concern in our family and I was supposed to help only. It became harder to work and bad luck pursued us.

On one trip my husband departed from the customs procedures in a big way by not declaring the whole amount of dollars that he took with him to Poland. When it was discovered the Customs confiscated all the money that he had concealed. In a moment we lost an amount of money equal to our yearly income, which meant that we had worked for nothing for the whole year.

With time, the Customs tightened the supervision of the import trade, limiting the quantity that could be imported and at the same time increasing the tariffs charged on imports. Of course, this increased the prices for Polish products and eventually reduced demand from customers. At the same time private enterprises began to increase the production of food in Ukraine, which was a bit cheaper.

These developments led to the situation where our incomes were equal to our expenses which forced us to borrow even more money in order to keep our business going. I felt that all this was wrong and tried to stop this escalation before it was too late, but my husband and son were afraid to find themselves without a business. "What will we do if we stop doing this business? Can you offer us another way out?" They asked.

Unfortunately I couldn't offer them anything else, because I thought that they knew everything better than me, but all of this time I tried to find a solution for this situation. From the moment we started doing this business the whole affair had stressed me a whole lot and my heart stopped at the thought of this business bankrupting us, the way it did to many other people.

At last the day came when my husband and son came back home and announced right away that they were going to stop the market business and had decided to go in for an international goods transportation business instead. This was a piece of good news for all of us, and we began to discuss the details of the new business and to allocate duties among us.

I personally was incredibly happy that I was supposed to deal only with the paperwork, and consequently, I would have more free time at last. It was not so easy to start a new business and it took us about a month to get things properly organized. We had to process different documents, get permissions, a license for the international transportation, etc.

All the documents were processed by an organization which was in Kiev so I had to go there quite frequently. However, it soon became obvious that starting this business was not as easy as we had first imagined, the hardest thing was to buy a vehicle necessary for such a business. Here we encountered a problem which we had never thought of. I was happy to start a new business and was hoping to stop borrowing money, stop paying the interest and stop working for the other people.

But my happiness came to an end very soon when I found out that a lorry, necessary for such a business, even a used one, cost several tens of thousands of dollars. Of course, we did not have such a large amount that was needed and we had to borrow again, not only that, but a far larger amount than before. This brought back my fear and not the happiness I had hoped for. This new business dragged us into a bigger debt and our life changed again for the worse and not for the better.

The only hope was that this business would be a successful one and we would soon pay back the debt and work for ourselves. In business, like a card game one needs a little bit of luck, which some have and others have nothing. For example all of us who went to trade at the market were in an equal situation at first, but over time some people prospered and others lost everything they had.

Many people often changed the type of business they conducted; trying to find a better one, but ill luck pursued them. Whilst other people worked seemingly the same way but they were lucky and business went well. I think we were the unlucky ones in business, but we couldn't stop because there wasn't anything else to do. I hated business and thought of those times when I had a job and didn't worry about anything.

During this time I couldn't sleep well at night, because I was constantly worried and asked God to help us. Because we had invested all our money (as well as the borrowed money) in a lorry and all our lives depended on how this lorry crossed the border and how it delivered the goods to destination, whether it broke down or got into an accident or not. It turned out that there were grounds for uneasiness, because every trip brought an unpredictable result.

We often paid fines for ill-timed deliveries, because due to the long queues at the Custom, the lorry stood there for a couple of days. There were delays during wintertime because of the weather conditions e.g. snow drifting on the road and edges. The lorry was an old one and required repair and parts replacement after every trip, which proved to be very expensive.

Once, when the lorry was entering one of the European Union countries, it was sent to the penalty area and after a maintenance check-up was forbidden to travel in the territory of the European Union. As a result of this we had to hire another lorry there and reload the goods on it and deliver them to the customer. Of course, this was an additional expense and we were shocked yet again.

After that my husband decided to buy another vehicle and he thought of a "cunning plan" – sell our flat and to live for a while in a rented one! "This way if something happens to one vehicle on a trip the other one would cover expenses. I estimate that if two vehicles work, we can pay the debts and buy a new flat in a year," he explained.

If he had offered me this earlier, I would have had gone off into hysterics, but at that moment I didn't care at all. I was tired of fighting for survival and of living without confidence in the future and of the constant worrying, worrying, worrying … I accepted his offer and found a buyer myself, and we sold the flat very quickly. Parents and friends couldn't believe this when they found out but I didn't care much because due to the disorders in our life I had never been happy in this flat.

Chapter 50

To Work in Great Britain

A year later I was walking into town when I met my friend, whom I hadn't seen for a long time. It turned out that she had lived for two years in Kiev and was working at a travel agency which was sending people abroad for contract employment. She told me of the wonderful opportunities there were by working abroad, and the guarantee of jobs in Spain, Czech Republic, and Italy. I knew it could not all be true and just laughed.

She then told me that there was a job under contract in England and they hired only those people who knew at least a little bit of English. Here is where she caught me! I knew a little bit of English and I had dreamed of going to Great Britain since school – to see London, Big Ben and the rest. She told me that a man who lived in London was working at the agency, and at that very moment he was sending people to work there under a contract for two years.

After the contract ended people could stay there and get permanent residence. The services of the agency cost 1300 dollars including 300 dollars for the job placement; however, I had to buy the plane tickets and other travel expenses for myself. She gave me a hundred percent guarantee and I agreed. I gathered documents and money and took them to Kiev.

Two weeks later I received a call and they told me that I had been granted a visa and I had to leave for London immediately. I was happy and thought, "They really didn't deceive me. At last I will leave." When I came to the agency I found out that I was a member of a group of bank workers who were going to London in order to improve their experience.

I was told that as soon as I arrived, I was to meet a man named Andrei at Heathrow airport, and it is he who would organise a job placement and housing. I was to buy a present for him – two bottles of champagne and two tins of salmon caviar. Since he was apparently employed at the café 'Fish & Chips' in the centre of London near the Victoria square and I was given a telephone number on which to contact him if necessary.

I bought a ticket and flew to London. I travelled for the first time abroad by plane and my heart soared with joy waiting for something new and unknown. The whole way I was thinking of where I would get a job and where I would live. At mid-day the plane landed at Heathrow airport and I entered and passed passport and customs supervision without any problems, and felt that I was in England at last!

At the arrivals exit stood people who met arrivals with the signs in their hands on which was written the surname of the expected person. Nobody was waiting for me. What should I do? The airport was so huge that I got lost at once. I started to look for the exit to the town on the signs. When I asked people something they could hardly understand me because of my bad English and when they tried to help me, I didn't understand them. Nevertheless they really tried to help me and I was thankful to them for that.

At last after much trouble and tribulation an old lady took my hand and led me out to the bus stop for buses going to the city centre. While I was sitting in the bus I was looking out of the window all the time. My Goodness! How beautiful it was there. My heart thumped. I couldn't believe I was in England. It was like a dream.

The Irish Bar at airport Boryspol in Kiev, 1989

When I reached Victoria square I got out of the bus and saw 'Fish & Chips' at once. I got excited that I had found it so fast. I entered and asked about Andrei from Ukraine. I was told that they didn't know him and nobody by that name had ever worked there. I could not understand this as I had definitely been told that he worked at the 'Fish & Chip' shop.

I went around the whole square back and forth and found several such shops, but nobody knew Andrei. Fortunately the weather was fine, and the sun was shining and it was hot. I didn't know what to do. Where would I go when the night came? It was around 5 p.m. before I remembered that I had been given a telephone number on which to contact Andrei. I just couldn't get to grips with the English telephone. I probably just dialled it wrong. I was very tired and hungry, I felt sick but I was afraid to faint.

I had no more strength to carry a bag with my clothes and the other one with two bottles of champagne. I hated that champagne and wanted to leave it near the waste bin. At last I came to the cab rank and asked a cabbie to drive me to the café "Fish & Chips". The taxi driver laughed and asked – "Which one?" How could I know that there were so many such cafes in London or even in England, and I couldn't answer his question, but just showed him the phone number.

The driver dialled the number from his cell phone and after he found out the address he took me there. It turned out that the shop was very close and I just had to go round the corner. It was 6 p.m. when I entered the café and asked for Andrei from Ukraine. Thank God he was there, and when he saw me with the bags, he bundled me outside at once. He told me: "Go outside the shop to the yard, and then up the stairs to the first floor and wait for me there. I'll come soon." I was waiting for more than an hour.

At last he came, he was outraged, "Why did you come here? Who gave you my phone number?" I told him everything. Then he explained to me that he didn't deal with job placements and that he worked himself at two jobs and didn't have any time, because he slept only for three hours a day.

"What should I do? I don't know anyone here. Help me," I begged him.

"All right, I'll think of something. Wait for me here. Don't enter the shop. If my boss finds out that people from Ukraine come here to me he'll fire me," he replied.

I was waiting for a very long time and I thought; maybe he had forgotten about me and had gone home.

It was 10 p.m., and dark by then, when at last the doors on the first floor opened and he called out for me. I went up the stairs and found myself in a small room with wardrobes where workers of the shop kept their uniforms. Andrei brought me some food to eat: a plate of chicken cream soup, some bread and a cake. By this time I was ravenous, as the last time I had eaten was on the plane on the way to London. I enjoyed this meal so much that I thought it was the tastiest thing I had ever tried in my life.

I then heard Andrei calling someone on his phone and telling them about me. A pretty young girl soon arrived whose name was Olga and she also had originally come from Ukraine. After she had listened to my story she laughed and told me that I had been cheated. There were no contracts and the people who came either had to work illegally or apply for political asylum. Olga, who rented a small room in a nearby three-storeyed house, said that I could stay with her short term if I agreed to sleep on a small sofa in her room.

In the morning before leaving for work, Olga told me she was calling a Russian lawyer and saying, "Don't go anywhere, wait for a lawyer. He will issue you a refusal." I was scared and asked, "What do you mean by a refusal?" She explained, "If you want to work and live in England you must within these two days ask for a political asylum." Two hours later, a lawyer arrived.

He looked at me and was outraged. "How do you look? Does a refugee from Ukraine look like this?

Go to the second hand shop and buy yourself some old clothes and prepare your story why you came to ask for a political asylum. I'll come back later for you," He said. "Wait! What story? I am not going to ask for asylum I came under contract for a job." Then he explained that I would be interviewed at the police station and I must tell them why I am a refugee from my country and ask for asylum in England.

Then I will give them my passport and will receive in exchange a temporary document for residence here, and also tickets for free food and housing. If my story is believed and I behave well I could be able to get a job in six months' time, but I would not be able to work during this time as there were often inspections at those places where foreigners work – cafés and hotels. If they found out that I was working illegally I would be deported immediately and without the right to come back to this country for five years.

I was shocked; I didn't know what to answer and asked him to give me some time till tomorrow. Olga came back from work at 10 p.m. She was so tired that she couldn't even talk and I waited until she had a little time to rest and revive herself. An hour later she told me about herself and her roommates. It turned out that all who lived in this house came from different towns of Ukraine in 1992.

Almost all of them came on busses as tourists and asked for asylum right away. Now everybody lived here legally and all work very hard and some of them even have two jobs in order to earn a little bit more. Olga had not been home for four years and hadn't seen her daughter during this time because she had no right to leave the country before she got a visa for permanent residence.

I then said to Olga "I don't want to stay in the country this way. I don't want to be a refugee and don't want to be an illegal immigrant. I am a lawyer myself and I don't like to deceive in this way, I'd better go back home." I felt myself deceived and unhappy and trusted nobody from that moment on. Olga helped me to call the agency in Kiev and I asked for explanations why I had been deceived, but they just talked to me in a very rude and abrupt manner.

"You were promised you would stay in the country and get a job and you will get one and the way this happens doesn't matter!" I told them that I didn't want to stay here like this and I was coming home immediately, and that they must give me back my 300 dollars for the job placement which has not happened.

Olga tried to persuade me not to be in a hurry to return back to Ukraine saying that as I had a return ticket I could spend a couple of days with her seeing the sights of London. The day before my departure, Olga took a day off work and we spent the whole day in London. She showed me the centre of the city, historical monuments, Big Ben, Trafalgar square, Tower Bridge, the Houses of Parliament, Buckingham Palace and the Westminster Abbey.

We walked around London until late at night; the city seemed to be in flames due to all the advertisements and lighting. The next day I departed for Kiev. I said good-bye to London with tears in my eyes – I looked out from the window and I repeated mentally: "I'll definitely come back here. Don't know when and how, but I know for sure that I will come back!"

It was another defeat in my attempt to move abroad and I was very reluctantly returning home, but at least I had seen something of the life that could be had abroad. While staying in Kiev for a day, and whilst waiting for my train to Chernovtsy I decided to go to the agency and try to get my money back. I had paid for a job placement, but this had not happened and I expected that I would have to prove that I was deceived.

However, to my surprise, I was given the 300 dollars at once and told that it was the first time that someone had returned home from Great Britain. So one attempt had not been a complete failure, and my mood was a little bit better at that moment. I was, however, still to have a conversation with my husband and I was afraid even to think about it.

I mentally prepared myself for this meeting and started to think about what I had obtained from my trip to Great Britain. On the one hand I couldn't find a job there and lost my money again, but on the other hand this trip gave me more than money. For the first time in my life I was in a capitalist country and saw what life was like there and how "bourgeoisies" lived, those we had been scared of since our schooldays.

This strengthened my thoughts that I had chosen the right way and I shouldn't give up because there was no other chance to change my life. These thoughts seemed to justify my own convictions, but I knew that my husband and his relatives thought the other way.

They wondered over my arguments about happiness and love, because they thought that a woman must only be happy because she had a husband and children. It was their belief that love and happiness did not concern women of fifty years of age!

All women of that age were traditionally doing chores around the house, gardening, raising grandchildren and having little ambition for anything more. Although by this time I had been divorced from my husband for a couple of years we continued to live together, but with separate lives.

This arrangement had now outlived its usefulness due to our unsettled state of life and the constant stress and worry, and I realised that this gave me the right to break off our relationship completely. When my husband had come

328

back from Kuban to Chernovtsy, I hoped that our marriage would return to normal, but the unsettled state of our lives, the constant stress and worrying had a negative effect on our personal relations and we parted from each other more and more.

We had different views in life, different interests and gradually we drifted further and further apart. I saw no hope for an improved future and finally understood that I would never be able accept the life I was having and despite previous unsuccessful attempts I would definitely go abroad. He didn't want to go and trusted that life in our country would get better in a couple of years.

When I eventually arrived back home he didn't even want to listen to me and began to repeat the same things as always: "I think you've understood this time that there's no use in looking for happiness abroad. You live no worse than anybody else, you are dressed and have shoes, you don't have to root through waste bins to survive, so calm down and live the way all normal people do. At your age it's time to calm down and raise grandchildren and think how to grow old and grey."

His words about how we would live out the rest of our lives put me in a temper and I told him everything I had in mind "What age are you talking about? I am under fifty and I'm not going to grow old and grey! I'm feeling young and want to rejoice every day of my life, be happy and love!" I blurted out. We quarrelled after that. I thought there was no use in staying together so I gathered my things and moved out to my son's place.

Chapter 51

Abroad To Get Married

So I began to live with the family of my son, and though I worked with documents concerning our business I had much more free time. I had the feeling that I had got rid of the chain that restrained me, and at that moment I could do anything I wanted without making excuses to anybody. Reconsidering my life, I was looking at myself as if from the outside and trying to decide who I was.

Before my arrival in Chernovtsy, I had always considered myself to be a modern business lady and a self-confident woman, but in the last few years, due to arguments in the family, together with stress of business and household duties I failed to keep pace with life and my confidence dropped. Everything around me changed quickly in the newly independent country, and I had the feeling that life was going past me and I was being left behind and would soon grow down to the expectations of an old lady.

I came to the conclusion that I had to do something urgently, not only to improve my own self-esteem, but also to present a public image of a confident business lady. In my opinion, a modern business lady should always look well, as they say "to be well groomed", should dress prettily and should drive a car, be able to operate a computer and speak foreign languages. So my old age was to be postponed and I was ready to start a new life at the age of fifty!

My first job was to reassess my current wardrobe. I shortened all my long skirts, began to wear only high-heeled shoes, changed my hairstyle, and had a full manicure including long artificial nails. Though I weighed only 57 kilos I joined an aerobics club. At the Computer Technologies Centre I learned how to use the computer and passed relevant examinations in computer operation. I also took a driving course and got my driving license after I had passed the test on the computer, although I have never driven a car because I have never had one.

The most important issue was still unresolved – learning the English language. I had studied English at school and at other educational establishments, but in those times, learning English was of secondary importance and only those who were going to enter a department of foreign languages at the university gave special attention to it. I therefore had no use for learning this language before contemplating a move to Great Britain. I quickly understood that I had forgotten almost everything about this new language.

At first I studied it by myself using a correspondence course from the ESCC – European School Correspondence Courses, I found English grammar was very difficult for me and I decided to continue my studies by taking a course in English language at the Centre for Business Information in Chernovtsy. There, the teachers were fully qualified and studying was in groups of students which allowed us to communicate with each other and thereby improving our speaking skills.

I went on the courses just to learn English and never thought that after them my life would change forever and I would gain a new sense of direction. There were 22 people in our group and the majority of them were young women who were going to get married abroad. Some of them were only just preparing to meet their fiancés whilst the others had already obtained their bridal visas and were busy with departure preparations.

Many of them were going to move to America, Canada, or Australia and to other English-speaking countries. When I looked at them I thought – "How young and lucky they are and the whole world is opening up for them – choose anything you want, the world is your oyster, and I am struggling desperately for nothing!" Soon I got acquainted with one woman, whose name was Anna.

She was 38; she was lonely, had a ten-year old son and was going to get married in America. She began to tell me how she met a man with a help of a dating agency. The man had already been to visit her in Chernovtsy and they had spent ten days together after which he proposed to her and she had readily accepted.

She was already in the process of preparing the documents for a bridal visa and before her departure to America was hoping to learn English. "And what do you learn it for?" She asked. I told her that I was going to get a job abroad and may be live there permanently if I could be happy in a foreign country. I also told her about my adventures while trying to go abroad and get a job.

"Are you out of your mind? You are just spending your time and money!" – She exclaimed and asked me "And what are your plans for the future in the other country, just work and that is all?" I began to tell her about myself, that I was divorced and I had lost the hope for happiness here, and that I would do anything to change my life for the better. "Of course I would like to get married there after I get settled because I am not used to living without a man and I feel lonely as a child without its parents." I joked.

"You should get married from here, the way we do and you'll go straight to a man you like in a country you want. It doesn't matter whether you get married now or then," she advised. "The thing is that there's a great difference between you and me, because I'm not so young and I don't speak English as well as you do. I think that at my age it would be easier to find a man when I'm there already," I answered. However, she insisted and gave me the address of the dating agency, the services of which she had used.

Previously I had my own plans and did everything to get employed abroad and then to take my family with me later. Many people did the same, and had already moved to Italy, Spain and Argentina with their families. But after my conversation with Anna I was distracted with doubts and saw a different way to make my dream come true. I knew that there were many dating agencies that invited girls and women at the age of 18 up to 35 to get married abroad, and that the young women got married to men 20-40 years older.

So if I was 52 that meant that my fiancé would be 70-90! It was funny even to think about this, and I was trying to get this idea out of my head, but I couldn't stop because the brain machine was working already, as Mikhail Gorbachev used to say – "things are really cooking" 'Why shouldn't I try, what if it works out well, I think fate has a purpose in bringing me together with this woman,' I thought.

After a while mustering up my courage I telephoned a dating agency and they told me to bring two photos and said that I would be required to fill in an application in order to add my profile on the dating website. I hadn't any photos so I went to a photo agency, where I asked them to take two pictures of me – one portrait and one full length. "Are the pictures for use on a dating agency?" asked a photographer girl.

I blushed beet-red and was so embarrassed as if I was caught in act of some indecent act, and that is why as soon as the girl turned her back to me I rushed out of the agency and went home.

I had an inferiority complex because of my age, moreover I was worried that if the picture was downloaded to a computer, my friends could see me and they would laugh at me. I understood that I was not ready to take this step and I forgot about the idea for a while.

In a couple of months I went to another photographer to take a picture for my passport and it turned out to be a pretty good photo.

Then I mustered up courage and asked to make a full length picture. "I should make a photo of myself while I look well, maybe it'll be the last photo in my life," I joked. The photographer was a friendly young woman called Natali Babinska and she didn't ask any awkward questions and just did her part very professionally.

When I saw my pictures I couldn't believe that I could look so well at my age. I was so glad that I told her what I needed the photos for, but I asked her not to tell anybody about this because I was very embarrassed. "You shouldn't! Many women are taking photos for the dating agencies now. They all are of different age and many of those whom I photographed have already got married," she calmed me down.

My photo for the dating agency, 2000

I felt myself ten feet tall, and banishing all the doubts in my mind I went to the dating agency. A young woman met me, and immediately asked me about my age, without even looking at the photos. I told her I was 51 and showed her my pictures. "The photos are very good, but we work with girls and women from 18 up to 35. So I'm sorry I can't help you," she said. I began to persuade her and explain that I know a bit of English and can use a PC. But it was for nothing because the conversation was over and she let me know this by her look.

I visited almost all the agencies that were in the town and the more of them I visited the less optimistic I became, because I was refused at all of them. I even asked one girl at one of the agencies to add my profile to the website despite my age. I even told her that I would pay some extra money for this. "Don't be ridiculous and put the idea out of your head! You will never get married at your age because we have many young and beautiful women on our website and even they can't get married," she said

It seemed to me that my blood boiled out of rage, I went hysterical and began to scream at her. "I will not get married? If I want to get married abroad I will!" And all your young beauties will stay single forever!" I blurted out and rushed out into the streets slamming the doors so hard that stucco began to fall down. My strength gave out and I went to pieces; after I had sat down on a nearby bench and had had a good cry, I went home.

But I couldn't accept the situation. 'I can't believe that my efforts were useless and that my dreams would never come true! What should I do? What should I do?' I thought. An idea suddenly struck me: 'The agencies don't want to take me and who are they to spoil my life? I can open my own agency and decide then whose profiles to add on the website and whose not!' I couldn't sleep the whole night long and the very next morning I went straight to the tax administration offices.

After I had shown my private enterprise certificate to an inspector I asked whether I could open a dating agency. "Of course you can because you have a clause called "other services" in your certificate and dating agency work can be considered legal under this category. But you have to record officially this kind of activity in an official register with numbered pages.

You will have to keep records of the customers and depending on the amount of money that you get from them you'll have to pay the taxes," he explained. "And that is all? – I exclaimed, jumping for joy. Oh my God, I need a simple register with numbered pages to make my dream come true! The same day I arrived back home with an opened dating agency and was thinking of what to do next. I needed somewhere to work, to advertise my business, and a computer, but I had none of these.

I went to see a friend of mine Elena Voroshilova, with whom I had worked at the company Neways she had her office in her home. I wanted to share my news as soon as possible and to get a piece of advice from her, where to rent office space for a small price. She didn't even let me finish before she told me – "You'll work at my office, for two hours per day.

You do not need to pay for the room because you have no money at present. You'll pay a little bit only for the time of using my computer." And laughing she added – "You'll also attract clients to my business!" she was a great and uncommon person and a good friend, and of course I had hoped for her help because she was local and had good local knowledge, but I didn't even expect that everything would be solved so easily and almost cried with happiness.

I printed some business cards at a printing establishment and placed an advertisement in the local newspaper and called my agency

"A happy couple":

If you are 18-50 years old and you are attractive –

You have a real chance of changing your life.

At your service: a catalogue, the internet,

The addresses of the fiancés and dates in

Chernovtsy.

The business card of my dating agency, 2000

In a couple of days there was a queue at the doors of the agency and half of the women were 40 to 50 years old. I took a small fee of 35 hryvnas (7 dollars) only, for the adding of the profile on the international website of a dating agency.

This is where I used my PC skills and English language knowledge. I didn't receive any profit from this, and I didn't even think of one, because this work carried me away and brought me pleasure.

I also used my communicating skills as well. Some of the women were depressed after divorces and I had to talk to each of them and give them hope for the future. I frankly told them about their drawbacks and explained what they had to do to prepare them for getting married to a foreigner.

They did everything I advised them: they bought vitamins from us, changed their hairstyles, began to lose weight, and when they had new photos taken they could not believe the difference in their own appearance.

Although many of them didn't get married they all were grateful to me because I forced them to adopt another outlook on life. After a couple of months a young man came to see me and I began to explain him that I worked with women only. But he stopped me and said – "Employ me please, I've graduated the foreign languages department of Chernovtsy University and I can operate a PC." "I would gladly do this but I have no money to pay you," I replied.

"You don't have to. I'll earn money from the women who are seeking husbands abroad by translating correspondence received in English from prospective husbands and writing their replies back in English. I'll also take money from men for the delivery of flowers and presents via the Internet," he answered. I couldn't believe my ears and thanked God for sending me Anton – this was the name of the young man.

He turned out to be a good worker and expertly translated all correspondence between men and fiancés which began to arrive with time. We broadened our services and began to meet the men at the airport, helped them with processing the bridal visa documents, etc. Thanks to Anton my dating agency became popular in the town and girls who couldn't get married using the services of the other agencies came to us and some of these got married with our help.

After I had worked for a year I learned all the issues from the bottom up connected to getting married abroad: marriage laws of different countries, document processing and emigration issues. During the course of running my agency I had another idea for starting another business at the same time. The thing was that many young women knew at least Basic English, but older women had already forgotten everything and couldn't go to the language courses because only those who had some basic knowledge were admitted to the courses.

I was asked many times where could they start learning English afresh. I couldn't advise them anything because there weren't such courses in the town and eventually I offered them to give English lessons myself at my home. We formed a class of six people right away and I promised them they would start lessons in two months and I began to prepare a teaching program named "English language courses for beginners who want to get married abroad."

While drawing up the programme I began to know English better and understood that at this stage I should think not of the courses, but of myself, before my age would make it impossible for me to marry abroad. I brought my photos to Anton and asked him to add them to the website. He was surprised because I had never told him about my wishes before. As soon as I appeared on the site the letters from men from different countries came in: Sweden, the USA, Germany, Great Britain and even Japan.

At first I corresponded with everybody, but then I began to reply only to those from Great Britain because I had already been there and I wanted to go back. This correspondence came from people all over Great Britain and continued for about a year, but I didn't take these communications any further because I didn't like some of them and the others just stopped writing. What surprised me the most and quite pleasantly was that all of them were of my age or a little bit older. One day, late at night, whilst I was considering whether to update my profile with some new photos, Anton called me suddenly and said:

"You have a very good letter from an English man; I think you'll like it." He was right, I really liked his photos and his letter was written with humour. He described his daily routine, wrote about England, his friends and family. He was 53 as well as I was and his name was Alan. After corresponding for a couple of months we were ready for a date. For a first date men usually came to Ukraine, but he invited me to his home for Christmas, as he was busy and sent me an invitation for the visitor's visa.

After I had gathered the needed documents I went for an interview at the British Embassy, which was in Kiev. I thought that the procedure of obtaining a visa would be a long one and I would have to go to the Embassy a couple times, but to my delight everything went fast. I wasn't asked many questions at the interview, but they did ask for how many days I was staying there. I replied that I was going for two weeks and not more because I had a business here.

After that they told me that I could collect my passport after 4 p.m. I was worried because I thought that if it took so little time, there would be a refusal and I could hardly wait for 4.00 p.m. to arrive. When I got the passport and looked inside, there was a visitor's visa for 6 months. I couldn't believe my eyes and I was in the seventh heaven for happiness. But then when I came to my senses I was beset with doubts and very soon fear replaced joy.

Great Britain – that is great of course but I'm going to visit the man whom I only know from the photo and correspondence. I liked his letters, but what kind of a man would he turn out to be in reality? What if I didn't like him, what would I do? Such things always happen in life, when one thing finishes well you began to worry about the other things. Before that I had been worried that I wouldn't get the visa and at that moment I was worried about our meeting.

Chapter 52

A Hard-Won Way to England

Despite my doubts, I came back home happy with a big green bag that I had bought in Kiev. After my son had seen me at the doors he exclaimed – "The visa was opened so quickly!" "How do you know that?" I wondered. "If it had not been you wouldn't have bought that bag," he replied. I was going to go to the ticket office to buy a ticket right away, but I decided to visit Anton first and tell him about my trip to the Embassy.

He didn't even ask me about the visa and told me that a letter was waiting for me in which a man was asking me which route I had chosen to travel to England because he was going to pay for my ticket. I replied, in response to this letter, that I was going to fly from Kiev to London, hoping that Alan would meet me at Heathrow airport. But after I had bought the ticket he wrote back to me the following:

'I'm very busy and will only be able to meet you in Birmingham; you will have to get by yourself from Heathrow. When you arrive at Heathrow, you must find the bus station and go into the office, where, if you give them your name they will give you a ticket to Birmingham, which I have already paid for.'

It was my opinion that the letter was a very strange one, and my disposition became very uneasy, and I began to think whether I should undertake the trip when Alan appeared to have so little time for me.

But I already had the visa and ticket and decided that I would go ahead with my journey and as I had already been to London I had a little experience of how to cope when I arrived. But, even so it occurred to me, "What if he doesn't meet me, what should I do then?" So I decided to take 600 dollars with me just in case I needed to buy a return ticket.

I usually prepared for the trips very quickly, but this time I was confused, and didn't know which clothes and things to take with me, what souvenirs to take for him, his children and his parents. I was visiting at Christmas time, but I didn't know for how long I was going to stay, this all depended on how our relationship turned out. Two people from different countries, with different culture, traditions and style of life would meet each other for the first time and at a relatively late stage in life.

Each of us had our own previous life, family, and children, each of us had our own character and habits and I had no idea how this all would work out. I departed for London on 22nd December, it was 17 degrees centigrade below zero in Kiev at that time and I was dressed according to the weather: a winter coat with a blue fox fur-collar, high leather boots with real sheepskin inside and a fur beret.

I had a big green suitcase and a small bag with me. To try and rid my mind of doubts and to cheer myself up whilst fastening my seat belt and preparing for the flight I was repeating inwardly "Dreams come true! Go ahead to your dream!" After a little more than two hours the plane landed at Heathrow airport. Following the other passengers I went through passport control and went straight through to the arrival hall where people were waiting for the arrivals.

I knew nobody was going to meet me so I went further trying to find the signs telling me where to collect my suitcase. Two and a half years before, when I arrived at Heathrow I had only hand luggage with me so I went straight to the exit without paying attention to the details of where to collect hold baggage. This time I had to find my suitcase and wandered in one direction after another until the moment dawned when I realised that I was completely lost and not only unable to find my suitcase but I couldn't even find the place where I had arrived.

I was in a panic and stopped every worker wearing a uniform and asked them where I could collect my luggage. Maybe because of my bad English or due to the strange question they couldn't understand what exactly it was that I wanted. One of them even thought that my luggage had been stolen and told me that I should go and report it to the police.

I kept looking at the clock with horror because the time for my bus departure was rapidly approaching and I had little time to continue searching for my suitcase. At last I got to some corridor and through the glass windows I saw people picking up luggage from a conveyer in the hall. I rushed to find an entrance to this hall, but all the entrances were closed and when I was trying to get over the barrier barring entry, a worker from the airport came over and stopped me. I gave him my ticket and began to tell that him that I just wanted to take my luggage pointing at the suitcases I could see through the glass.

"This luggage isn't from your flight and moreover if you have already gone through the passport control you can't go back there." he said, offering no more explanation. I sat at the windowsill and took out my English dictionary and wrote with big letters everything I wanted to say. After that I approached a woman wearing a uniform and gave her this piece of paper on which I had just written, together with my ticket and my invitation and did not say a word. She immediately said "Follow me, please," and took me in the opposite direction.

We walked for quite a while until she told me to stop and to wait for her. She disappeared into the back of the airport and in a couple of minutes returned with my suitcase. Thank God I gasped, but as I took hold of my suitcase I realised that it was only a few minutes until the departure of my bus to Birmingham. But, in which direction was the bus station? What direction to choose? I won't tire you by telling you how much time and strength and nerves I spent to getting to the bus station and finding the office, which almost no one knew about.

When I eventually arrived, totally exhausted, and presented my ticket I found that my bus had already departed. It was explained to me by the lady in the office that as I had missed my reservation, my ticket was no longer valid and that I would have to purchase another for a later bus which was due to depart a 9 p.m.

This piece of news almost knocked me out, it was nearly the last straw, but gathering my last strengths and the words that I knew I began to tell her that I was late because of the flight delay, that I had no pounds with me because I arrived from Ukraine and the man who had paid for my ticket would meet me in Birmingham … I was going to go on and on but I stopped when I saw the ticket for the 9 p.m. bus in front of my nose. God, how grateful I was to that lady office worker.

There was still some time before the departure of the 9 p.m. bus and I sat on a bench, and looked around. I was exhausted, tired and all wet because it was 4 degrees above zero in London and the flowers were blooming in flowerbeds! I couldn't believe that it could be so warm in the middle of winter in England!

'Oh, why am I sitting here? I should call Alan and let him know that I was going to be three hours late,' I worried. As there was a pay phone call-box not far from me I decided to try and call Alan to make him aware of my circumstances. When I entered this red box I began to read a manual on how to make a call and I understood that I needed 50 cents to make a call. Ten American dollars was the smallest note that I had, so I went back to the office again to try and change the note, I was afraid to go further for fear of getting lost again.

The lady behind the counter was looked at me silently with amazement when I produced a ten-dollar bill and asked her to exchange it for pounds. She patiently began to explain that I had to go back to the airport and find an exchange office that could do this for me. I looked at her with a faraway look knowing that I wouldn't go back into the airport at any price. I returned to the call box and stood there in the hope that somebody passing by would help me to make the call.

There were very few people passing by, but after a while I saw a man who was passing not too far away and I stopped him and asked him to help me make the call. I gave him the letter with the phone number together with the ten-dollar bill. The man refused to take dollars dialled the needed number and dropped his 50p coin into the box, and when Alan replied he handed me the receiver.

I began to tell quickly that due to the flight delay I would be in Birmingham at midnight and after I had heard the "OK" reply I hung the receiver with a sigh of relief and turned around to say thank you but there was nobody there ... I was extremely grateful to this Good Samaritan and thankful that such Englishmen existed.

The bus was very comfortable but despite the tiredness I couldn't sleep, and was looking out of the window and everything I saw was new to me and I did not want to miss a thing. We were going along a motorway at night and one can think that there wasn't anything interesting to look at. But I was scrutinizing everything because it was all interesting for me and the things that local people considered to be ordinary were amazing and unusual for me.

For example, 'Why haven't we passed by a single centre of population where people live?' All the roads were lit and it was as light as during daytime, which amazed me a lot. I thought, "How much electricity does this require to light all the roads in England?" When the bus arrived at Birmingham Airport at midnight there seemed to be nobody about, neither near the airport building nor at the bus station which was opposite.

There was only one car not far from the entrance to the airport and it seemed to me that there wasn't anybody in it. I was frightened and thought, 'That's all I need! He hasn't come to meet me, maybe he got angry because I am late, maybe he fell asleep because he had worked all day long, got tired and it's midnight right now.' There could be very many reasons, but the result was the only one – he wasn't there. Of course, I had his address but how I could get to that strange town alone and at night.

All the passengers went out of the bus and began to take their luggage. I took mine and was standing at the pavement looking around trying to find something. Suddenly, the doors of the car which I had noticed from the very beginning opened and a man came out of it and began to make his way towards the bus very slowly. When he came closer I saw that it was Alan, he was the same as his photograph.

He was embarrassed and didn't feel himself quite at ease; I also didn't know what to do and began to tell him about the weather in Kiev as if making an excuse for my warm clothes.

Whilst we were driving to his house he told me that he lived in a town not far from that airport and I could have flown into Birmingham Airport.

'Why didn't you write me about that?' I wondered. I thought that Great Britain was a small country and had only two airports – Heathrow and Gatwick. Great Britain is almost two and half times smaller than Ukraine and how could I know that it had 29 International airports and one of them was in Birmingham? As we were talking to each other I didn't notice that we were in his town already, he stopped the car in front of a long house and said: "We've arrived – welcome to my house."

Chapter 53

My Life in Great Britain

I arrived to Alan's house late at night, when it was already dark and I couldn't look around well. After everything that had happened to me during that day I was falling asleep on my feet and that is why I fell asleep right away ... and woke up in a fairytale the next day! His entire house was decorated for Christmas and there was a Christmas tree in the corner of a living room, which was lit with sparkling lights and was so beautiful that it didn't need any other decoration.

I was amazed at it because I'd never seen anything like it before and Alan explained to me that that was a fibre optic effect. I must say that from the very first day of my stay in England I was filled with amazement all the time and I was sometimes embarrassed because of that, as if I'd lived all my life in more austere surroundings and hadn't seen anything like this before. Of course I'd seen a lot in my life and had even visited London three years ago, but this was totally different.

I had arrived in a small town and to an English family and was now, for the first time, experiencing the atmosphere of real English life with its customs and traditions, which were of great interest to me. I came from Ukraine where everything was totally different and everything I saw during my stay in England I compared, at the back of my mind, to my life in USSR.

For example, as soon as I entered Alan's house, I saw that the rooms were small, but later I understood why. United Kingdom is much smaller than Ukraine and its population is much bigger, but despite that, parents, their children and grandchildren don't live together under one roof and each family, even single people live separately.

Besides that each house has a main entrance, the front door, and a back door out to a garden where people grow ornamental plants and have an area set aside for sitting and eating in the summertime. In the USSR houses usually have only one entrance and gardens in USSR are just used for growing fruit and vegetables (potato mainly).

Despite hearing many stories about Great Britain being overpopulated it was interesting to note that Great Britain isn't completely built-up and there are many places with green spaces and parks in the towns. Particularly interesting for me was an out-of-town view, where there were many manicured fields, divided from each other with not-too-high green hedges or stone barriers, built using old technology without cement or any other binder, the techniques having been preserved for hundreds of years.

While driving along the country roads away from the towns, one can see fields where sheep and other livestock feed. Once when Alan and I were driving along a country road, I saw a field in which there were lots of small buildings. I couldn't understand at first what the reason was for these, I thought that they might be hiking tents, but it seemed strange for me that they weren't triangular as usual, but semi-circular.

When Alan told me these were pig farms I thought he was kidding, upon taking a closer look at these huts, I saw pigs walking in the field and around feedboxes. In answer to my question why the pigs were kept in such small buildings, he told me that they were not small, but just big enough to keep four pigs in. I was shocked at this revelation of just four pigs to a hut: In the USSR, because of the severe weather, pig farms are on a large scale with a couple of hundred pigs in one building I was so amazed that pigs could be housed in small structures and continued to think about it.

I then asked him "How do they know which building to come back to for the night time?" He replied with a smile on his face "Each of them has a number on it. I immediately realized he was kidding, but couldn't resent him, because I asked such a silly question myself. I was particularly impressed with the huge supermarkets which had so many different products, that even if one bought something different each time, it would not be possible to try everything in a year!

What was even more impressive was the fact that the big supermarkets had up to thirty cash desks and each of them had a queue at it with carts full of products, which suggested a big buying ability by the population of the country. Besides the usual range of vegetables and fruit produce that I was familiar with, there were others that I had never encountered before.

There were also huge quantities of ready-made dishes and half-finished products, which could be cooked for 5 minutes using a microwave oven or for 20 minutes in the oven. Looking at all that, I involuntarily thought that women were probably very happy in England because they don't spent much time cooking, don't have to preserve fruit and vegetables for winter and don't need to think of how to feed the family as cheap as possible.

Every day during these first couple of weeks I encountered something new and not always wonderful because, due to the differences in customs, the same behaviour in one country has a different meaning in another. For example I was shocked when I first visited the local pub which Alan visited almost every Friday and traditionally met his friends there.

On this occasion as soon as I entered the room, the men who were already drinking there started whistling at me. For this important occasion of meeting

343

Alan's friends I dressed up smartly wearing a blouse and a skirt which revealed my knees, together with fashionable high-heeled shoes. I didn't understand what was going on. I almost tripped and fell with the embarrassment and blushed bright red.

However, Alan appeared pleased and displayed no other reaction. I just sat at the table, confused, but pretended nothing had happened. Later, when after I had composed myself I asked him: "Why did the men whistle when I came in? Do I look so bad or I look like a whore?" He was stunned and began to calm me down. Saying:

"No way! On the contrary, this means you look great!" I was amazed and thought 'How different from the other countries that I knew where men only whistle when they see a woman with a bad reputation.' I was very glad to have an opportunity to see Christmas celebrations in Great Britain. Everything was uncommon for me here: Christmas dinner with turkey and vegetables baked in an oven, plenty of greeting cards from all the relatives and friends, presents under the Christmas tree for all the members of the family, etc.

It was the first time in my life that I saw the way towns, supermarkets and private houses were decorated for Christmas. As they say, time flies when you are enjoying yourself, and the Christmas holidays raced by. I had to go back home in two weeks because I had a return ticket to Kiev, but I began to think that it would be better to flesh out our relationships with Alan before my departure.

I liked him, and regarded him to be a good man and I'd already got used to him, his house and his relatives. He had such a good sense of humour that I had never laughed so much in my life as I did with him. I felt he liked me as well, his parents and children accepted me very well, but two weeks only had passed since we first met and this was too early to make any sense of our feelings. More time was needed to think everything over and make any serious decision.

However, it turned out that I had no time for thinking because Alan proposed very soon. This was so unexpected and unusual that I had tears in my eyes. According to British tradition he set on one knee and after he had asked to marry him he held out an engagement ring. I couldn't believe this to be really happening to me in real life, before this I'd only seen such proposals in foreign movies.

Here and now was an Englishman offering me marriage in such a traditional way. How could I have possibly refused? Of course not! I gladly agreed. It was another three months before we were able to arrange a wedding ceremony and from the very beginning of our wedding preparations I was nervous, because without asking me he began to invite around 90 people for the wedding party.

He had very many friends and he wanted to invite all of them. I was in a panic when I imagined how much time, strength and money we would need to prepare food for all of them. "Don't worry, I'll organize everything myself and you'll only be helping me. This is not my first wedding and I know exactly what to do," he said.

I didn't know what weddings were like in Britain and remembered my Ukrainian wedding and thought he was joking about being able to organize a wedding by himself. It wasn't funny for me, though, with only two weeks until the wedding my mind raced with thoughts of where would we find so many tables and where would we put them to host so many people?

My panic continued when Alan announced that we would celebrate our wedding in the garage using our existing dining table! It was incredible to me that I could have a wedding party in a garage and hoped that no one from Ukraine would find out about that! According to British tradition, all women who were invited for the wedding organized a bridal shower for me at a disco-club the night before the wedding.

They put a bridal veil and a crown with twinkling lights on my head and other people who were also there congratulated me, knowing what we celebrated. We had great fun and I felt myself a real bride! Alan went with men to the local pub. We cleaned up a garage a couple of days before the wedding and put a table and chairs inside. I hung out wedding decorations that we had bought, and it became kind of cosy there, but it was hard for me to believe that there could be such weddings.

Then we went to the supermarket and bought some beer, wine, several packets of different food stuffs and sandwiches. The day before the wedding I reminded Alan that we had to cook something for the next day, but he was completely calm and I just stopped worrying and waited for what was going to happen next. At last at 4 p.m. he said it was time to prepare for the wedding and went to the fridge. We took out of the packets some small sausages and chicken legs and placed them in the oven.

We put sandwiches, plates with crisps and bread sticks on the table in the garage as well as drinks and disposable tableware, we brought a tape-recorder with speakers, and after that Alan told me everything was ready for the wedding and we can go and have a rest. The wedding ceremony went wonderfully and after that the closest relatives and friends were all invited to a restaurant for dinner.

Later in the day around 70 people visited the party in the garage, and only after I saw that all guests were satisfied and having fun did I calm down and began to celebrate my wedding. I was very glad to marry a good man whom I like a lot and I sincerely hoped that we would make each other happy. There is an English saying "Marry in Haste. Repent at Leisure," and this proved to be the case with us.

Euphoria ended about four months after the wedding, when I got to know better his unpredictable temper and understood that I had made a terrible mistake by agreeing to marry him. At first I tried to repair, somehow, our relationship, but my efforts were useless there was an unbridgeable difference in our intellect and cultures and I found it impossible to change his habitual way of life.

Likewise, I was from a different cultural background and he did not seem to understand or make any allowances for this. I eventually could not tolerate his behaviour or manners and accept his lifestyle, because all this was not my thing and not for me, it would seem we were completely different people and had different views of life. This was a funny marriage and several months later we parted company because we couldn't put up with each other any longer.

This was a hard period in my life, I lost self-confidence, I had a depression and I couldn't imagine how to survive in a foreign country all alone. I eventually moved into a flat of my own and lived a single life for the next 8 years. During this time I acquired full British citizenship and a UK passport. I'm grateful that life gave me this opportunity and the chance to meet such great people like Sue Cardus, Eileen and Vincent Murphy, Pauline and Michael Devlin, who became real friends for me for many years. Their help and support revived me and boosted my self-confidence, and for this I will always be grateful to them.

However, the prospect of a suitable professional job still seemed to be beyond my grasp. I realized that my work experience, education and all the diplomas received in my previous country weren't appreciated in Britain and that is why I had no chance in finding any appropriate professional work for myself. However, I was lucky that in this country there are always opportunities to change one's life for the better when there's a desire so to do.

I started to believe in myself once again and understood that in order to develop in my new country I had to return to education. I began to take English language courses at a college and also courses in "Food preparation and cooking", "Pastry Cooks and Patissiers" and "Food Safety in Catering" in all of which I successfully passed exams after two years of study.

I did consider the possibility of opening my own Russian café, with an assortment of Russian and Ukrainian specialities as I had received many compliments about my style of cooking. However, the prospect of running a business again, particularly after my experience in Ukraine, did not appeal.

It was one of my friends, who after hearing about some of my exploits in Siberia suggested the idea of writing a book about my life. They considered my life to be very interesting and unusual and thought it probably would be of interest to many other people, as well as being a family history for future generations.

At first, I just laughed and told them that I would find it difficult because I had never written a book before. However, after giving this matter some thought I came to the conclusion that my friends Eileen and Vincent had put a good idea into my head and I just took a pen and a notebook and began to scribble some notes.

This way thanks to my friends a book gradually appeared that recollected all the facts and events (good and not very) about my life and I felt that I lived

346

my life twice. It seemed things got better from that moment on and everything was great, but I was still lonely and it made me sad. Despite my unfortunate previous marriage experience I didn't lose hope of meeting a good man with whom I would be happy – and completely by accident he came into my life.

After I had been writing my book for a little while, I realized that I needed help as my English vocabulary, whilst adequate for everyday use, was not quite good enough to write my book. I therefore started to look for someone who had a good command of the English language and could help me. I placed an ad on the Internet that I was looking for a person who would help me in editing my book.

Several people responded to my ad, but I selected someone who seemed to have the right credentials and who lived not far from my town. It turned out that he was a widower and lived alone, and was looking for something to occupy his spare time and after hearing my story began helping me with pleasure. From the very first meeting I fell in love like a girl and understood that he was my destiny. He was an intelligent, elegant, lively and interesting English gentleman. We continued to meet regularly, and after about 18 months we were married.

After a long period of losses and misfortunes I was really happy at last. Our wedding was a romantic dream – taking place at sunset on a Caribbean Beach, it really seemed like heaven to me with a warm turquoise sea, unusual plants, the most beautiful sunsets and a friendly atmosphere.

Now I'm all fine, I have a husband I love and am happy with. I'm proud to live in Great Britain, a wonderful country where there are ancient castles and a Queen like in a fairytale. I'm thanking fate that all my dreams came true and God gave me more than I've ever asked for! However, I still think fondly of the people and my past life in USSR and still celebrate, in my own quiet way, many of the traditions and customs of my Russian and Ukrainian heritage.

My wedding on May 2012

References

An unused chance: One and half year in government, Abalkin L.I., Politizdat, 1991

Archive documents and photos of the Donetsk Regional Natural History Museum (permission to use)

Attention, mammoths! Rusanov B., Magadan, 1976

Alaska-Siberia. A track of courage. Negenblya I.E., Yakutsk, 2000

A Citadel on Prut. (From the history of Chernivtsi origin) Timoschuk B., Uzhgorod, Carpathians, 1978

An investment tourist Bukovina. Dumitraschuk V.D., Zubovich T.I., Chernivtsi, 2004

Articles of the 22nd Congress of the CPSU, October 1961

Brief geographical dictionary-reference book "Yakut ASSR", Mostahov S.E. Nekrasov I.A., Dmitrieva Z.M., Kalmykova A.I., Yakutsk, 1980

Chernivtsi. City itinerary. Kolodiy V.I., Uzhgorod, Carpathians, 1967

CPSU Resolution "About measures to overcome alcohol abuse and alcoholism", May 1986

Donetsk yesterday, today and tomorrow. Boroday A.S, Kishkan V.P, Donetsk, Donbass, 1970

Everything about Donetsk. An itinerary, 1987

Excursion in Kiev. Briukhovetsky Y, Kiev, 2008

From the history of the Kolyma camps (Materials of Zyryanka museum of the peoples history and culture)

Kiev- "Encyclopedic Reference Book" USE Kiev, dp 1982

Kiev. Glance at the Crisis of the century. Petrov S., Kiev, 2010

Kolyma tales. Varlam Shalamov, Eksmo, 2005

Materials of the 19th CPSU Union Conference, June 1988

Materials of the 3rd Congress of People's Deputies, March 1990

Materials of the 3rd Extraordinary Congress of People's Deputies, March 1990

Materials of the 1st Congress of People's Deputies of the USSR, May-June 1989

Materials of the Soviet Union Referendum, March 1991

Materials of the currency reform in the Soviet Union, January-April 1991

Materials of the newspaper "Sovetskaya Kolyma" of November 6, 1977 (permission to use)

Materials of Ukrainian independence referendum, December 1991

One day of Ivan Denisovich. Alexander Solzhenitsyn, Terra, 2004

Old Vladivostok. A Russian morning. 1992

Power, democracy and perestroika. Karelsky V.M.M, 1990

Strategy and tactics of perestroika. Rakitskiy B. Rakitskaya G.M., 1990

Soviet Encyclopedic dictionary. Prohorov A.M., Moscow, Soviet Encyclopedia, 1987

Resolution of USSR Council of Ministers №410 "About measures to overcome alcohol abuse, alcoholism and elimination of self-combustion", May 1986

The Kremlin Chronicle. Grachev A.M., 1994

The documents of the Central State Archive of Yakut ASSR.

The history of Chernivtsi city. Kayndl R., 2003

To be kept forever. Kozlov N.V., Magadan, 1974

Trans-Siberian line. Itinerary. Yudin A., Vokrug Sveta, 2009

USSR Law "About self-employment", November 1986

USSR Law "About Cooperation in the USSR", May 1988